COWBOYS
of the Americas
Richard W. Slatta

YALE UNIVERSITY PRESS NEW HAVEN AND LONDON

*For Jerome David Slatta—*many happy trails to my little cowboy

This volume is part of the Yale Western Americana Series. The editorial committee for the series consists of Archibald Hanna, Jr., Howard Roberts Lamar, and Robert M. Utley.

Designed by Richard Hendel and set in Century Expanded type by G & S Typesetters, Inc., Austin, Texas

Printed in Singapore by C S Graphics PTE Ltd.

Library of Congress Cataloging-in-Publication Data
Slatta, Richard W., 1947–
  Cowboys of the Americas / by Richard W. Slatta.
    p.   cm. — (Yale Western Americana series)
  Bibliography: p.
  Includes index.
  ISBN 0–300–04529–8 (cloth)
  ISBN 0–300–05671–0 (pbk.)
  1. Cowboys—West (U.S.)—History. 2. Cowboys—America—History. 3. Frontier and pioneer life—West (U.S.) 4. West (U.S.)—Social life and customs. 5. Cattle trade—West (U.S.)—History. 6. Cattle trade—America—History. I. Title. II. Series.
F596.S63 1990
978—dc20   89–31880
            CIP

A catalogue record for this book is available from the British Library.

The paper in this book meets the guidelines for permanence and durability of the Committee on Production Guidelines for Book Longevity of the Council on Library Resources. ∞

10 9 8 7 6 5 4 3 2

Publication of this book is supported by a grant from the National Endowment for the Humanities, an independent federal agency.

CONTENTS

ILLUSTRATIONS

Following page 50

Gauchos and horses. Painting by Juan Léon Pallière, date
unknown.

Argentine gaucho on horseback. Photograph, c. 1890.

Group of gauchos. Illustration by Emeric Essex Vidal,
c. 1820.

Gaucho wearing *chiripá*. Photograph, date unknown.

Chilean *huaso*. Anonymous drawing, nineteenth century.

Huaso on horseback. Anonymous drawing, c. 1850.

Llaneros crossing Venezuelan plains. Anonymous drawing,
c. 1862.

Llaneros on horseback. Anonymous watercolors, c. 1850.

Mexican *charro*. Drawing by José Cisneros.

Baja California cowboy. Drawing by José Cisneros.

Mexican *vaquero*. Drawing by Frederic Remington, 1893.

Vaquero on horseback. Photograph, c. 1900.

Hawaiian *paniolo*. Photograph, c. 1900.

American cowboy. Lithograph by J. R. McFarren, 1887.

Cowboys in New Mexico. Photographs, c. 1900.

Wild Horse Hunters. Painting by Charles M. Russell, 1913.

Arizona Cowboy. Lithograph by Frederic Remington, 1901.

Black cowboys in Texas. Photograph, c. 1910.

Bill Pickett in *The Bull-dogger*. Film poster, 1923.

Indian cowboys in Oklahoma. Photograph, c. 1890.

Cowboys and cattle on the open range. Photograph, date
unknown.

"Montana Girl." Photograph, 1909.

Woman riding sidesaddle. Photograph, date unknown.

Canadian cowboys. Photographs, 1880s.

Following page 82

Cowboy roping calves on Texas ranch. Photograph, 1905.

Cattle crossing stream in Texas. Drawing by A. R. Waud,
1867.

ACKNOWLEDGMENTS

I have benefited from a good deal of editorial and financial assistance for this project. I thank the Tinker Foundation for a year-long fellowship in 1984–1985 that allowed me to conduct research in the United States, Canada, and Venezuela. I would like to think that Edward Larocque Tinker, an avid student of equestrian life, would have been pleased with the use of his money. Earlier research on the gaucho in Argentina was funded by the Fulbright-Hayes Doctoral Dissertation Abroad Program and by the Social Science Research Council. A grant from the North Carolina State University Professional Faculty Development fund permitted further research on the dictatorship of Juan Manuel de Rosas.

During my stay in Venezuela, I had assistance from Miguel Izard of the Universidad de Barcelona, Arturo Alvarez D'Armas, Judy Ewell of the College of William and Mary, Susan Berglund of the Universidad Central de Venezuela, and Adelina C. Rodríguez M. of the Universidad Santa María.

José Antonio de Armas Chitty heads Venezuela's Academia Nacional de Historia. A *llanero* himself, he shared his considerable knowledge and congenial company in several interviews. Manuel Pérez Vila, then director of historical research for the Fundación John Boulton, served as a gracious sponsor during my Tinker fellowship.

Staff at a number of archives and libraries assisted me, including the Archivo General de la Nación and the Biblioteca Nacional in Caracas (where Gladys Chacón was especially helpful), and the library of the Fundación Boulton.

In Alberta, Canada, I was ably assisted by Chris Archer of the University of Calgary. Staff at the Glenbow Archive and the library of the University of Calgary quickly located relevant sources. Howard Palmer, Graham Knox, and Tim Travers offered helpful comments.

At the University of Washington, the late Carl E. Solberg, Dauril Alden, and several graduate students, including Dan Greenberg, offered constructive criticism on the project. Many other colleagues, including Deborah Jakubs, Mary Lou LeCompte, John David Smith, Bill Beezley, John Chasteen, and Charlie Seemann, offered suggestions for sources or editorial revisions. Rodolfo Borello, Sandra Thomas, Mark McCaffrey, Dennis West, Bill Katra, and Deborah Schwartz, participants at a conference entitled "Gauchos and

Nation Builders in the Río de la Plata" (LaCrosse, Wisconsin, April 1988), provided important sources and advice. Friends outside of university circles, Fred Jerome and Elmo Jensen, commented on the readability and clarity of the text. My wife, Maxine P. Atkinson, helped keep the project in proper perspective by reminding me that there is more to life than cowboys. To all, *gracias.*

Brief passages of text are based on previous publications. My thanks to the Center for Great Plains Studies for permission to use sections of my article "Comparative Frontier Social Life: Western Saloons and Argentine Pulperías," *Great Plains Quarterly* 7:3 (Summer 1987). The *Journal of Sport History* permitted me to use parts of "The Demise of the Gaucho and the Rise of Equestrian Sport in Argentina" (13:2 [Summer 1986]). A final thanks to the many scholars whose cited works provided pieces of the large puzzle that I have called "Cowboys of the Americas." We still have a lot of range to ride. I hope that this book helps point the way up the trail.

CHAPTER 1

Introduction

Colorful, often dangerous men on horseback have awed and fascinated pedestrians through the ages. Civilizations ancient and modern have granted special prestige to horsemen. In premechanized eras, mounted workers played important economic roles in livestock herding, transportation, and communication. Cavalry often determined the outcome of military conflicts. People around the world thrill to galloping hooves, stampeding cattle, blazing gunfights, and other real and imagined elements of cowboy culture.[1]

The Spanish culture, in particular, endowed horsemanship with high status. Official portraits of Spanish kings depicted them astride pawing, rearing horses. The conquistadors brought Hispanic equestrian values and practices to the New World. The "man on horseback" epitomized military and political leadership. Indeed, it is a thesis of this book that Spanish influence is primary in all open-range cattle frontiers of North and South America.

Horses and cattle spread quickly across the fertile American plains. Distinctive equestrian subcultures and livestock economies developed from the Río de la Plata of southern South America to northern New Spain (today's Mexico). Over the centuries Iberian and indigenous practices intertwined on the cattle frontiers of Latin America. In the United States and Canada, Anglo-Saxon influences were added. In spite of the radical changes brought about by industrialization and urbanization, the history and mythology of equestrian plains cultures remain significant in many Western Hemisphere nations.

The master historian of the Spanish Borderlands, Herbert Eugene Bolton, delivered the presidential address at the forty-seventh meeting of the American Historical Association in Toronto in 1932. "Who," he asked, "has written the history . . . of the spread of cattle and horse raising from Patagonia to Labrador?" Few of Bolton's students took up the challenges of comparative frontier research. More than a half-century later, this book aspires partially to fill this historiographical void.[2]

In North American historiography, the Spanish Borderlands is now getting proper attention. But as Cecil Robinson, Don Worcester, David J. Weber, and others have pointed out, biases mar Anglo-American perceptions of Hispanic culture. Comparative analysis drawing on documentary sources from both cultures is one way to help correct these historical biases.[3]

This book traces the rise and fall of cowboy types in the major Anglo-American and Spanish-American ranching areas of the Western Hemisphere. It compares and contrasts the social, economic, and cultural formation of horsemen from the Argentine pampas to the western Canadian prairies. Primary attention is given to the classic era of open-range ranching during the late nineteenth century, with special emphasis on the environmental and cultural factors that shaped frontier life. Table 1 summarizes the groups and regions covered.

Such a sweeping hemispheric perspective mandates a degree of selectivity. I have focused on the cowboy groups that achieved the status of national or regional types. As Alistair Hennessy has noted, "Cattle and horse frontiers produce independent herders who are often taken to symbolize the national virtues." My treatment of Latin America concentrates on Spanish-speaking areas; only occasional references are made to Portuguese-speaking Brazil's *vaqueiros* and *gaúchos*, important though they may be. I have included a few passages about Hawaii's cowboy, the *paniolo* (or *paniola*), because his origins are linked to those of Mexico's *vaquero*. Even the Hawaiian cowboy's name, a corruption of *español*, shows his Hispanic roots.[4]

Another criterion that I have taken into account is the relative significance of a cattle-raising region in the national economy. This means that riders of Peru, the Gran Chaco (Paraguay), western Patagonia, and south-central Bolivia are not discussed. Likewise, I mention only in passing the "cowpens" of the Carolinas and the small ranching industry of Spanish Florida. For the United States, I give greatest attention to Texas and the Great Plains, with a few words about the Pacific Northwest. Similarly, for the *llanos*, the tropical plains of northern South America, evidence is drawn primarily from Venezuela rather than Colombia.

This is a work of social history. As with all social history, the focus is on people—in this case, cowboys—and how they lived their lives. It probably fits into what Robert P. Swierenga has termed the "new rural history." I think of my work as "new rural social history." While some descriptions of animals, landscape, and material culture are given, this is not a study of ranching tools, technology, ecology, or livestock. Nor is it a work of political economy, although economic and political matters receive some attention. I do not at-

Table 1. Cowboys of the Americas

Group*	Location	Region
Cowboy	Alberta, Canada	Prairie
Cowboy	Western United States	Plains
Vaquero	Northern Mexico, Spanish Southwest, and California	Plains
Gaucho	Argentina	Pampas
Huaso (guaso)	Chile	Central Valley
Llanero	Venezuela	Llanos

*The following groups are mentioned in the book, but not studied in detail: llanero (Colombia), vaqueiro (sertão of northern Brazil), gaúcho (Rio Grande do Sul, Brazil), gaucho (Uruguay), charro (Mexico), and paniolo (Hawaii).

tempt a "total history" of cattle frontiers; women, ranchers, city folks, Indians, farmers, and others are discussed only in relation to the cowboy. Female ranch hands appear nowhere in the sources that I examined, so the only "cowgirls" mentioned are rodeo performers.[5]

Whenever possible, I have included substantial quotations from firsthand observers. These descriptions of cowboy dress, equipment, work habits, and the plains environment are meant to transport the reader back to the historical period. The writing styles and viewpoints of contemporary witnesses help us to recapture past perceptions of the cowboy. For example, I could describe the attitude of cattlemen toward rustlers, but why not let Colonel E. P. Hardesty, an Elko County, Nevada, rancher, speak for himself? He instructed his cowboys how to handle a man who stole any of his cattle: "If he stole it to eat, tell him to enjoy it and bring me the hide. If he stole it to sell, bring me his hide."[6]

I would liken this book's structure to that of a Western film. It opens with quick vignettes that highlight the many cowboy types. Flashbacks reveal the distant, shadowy origins of the cowboy as a wild-cattle hunter. The cowboy hero rides onto the plains. Closeups reveal his appearance and something of his character and values. The camera then draws back for a sweeping wide-angle shot of the cowboy's environment—the great, grassy plains stretching toward an infinite horizon. Like the cowboy himself, the plains have generated a melange of positive and negative images.

The cowboy remains at the center of the action. The dust, smoke, and sweat of his hard work and life on the range occupy the book's central chapters. We ride with him on roundups and trail drives; we see him in relation to his rancher/employer; and we eat a meal with him by a campfire. His pastimes on horseback and afoot take us to horse races, saloons, and houses of ill repute. No cowboy movie is complete without Indians; the chapter entitled "Cowboys and Indians" examines the harsh reality of frontier racial conflict and Indian wars.

Our "movie" concludes with scenes at twilight. A larger plot overtakes the protagonist. Rapid changes in the ranching industry deeply and permanently alter the cowboy's work and way of life. A few villains make appearances and powerful political and socioeconomic forces go to work. A procession of farmers, immigrants, and new gadgets pushes across the plains, cutting off the cowboy from his accustomed way of life. Finally, the cowboy rides off into a brilliant western sunset. But his image and memory live on in myth and popular culture.

Etymologists trace the use of the term *cowboy* back to AD 1000 in Ireland. Swift used it in 1705, logically enough, to describe a boy who tends cows. But its modern usage, first in hyphenated form, dates from the 1830s in Texas. Colonel John S. "Rip" Ford used the word *cow-boy* to describe the Texan border raider who drove off Mexican cattle during the 1830s. This early tinge of life at the fringes of the law—of an indifference to the strictures of "civilization"—also taints South American equestrian groups, such as gauchos and llaneros.[7]

After the American Civil War, Westerners applied the term *cowboy* to ranch hands, not cattle thieves. The Denver *Republican* observed in its issue of October 1, 1883, that "it matters not what age, if a man works on a salary and rides after the herd, he is called a 'cowboy.'" The term *cowboy* is used in this book to mean a man who works at least part of the year as a salaried ranch hand.[8]

Cowboys are defined by what they do—work cattle on horseback. "Cowboy work is more than a job; it is a life-style and a medium of expression," writes John R. Erickson. They are also defined by their social position. Ranchers or "cowmen" owned land and cattle; cowboys did not own land and seldom owned cattle. As will be seen, many equestrian groups of Latin America labored for generations as wild-cattle hunters before the rise of organized ranching. They did eventually work on ranches as cowboys, however, so the term applies with equal validity to gauchos, llaneros, vaqueros, and *huasos*.[9]

Are the similarities among the various types of cowboys stronger than their differences? In the 1880s Emilio Daireaux asserted that the plains "imprint" similar characteristics on their inhabitants around the world. Analogous equipment, riding techniques, types of labor performed, and social roles prompted Edward Larocque Tinker to label the horsemen of North and South America brothers under the skin. "Not only did they all get their original horses and cattle from Spain, but they learned their superlative horsemanship from the same source, as well as their methods of branding and handling large herds. . . . They were all molded, North and South, by the same conditions the frontier and the cattle business imposed on them, and naturally developed the same characteristics of pride, daring, and fierce independence."[10]

Laureano Vallenilla Lanz, an apologist for Juan Vicente Gómez, who ruled Venezuela as dictator from 1908 to 1935, extended the comparative imagery: "In all pastoral peoples, from the Bedouin, Tartar, Turk, Kurd, and Cossack to the gaucho of the Río de la Plata, is the feeling of independence, of profound contempt for agricultural towns." Other commentators have noted resemblances among Argentine gauchos, Mexican vaqueros, American cowboys, South African Boers, Russian cossacks, and Hungarian *csikos*.[11]

Real and imagined similarities notwithstanding, close examination reveals major differences between equestrian groups of the Western Hemisphere. I will try to highlight both the distinctive traits of individual cowboy types and those characteristics that they share with other riders. The length of time they flourished, the degree of change they underwent, and the sociopolitical contexts of the cowboy cultures differed substantially. I seek a balance between the broad, comparative perspective and the details and nuances that add texture and richness to the general picture. The reader must determine whether the result both does justice to specific events of history and offers insights into wider social processes that transcend a particular place and time.

A. A. Hayes commented in late 1880 that "the 'cow-boys' of the Rocky Mountain regions are a race or a class peculiar to that country. They have some resemblances to the corresponding class on the southern side of the Río Grande, but are of a milder and more original type." Horsemen of Latin America also have been described as a peculiar race or class of people. For the most part, however, such depictions are inaccurate and inappropriate. Even if a satisfactory definition of class could be developed, it is doubtful whether these frontier types would conform well to it.[12]

Peter Calvert has warned that a "state of considerable confusion" surrounds the concept of class today. I will refer to cowboys in their respective nations as distinct social groups, not as classes. Nor do they qualify as peasants, campesinos, or freeholders. Cowboys held distinctive cultural values. These values and their way of life set them apart from others in society. In some cases, they occupied a unique legal status—that of rural outlaws or vagrants. By definition, they never owned land, exercised political power, or held high social position.

I avoid labeling cowboys as a class, but this does not deny the existence of class conflict, particularly in the Latin American plains regions. Landed elites existed and functioned as self-conscious ruling classes. Their class interests conflicted sharply with those of the rural poor, including horsemen of the plains. I favor adopting the phrase of Argentine intellectual Ezequiel Martínez Estrada, who termed gauchos "a class of the unclassified."[13]

Cowboys are imbued with an aura of romance and violence. In the popular mind, they are archetypal frontiersmen. Frederick Jackson Turner linked frontier environments with character traits in his famous 1893 treatise. Since then generations of scholars, particularly in the United States, have wrestled with the frontier concept. Rather than splitting more hairs, I will use the term *cattle frontier* to refer to sparsely populated areas, remote from political and population centers, where the legal and illegal slaughter of livestock provided the main source of income and employment.[14]

Cowboys lived and worked primarily in frontier areas. Their actions played a major role in shaping our perception of frontiersmen. In some countries, notably the United States, Uruguay, and Argentina, cowboys became cultural symbols of national importance. In the northern and southern plains of Brazil (the *sertão* and pampa, respectively) and in the prairies of western Canada, the cowboy's impact remained regional. Hawaii is only now uncovering and recognizing its own cowboy culture.[15]

Whatever its explanatory shortcomings, Turner's frontier thesis provoked numerous comparative studies. Alistair Hennessy's *Frontier in Latin American History* is the most ambitious recent critique of Turnerian thought for the region. This book builds on and refines Hennessy's presentation of plains frontiers. Hennessy's general view that "frontiers of exclusion" did not typify Latin America is correct. But "hard-edged" frontiers sharply divided whites from Araucanian Indians in Chile, from pampas tribes in Argentina, and, initially, from Chichimecs in northern Mexico. Hennessy repeats Arnold Strickon's erroneous statement that "slavery and forced labor systems were incompatible with open-range ranching." On the contrary, slaves worked cattle in Venezuela, Brazil, and Argentina.[16]

Hennessy also argues that no frontier myth has stirred massive Latin American migrations. This view ignores the recent gold rush to the Amazon Basin. The great tide of European immigration to the Argentine plains from 1880 to 1910 is another example. To be sure, Turner's somewhat romanticized link between the frontier and democracy did not function in Latin America. But equally powerful myths, such as that of "El Dorado" in Colombia, drew generations of Spaniards to the region. Today, the "West" in Brazil and the "South" in Argentina continue to exert important political and psychological influences. Argentina went so far as to rename its national currency the *austral* in honor of its southern region, symbol of the future.[17]

I also take issue with the "cowpens" school that traces western ranching to roots in the colonial Carolinas. The meager cultural trickle from the Carolina Piedmont through the Old South to the coast of east Texas was a minor sideshow. The Spanish influence dominated and shaped the western cattle frontier. The Anglo-American cowboy learned his trade from the vaquero. Spanish terminology, equipment, and technique spread from Texas and California throughout the western United States. In the 1880s a ranch foreman was called "major domo" (from the Spanish term *mayordomo*), whether he was in eastern Oregon, southern Idaho, or Nevada. Cowboys in the region were called vaqueros. Hispanic influences also crossed the border into Canada, carried by cowboys from the United States.[18]

Beyond correcting some notions about the frontier in both Latin and Anglo-America, this book aspires to contribute conceptually to comparative studies. I agree with Frederick C. Luebke's assessment that regions are "best conceptualized in terms of the interplay between environment and culture; they are best described and analyzed through appropriate comparisons in time, space, and culture." Regional histories have made important contributions to our understanding of plains frontiers. But the findings from regional studies are enriched when they are placed into a broader, comparative framework. I hope that other scholars will take up the challenge of probing the lives of cowboys in those regions in need of further study, which are indicated in my bibliographical essay.[19]

Comparison is implicit in most studies. Donald Denoon, author of a fine comparative work, goes so far as to say that "only one analytical method is to be found anywhere in the social sciences: the comparative method." But explicit comparative analysis is relatively rare. Theoretical and typological arguments are rarer still.[20]

George M. Fredrickson and Philip Curtain, among others, have lamented the dearth of truly comparative analysis. Comparative historical study, notes Fredrickson, "is characterized by its relative sparseness and by its fragmentation." Explicit comparison enhances the analyst's explanatory power. It also illuminates the structures and processes essential to historical understanding. In his presidential address to the 1983 meeting of the American Historical Association, Curtain urged comparisons of the United States, Canada, and Latin America. "It can be argued," he said, "that the fullest understanding of New World history requires a comparative study of what went on in all three of these zones." It is with these promptings in mind that this study was written.[21]

Specialists in national or regional history will likely find cause for discontent in a work of this scope. I have taken pains to keep particularistic variations in mind, but the search for larger, comparative themes may at times do violence to the subtleties of local events. This is a necessary tradeoff in comparative and interpretive studies. Professor Bolton, in his eightieth year, offered this advice to one of his students: "Don't ever write a definitive work, young fellow; it kills off the subject. Leave a few mistakes and your students will have great fun catching up the old man." I have no doubt followed Bolton's advice, and I hope that you enjoy the ride.[22]

CHAPTER 2

From Wild-Cattle Hunters to Cowboys

Spanish Caribbean Origins

Herding and herdsmen go far back in history. But mounted herding and open-range ranching did not begin in the New World until the time of Columbus, who introduced cattle and reintroduced the horse on his second voyage. On January 2, 1494, he unloaded twenty-four stallions, ten mares, and an unknown number of cattle on the island of Hispaniola (today shared by the Dominican Republic and Haiti). Because importing livestock from Spain was expensive, and many animals died en route, ranching quickly became established in the Caribbean islands.[1]

Three elements of the pioneering Caribbean livestock industry stand out because they later recurred throughout the Latin American mainland. First, animals proliferated with tremendous rapidity, creating huge herds of wild, ownerless cattle and horses and an abundance of meat. Second, horsemen adapted Spanish equipment and techniques to their New World environment. Third, ranchers worked assiduously to monopolize markets. José de Acosta, writing of West Indies ranching in 1590, confirms the first two points: "The cattle have multiplied so greatly in Santo Domingo, and in other islands of that region that they wander by the thousands through the forests and fields, all masterless. They hunt these beasts only for their hides; whites and Negroes go out on horseback, equipped with a kind of hooked knife, to chase the cattle, and any animal that falls to their knives is theirs. They kill it and carry the hide home, leaving the flesh to rot; no one wants it, since meat is so plentiful."[2]

Caribbean island livestock producers immediately set out to protect their economic interests. They sought to maintain a monopoly on livestock production by prohibiting animal exports to the mainland. Smugglers could be punished by death. Similar monopolistic tactics (with less drastic penalties) would be used well into the nineteenth century in Venezuela and Chile. In general, regulations stimulated contraband cattle trading, which was commonplace throughout the Spanish Empire from Florida to Argentina. Restrictions notwithstanding, smuggled animals reached mainland areas well before Charles V lifted the export ban in 1526. Horses and cattle escaped, and wild herds proliferated rapidly. The abundance of wild livestock in plains regions gave rise to customary rights for killing the animals.[3]

From the islands of the Caribbean, livestock spread to many areas of the mainland within the next few decades. Cattle reached the Panamanian isthmus in 1510. In 1519 Hernando Cortés took horses into New Spain (Mexico). By 1524 cattle had appeared on the northern coast of South America; a decade later they reached the west coast of the continent. The conquistador Pedro de Valdivia brought the first cattle to Chile, where livestock development centered on the capital, Santiago (founded in 1541). By the end of the sixteenth century, livestock had penetrated all of the major colonial ranching areas of South America: the llanos, Peru, Chile, and the Río de la Plata.[4]

Spanish explorers took horses and cattle northward to Florida, beginning with Ponce de León's second trip in 1521. Hernando de Soto followed, carrying more than three hundred horses and some cattle in 1539. It was there that the Spanish established the first stock raising in what is now the United States. As elsewhere on the frontier, missions spearheaded settlement. Some stock raising was established by about 1565 around St. Augustine and Tallahassee. Early ranchers produced for local markets but also smuggled cattle to Cuba. Tropical disease and hostile Indians took their toll, however. By the end of the seventeenth century, tax rolls showed only thirty-four ranches in Florida with a total of fifteen to twenty thousand cattle. The first ranching area in the United States never developed anything like the vast herds found in South America and Mexico. By the time the United States annexed Florida in 1821, very few vestiges of the original Spanish cattle culture remained.[5]

In Brazil, where active settlement did not begin until 1550, ranching accompanied plantation agriculture in the northeastern hump. Vaqueiros herded cattle in the dry inland plains called the sertão. Cowboys received a share of the calves born on the large ranches, enabling some to establish herds of their own. The ranches of the Northeast produced both meat on the hoof and dried beef. But recurrent drought and the general economic shift of Brazil to the south led to a decline in the sertão livestock industry toward the end of the eighteenth century. It thrived instead in the southern state of Minas Gerais, stimulated by the expansion of mining and agriculture there and in São Paulo. Less prone to droughts, Minas developed a diversified livestock industry that supplied pack animals, meat, and dairy products.[6]

Jesuit missionaries brought some livestock to southern Brazil in the 1620s, and major introductions came during the following decade. The southern plains, called Campo Gerais during the colonial era, were blessed with well-watered pastures. Spanish-Portuguese conflict in southern Brazil during the eighteenth century and civil wars during the nineteenth century disrupted ranching. Warfare also created large herds of wild, unclaimed cattle. Cattle smuggling across the Brazilian-Uruguayan border became commonplace during the nineteenth century. A robust if primitive dried beef industry developed in Rio Grande do Sul and northern Uruguay. Open-range ranching and mostly unimproved livestock characterized this border region into the twentieth century.[7]

Wild-Cattle Hunters of the Río de la Plata

By the late seventeenth century, the foundations for Western Hemisphere equestrian cultures had been laid: horsemen and livestock coexisting in plains environments. Throughout Latin America, plains horsemen hunted and slaughtered wild cattle for their hides, tallow, and by-products. These wild-cattle hunters evolved with the livestock industry and became the cowboys of Latin America. Either working for merchants with official licenses or free-lancing illegally, hunters performed the grisly labor on the plains. Riders hamstrung the cattle with long hocking blades. They then slit the animal's throat, perhaps sliced out the tongue for a meal, and stripped off the hide. Staked out on the plains to dry, the hides were later collected for export. Organized ranches, domesticated cattle, and slaughterhouses would come later.[8]

Gradually, the depletion of livestock and the desire to extract greater profit from the livestock economy led to changes in cowboy work. Spanish colonial officials moved to preserve the wild-cattle herds and limit the free-lance activities of gauchos. Elites in all ranching areas began to extend their domination over the resources of the plains (land, livestock, water, and labor). The rise of ranches and an organized livestock industry changed the cowboy's life and work.[9]

Enormous herds of wild horses and cattle roamed the Mexican plains, the pampas of the Río de la Plata, and the llanos by the mid-seventeenth century. Despite formidable predatory enemies, such as the jaguar of the llano and terrifying packs of wild dogs on the pampa, livestock numbers increased mightily. Indians in plains regions expanded their traditional hunting activities to include the new animals. They also developed equestrian skills that would make them dangerous adversaries to the encroaching Spanish. Mestizo horsemen joined in the hunts, because the hides and by-products from cattle offered a ready source of income to anyone with the skill and energy to chase, kill, and skin cattle. By the mid-eighteenth century, these mestizo wild-cattle hunters had developed a set of practices and values and a life cycle that were both appropriate and peculiar to the plains they inhabited.[10]

By 1603, some sixty years after Valdivias's arrival, Spaniards in Chile had established horse breeding ranches. A shortage of mounts in the sixteenth century forced Chilean riders to the unthinkable and unmanly expedient of riding mares. Herds of horses multiplied, and by the nineteenth century huasos reasserted the cultural prejudice against mares. Cowboys throughout Latin America refused to ride mares, and the Mexican vaquero passed this aversion along to Anglo cowboys in Texas.[11]

Wild cattle multiplied readily in Chile as in other parts of the Americas. As ranchers sought to establish control over rights to the livestock and land, complaints of rustlers increased. In northern Mexico, on the Argentine pampa, and in southern Chile, hostilities with Indians made cattle and horses important allies in the conquest of frontier regions. By 1568 the fierce Araucanians had become dangerous cavalrymen, often armed with weapons captured from the Spanish. By 1600 the Indians had more horses than the Spanish. Repeated and prolonged conflict with the Araucanians created a sizable internal market for livestock to mount and feed the Spanish armies in Chile.[12]

Hunting wild cattle, like battling Indians, required many cowboys. Spaniards brought with them several tools for working cattle. They used the *desjarretadera*, or hocking blade, to hamstring wild cattle. The *garrocha*, or pike, could be used to prod animals or to attack enemies. These Spanish tools, along with the *lazo*, appeared throughout cattle regions of Latin America.[13]

Amerindians also contributed to the cattle culture. In southern South America, gauchos and huasos adopted an effective tool and weapon called the *bolas* or *boleadoras*. A Flemish soldier, Hulderico Schmidel, described the use of the bolas by Indians on the pampas in 1585: "They have certain balls of stone tied to a long string like our chain shot; they throw them at the legs of the horses (or of the deer when they hunt), which brings them to the ground, and with these bolas they killed our Captain" [Diego de Mendoza, brother of the explorer who founded the city of Buenos Aires, Pedro de Mendoza]. Gauchos developed variants of the weapon for large game (three balls), small game (two balls), and hand-to-hand combat (a single ball, called the *bola perdida*).[14]

Beginning in 1535, Jesuits established livestock raising on their missions in the Río de la Plata and farther north in the interior of South America. But the missions of northern Argentina, Paraguay, and Brazil faced a dire threat from *bandeirante* slaving raids. Bandeirantes, based in São Paulo, launched large expeditions into the South American interior that often lasted for years. They found it much easier to capture and enslave mission Indians than to chase nomadic tribes. Bandeirantes destroyed many Jesuit missions and left thousands of cattle abandoned. From about 1637 to 1687, feral cattle in Rio Grande do Sul were considered unowned and available equally to anyone.[15]

Juan de Magalhaes re-established ranching in Rio Grande do Sul in 1715 with his *estancia*, or small farm. The rise of organized ranches in the eighteenth century set up conflict between wild-cattle hunters and established ranchers who claimed both land and cattle. Public rights to livestock on the range were still claimed through the mid-nineteenth century from Argentina to south Texas. These wild-cattle hunters who claimed use rights from the late sixteenth and seventeenth centuries were the precursors of the cowboys of the Americas.[16]

In most ranching frontiers, missions established by various religious orders played an important economic role. Like the bandeirantes, the Minuane and Charrúa Indians of the Río de la Plata became formidable adversaries to Spanish expansion and settlement. They hunted wild cattle and raided Jesuit missions. In southern Brazil and Uruguay, the Jesuits established important missions and gathered tens of thousands of Guaraní Indians under their care. About 1720, Jesuits drove an estimated eighty to one hundred thousand head of cattle from Vaquería del Mar in Uruguay north to Campos da Vacaria. The impressive drive of more than three hundred miles necessitated cutting a seventeen-mile stretch of trail through dense forest. The mission the Jesuits established became the town of Vacaria dos Pinhais in Rio Grande do Sul.[17]

The growth of cities in the Río de la Plata generated further markets for livestock for local consumption and export. The founding of Santa Fe in 1573 and Juan de Garay's refounding of Buenos Aires in 1580 spurred hinterland development insofar as hostile Indians permitted. Cattle appeared in the Mesopotamian provinces of Corrientes and Entre Ríos by 1583. Unlike *hateros*, who established ranches in the llanos beginning in the sixteenth century, Argentine ranchers (*estancieros*) preferred to live in cities. The hostility of pampas Indians and the great abundance of wild cattle largely explain their early failures to establish ranches. *Vaquerías*, or wild-cattle hunting expeditions, continued as the main means of livestock exploitation into the eighteenth century. In 1609 the *cabildo*, or town council, of Buenos Aires began granting licenses (*acciones*) to round up escaped cattle. The concept became generalized to include unbranded cattle as well. The number of wild cattle permitted was in proportion to the number of branded animals owned. This system, of course, benefited the wealthiest.[18]

Penetrating the Llanos

Livestock existed in most plains areas of Latin America by the mid-sixteenth century. Established ranches, with claims to land and water resources, appeared soon thereafter. For example, Cristóbal Rodríguez is commonly credited with importing livestock into Venezuela during his expedition in 1548. In neighboring Colombia, cattle were driven over the Andes from Santa Marta to Santa Fe in the llanos in 1541. In 1569 Diego Fernández de Serpa brought in eight hundred head via the island of Margarita. The important livestock center of San Sebastian de los Reyes was founded in 1584 or 1585, and *hatos* (ranches) proliferated thereafter. By the early seventeenth century, ranches had extended to the areas of Tocuyo, Barquisimeto, Valencia, and the valley of Caracas. By 1665 hides ranked first among Venezuela's exports. On the Colombian llanos, herds of Casanareño (a small, jersey-tan breed) and San Martinero (a larger, dark-red breed) became common by the seventeenth century. Over time, the coastal *cacao* (chocolate) plantations overtook livestock in importance. But hide prices tended to fluctuate much less than those for cacao, so the livestock industry enjoyed gradual, relatively stable growth during most of the colonial period.[19]

As elsewhere in the Americas, religious as well as military missions penetrated frontier regions. Franciscans and Capuchins established villages in the llanos by the mid-seventeenth century. Cattle herding became an important economic activity for profit and for indoctrinating the Indians. During the eighteenth century, the original mission villages gradually became secularized. After independence came to Venezuela in 1821, the authority of the religious orders in the llanos gave way to that of *caudillos*, local political bosses backed by private armies.[20]

In cattle frontiers throughout Spanish and Portuguese America, contraband was a way of life. Both free-lance (often illegal) and sanctioned, organized cattle hunts took place. In the Venezuelan llanos, wild-cattle roundups took place in late July and August. Neighboring landowners named a *caporal* (range boss) to call together workers of a given region. Each ranch contributed a number of peons and provided them with six or more mounts each. The workers traveled the region rounding up the cattle that had grazed wild and unattended during the past year. In 1723, for example, landowners of Parapara on the llanos requested permission to hold a communal hunt. The riders swept the area of Guesipe in search of livestock. California vaqueros performed similar labors in the *matanza*, the slaughter of cattle for hides and tallow. These hunts continued in Spanish California from the eighteenth century until the gold rush of 1849 absorbed all available livestock.[21]

Independent Frontiersmen or Outlaws?

The lives and character of the Latin American plainsmen were strongly molded by their principal early economic activity—wild-cattle hunting—and by their remoteness, both geographical and cultural, from central governmental authority. Plainsmen lived by values and goals that were very different from those of the ruling urban elites. Conflict developed early, as Spanish officials tried to extend their monopolistic economic policies to frontier regions, and to subdue and regulate the mestizo and Amerindian inhabitants of the plains. For example, officials in New Spain, concerned about the rapid slaughter of wild cattle, forbade use of the hocking lance in 1574.[22]

The town council of Buenos Aires continued to issue government licenses to hunt wild livestock, but contraband hunting remained common. By the 1640s officials increased their efforts to maintain a monopoly for the favored few. Labeling the landless rural population vagrant and criminal, officials initiated two centuries of ultimately successful legal repression to control the gaucho. As Alistair Hennessy has noted, pastoral workers were "relatively free men," controlled by "internal rather than by external restraints." But we must remember that many ranch hands were slaves, their lives circumscribed by all the strictures of that labor system. And we must not ignore the large body of Hispanic legislation aimed at controlling the rural masses during both the colonial and national periods. Cowboys in Latin America retained their freedom only insofar as they could evade the oppressive legal measures directed against them and their way of life.[23]

Smuggling remained an important element of the Río de la Plata economy even after Argentina became independent in 1816. Bribery of public officials was commonplace. Smugglers bribed Spanish and later Argentine officials with liquor and fine furnishings as well as satin dresses and silk stockings for their wives and daughters. As one source complained in 1821, "In all parts were poachers allowed to infest the domains of the public revenue." As we will see, the American cowboy also got his start in Texas as a wild-cattle hunter and rustler.[24]

Insofar as possible, any strictures emanating from Buenos Aires, Mexico City, or Caracas went ignored on the plains, unless accompanied by sufficient military force. Illegal hunting and contraband trade were the normal forms of economic activity. To plainsmen, the fruits of the earth belonged to anyone who could gather them. Itinerant merchants willingly traded with anyone, mestizo or Indian, to acquire marketable hides or other produce. From the mid-seventeenth through the early nineteenth centuries, the Río Apure served as a principal transportation route for the llanos. Smuggled hides traveled down the river and out of the country to cooperative Dutch and English merchants. In late eighteenth-century Venezuela, fifty thousand hides per year—nearly 25 percent of total exports—may have been contraband. Such rampant illegal activity gave rise to an economic system of "contraband capitalism" in which both the powerful and the poor participated.[25]

Wild-livestock hunters were frontiersmen who lived and worked in regions of sparse population, in contact (and often conflict) with indigenous societies, far from urban, civic authority, and possessing ample natural resources for near self-sufficiency. Miguel Izard, a leading scholar of the Venezuelan llaneros, argues convincingly that they came to constitute a separate people, distinct from the Spanish/creole population of the northern coast and valleys.[26]

Static Frontiers

During the nineteenth century, some ranching areas, notably the Argentine pampas, improved breeds and introduced new livestock tools and management. The life and work of the gaucho changed accordingly. But reports from the llanos indicate that ranchers and their hired hands lavished little unnecessary care or attention on livestock or horses. Nor did they adopt more "scientific" range management techniques. The leading scholar of the Colombian llanos has described the region as a "static frontier," largely unchanged over centuries. The same description applies to the Venezuelan plains.[27]

Accounts of wild-cattle hunts on the llanos during the early nineteenth century could well have been written more than a century before. Richard Vowell, who observed the llanero at work in 1818, wrote: "Although usually styled and considered herdsmen, their habits and mode of life were in reality those of hunters; for the cattle, which constituted their sole wealth, being perfectly wild, the exertions requisite to collect a herd, and to keep it together in the neighbourhood of a farm-house, were necessarily violent and incessant."[28]

George Flinter detailed the llanero technique of wild-cattle hunting in 1819. The llanero "at full speed, hamstrings the animal in both legs, which brings it immediately to the ground; he then alights, and, with the point of his spear, strikes the bull in the nape of the neck. . . . He next skins it, takes out the fat, and, after having cut up the flesh in long pieces, brings it to the hato, where it is sprinkled with salt, and hung up to dry in the sun."[29]

Ranching techniques on the llanos remained backward for many years. Ranchers, indifferent to the niceties of selective breeding or to careful husbandry, changed their approach to ranch management little from the eighteenth through the twentieth centuries. As one nineteenth-century rancher, Zoilo Navarro, observed, "God nourishes the cattle and I sell them. It's a profitable deal." Well into the twentieth century, llanos ranches suffered from overgrazing as well as a lack of fences and roads.[30]

The cattle frontier of southern Brazil and northern Uruguay also remained static. Visiting Rio Grande do Sul, Brazil, early in the 1820s, Auguste Saint-Hilaire commented that "the cattle are left completely to the laws of nature. They are not cared for in any way. They are not even given salt as the cattle in Minas [Gerais] are. They are almost wild." A German visitor to the region commented in 1829 that "the cattle are not well cared for" and "horses are badly treated too." Not until the mid-nineteenth century did ranchers in southern Brazil begin to furnish cattle with salt. Some ranchers added wire fencing after the 1880s, but borderlands cattle production, work techniques, and social relations changed very little.[31]

The rich valleys of central Chile occupied a middle ground between the pampas and the llanos in terms of nineteenth-century change. Ricardo Price imported purebred Durham bulls during the 1840s, and Tomás Gallo and Anacleto Mott followed suit in 1850. The Agricultural Society, the political organization of the Chilean landed elite, established a Durham registry in 1883.

Nevertheless, many ranches continued to produce mestizo cattle for the internal market. The tradition-bound elite did not adopt new breeds and techniques to compete with Argentina, Canada, Australia, and the United States in the international chilled beef trade.[32]

From Cattle Hunter to Cowboy in the United States

Cattle herding in the United States began at opposite poles, the Southeast and the Southwest. The Spanish brought livestock to Florida in the sixteenth century, but these early efforts had little long-term impact. It is doubtful whether cattle, horses, or ranching techniques ever spread from Spanish Florida to British North America. But the British colonies were developing their own version of the cattle culture. In 1611 cattle were first imported to Jamestown colony. As Terry G. Jordan, Gary S. Dunbar, and others have documented, herders tended cattle in the "cowpens" of colonial South Carolina. The practice spread north to North Carolina and Virginia and southwest to Georgia during the eighteenth century. These "cattle hunters" (more rarely called "cowboys") worked on foot for the most part, with the aid of stock dogs and whips. Piedmont herders branded their animals to show ownership, a common practice dating back thousands of years in other cultures. Black slaves often performed the hard labor of hunting wild cattle. Herds of one to three hundred head of cattle appeared in the Ohio Valley by the 1820s. By the 1830s herding techniques had diffused through the Deep South into the humid coastal plains of east Texas. Moving further west to the semi-arid plains, the habits and techniques of southeastern Anglo cowboys changed substantially under the influence of Mexico's vaqueros.[33]

Early Anglo cowboys in east Texas hunted wild cattle in much the same fashion as their Latin American counterparts. Illegality tinged the Texas cattle hunts as it did those in South America. Many Anglo cowboys exhibited a ready indifference to the legal ownership of the cattle they hunted. Anglo cowboys raided Mexican stock, which they then drove to markets in Louisiana. Some Anglos exchanged arms for livestock with Indians in Texas. They also scoured the coastal plain for semiwild cattle, or "swampers," during annual roundups and branding.[34]

Anglo cowboys were following in the footsteps of vaqueros, who had driven

cattle illegally from Texas to Louisiana for generations. Throughout the eighteenth century, Spanish ranchers drove cattle to French Louisiana. In 1750
the Spanish governor proposed to no avail that the heavy traffic be licensed
and regulated. Spain acquired Louisiana in 1763, thereby removing the
stigma of illegality. But after the United States acquired the Louisiana Territory in 1803, cattle movements east from Texas continued—again illegally.[35]

Spanish colonial ranching in Texas was neither so haphazard nor so completely decimated by Indians attacks as might be thought. By 1800 major
livestock economies flourished in three areas. Nacogdoches included many
horse ranches. Large herds of cattle and horses grazed in the Río Grande
Valley all the way north to the Nueces. Well-established ranches dotted the
countryside around San Antonio, east to the Guadalupe River, and south to
La Bahía. The Spanish made no extraordinary efforts to tame their cattle.
They grazed on accustomed ranges but generally ran free. By leaving the
cattle semiwild, Spaniards made it more difficult for raiding Indians to drive
them off. Thus, many of the "wild" animals appropriated by Anglo immigrants belonged to Hispanic ranchers and had been tended by vaqueros.[36]

Anglos helped themselves to the livestock bounty bequeathed by Spanish
settlers. The *Texas Almanac* for 1861 reveals that those working in the "Cow
Boy System" did not "scruple to push their expeditions to the very doors of
the Mexican on the Río Grande and drive off their gentle cattle." Many Anglo
settlers considered the wild cattle they found in Texas to be open game, free
for the taking. They called the animals mustang cattle (from *mesteños*) or
Spanish cattle. A 1935 evaluation of the grazing industry concluded that "Texans did not create their cattle industry, they simply took it over."[37]

We do find Anglo-Spanish fusion in Texas livestock, beginning in the 1830s.
The storied Longhorn was the result of cross-breeding between Spanish cattle, primarily the Retinto, and animals brought to Texas by early Anglo settlers. Immune to tick fever and accustomed to life in the tough brush country
of south Texas, the Longhorn became the mainstay of the western livestock
industry. During the decades following the Civil War, cowboys trailed some
eight to ten million Longhorns north from Texas. The hardy animals gradually gave way to other breeds and are now largely a curiosity of folklore, like
the bison.[38]

By the 1860s "cow hunts" took men into the brush country of south Texas
in search of wild cattle. James C. Shaw, born in 1852, recalled such hunts
during his childhood near Elgin, Texas. Five men riding "Spanish ponies"
would go in search of wild cattle. They augmented their diet of coffee and

biscuits with fish, deer, and wild turkey. Unbranded wild mavericks could be taken by anyone with a rope. Outlaw skinners seldom worried about who might own the hides they took. Coastal "factories" processed the tough, rangy Longhorns into marketable hides, tallow, and beef jerky until the mid-1870s.[39]

The Vaquero Rides North to Texas

Spanish influence arrived on the Great Plains from the south and west. J. Frank Dobie, Jack Jackson, Sandra Myres, and others argue convincingly that, for Texas, the Hispanic element is key. The Anglo ranching component, traced by Jordan to the cowpens of the Carolinas, is marginal in terms of its impact on western ranching technique, equipment, vocabulary, and folklore. The prior experience of Anglo settlers from the South with tame, often penned cattle hardly prepared them to face Longhorns. Handling wild cattle on the arid, open range was something new. New perhaps to Anglos, but centuries-old to the vaquero. Texas and, by extension, Great Plains ranching exhibits far more Hispanic than Anglo roots.[40]

Barriers of race, class, and culture separated the cowboys of the Americas from the elites who controlled the land. By the mid-sixteenth century, ranch hands (vaqueros) were needed to tend the multiplying cattle herds of Mexico. Frontier missions trained their Indians and other nonwhite charges to tend cattle—labor that was considered undignified for Spanish gentlemen. Similarly, Argentine gauchos lived as a distinct social group on the fringes between urban-based Spanish/creole and indigenous frontier societies. Spanish landed gentlemen rode horses but never actually worked cattle. Their aversion to manual labor left livestock hunting and tending to the *castas*, the nonwhite lower classes. In the Franciscan missions of Texas, New Mexico, Arizona, and California, Indians herded the livestock.[41]

Livestock made a brief appearance in what is now the American Southwest in 1540–1541. Francisco Vásquez de Coronado and his men gathered five hundred cattle and some smaller quadrupeds for their long journey northward. But it is unlikely that any animals remained in the American Southwest after the expedition passed through. Indians and predators likely dispatched any animals that may have strayed. The burgeoning silver mining industry, spurred by booms in Zacatecas in 1546 and Guanajuato in 1554, created a strong internal demand for cattle, horses, and mules. Tallow for candles in the mines, hides for ore and water bags, clothing, harnesses, hinges, and countless other necessities all boosted demand for livestock.[42]

Once the hostile Chichimec Indians had been bought off by a more accommodating Spanish policy in the late sixteenth century, livestock spread northward into northern Mexico and what is today New Mexico and Arizona. San Juan de los Ríos, Mexico, situated at an important river ford, became a major livestock center. By 1582 an estimated one hundred thousand cattle, two hundred thousand sheep, and ten thousand horses grazed on the range near San Juan. Organized ranches (estancias) with domesticated animals began to appear in the region before 1600. Juan de Oñate can be credited with breeding livestock for the first time in 1598 in the American Southwest. Not for another half-century were settlements established near El Paso del Norte in west Texas.[43]

East and south Texas also experienced considerable Spanish influence prior to Anglo occupation. An expedition in 1690, led by Captain Alonso de León, brought livestock to the first Spanish mission in east Texas, San Francisco de los Tejas. Domingo de Terán further stocked the mission the following year. By the early eighteenth century, cattle grazed along the Neches and Trinity rivers. The Marquis de Aguayo spurred Texas ranching in 1721 when he brought four hundred sheep and three hundred cattle into south Texas from Nuevo León. José de Escandón pushed northward to Nuevo Santander from Querétaro with four thousand colonists in 1748. This drive established stock raising in the diamond-shaped area formed by the Nueces and Río Grande valleys. Spanish ranchers illegally drove livestock to Louisiana. The Bourbons finally legalized the trade in 1780 as part of their economic liberalization policies. Hence, the Spanish operated a lively livestock economy in Texas well before the arrival of Anglos from the southern United States.[44]

Missions in Texas, as elsewhere, served as focal points for early ranching efforts. Franciscans founded a number of missions in the area of San Antonio de Bexar. These included San Antonio de Valero, established in 1718, and San José, built two years later. Indian depredations in east Texas forced the relocation in 1731 of three more missions: Concepción, San Juan Capistrano, and Espada. All three sat along the San Antonio River.[45]

As the eighteenth century progressed, ranching in Spanish Texas suffered from disease, drought, Indian raids, and lack of legitimate markets. As in livestock regions of South America, illegalities marked the early Texas range. Cattle smugglers moved herds surreptitiously into Louisiana. Legal trade expanded in the 1770s, but smugglers continued operations to avoid the export tax of two reales per head. By the late eighteenth century, some fifteen to twenty thousand head moved eastward to Louisiana each year. In the early 1800s illegal horse and mule trade joined the contraband cattle drives. The movement of Anglo settlers into the Mississippi Valley provided another market for livestock. Meanwhile, problems plagued the economic and religious activities at the missions. Unable to convert the hostile Indians, priests abandoned the missions in east Texas. But livestock remained.[46]

Missionaries also played a leading role in establishing ranching in Arizona, New Mexico, and California. In 1687 an Italian Jesuit, Father Eusebio Francisco Kino, established the mission of Nuestra Señora de las Dolores. This and subsequent missions brought livestock to the Pimería Alta region (today southern Arizona and northern Sonora, Mexico). During his active missionary career (he died in 1711), Father Kino established stock ranches in at least twenty locations in the Santa Cruz Valley of Arizona. He viewed the role of livestock tending as essential in converting and feeding the Pima Indians on the northern frontier of New Spain.[47]

Vaqueros in California and the Southwest

The vaquero in California, as in Old Mexico, began his life on the frontier missions. Beginning with the establishment of San Diego in 1769, Father Junipero Serra's string of Franciscan missions spread along the California coast. As in Mexico, Indian vaqueros tended the livestock. The Spanish, ever fearful of attacks by their Indian charges, had forbidden Indians to ride horses. The law had to be amended to permit mission neophytes to tend cattle on horseback. Mission Indians quickly became skilled at all aspects of ranch work. They made and threw lariats, herded, and branded. Unfortunately for the Spanish, hostile Indians, especially the Apaches of the Southwest, also became excellent horsemen and formidable enemies.[48]

Father Kino's work in Arizona also bore fruit in California. In 1775 and 1776 Juan Bautista de Anza brought settlers and trailed livestock from Arizona to Monterey and then on to San Francisco. This route fulfilled one of Kino's ambitions—to supply California with livestock from Arizona.[49]

Raiding Apaches, however, constantly threatened livestock raising and the Spanish presence on the northern frontier of New Spain. The usually friendly Pima rose up in 1751 and drove out the few Spanish settlers in Arizona. The Yuma Indians attacked in 1781. These and other depredations often left livestock untended. Herds of feral horses and cattle multiplied in the American Southwest and in northern Mexico. In 1802 F. A. Michaux wrote that the wild horses "have a very unpleasant gait, are capricious, difficult to govern, and even frequently throw the rider and take flight." Ranchers retained a tenuous hold on their lands and livestock from the 1790s through the disruptions of Mexican independence in the early 1820s. Raiding Apaches and other Indians then destroyed most ranches in Arizona. The livestock industry did not recover in the region until the mid-nineteenth century.[50]

During the late 1840s and after, a series of incidents created minor booms and internal markets for livestock in the Southwest. Provisioning troops in New Mexico, beginning in 1846, spurred livestock production. Ranchers also traded stock with emigrants headed west during the 1850s. The Gadsden Purchase of 1853 stimulated regional growth for both Hispanics and Anglos. The Colorado gold rush of 1859, an Arizona mining boom in 1862, and the coming of the railroad in 1883 created other boomlets. But by the early 1890s, a combination of drought and falling livestock prices effectively ended open-range ranching and the heyday of the vaquero in Arizona.[51]

While Indian attacks devastated ranches and missions in the Southwest, a political turn of events led to the destruction of the California missions. Liberal leaders of the new Mexican nation, anxious to diminish the Church's power and wealth, ordered the secularization of the missions in 1834. The missionaries responded by ordering the destruction of their herds. In 1834 some 31,000 mission vaqueros tended an estimated 396,000 cattle and 62,000 horses. The animals were killed with the cooperation of local ranchers, who promised but usually failed to return half of the hides to the missions. The mass slaughter set ranching in California back decades, but the skilled labor force of Indian vaqueros remained. These ranch workers provided the manpower for Hispanic ranchers and later Anglo settlers who replaced the Franciscans as vital forces in the California livestock industry.[52]

Vaqueros Train Hawaii's Paniolo

Just as this massive destruction of livestock struck the California missions, the vaquero moved unexpectedly across the Pacific Ocean to the Hawaiian Islands. In this unlikely fashion, he become the cultural ancestor and tutor of Hawaii's cowboy, the paniolo. George Vancouver had first brought cattle to Hawaii, as a gift to Kamehameha I, in 1793. The animals received royal protection for more than thirty years, permitting vast herds of wild cattle to proliferate in the fertile island environment. In 1803 Richard J. Cleveland brought a gift of horses—mustangs from Spanish California—to the Hawaiian king. The raw materials for a ranching industry—land, water, and livestock—were now present; all that was lacking was the cowboy.[53]

By the late 1820s, European pioneers and native Hawaiians had begun hunting wild cattle for their hides, tallow, and meat. As in South America, the island livestock industry progressed from wild-cattle hunts toward domesticating animals and organizing ranches. Kamehameha III, recognizing that more skillful labor would be required to handle the burgeoning herds, arranged for Mexican vaqueros to come from California to Hawaii in 1832 to teach ranch skills to the Hawaiians. Pioneers of the Hawaiian livestock industry, such as John Palmer Parker, also benefited from vaquero expertise. Vaquero-trained paniolo worked cattle in Hawaii decades before the heyday of the American cowboy.[54]

By the mid-nineteenth century, an estimated thirty-five to forty thousand cattle, about one-third of them tame, roamed the volcanic slopes of Hawaii. The vaquero passed along his cattle-handling and leather-working techniques and much more. The paniolo adapted vaquero equipment—notably the saddle, the Mexican sombrero and spurs, and probably the Spanish guitar—to the Hawaiian environment. By the twentieth century, ranches existed on six of Hawaii's eight islands (all but tiny Lana'i and Kaho'olawe). The big island of Hawaii had the most ranches, including the huge Parker spread, founded by John Palmer Parker. Vaqueros carried Hispanic influences to the fiftieth state more than a century before Hawaii joined the Union.[55]

Road Ranching on the Great Plains

On the mainland, Texas, California, Arizona, and New Mexico were the earliest ranching frontiers of the American West. Ranching has its roots in the northern plains during the 1840s, but sizable numbers of animals and cowboys did not arrive until the latter decades of the nineteenth century. Joseph Nimmo erroneously records the beginning of northern plains ranching as December 1866, when a government trader, caught in a blinding snowstorm on the Laramie plains of Wyoming, set his herd loose. Some of the animals wintered over, thereby proving that cattle could be grazed. But "road ranching," whereby plains settlers traded stock with emigrants bound for Oregon or

California, had established decades earlier that cattle could survive northern winters. Richard Grant traded animals with western emigrants at Fort Hall, Idaho, as early as 1843. Lancaster P. Lupton did so in Colorado and Granville Stuart in western Montana by the 1860s. These pioneers in road ranching were cattle traders, not ranchers, although Stuart did go on to become, among other things, a prominent rancher and vigilante leader. It was, of course, the great trail drives northward from Texas, beginning in 1866, that made the northern Great Plains cowboy country. The Cavalry's removal of the Indian threat during the 1870s eliminated the last major barrier to northern plains ranching.[56]

Trailing from Oregon to Canada

The Canadian ranching frontier lacked the violence and drama associated with the rise of ranching in Mexico and the American Southwest. The Canadian West, aside from occasional outbursts, proved to be a rather peaceful frontier. Cattle made an appearance there well before cowboys. By the early eighteenth century, livestock were kept at northwest fur trading posts. The Spanish carried livestock during the early 1790s from Mexico or California to their outpost at Nootka Sound. They abandoned the post and their northwest claims soon thereafter. By the War of 1812, cattle could be found along the Red River and by the 1840s at Fort Edmonton. To the south, American settlers had brought a few cattle to Oregon Territory as early as 1834. Growing numbers arrived with immigrants during the 1840s. In fact, much of the livestock consumed by the Forty-niners during the California gold rush came from Oregon valleys. But Oregonians also moved their animals northward into British Columbia.[57]

Between 1859 and 1870, some twenty-two thousand Oregon cattle entered Canada, mostly along the Okanagan Trail that ran through eastern Washington to the port of entry at Osoyoos. Some of the American drovers settled in British Columbia. Cattle multiplied during the 1850s and 1860s in the areas of Lytton, Lillovet, Caribou, Quesnel, and Williams Lake. As in Mexico, Brazil, and the American Southwest, a mining boom, this one along the Fraser River, fueled demand for livestock. But when the mines went bust in 1868, the Oregon cattle drives dwindled. Ranching in British Columbia also suffered from continued overstocking, overgrazing, and harsh winters.[58]

Ranching came even later, and very briefly, to the prairies of Saskatchewan. Charles Reid established a ranch in 1886, but there were few other ranches or cowboys until the mid-1890s. A report in 1899 by a North West Mounted Police officer provided a glowing description of the Swift Current-Maple Creek region: "The district is in the most prosperous condition, and the livestock industry, in which almost the entire population may be said to be engaged, to a greater or a lesser extent, is bringing large sums of money into the country." Ranching enjoyed an ephemeral heyday during the first years of the twentieth century. Ranch hands, about half Canadian and half from the United States, found good, steady work. But by 1905, farming rapidly swept aside cattle on the western Canadian prairies. Cowpunchers faced unemployment or "sod busting" as their unpalatable alternatives.[59]

The Alberta Range

It was Saskatchewan's western neighbor, Alberta, that developed a flourishing cowboy culture. As in the United States, the first phase of Alberta ranching depended on access to free grass on the open range. From about 1874 to 1881, cattle slowly supplanted bison on the range. Again, local markets—supplying the Mounted Police and reservation Indians with beef—stimulated early ranching. As on the American Great Plains, the bison disappeared, Indians were reduced to reservation life, and the rich grasses were left to the cattleman. Calgary became the economic and social center of cowboy life, not unlike Fort Worth or Cheyenne. The ranching boom began about 1881 and peaked between 1885 and 1895. As in Saskatchewan, ranching lost its pre-eminence to agriculture during the first decade of the twentieth century.[60]

The first roundup in Alberta took place during the summer of 1879 in the Macleod district, when sixteen cowboys gathered some five to six hundred head. Disappointed with the number of cattle, some ranchers moved their herds south across the border to Montana. Many believed that despite government grants of beef to reservations, Indian depredations continued to take a toll on Alberta livestock. A leasing system, established in December 1881, permitted leases of up to one hundred thousand acres—a provision that aided big ranchers at the expense of small stockmen (just as public policy did in Latin America). The leases obligated ranchers to establish one head per ten acres within three years' time.[61]

The boom of the eighties stimulated a healthy demand for cowboys. Alberta's cowboys initially came from a variety of sources. Early ranchers in the 1870s hired Indians and ex–mounted policemen. Frank G. Roe recalled that in those early days "a large percentage of the labor employed on the ranches was either half-breed or Indian." Canadians often used the term *half-breed* to mean the Métis—mestizo trappers, hunters, and subsistence farmers of mixed Indian and French parentage. In Latin America most cowboys were Indians, mestizos, or otherwise of mixed blood. But in Canada the Métis, a large mixed-blood population, seldom worked on cattle ranches. Captain John Stewart developed a substantial cattle ranching operation and raised horses for sale to his ex-colleagues of the Mounted Police. Thus, the Mounted Police provided both market and manpower to the incipient ranch industry. Cowboys also rode up from the United States to work the Alberta range. By the late 1880s, Canadian and British hands had replaced most of the earlier cowboys, although ranchers still added American hands during trail drives and roundups.[62]

CHAPTER 3

Cowboy Character and Appearance

The character of cowboys of the Americas—even the definition of who they were—has aroused great and extended controversies. Contradictory images arose in all countries. One view held that cowboys were paragons of national virtue—patriotic, honest, principled. An opposing image presented cowboys as lazy, immoral, backward, low-class drifters. As is often the case, reality lay somewhere between these two caricatures. Cowboys were often defined by their dress and ability to ride. "I see by your outfit that you are a cowboy," runs the line from the old song "The Cowboy's Lament." Distinctive clothing and equipment set cowboys apart from others in their societies, but wearing the outfit did not necessarily make a man a cowboy. This chapter examines the appearance of the cowboys of South and North America, as well as varying appraisals of their character.

The Chilean Huaso

Of the many cowboys of the Americas, none remains as shrouded in mystery and contradiction as Chile's huaso. To some he is a middle-class gentleman rancher, akin to the *charro* of Mexico. The huaso lives on and loves the land, but he does not perform manual labor. Socially and economically, he is below the landed elite but above the landless rural worker, variously called a *gañan*, *roto*, or *labrador*. Racial arguments come into play, the mestizo huaso being depicted as heir to Hispanic pride and arrogance. René León Echaiz, a leading exponent of this view, contrasts the huaso with the roto, who he claims is depraved and debilitated by alcohol. According to this school of thought, the roto inherits from the Indian an indolence, weakness for alcohol, and other negative traits, whereas the superior huaso imbibes only at fiestas and with meals and is not dominated by strong drink.[1]

Nineteenth-century usage of the term *huaso* contrasts with the portrait drawn by Echaiz. Rather than a middle-class estanciero, the huaso appears as a rural, lower-class outlaw or common laborer. The word often meant vagrant or outlaw, and it sometimes appears in the same context as "gaucho," which carried similarly negative connotations. Horsemen in Chile were termed "gauchos" as well as "huasos." On the other hand, foreign visitors to Chile equated the huaso not with the criminal element but with the *inquilino*, the rural laborer tied to one of the large estates in the central valley of Santiago.[2]

In Mexico, different terms evolved for the working cowboy (vaquero) and the gentleman rancher (charro). But in Chile, *huaso* was applied indiscriminately to a wide range of rural social classes. A British visitor, George Byam, used it describe a middle-class rancher in 1850:

> The guasso [*sic*] dress for a person in easy circumstances is as follows:—A straw hat with narrow brim, tied under the chin with black silk tassels; a blue, round jacket, more or less embroidered, with a poncho thrown over it, the colour and texture of which depends upon the taste and purse of the wearer. A pair of tightish trousers, with a red silk sash round the waist, a pair of over-all boots, drawing up above the knee, and of divers colours; sometimes double-strapped with black Cordova leather, and confined below the knee by handsome black and silver gaiters; the costume being completed by an enormous pair of silver spurs, with steel rowels.[3]

In reality, the huaso was a working cowboy, a ranch hand. He labored hard but seasonally. He went barefoot or wore sandals (*ojotas*). A simple apron or flour sack tied about his waist protected him during his labors. Only after completing the day's work did he don a jacket. Uneducated and landless (as were the vast majority of Chileans), he worked whenever possible on horseback, but he also engaged in agricultural labors when necessary. Like the gaucho, the huaso faced severely limited avenues of legitimate employment; some became vagabonds or rustlers. Like the gaucho and llanero, he served as a soldier. The long wars against the Araucanian Indians made the huaso indispensable to the defense of the frontier.[4]

The vastly different descriptions of the huaso arise from a number of factors. Many commentators have been imprecise and sloppy in their terminology. For example, in his book about the huaso, Tomás Lago reproduces a late nineteenth-century print titled "A Hacendado." He relabels the print "huaso rico"—an oxymoron if one accepts the definition of the huaso as a lower-class rural worker. But a more important factor is the ruling elite's desire to mitigate or even hide the deep class lines that have divided Chile since the colonial era. The Chilean elite manipulated the historical huaso into a political and social symbol. Thus was born the "postcard" or "tourist" huaso.[5]

Like drugstore cowboys in the United States or the Mexican charro, the elite's huaso wore a richer, more embellished costume than working cowboys. Chilean romanticizers tend to have their cowboy dressed in fine silks, trimmed in silver or gold braid, with huge silver spurs. The charro and the postcard huaso could well afford such expensive ceremonial trappings and blooded horses. But the huaso of reality was an ill-dressed, lower-class mestizo cowhand. As we will see, the ranching elite of Argentina contrived a similar transformation of the gaucho's image. The gaucho of mythology becomes a pure-blooded Spaniard, laden with silver ornamentation and cloaked in fine cloth.[6]

The working ranch hand in Chile wore simple, functional riding clothes. The high-crowned hat worn during the colonial era gave way to one with a lower crown during the nineteenth century. His knee britches became full-length trousers. High-heeled boots became more common, in place of the colonial sandals and low-heeled shoes that let the large Chilean ceremonial spurs (*marinos* or *moriscos*) drag the ground. Regular working spurs (*medio celemin*) were not so large. Brightly colored ponchos served many purposes—protection from rain and wind, blanket at night. The huaso used chaps, like many of his counterparts in North and South America. The leather chaps protected the legs from raking thorns and brush, particularly during busy roundups. At ranches near the coast, huasos also used chaps fashioned out of sealskin.[7]

What never failed to impress observers, regardless of their estimates of the huaso's social status and character, was his ability to ride and rope. Thomas Sutcliffe, who lived in Chile and Peru from 1822 until 1839, visited the ranch of Juan de Dios Correa de Saa and watched the huasos at work during a *rodeo* (cattle roundup).

> It is during a rodeo that the Chilian Huassos [*sic*] are seen to advantage, whilst they are scouring the woods, and riding at full gallop up and down the steep hills, and almost impervious thickets of thorns, "algaroba" [*al-*

garroba, a variety of vetch], and patches of cardoon [perennial thistle related to the artichoke], where a stranger could scarcely find a passage, or be able to ride without incurring the danger of breaking his neck, or being sorely lacerated. I have often seen them throw their lasso at full speed, and entangle and secure the wildest animal in situations that have surprised me; and still more so, to see them bring a strayed one back to the herd in perfect safety.[8]

Sutcliffe also described the huaso's skill with the bolas, a weapon generally associated with the gaucho. The bolas (or boleadoras) and the method of throwing it were similar on both sides of the Andes.

In the southern provinces [of Chile] a missile is used, called "bolas," that are made from three stones, or round pieces of iron or lead, enclosed in a piece of leather; these weigh from six to eight ounces each, and are attached to thongs of about three feet in length, which, when, knotted together, complete the bolas. The person who uses this missile takes the bolas by the knot, and gallops after the animal, or ostrich, he may be in pursuit of, and when he arrives at a convenient distance he lets two of the balls slip through, and retains the other in his hand, and begins twirling them round his head, and casts them from him, as a stone would be propelled from a sling. An expert huntsman, or what is called a good "boleador," can almost ensure his aim at the distance of one hundred paces. The bolas generally entangle the legs of the animal, and causes it to fall, or otherwise impede its flight; then the huasso is enabled to secure it with his lasso; the bolas is also used in warfare both by the Chilian cavalry and the Indians, and is a fearful missile.[9]

The many commonalties between huaso and gaucho show that the Andes did not form an impenetrable barrier.

The Argentine Gaucho

The gaucho attracted the same mixture of admiration and vituperation, and suffered from the same confused definition of identity, as the huaso. Gauchos roamed the broad plains of the Río de la Plata through what is today Argentina, Uruguay, Paraguay, and Rio Grande do Sul, Brazil. Colonial officials throughout this vast region branded wild-cattle hunters as outlaws. To officialdom and the colonial Spanish elite, the terms *gaucho* and *gauderio* conjured images of vagrancy and rustling. The gaucho was unlettered, uncultured, uncivilized—in short, a barbarian not significantly superior to the Indians of the pampas. Only a shallow, superstitious acquaintance with the symbols of Catholicism separated the gaucho, in the official eye, from the "savages" of the plains.[10]

Military service against Indians on the frontier, against the British who invaded Buenos Aires and Montevideo in 1806 and 1807, and against the Spanish Royalist forces during the independence wars, improved the gaucho's image somewhat. By the early nineteenth century, he took on the trappings of valor and patriotism. The word *gaucho* became less an epithet than a description of plainsmen in general who rode horses and tended cattle. Landownership qualified one as an estanciero, or rancher; the landless worker was called *jornalero, peón*, labrador, and, increasingly, gaucho. On his visit to the pampa in the early 1830s, Charles Darwin noted the generic use of the term.[11]

Darwin recorded his impressions of gaucho character and appearance during a critical period in Argentine political life—the rise of Juan Manuel de Rosas as governor of the province of Buenos Aires and de facto dictator of the young nation.

> At night we stopped at a pulpería, or drinking-shop. During the evening a great number of Gauchos came in to drink spirits and smoke cigars: their appearance is very striking; they are generally tall and handsome, but with a proud and dissolute expression of countenance. They frequently wear their mustaches, and long black hair curling down their backs. With their brightly-coloured garments, great spurs clanking about their heels, and knives stuck as daggers (and often so used) at their waists, they look a very different race of men from what might be expected from their name of Gauchos, or simple countrymen. Their politeness is excessive: they never drink their spirits without expecting you to taste it; but whilst making their exceedingly graceful bow, they seem quite as ready, if occasion offered, to cut your throat.[12]

Robert B. Cunninghame Graham recorded a memorable if slightly romanticized vision of the gaucho somewhat later in his essay "La Pampa."

> Nothing could be more typical of the wild life of forty years ago [about 1862] upon the plains than was the figure of a Gaucho dressed in his poncho and his *chiripá* [baggy, diaper-like pants], his naked toes clutching the stirrups, his long iron spurs kept in position by a thong of hide dangling below his heels, his hair bound back by a red silk handkerchief,

his eyes ablaze, his silver knife passed through his sash and *tirador* [belt], and sticking out just under his right elbow, his *pingo* [horse] with its mane cut into castles and its long tail floating out in the breeze, as, twisting *las tres Marías* [bolas] round his head, he flew like lightening down a slope, which a mere European horseman would have looked on as certain death, intent to 'ball' one of a band of fleet *ñandús* [rheas] all sailing down the wind.[13]

The generalization of the term *gaucho* to cover virtually anyone who rode a horse on the pampas further blurred and multiplied his putative attributes. Most gauchos worked as ranch hands only a few weeks or months a year— that was all that ranchers required. Gauchos hired themselves out by the day during the roundup and branding season. The most skilled horsemen worked as *domadores*, or broncobusters. They, too, traveled from ranch to ranch and were paid by the day. These migratory ranch hands circulated to many different ranches and worked as needed a few days at each.[14]

A small minority of gauchos occupied permanent positions as year-round ranch peons. But even permanent workers were prone to quit their jobs and ride off. In some cases, such departures were prompted by the chance to earn higher wages by the day during roundups. Many ranchers felt that both day laborers and permanent peons drank and gambled too much. The landed elite worked assiduously to tame the free-riding gaucho. They wanted docile peons, willing to work hard for low wages. By the latter decades of the nineteenth century, the ranchers succeeded in stripping the gaucho of his freedoms.[15]

At most times of the year, ranch day labor was not needed. A small staff of permanent peons could tend the animals adequately. At these times, many gauchos hunted ostriches for the prized feathers, exported to satisfy the vanities of European fashion. Gangs of ostrich hunters (*boleadores*) drew the wrath of ranchers, because they scattered livestock and sometimes set range fires to drive ostriches (technically rheas) into the open plains where the bolas could do their work. Wild cattle remained on much of the pampas through the mid-nineteenth century. Gauchos would kill these animals and sell their hides and tallow to the local *pulpero* (tavern keeper). These migratory types, whom Darwin found lounging about the tavern, smoking, drinking, and gambling, were widely held responsible for most rural crimes, especially rustling.[16]

To be sure, some gauchos were bandits and rustlers. Juan Moreira, for example, worked as a bandit and bodyguard for a political party. After his death at the hands of the police, he came to be celebrated in Argentine poetry and prose. In the early 1880s, a bandit gang led by the Barrientos brothers terrorized the Tres Arroyos area of Buenos Aires province. But such gaucho criminals were in the minority. More often, gauchos' lawbreaking reflected their traditional belief in common-use rights; they became bandits because they lacked legitimate alternatives.[17]

Gauchos did not believe the resources of the pampa to be private property. Rather, they believed in communal access to animals, grass, and water. During the colonial era the vast herds of wild cattle and horses on the plains seemed inexhaustible. Gauchos scorned or were ignorant of a remote, invisible government that tried to dictate who could kill cattle and who could not. They consistently fled from or resisted official attempts to dominate, direct, and draft them.

Gauchos held a simple, clear worldview and set of life goals. They wished to ride freely about the plains wherever and whenever they chose. They resisted, sometimes successfully, attempts to alter or regulate their lives. The abundance of the plains permitted gauchos to live doing little or no wage labor, as long as wild livestock and game animals roamed the plains. Gauchos had little need of money, since they could exchange hides or ostrich feathers for mate (a bitter, caffeine-rich tea), tobacco, and liquor. The toss of a lasso brought a tasty beef dinner, washed down with large amounts of mate.[18]

During the colonial era of wild-cattle hunts, hostile plains Indians, and weak governmental authority, gauchos stood a chance of maintaining their free-riding lives. A horse, a knife, beef, mate, and tobacco accounted for most of the gaucho's worldly needs. The pampa provided for his simple needs. From the legskins of a colt, he fashioned his supple boots (*botas de potro*). His road belt (tirador) and riding gear were made of leather, among the most abundant resources of the plains.[19]

William Henry Webster, a British naval surgeon, described the traditional dress and demeanor of an Uruguayan gaucho of the late 1820s: "His complexion is a swarthy brown, his hair is generally black and long, sometimes platted and surmounted by a small-brimmed neat-looking hat. His shoulders and body are concealed by his poncho, and by the variety and mixture of its colours, in which bright scarlet and yellow are sometimes particularly conspicuous adds much to the general effect. It descends only low enough to leave the fringe of his white trousers conspicuous, over the feet, which frequently are uncovered."[20]

But as the nineteenth century progressed, the landed elite in combination with Europeanized politicians gradually subdued the gaucho and radically altered his life. New laws forbade his homemade boots in order to reduce the killing of colts. (As early as 1856, ranchers demanded laws against homemade boots and leather saddle linings.) Imported textiles and machine-made boots appeared throughout the pampa. The chiripá yielded to bloused trousers (*bombachas*) imported from Europe. (These pants are the model for the high-fashion gaucho pants favored by American and European women that make an appearance every decade or so.) The gaucho retained his long hair, beard, and poncho. To be sure, gauchos remained, just as cowboys persisted after the closing of the open range in the American West. But their ability to maintain the traditional way of life and to live by their equestrian values largely disappeared during the last third of the nineteenth century.[21]

The Venezuelan Llanero

The horsemen of the Venezuelan llanos faced tribulations not unlike those of the gauchos of the Río de la Plata. Like the gaucho, the llanero's dearest dream was to ride freely, unfettered by authority or responsibility. His tropical plains environment imposed additional constraints but also provided benefits. With his keen eye to equestrian life, Cunninghame Graham recorded some attributes of the llanero:

Unlike the gauchos and the Mexicans, the Roman Butari, the Arabs of North Africa, the Western cowboy (before fell cinemas made a puppet of him), any old saddle, any clothes, content the dweller on the plains of the Apure. His horse is almost always thin, often sore-backed, and always looks uncared for, while the ungainly pace at which he rides, a shambling *pasitrote*, or tied camel waddle, moving both feet on the same side at once, deprives him of all grace. Still few can equal, none excel, him for endurance. Nothing daunts him, neither the peril of the rivers, with all their enemies to mankind ever awake, to tear or numb the unlucky horseman who may come near their fangs or their electrically charged bodies, or any other danger either by flood and field. He, of all wielders of the rawhide noose, alone secures it, not to the saddle, but to his horse's tail, fishing for, rather than lassoing, a steer, playing it like a salmon with a rope a hundred feet in length, instead of bringing it up with a smart jerk, after the fashion of the Argentines or Mexicans. Abominably slow and tedious in his methods to the eyes of commentators; still it is never wise, in matters of such deep import, to criticize or to condemn customs that use and wont have consecrated.[22]

Sir Robert Ker Porter represented the Queen's interests in early republican Venezuela. He recorded his impressions of the region and its leading citizen, General José Antonio Paez, a political leader from the llanos. Porter was not taken with the llaneros. "Their manners were the most unpolished and almost uncivil I ever met with," he observed. Paez, illiterate himself, was served by a secretary who could barely read. An independence hero who rallied llaneros to the side of the patriot forces, Paez subsequently became a political caudillo. Porter found his typical dress striking: "The General was dressed quite in his llanero costume; a low-crowned broad brimmed straw hat, white calzoncillos (a sort of linen short trouser), black, unpolished long leather garters lacing up the sides, shoes, with spurs, and over his person a white linen cobija [poncho], ornamented round the edges and corners with needle work. A scarlet, broad belt embroidered with golden oak leaves crossed his shoulder, from whence hung his trusty sword."[23]

The llanero adapted his dress to the vagaries of the tropical plain. He faced searing heat during the dry season and massive floods during the rainy season. Ramón Paez described several elements of llanero dress. When he traveled in the region, he

adopted the less cumbrous attire of the Llaneros, consisting mainly of breeches tightly buttoned at the knee, and a loose shirt, usually of a bright checkered pattern. Shoes are altogether dispensed with in a country like the Llanos, subject to drenching rains, and covered with mud during a great portion of the year, besides the inconvenience they offer to the rider in holding the stirrup securely when in chase of wild animals. The leg, however, is well protected from the thorns and cutting grass of the savannas by a neat legging or *botín*, made of buffskin, tightly buttoned down the calf by knobs or studs of highly polished silver. Another characteristic article of dress, and one in which the wearers take great pride, is the linen checkered handkerchief, loosely worn around the head. Its object is ostensibly to protect it from the intensity of the sun's rays; but the constant habit of wearing it has rendered the handkerchief as indispensable a headdress to the Llaneros as is the cravat to the neck of the city gentleman.[24]

Wealthy ranchers of the plains used more expensive materials for their clothing and spurs. These richer garments were worn for special occasions, such as visits to town. On the plains, even the rich retained the basic llanero dress. Landowners might wear a more expensive type of poncho, a garment common to many different cowboy types. Ramón Paez described the more costly poncho and its humbler version, the *cobija*: "The *manta*, or white linen poncho, is worn when the sun is very powerful, the color in this instance repelling the rays of light more readily than the red surface of woolen materials. The *manta* is a very expensive luxury on account of the embroideries that usually decorate it, and which might rival in elegance the finest skirt of a New York or Parisian *belle*."[25]

Of course, the dress of the common llanero peon or soldier of the time lacked such rich embellishment; most llaneros rode about half-naked and barefoot. But all carried the indispensable cobija, well adapted to the vicissitudes of the tropical plains, which Ramón Paez described as follows:

It is fully six feet square, with a hole in the centre to admit the head, and its office is twofold, viz., to protect the rider and his cumbrous equipment from the heavy showers and dews of the tropics, and to spread under him when there is no convenience for slinging the hammock. It also serves as a protection from the scorching rays of the sun, experience having taught its wearer that a thick woolen covering keeps the body moist and cool by day, and warm by night. The poncho in Venezuela is made double, by sewing together two different blankets, the outside one being dark blue and the inner one bright red, which colors, as is well known, are differently acted upon by light and heat. By exposing alternately the sides of the poncho to the light according to the state of the weather, those modifications of temperature most agreeable to the body are obtained. Thus, when the day is damp and cloudy, the dark side of the poncho, which absorbs the most heat, is turned towards the light, while the reverse is the case when the red surface is presented to the sun.[26]

Another portrait by Cunninghame Graham captures other elements of typical llanos life: "Beef is the staple, almost the only food of the Llanero; his ordinary drink is the muddy water of the neighboring stream or the lagoon. His luxuries, coffee, and the rough brown sugar full of lye, known as Panela; his bed a hammock, that he carried rolled up, behind his saddle; his pride, his horse, the companion of his dangers and his toil, sober and hardy as himself."[27]

Like the gaucho, the llanero always carried a knife or machete. The diplomat Porter termed the knife "an appendage no llanero ever is without, and which amongst the poorest classes, answers likewise for a spear head." Laws in San Fernando for a long time prohibited llaneros from wearing the shirt outside the pants. This odd dress code was to prevent machetes from being concealed under the shirt. Similar restrictions in Argentina were enacted to limit the gaucho's use of his long knife.[28]

Llaneros shared another characteristic with the gaucho: both believed in use rights and the value of cattle, not land. Custom and law had long held that grass and pastures were to be used in common—the same primitive communalism found in the Río de la Plata. In fact, the caudillo General José Antonio Paez codified use rights into official regulations permitting communal access to the water and grasses of the llanos. The new patriot elite overturned the old llanos assumptions and instituted a regime of private property and latifundia. Like the gaucho, the llanero paid a heavy price for his "archaic" values.[29]

Europeans and Venezuela's own elite looked disdainfully upon the backward llanos and its crude inhabitants. Ramón Paez, European-educated, found many shortcomings in the "barbarous" life of the "mongrel breed" inhabiting the plains. But like other educated observers, notably the Argentine Domingo F. Sarmiento, he also found some fascinating strengths and virtues in the primitive cowboy.

> The Modern Centaur of the desolate regions of the New World, the Llanero spends his life on horseback; all his actions and exertions must be assisted by his horse; for him the noblest effort of man is, when gliding swiftly over the boundless plain and bending over his spirited charger, he overturns an enemy or masters a wild bull. . . . Like the Arab, he considers his horse his best and most reliable friend on earth, often depriving himself of rest and comfort after a hard day's journey to afford his faithful companion abundance of food and water.
>
> Few people in the world are better riders than the Llaneros of Venezuela, if we except perhaps the Gauchos of Buenos Ayres, or equal to either in the dexterity they display in the wonderful feats of horsemanship to which their occupations in the field inure them from childhood.[30]

Like the Mexican vaquero, the llanero was very superstitious. Both feared ghosts and evil spirits. The powerful novel of the llanos, *Doña Bárbara* by Rómulo Gallegos, highlights the prevalence of superstition on the plains. The novel is filled with supernatural happenings. The leading lady, Doña Bárbara, is a witch, in league with a wizard (Melquíades) and the Devil (her "Partner").

Mysterious dancing lights, generated by decomposing matter in swamps, are only one of the apparitions imbued with supernatural meaning.[31]

Despite his penchant for romanticism, typical of his epoch and class, Ramón Paez identified the raison d'être of the llanero—remaining on horseback. Indifferent to religion, political philosophy, education, and "high culture," the llanero lived to ride. Strong of body and spirit, he clung to his life in the saddle despite sharp outside pressures. He also pursued another passion—gambling—with a zeal common to cowboys in both North and South America. A card game or a cockfight was sure to attract his interest and absorb his meager earnings.[32]

Life changed far less on the llanos than on the Argentine plains over the course of the nineteenth century. Following a visit to the llanos in 1925, Cunninghame Graham described the llanero in terms that might well have been used a century earlier: "His well-greased *lazo* ready coiled in front of his right knee, his brown, bare toes sticking out through his alpargatas [sandals], clutching the light Llanero stirrup with its crown-like prolongation underneath the foot, the llanero scans the horizon as his horse paces rapidly along, leaving a well-marked trail upon the dewy grass. He sits so loosely in the saddle that one would think if his horse shied it must unseat him, but that he also shies. High on his vaquero saddle, so straight and upright that a plummet dropped from his shoulder would touch his heel, he reads the llano like a book."[33]

The Mexican Vaquero

The vaquero, the working cowboy of Mexico's missions and ranches, suffered the same stigmas of race and class as his South American counterparts. Spaniards and creoles attached racial stereotypes to mestizos and other nonwhites. Mestizos (persons of mixed Indian and Spanish ancestry) were considered untrustworthy, criminal, ignorant by birth. The Spanish had originally barred nonwhites from riding horses. The equestrian life was reserved for "decent people;" it was too dangerous and democratic to let nonwhites rise up from the ground to mount a horse. But the demands of ranching, coupled with the Spanish aversion to work, opened riding to Indians, blacks, and mestizos. Later vaqueros in the American Southwest encountered Anglo racism that was if anything more virulent than that of the Latin American white elites.

Regrettably, Anglo-American racism tinges most contemporary portraits of the vaquero recorded in English. (See chapter 10 for details.) "Untrustworthy," "lazy," "drunken," and "debauched" are among the adjectives generally applied to vaqueros by Anglos. The observations of Theodore Roosevelt, who was deeply concerned with maintaining Anglo-Saxon superiority, are unfortunately typical: "Some of the cowboys are Mexicans, who generally do the actual work well enough, but are not trustworthy; moreover, they are always regarded with extreme disfavor by the Texans in an outfit, among whom the intolerant caste spirit is very strong. Southern-born whites will never work under them, and look down upon all colored or half-caste races."[34]

J. Frank Dobie recognized and tried to correct the Anglo biases that colored the image of the vaquero. In 1931 he recorded a more accurate portrait of the Mexican cowboy. Dobie found the vaquero superstitious, a bit cruel to animals, close to nature, faithful, and hospitable.

> He is full of stories about buried treasures, which priests and *gachupines* [Spaniards] are usually somehow connected with and which are guarded by white *bultos* [ghosts], clanking chains, eerie lights and other mysteries. If he does not know a witch, he knows of one. If he does not fear the evil eye, he respects it. If he or any of his family become very ill, he wants a doctor, but at the same time he yearns for a *curandero* [folk healer] (a kind of quack that a whole essay would be required to picture forth). He is familiar with the habits of every creature of his soil. For him every hill and hollow has a personality and a name. He regards the stars; he watches the phases of the moon. He knows the name and virtue of every bush and herb. He is a child of nature; he is truly *un hombre de campo* [a man of the land].
>
> Either despite or because of his nearness to nature, he is as insensible to the sufferings of nature's progeny as nature is herself. He will run his horse into thorns and then have no thought of pulling the thorns out; he will ride a thirsty horse within fifty yards of a water hole and unless he himself is thirsty will not turn aside. He will rub sand into the eyes of a wild cow that he has roped, though in this he is no more cruel than the average old-time cowpuncher. He will sit all day in the shade of his *jacal* [hut] and never offer to carry a bucket of water for his over-worked wife.
>
> For all that, the *vaquero* is kind to his family, sets no limit to his hospitality, and probably goes beyond the average human being in faithfulness. He will divide his last *tortilla* with any stranger who happens by. He will take the side of his *amo* [master], if he likes him, against any

Mexican that tries to do his *amo* an injustice. The reputation he has somehow acquired in literature for being treacherous is, I believe, altogether undeserved.[35]

Folk sources reveal the vaquero's pride, machismo, and vanity. "The Ballad of Manuel Rodríguez," supposedly based on a true incident at the King Ranch in Texas, depicts these characteristics. An especially bad horse threw Rodríguez in front of his fellow riders. An excellent broncobuster, the humiliated Rodríguez quit the ranch and vowed to go pick cotton—to the cowboy a particularly demeaning type of footwork. Like his equestrian fellows elsewhere, the vaquero looked upon the lowly farmer (as well as goat- and sheepherders) with mixed pity and contempt.[36]

Vaqueros admired their fellows who were long-suffering, patient, uncomplaining, and persevering, just as Anglo cowboys esteemed men who worked in bad weather or with pain, went without food, and tracked down stray animals at all costs. Courage—riding into the midst of a milling herd, for example—represented another vaquero virtue. The vaquero and cowboy expected and valued these qualities. Virtuous actions would not bring praise, but failing to measure up to the vaquero standard could bring criticism, censure, or ridicule.[37]

The vaqueros' virtues remained constant, but their dress varied with the terrain they rode. Most, like the llanero and the gaucho, wore a poncho, also called a *serape* in Mexico. The broad-brimmed sombrero, another necessary item of clothing, was made from a variety of materials. Theodore Dodge described the vaquero dress of northern Mexico in 1891: "Our Chihuahua vaquero wears white cotton clothes, and goat-skin chaperajos [*chaparejos* or chaps] with the hair left on, naked feet, and huarachos [*huaraches*], or sandals, and big jingling spurs. A gourd, lashed to his cantle, does the duty of canteen . . . and his saddle is loaded down with an abundance of cheap plunder."[38]

A slightly more detailed description, written in 1912, offers insight into the little flourishes that a vaquero might make in his wardrobe.

[His dress] consists of a short jacket made of some cheap coarse material, usually in colors, and tight-fitting pantaloons belled out at the bottom just enough to permit easy foot action. Down the outside seam of his trousers runs a broad strip of brilliant cloth. Instead of a belt he wears a *faja* (sash) which is wrapped around his body several times with the ends tucked in. It is always of some bright color, usually red or blue. His sombrero, of course, is an object of almost universal conjecture, often having a three-foot expanse of brim, which is dipped at a rakish angle, with a conical-shaped crown. It is made of braided straw and is invariably decorated with bands of brilliant colors.

On the range he always has about him somewhere his beloved *serape*, which seems indestructible. He wears it thrown over his shoulder like a shawl, and how he keeps it on, in the thick of a round-up, always puzzles the American cowboy. He also uses it as his bed at night; and when it rains, one will see him stoically sitting his horse (he rides a horse on the plain but not in the mountains), enjoying the full glory of it like an Indian chief on dress parade. His foot-gear is almost laughable, for instead of the high-heeled graceful boot worn by American cowboys, he wears the *charro* shoe, which is low-heeled, thin-soled, and very pointed at the toe, resembling, in every respect but the toe, the old-style congress shoe. It is usually of russett leather of very soft texture. As a rule, he wears no kerchief round his neck, and his chaps fit tight and flare at the bottom like his trousers.[39]

Jo Mora described the appearance of the *californio*, the vaquero of Spanish California:

A kerchief was bound about his head, atop which, at a very rakish, arrogant angle, sat a trail-worn weather-beaten hat, wide of brim, low of crown, held in place by a *barbiquejo* (chin strap) that extended just below the lower lip. His unkempt black beard scraggled over his jowls, and his long black hair dangled down his back to a little below the line of his shoulders. His ample colonial shirt was soiled and torn, and a flash of brown shoulder could usually be seen through a recent tear. The typical wide, red Spanish sash encircled his lean midriff. His short pants, reaching to his knees, buttoned up the sides, and were open for six inches or so at the bottom. Long drawers (which were once white) showed wrinkles at the knees and were folded into wrapped leather *botas* (leggings). He wore a rough pair of buckskin shoes with leather soles and low heels, to which were strapped a pair of large and rusty iron spurs. This costume was finished off by a *tirador* (a heavy, wide-at-the-hips belt) that helped him to snub with the *reata* (rawhide rope) when lassoing on foot. The ever-present long knife in its scabbard was thrust inside the garter on his right leg.[40]

In the deserts of Baja California and northwestern Mexico, vaqueros of the colonial era rigged their saddles with *armas*—large, stiff leather skirts hanging off the saddle. The leather protected riders from thorns and cacti. Later riders attached smaller skirts (called *armitas* or *polainas*) to their legs. These leather protectors were of course the forerunners of the vaquero's *chaparreras* and the chaps used by American cowboys. Leather comprised practically the entire outfit and equipment of the rider in Baja California. He wore a leather hat (*vaqueteada*) and a long, leather wrap-around coat (*cuera*). His stirrup coverings (*tapaderas*), saddle bags (*cojinillos*), and lariat (*reata*) were also made of leather. Vaqueiros of Brazil's arid northeastern sertão wore much the same garb.[41]

Both vaqueros and gauchos disdained firearms, which were considered unmanly. Vaquero folklore emphasized the value of outwitting an adversary, rather than confronting him with a gun. The gaucho relied on his long knife and the bolas, the vaquero on his rope, which served as both a tool and a formidable weapon. Vaqueros looked disdainfully at the gun-toting Anglo who could not protect himself like a real man.[42]

Class and race sharply divided society in New Spain and in independent Mexico. An elite equestrian culture developed parallel to that of the lower-class vaquero. The legacy of the Spanish gentleman rider was perpetuated by the charro. The first charros were the Spanish elite who were rewarded with encomiendas, royal grants of Indian labor. They became the landed elite of New Spain. They retained *jinetea*, a short-stirrup riding style. The Spanish adopted the style from the Moors, who originated it for cavalry warfare. From the short stirrups, riders could stand high above an enemy and slash downward with sword or lance. Richly dressed and well mounted, the *caballeros* (gentlemen) of New Spain would ride out and survey their estates and perhaps offer a few words of instruction to the ranch manager. Their stylized riding evolved over time into the distinctively Mexican mounted exhibitions called the *charrería*. But between these wealthy, landed riders and their vaquero hands stood a great social and economic gulf.[43]

The gentlemanly equestrian tradition remained after independence came to Mexico. The great upheavals of the Mexican Revolution (1910–1920) put a new revolutionary elite in power in place of Porfirio Díaz and the clique that had ruled and profited with him since 1884. This new elite resurrected and ritualized caballero dress and riding, just as the Argentine elite "civilized" equestrian sport in Argentina. In 1921 a Tamaulipas lawyer named Ramón Cosío González organized the National Association of Charros. These exhibitions perpetuated the upper-class equestrian values of the past. *Charreadas* of rodeo-style events exhibited the stylized riding and showmanship dear to the hearts of Mexico's rural middle and upper classes.[44]

Much of the dress, language, equipment, and values of the Mexican and California vaquero passed to the Anglo-American cowboy. *La reata* became the cowboy's lariat. The name *vaquero* became corrupted in English to buckaroo. So, too, *chaparejos* became chaps. *Dar la vuelta* (take a turn) became "dally," meaning to twist the end of a lariat around the saddle horn rather than tying it down. A veneer of Anglo influences wandered westward to Texas from the Carolina coast. But cowboy life developed a distinctly Spanish flavor throughout the American West.

The Hawaiian Paniolo

When Mexican vaqueros traveled to Hawaii in the 1830s to train ranch hands in the islands, they carried more than skills with them. Their cultural baggage included attitudes about animals as well as their distinctive dress. The paniolo adopted Mexican techniques and dress to suit local conditions. For example, the Hawaiian cowboy retained the general shape of the Spanish felt sombrero worn by the vaquero, but he constructed his hat (*papale*) from locally available materials. The woven leaves of the *hala* (pandanus tree or screw pine) proved well suited to hat making.[45]

The paniolo also added his own touches to the quintessential cowboy headgear. Hawaiian cowboys decorated their hats with beautiful, richly hued local shells and feathers. And they bedecked their hats and necks with a lei of vivid flowers, vines, or feathers. The paniolo is a colorful figure, but very different in dress from other cowboys. One old paniolo, sensitive to his image, defended the practice of using the lei: "Even the roughest, toughest, rowdiest, most rugged and most manly of us wear *lei*. We do it for the pure joy and pleasure of it and you cannot tell me that we don't look handsome as men should!"[46]

At least two practical reasons have been suggested for wrapping a cowboy hat with a lei. The first and more convincing is that the costume is useful for impressing women. "The flower *lei* makes you feel good, special, and *paniolo* like to make fancy sometimes. We like to show off. The girls all look at you when you wear *lei*!" said one paniolo.[47]

Another explanation is that the flower wreath helps secure the paniolo's hat in the gusty island winds. Since a simple chin strap would do that job better, I find this argument weak. Making a lei on the job gives the paniolo another way to help pass the time; the lei also provides a memento of a place and perhaps a special event. But there is no denying the alluring beauty and fragrance that a well-constructed lei adds to a paniolo hat. Regrettably, the custom is not as popular with youngsters today as it was earlier in the century.[48]

The vaquero also brought his knowledge of leather work to the islands. Like his Mexican mentor, the paniolo learned to work rawhide into functional but intricately decorated tools. The making of saddles, ropes, bullwhips, bridles, and other riding gear became a specialized craft in Hawaii. Nineteenth-century paniolo made and used braided rawhide ropes (*kaula 'ili*) or ropes made of horse or cow hair (*kaula hulu*). But the salt water, rain, and tropical heat of the islands took a toll on rawhide; today's Hawaiian cowboys have switched to nylon ropes.[49]

The folklore and history of the paniolo is only now attracting interest. Consequently, little is known of his daily life beyond the reminiscences that have been recorded by the Hawaiian State Foundation on Culture and the Arts. Little of the negativity associated with most other cowboy types appears to be connected to the paniolo. He is a positive figure of Hawaiian folklore. The existence of a number of large, working ranches in the islands should insure the perpetuation of paniolo culture and skills.

The Anglo Cowboy of the American West

Like his Latin American counterparts, the cowboy of the American West generated conflicting appraisals. When observed at the end of a long trail drive, "hellin' 'round town," cowboys attracted little praise. The *Topeka Commonwealth* of August 15, 1871, painted an unflattering portrait of the cowboy on a tear:

> The Texas cattle herder is a character, the like of which can be found nowhere else on earth. Of course he is unlearned and illiterate, with but few wants and meager ambition. His diet is principally navy plug and whiskey and the occupation dearest to his heart is gambling. His dress consists of a flannel shirt with a handkerchief encircling his neck, butternut pants and a pair of long boots, in which are always the legs of his pants. His head is covered by a sombrero, which is a Mexican hat with a high crown and a brim of enormous dimensions. He generally wears a revolver on each side of his person, which he will use with as little hesitation on a man as on a wild animal. Such a character is dangerous and desperate and each one has generally killed his man.

The unsympathetic writer went on to catalog the cowboy's additional sins of swearing, fighting, and aversion to authority.[50]

Even as the ranching industry matured during the 1880s, many writers found cowboy character little improved. The *Las Vegas Optic* (New Mexico) reported unfavorably in its issue of June 28, 1881:

> It is possible that there is not a wilder or more lawless set of men in any country that pretends to be civilized than the gangs of semi-nomads that live in some of our frontier States and Territories and are referred to in our dispatches as "the cow boys." Many of them have emigrated from our States in order to escape the penalty of their crimes, and it is extremely doubtful whether there is one in their number who is not guilty of a penitentiary offense, while most of them merit the gallows. They are supposed to be herdsmen employed to watch vast herds of cattle, but they might more properly be known under any name that means desperate criminal. They roam about in sparsely settled villages with revolvers, pistols and knives in their belts, attacking every peaceable citizen met with. Now and then they take part in a dance, the sound of the music frequently being deadened by the crack of their pistols, and the hoe-down only being interrupted long enough to drag out the dead and wounded.[51]

A few years later, a similar assessment of cowboys appeared in the *Rio Grande Republican* of Las Cruces, New Mexico:

> Out in the Territories there are only two classes—the "cowboys" and the "tenderfeet." Such of the "cowboys" as are not professional thieves, murderers and miscellaneous blacklegs who fled to the frontier for reasons that require no explanation, are men who totally disregard all of the amenities of Eastern civilization, brook no restraint, and—fearing neither God, nor man or the devil—yielding allegiance to no law save their own untamed passions.
>
>   He is the best man who can draw the quickest and kill the surest. A "cowboy" who has not killed his man—or to put it more correctly his score of "tenderfeet"—is without character standing, or respect. The "tenderfoot" who goes among them should first double his life insurance and then be sure he is "well-heeled."[52]

These negative portrayals are not unlike those depicting Latin American horsemen as violent frontier criminals and ruffians living beyond the pale of civilization. While some cowboys in both hemispheres fit this mean stereo-type, the majority did not. In fact, some writers recorded in glowing images the character of the American cowboy. William G. "Billy" Johnson, who worked the range during the 1880s, recalled that "cowpunchers were square shooters, upright, and honest men. I never heard of a cowpuncher insulting a woman. If they were not up to par they were soon run out of the country."[53]

Two other sources from the 1880s attest to the positive qualities of cowboy character. The *Texas Live Stock Journal* (October 21, 1882) wrote glowingly of the cowboy's courage, chivalry, and loyalty:

> We deem it hardly necessary to say in the next place that the cowboy is a fearless animal. A man wanting in courage would be as much out of place in a cow-camp, as a fish would be on dry land. Indeed the life he is daily compelled to lead calls for the existence of the highest degree of cool calculating courage. As a natural consequence of this courage, he is not quarrelsome or a bully.
>
> As another necessary consequence to possessing true manly courage, the cowboy is as chivalrous as the famed knights of old. Rough he may be, and it may be that he is not a master in ball room etiquette, but no set of men have loftier reverence for women and no set of men would risk more in the defense of their person or their honor.
>
> Another and most notable of his characteristics is his entire devotion to the interests of his employer. We are certain no more faithful em-ployee ever breathed than he; and when we assert that he is, *par excel-lence*, a model in this respect, we know that we will be sustained by every man who has had experience in this matter.[54]

John Baumann, writing in the *Fortnightly Review* in 1887, decried the myth of the cowboy as a "long-haired ruffian. He is in the main a loyal, long-enduring, hard-working fellow, grit to the backbone, and tough as whipcord; performing his arduous and often dangerous duties, and living his comfort-less life, without a word of complaint about the many privations he has to undergo."[55]

How can we account for such sharply conflicting visions of cowboy charac-ter? First, where the writer observed cowboys is important. Those who saw gauchos, for example, lounging about taverns, gambling, drinking, and fight-ing, formed an almost entirely negative appraisal. Those who saw them at work on the range, riding, roping, and branding, were struck by their strength, skill, courage, and hard work. Likewise, writers who saw cowboys in town, letting off steam after months on the trail or range, saw only law-lessness and debauchery in the cowboy's life. The few observers who actually spent time on the range with working cowhands formed an entirely different and more positive view.

The time period of the observation can also be significant. The heyday of cowboy life lasted only a few brief decades. In the early 1870s, when Texas cowboys drove hundreds of thousands of cattle north to various railheads, unbridled frontier exuberance dominated their lives and actions. As a British traveler noted, "The Texans are, as far as true cowboyship goes, unrivaled: the best riders, hardy, and born to the business, the only drawback being their wild reputation. The others [from Missouri and Oregon] are less able but more orderly men."[56]

Joseph G. McCoy offered the wealthy cattleman's vision of the cowboy. He recorded a reasonably balanced, if slightly condescending, view in his 1874 treatise on the cattle trade:

> He lives hard, works hard, has but few comforts and fewer necessities. He has but little, if any, taste for reading. He enjoys a coarse practical joke or a smutty story; loves danger but abhors labor of the common kind; never tires riding, never wants to walk, no matter how short the distance he desires to go. He would rather fight with pistols than pray; loves tobacco, liquor and women better than any other trinity. His life borders nearly upon that of an Indian. If he reads anything, it is in most cases a blood and thunder story of a sensational style. He enjoys his pipe, and relishes a practical joke on his comrades, or a corrupt tale, wherein abounds much vulgarity and animal propensity.[57]

Anglo cowboy dress, like that of Latin American riders, varied with climate and terrain. Cowboys in Canada and the United States had access to mass-manufactured equipment and clothing. As a result, Anglos made far fewer items by hand. Vaqueros would weave intricate leather lariats; cowboys bought hemp rope. Gauchos fashioned their boots from the legskins of cattle; cowboys in the West purchased high-heeled boots at the store.

As William Timmons recalled from his days on the range, cowboys had a particular ritual for dressing and undressing: "A cowboy undresses upward: boots off, then socks, pants, and shirt. He never goes deeper than that. After he has removed the top layer he takes his hat off and lays his boots on the brim, so the hat won't blow away during the night. Spurs are never taken off boots. In the morning a cowboy begins dressing downward. First he puts on his hat, then his shirt, and takes out of his shirt pocket his Bull Durham and cigarette papers and rolls one to start the day. He finishes dressing by putting on his pants, socks, and boots. This is a habit that usually stays with a cowboy long after his days in the saddle are over." [58]

The cattle frontier in the United States did feature more firearms than any other. However, cowboy gunplay has been exaggerated to titillate movie and pulp novel fans. Self-conscious of their image, most cowboys appeared in photographs with a six-shooter. But a sidearm was heavy and uncomfortable. On trail drives or at roundup, most cowboys left their sidearms in the chuckwagon. [59]

During the 1880s, particularly on the northern ranges, cattle raising took on the trappings of a big business. Cowhands were employees in a large corporate enterprise with obligations to eastern and foreign stock holders who expected handsome returns on their investments. Ranchers under these circumstances ran businesses that showed little evidence of the wildness of the "Old West."

Few ranchers in the American West faced labor shortages. Green kids, college graduates, immigrants, and sundry other men seemed willing to try their hand at cowboying. Ranchers could impose restrictions on their hands, such as forbidding gambling and drinking, and make them stick. Any grumblers or violators could be replaced quickly and easily with other men. Joseph Nimmo in 1886 recorded that "organization, discipline, and order characterize the new undertakings on the northern ranges." The northern cattle industry made cowboys less independent and more akin to other regimented workers of their time. The supposedly wild, hard-riding Texas cowboy gave way to responsible, loyal ranch hands. This transition occurred in Argentina as well, where obedient peons replaced the free-spirited gauchos of the plains. [60]

Cowboys were no paragons of virtue, as many romantics and popularizers would have it. Nor were they the uncouth barbarians of the plains described by self-anointed spokesmen of civilization and culture. Externalities—principally the law and employers—imposed restrictions that shaped the lives of all horsemen. But cowboys lived as much as possible by their own internal codes of conduct. The cardinal virtues for the American cowboy were to do his best and to be cheerful, courageous, uncomplaining, helpful, and chivalrous. Of course, few cowboys maintained these ideals at all times in their lives. [61]

Honesty, a man's word as his bond, is also associated with the cowboy in the popular mind. But examples of cowboy indifference to the truth and to the rights of others emerge in a diary kept by Perry Davis. The document describes a trail drive from South Dakota to Texas in 1894. Davis notes that in Wyoming they passed "a nice stream through a pasture where they charge twenty dollars for watering a herd. Watered before anyone sees us; no pay." A little further along, their horses ran through a fence. "Didn't pay for fences," records Davis. In fact, this trail crew committed so many misdemeanors that they became notorious. In northern Colorado, the boss of the "7D" outfit passed the crew Davis worked with. "Says he is glad to get ahead because we left a hard name and everyone was watching him whenever he stopped fearing he would steal fence posts or water as we did."[62]

It may be that Davis simply fell in with a trail boss a cut below the standards of the range. But his comments reveal a sense of use rights—open access to resources on the plains—that was typical of an earlier era in cowboy life. Latin American cowboys held the same view of open access to animals, water, and grass on the plains. As laws imposed a private property ethic in place of communal use rights, conflict between politically dominant ranchers and range cowboys increased.

Fences were perhaps the foremost symbol of the changing nature of the range. Like their South American counterparts, American and Canadian cowboys hated fences with a passion. Fencing cut against the grain by limiting access to grass and water. Fencing, to the cowboy or the gaucho, meant farmers—anathema to cowboys everywhere. (The exception may be Chile, where cowhands often worked in agriculture as well.) Fencing also meant work on foot, something that most cowhands avoided like the plague.[63]

Old-time Alberta ranchers well expressed this loathing for fences:

Well you know, I've always maintained that next to good whiskey and bad Indians, nothing caused as much hard feelings or stirred up as much trouble as those pesky sheep did when they first came across the line.

Oh, I wouldn't say sheep were so bad. I'd say barb wire is what ruined this country. At first we could keep it cut pretty well, and use the posts for firewood, but it got so, after a while, they were putting up the d—— stuff faster than a guy could cut it down.

Every homesteader had his little bit fenced off, and there was that whole stretch between Standoff and Fort Kipp. The Cochrane ranch had three strands running for 25 miles, and fence riders straddling it all day. When I saw that I said to myself, I says, "This country's done for"—and you see now I was right.[64]

The cattle and horses *brought by the Spanish to the New World laid the basis for livestock industries that continue today. Working first as wild-cattle hunters (pp. 10–15), horsemen adapted their dress, equipment, work, and play to the varied plains environments of North and South America. By the 1700s in Latin America and the 1800s in the United States, cowboys worked on organized ranches, tending herds of domesticated cattle. Wild-cattle hunting had given way to salaried ranch work, but much of old cowboy culture persisted.*

The gaucho *(and his Brazilian counterpart, the* gaúcho*) hunted wild cattle and horses on the pampas of southern Brazil, Uruguay, and Argentina (pp. 13–14, 17). This mid-nineteenth-century painting by the Frenchman Jean León Pallière shows the traditional gaucho dress, which included a baggy diaper-like* chiripá *worn over lace-trimmed leggings (*calzoncillos*). Through his broad leather belt, often decorated with silver coins, the gaucho thrust a long, sword-like* facón. *(Prints and Photographs Division, Library of Congress)*

Argentine horsemen *became expert with lasso and* bolas. *Over the course of the nineteenth century, shrinking herds of wild livestock and proliferating fences reduced the gaucho's independence. By century's end, most of these hardy riders, like those shown in these late nineteenth-century photographs, had lost the freedom to roam. Traditional dress and equipment remained, but their customary free-riding lifestyle was gone forever (pp. 184– 85). (Archivo General de la Nación, Buenos Aires)*

Gauchos worked *at a variety of jobs, but all involved livestock. Some, such as those portrayed in the 1820s by Emeric Essex Vidal, transported goods across the vast pampas in high-wheeled oxcarts. The gauchos wear the staples of traditional dress, in-cluding a striped poncho,* chiripá, calzoncillos blan-cos, *and* botas de potro, *boots fashioned from the legskin of a colt (p. 34). They feast on a tasty* asado, *spitted beef roasted by an open fire (p. 112). (From* Vidal's Views in Buenos Ayres and Monte Video, *London, 1820, Yale Collection of Western Americana, Beinecke Rare Book and Manu-script Library)*

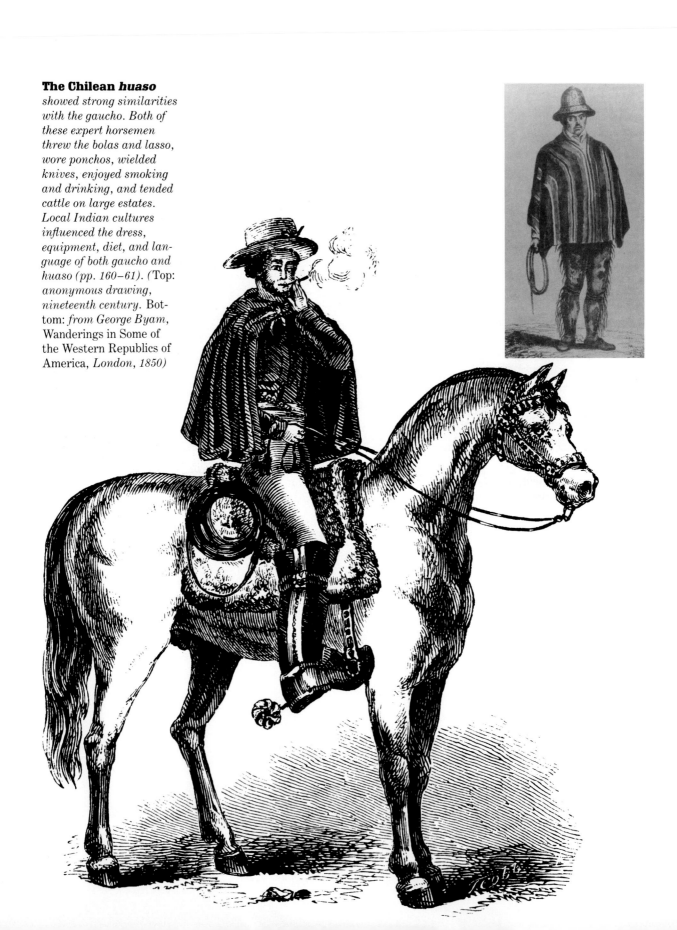

The Chilean *huaso* *showed strong similarities with the gaucho. Both of these expert horsemen threw the bolas and lasso, wore ponchos, wielded knives, enjoyed smoking and drinking, and tended cattle on large estates. Local Indian cultures influenced the dress, equipment, diet, and language of both gaucho and huaso (pp. 160–61). (Top:* anonymous drawing, nineteenth century. *Bottom:* from George Byam, Wanderings in Some of the Western Republics of America, *London, 1850)*

In the llanos, *the tropical interior plains of Colombia and Venezuela, horsemen faced seasonal floods and droughts (p. 58). During the rainy season, depicted above, llaneros moved cattle from flooded lowland pastures to higher ground. Long lances served as tools to work cattle and as formidable weapons in the many battles that raged in the llanos. (From Ramón Paez,* Wild Scenes in South America, *New York, 1862)*

Llaneros, *such as those shown in these watercolors by an unknown artist in mid-nineteenth-century Colombia, often rode barefoot, went shirtless, and used a light saddle (pp. 35–37). The hot and seasonally wet conditions on the llanos dictated minimal dress. Like other Latin American horsemen, the llanero shielded himself against sun, rain, and cold with a hat and poncho (called a* manta *or* cobija*). (Prints and Photographs Division, Library of Congress)*

Gentlemen riders *in New Spain created the* charro *tradition rooted in the equestrian pursuits of Spanish nobility (p. 43). Middle- and upper-class charros could afford elaborate, ostentatious costumes and saddles, trimmed in silver. Even today,* charrería *riding contests remain the pastime of wealthy Mexicans. (From José Cisneros,* Riders Across the Centuries, © *1984 by Texas Western Press of the University of Texas at El Paso)*

The *vaquero, or working cowboy, contributed another equestrian tradition to Mexico. The arid plains and valleys of northern Mexico forced him to adapt differently from the tropical llanero. Leather clothing and equipment protected vaqueros of Baja California and northern Mexico from thorny cactus and brush. The "taps" (*tapaderas*) hanging down over the stirrups protected the feet and prevented them from slipping through the stirrups (pp. 42–43). (From José Cisneros,* Riders Across the Centuries, © *1984 by Texas Western Press of the University of Texas at El Paso)*

Vaqueros made *excellent leather and horsehair ropes, which they threw with great skill (p. 86). Vaqueros generally could be found with a rope, a tall, wide sombrero, and, depending on local conditions, high leather boots and leggings or sandals. Vaqueros might wear a short, trim charro jacket or use a poncho. (Drawing by Frederic Remington,* Harper's Monthly, *December 1893, courtesy of Yale University Library)*

In mountainous regions *of northern Mexico, vaqueros used sure-footed mules rather than horses, but still wore wide sombreros and protective leather skirts (*armas*). This horseman was photographed around 1900 in Berino, New Mexico. Argentine gauchos in the northern mountains of Salta likewise rode mules rather than horses. (Rio Grande Historical Collections, New Mexico State University Library)*

In the 1830s *California vaqueros traveled to Hawaii to train island cowboys (paniolo) to handle wild and later domesticated cattle (pp. 24, 44– 45). Mexican-inspired rawhide ropes and saddles with taps became part of Hawaii's cowboy culture, as shown in this turn-of- the-century photograph of Kaholuamanu riders and their children. Even the Hawaiian cowboy's name is derived from* español. *Pacific-Polynesian cultural elements, such as the use of traditional flower or shell lei to decorate hats, mixed with the Hispanic influence in Hawaii. (Gartley Collection, Bishop Museum, Honolulu)*

In reality *and in romanticized images, such as J. R. McFarren's 1887 lithograph, the cowboy of the American West was strongly influenced by Mexico's vaquero. Language, equipment, dress, work techniques, stockman's organizations, roundup procedures, and range law all showed strong Hispanic roots. American saddlemakers modified many elements of the vaquero saddle, but in some cases kept the taps, as shown in this photograph taken in the Sacramento Mountains near Cloudcroft, New Mexico, around 1900. (Above:* Prints and Photographs Division, Library of Congress. *Below:* Rio Grande Historical Collections, New Mexico State University Library)

Some cowboys, *such as those depicted in Charles M. Russell's 1913 oil painting* Wild Horse Hunters, *became "dally men," copying the Mexican vaquero's practice of wrapping the rope around the saddlehorn (pp. 44, 86). Techniques to tame wild horses also passed from the vaquero to the cowboy. One significant difference is the six-shooter strapped to the cowboy's hip. Like gauchos, vaqueros considered firearms unmanly and preferred a knife to a pistol (p. 43). (Amon Carter Museum, Fort Worth, 1961. 209)*

Frederic Remington, *like Russell, popularized and romanticized the American cowboy. But one sees accurate details in Remington's 1901 lithograph entitled* Arizona Cowboy: *heavy leather chaps (from the vaquero's* chaparreras*), lariat tied to the stock saddle within easy reach of the right hand, and the ubiquitous kerchief around the neck (pp. 89–90). (Prints and Photographs Division, Library of Congress)*

Frederic Remington
1901

Black cowboys *worked first as slaves in the Old South and later on ranches in western states and Canada (pp. 167–69). In the turn-of-the-century photograph taken in south-central New Mexico (above), the rider on the right is black. Erwin E. Smith's photograph (below) shows a group of black cowboys in Bonham, Texas, about 1910. Like Hispanics, blacks faced discrimination on the ranching frontier.* (Above: *Rio Grande Historical Collections, New Mexico State University Library.* Below: *Erwin E. Smith Collection, Amon Carter Museum, Forth Worth*)

THE NORMAN FILM MFG. CO.
PRESENTS

BILL PICKETT
WORLD'S COLORED CHAMPION IN
'THE BULL-DOGGER'
Featuring The Colored Hero of the Mexican Bull Ring
in Death Defying Feats of Courage and Skill.
THRILLS! LAUGHS TOO!
Produced by NORMAN FILM MFG. CO.
JACKSONVILLE, FLA.

Rodeo star Bill Pickett is credited with the invention of bulldogging, now called steer wrestling (pp. 168–69). In the 1880s Pickett developed his technique as part of the Miller Brothers' 101 Ranch Wild West Show. Pickett would bite a steer's upper lip to control the animal as he wrestled it to the ground. In 1923 he starred in a Western movie that featured his special rodeo skills. Pickett died in 1932 after being injured breaking horses at the 101 Ranch in Oklahoma. *(American Folklife Center, Library of Congress)*

Indian cowboys *also worked the range, especially in Oklahoma, where this photograph was taken around 1890. Indian reservations provided ready markets for beef and horses in both the United States and Canada. However, the cowboy culture of the United States shows far less direct Indian influence than Latin America. (Western History Collections, University of Oklahoma Library)*

A few hardy men *mastered millions of cattle and horses and created the cowboy cultures of North and South America. Black, Indian, mestizo, and white cowboys handled large herds of wild and semiwild cattle on the vast plains of the Americas until fencing and other changes ended open-range life. Cowboys worked, played, and even rested on horseback. Underpaid, often unemployed, cowboys clung to life on the range as long as they could, despite economic and natural adversity. (Prints and Photographs Division, Library of Congress)*

Women were not *absent from the ranching frontier, although ranch records that I have examined for both North and South America show no women working as salaried cow hands (pp. 3, 117–18). On small ranches, wives and daughters helped with all types of work, which included tending animals. Middle- and upper-class ranch women rode for pleasure, and widows sometimes ran ranch operations. This photograph was taken in Montana in 1909. (Prints and Photographs Division, Library of Congress)*

Victorian concern *for "ladylike" behavior inspired some women to opt for the somewhat dangerous and debilitating sidesaddle. (Prints and Photographs Division, Library of Congress)*

Canadian cowboys
in Alberta, such as these photographed in the 1880s, dressed and worked much like their neighbors across the border in Montana (pp. 51–54). The colder climate dictated buckskin or wool shirts and full leather or sheepskin chaps. Canadian saddle-makers took the western stock saddle as their model, and some retained the taps traceable back to Mexico. (Glenbow Archives, Calgary)

The Canadian Cowboy

Canadian cowboys appeared very similar to the cowhands across the border in the United States. A broadbrimmed hat for shelter from sun and rain, snug jeans, and high-heeled boots were standard garb. Although unpolished by the urban standards of Montreal or Quebec, Alberta cowboys could likely read and write. Cowboys everywhere prided themselves on their ability to ride and perform the necessary labors of ranch life. Demeaning footwork—haying, milking, fencing, and the like—they loathed. At Macleod, an early Alberta cowtown, a policeman complained that he could not hire someone to dig a well, explaining that "a man cannot dig a well from a horse's back." In 1888 a Mounted Police commissioner related rancher complaints that "cow-boys will not work on foot." Before masses of European immigrants arrived, Argentine ranchers faced similar difficulties finding men to work on foot.[65]

Ranch hands in Canada stand alone among the cowboys of the Americas in having very little negative imagery associated with them. In fact, Canadians go to considerable pains to distinguish their "civilized" and cultured West from the violent, rough-and-tumble frontier to their south. John R. Craig insisted that "there was very little of what is termed the 'wild and woolly' West in evidence; the people were law-abiding, and there was absolute freedom from such objectionable incidents as were encountered south of the boundary line." Historian L. G. Thomas noted of the not-so-wild Canadian West that "the body is American but the spirit is English."[66]

Nineteenth-century sources recorded considerable differences in cowboy country north and south of the Forty-ninth Parallel. In reaction to press criticism of cowboys, Canadian rancher Duncan McEachran wrote in 1881 that "never were a more respectable body of men more maligned than the hard working, manly fellows who are found at work on properly conducted cattle ranches." The Calgary *Herald* in 1884 contrasted the cowboys of Canada and the United States. "The rough and festive cowboy of Texas and Oregon has no counterpart here. Two or three beardless lads wear jingling spurs and ridiculous revolvers and walk with a slouch, [but] the genuine Alberta cowboy is a gentleman."[67]

Unlike the situation on other frontiers, law and order, in the form of the Mounted Police, predated the cattle industry in Alberta. Gunplay—indeed guns in general—played a smaller role than in the American West. Herbert Church recalled that by the late 1880s "it was the regular custom to leave your gun at the livery stable with your horses and saddle outfit. Guns were seldom carried on the range." But a gun could be a useful tool at times. Cowboys could use a sidearm against rattlesnakes and two- or four-legged predators. J. Frank Dobie doubts that hands fired shots to turn aside stampedes, a scene very popular in Western movies.[68]

Carrying guns was not unknown in Alberta, however, as is shown by an unhappy event in Lethbridge in 1912. Richard Christian, a cowpuncher in his late twenties, shot and seriously wounded a former city detective named Pat Egan. A police sergeant immediately caught the perpetrator, who confessed and remained unrepentant. Christian told police that "Egan had ordered me out of town on several different occasions and at one time was instrumental in having me sent up for stealing a watch. When he passed me on the street he applied a vile name to me and I promptly pulled my gun and shot. I am not sorry that I shot him, and would do it again under the circumstances, as I will not take the name he called me under any circumstances from anyone, and if I was to swing for it tomorrow I would still be glad that I committed the deed."[69]

Alberta cowboys were seemingly more cultured and less violence-prone than their counterparts in the States. But the two did share some characteristics. In *Wolf Willow*, his reminiscences of life along the U.S.-Canadian border, Wallace Stegner stresses the commonalties that united cowboys of the two nations. In his mind, cowboy culture and character transcended national boundaries.

> The outfit, the costume, the practices, the terminology, the state of mind, came into Canada ready-made, and nothing they encountered on the northern Plains enforced any real modifications. The Texas men made it certain that nobody would ever be thrown from a horse in Saskatchewan; he would be piled. They made it sure that no Canadian steer would ever be angry or stubborn; he would be o'nery or ringy or on the prod. Bull Durham was as native to the Whitemud range as to the Pecos, and it was used for the same purposes: smoking, eating, and spitting in the eye of a ringy steer. The Stetson was as useful north as south, could be used to fan the fire or dip up a drink from a stream, could shade a man's eyes or be clapped over the eyes of a bronc to gentle him down. Boots, bandanna, stock saddle, rope, the ways of busting broncs, the institution of the spring and fall roundup, the bowlegs in batwing or goatskin chaps—they all came north intact. About the only thing that

COWBOY CHARACTER AND APPEARANCE 53

changed was the name of the cowboy's favorite diversion, which down south they would have called a rodeo but which we called a stampede.

Many things that those cowboys represented I would have done well to get over quickly, or never catch: the prejudice, the callousness, the destructive practical joking, the tendency to judge everyone by the same raw standard. Nevertheless, what they themselves most respected, and what as a boy I most yearned to grow up to, was as noble as it was limited. They honored courage, competence, self-reliance, and they honored them tacitly. They took them for granted. It was their absence, not their presence, that was cause for remark. Practicing comradeship in a rough and dangerous job, they lived a life calculated to make a man careless of everything except the few things he really valued.[70]

An anonymous source from the early twentieth century offers another picture of the dress of Alberta cowmen: "Rancher's attire was not nearly as picturesque as we are led to believe; 10 gallon hats of today would have been more ornamental than useful. The narrow-brimmed gray Stetson, a shirt open at the neck, sometimes a scarf about the neck, pant overalls with a leather belt, and hand-made riding boots with spurs completed the outfit. In winter weather hair chaps were worn over the pants, giving added protection to the legs."[71]

The rough edges typical of ranch hands elsewhere in the Americas were smoothed considerably on Alberta's ranches. The putative chivalry of the cowboy appeared both north and south of the border. Mary Ella Inderwick, an English bride newly arrived on her husband's ranch, described the hands in 1884: "They are a nice lot of men. I love their attempts to help me to appear civilized. Though they ride in flannel shirts they never come to the table in shirt sleeves. They have a black alpaca coat hanging in the shack and each one struggles into it to live up to the new regime which began with a bride at the ranche—and this is done so enthusiastically and with such good will that I have no qualms of conscience that I am a nuisance."[72]

Some of the impositions of "civilization" and chivalry weighed too heavily even for gentlemanly Alberta cowboys. They performed their duties as gentlemen as best they could, but they were capable of rebelling against excessive demands of high culture with guerrilla tactics. Another frontier bride, Monica Hopkins, lived on a ranch near Priddis. In a letter written in 1909, she related the results of her decree that cowhands would use napkins and napkin rings at meals: "Deadly silence followed this announcement, but at least they did put the napkins into their laps. After they left I retrieved them (the napkins) from the floor. They looked as if the men had wiped their feet on them. I put out clean napkins for the next meal and the same thing happened so I picked them up, and put them in the rings, and there they have stayed ever since."[73]

About the only riders on the Canadian range who drew criticism were "remittance men." These young English gentlemen came to make their fortunes on the frontier. Few succeeded; many ended up squandering the remittances sent by their families for their maintenance. Frank Gilbert Roe painted an unflattering portrait of these equestrian dandies as ignorant, drunken wastrels: "Although in many cases anything but the most docile old sheep of a horse was beyond their skill, nothing less in saddlery than a sixty-pound Cheyenne steel tree was worthy of their patronage. They were seldom seen, and never in the public eye, without the full regalia on the range."[74]

CHAPTER 4

American Plains Frontiers
Geography and Imagery

If the images and reputations of cowboys in many countries are varied and contradictory, so are the descriptions of their habitat—the great plains regions of North and South America. Plains have been represented historically as "deserts"—remote areas devoid of culture, sparsely populated, dangerous, and arid. But plains have also represented regions of opportunity and optimism where hard work and nature's bounty could bring substantial livelihood, if not excessive wealth, to millions. As with perspectives on the cowboy, love and hate tinged views of the plains. To some, the great plains of the Western Hemisphere were bleak deserts; to others, utopian gardens.

Pampas of the Southern Cone

The haunt of the cowboy varies considerably in its physical features. We will survey the plains beginning in southern South America and traveling northward. The pampas of the Río de la Plata are probably the world's richest natural grazing lands. A temperate climate and adequate, but not excessive, rainfall combine to provide a near ideal environment for livestock. Ranging from flat to gently rolling, the pampas stretch nearly unbroken by hills for several hundred miles from the Atlantic Ocean inland. Only two ranges of hills, one in southern Buenos Aires province and another in Córdoba province, interrupt the vast grasslands. These continue northward across the Río de la Plata in the Banda Oriental (today Uruguay) and into the *campanha* of Rio Grande do Sul, Brazil.

An oddity of the pampa, compared with other plains regions, was its nearly total lack of trees. This condition may have been natural or induced by man. But upon their arrival, the Spanish found only an occasional, twisted ombu tree. Tall, coarse grasses, thistles, wildflowers, and, in swampy areas (called *pajonales*), low shrubs covered the plains. The spongy ombu is worthless as lumber or firewood. Europeans had to plant fruit, eucalyptus, and other usable trees that gradually changed the physiognomy of the pampas. But the rich, natural pastures remained the mainstay of ranching until the advent of alfalfa, wheat, and corn farming in the latter half of the nineteenth century.[1]

George Catlin visited the pampa in the 1860s and compared it with the Great Plains of the United States that he knew so well.

> The pampas in various parts of South America are vast level plains, not unlike the great prairies of the Platte and the Arkansas, excepting that they are covered with high weeds instead of short grass; and amongst these weeds, of which there are many kinds, there are wild flowers of all colors. And on the eastern borders of the great pampas, stretching off from Buenos Ayres to Patagonia on the South and to the base of the Andes on the west, there are vast forests of thistles, which, sometimes for a great many miles together, though they grow in patches and as high as a horse's back, are almost impassable, even for a man on horseback.
>
> These thistles are the covers and asylums for the ostrich, which feeds mostly out in the open plains and in the ravines; and when pursued runs for the thistles for cover, where it is excessively difficult to follow it.[2]

Chile, wedged tightly between the towering Andes to the east and the Pacific Ocean to the west, did not enjoy the wide expanses of open range available in the Río de la Plata. Suitable grasslands for livestock existed near Santiago, in the central valley of Chile, where agricultural food production and grazing developed side-by-side.

Chile's frontier extended to the south, encompassing some forty thousand square kilometers between the Bío Bío and Toltén rivers. Today the area includes the provinces of Arauco, Bío Bío, Malleco, and Coutín. But the Spanish military faced stiff, successful opposition from Araucanian Indians, and the southern frontier could not be opened to European settlement until nearly the twentieth century. The long period required to subdue the Indians generated a frontier ambience of violence, brutal repression, coercion, and disrespect for law.[3]

Topographically, southern Brazil is a slightly more tropical extension of the pampas of the Río de la Plata. Summer temperatures in January and February are a mild seventy-two degrees at night but soar to the mid-nineties during the day. Fresh breezes moderate the climate and blow early morning fog from the hills during the less oppressive autumn months. The rich, rolling hills of the campanha region of Rio Grande do Sul proved well suited to grazing livestock. As a result, the area that later became the counties of Alegrete, Bage, Dom Pedrito, Livramento, Quarahy, Rosario, and Uruguayana developed a robust livestock economy. The southern mountains (serra) and coastal plain (litoral) bound the campanha to the north and east.[4]

But rich land does not always mean prosperity. In its political and economic development, the borderlands plains region of southern Brazil and northern Uruguay has more in common with the llanos than with the pampas of nearby Argentina. Ranching areas in Argentina, the United States, and Canada were modernized in the late nineteenth century. The Colombian and Venezuelan llanos and the Campanha of southern Brazil remained technologically backward compared with Argentina, the United States, and Canada. A few Colombian ranchers did bring fencing, hybrid cattle, and improved pasturage to their estates. But they produced for a local meat market and exported a few hides. The llanos in general did not compete in the profitable cereals and chilled beef export booms that boosted other livestock economies.[5]

Brazil's southern plains served as an important military buffer against the Spanish in the Río de la Plata. Spain and Portugal both sought to expand and control the lush grazing lands of the Banda Oriental, modern-day Uruguay. Seesaw battling over the area persisted for decades. Brazil invaded and occupied the territory in 1817. Brazilians stole large herds of Uruguayan cattle and drove them over the border to Rio Grande do Sul. Ranchers there, covetous of the fertile grasslands to the south, vigorously supported the Brazilian cause. Eight years later Uruguayan exiles, supported by Argentina, launched an attack to oust the Brazilians. To preserve the regional balance of power and the profits of trade, the British denied the lands to both contenders and insisted on a new, weak, independent country as a buffer between Argentina and Brazil. In this fashion, the small nation of Uruguay was born in 1828. Like Buenos Aires in Argentina, Montevideo developed as a large, dominating city that profited from and dominated the surrounding plains.[6]

Llanos of Northern South America

The llanos of Venezuela and Colombia are topographically very different from the great southern plains of the Río de la Plata and the Great Plains of the United States. The latter two regions lie within the temperate zone, whereas the llanos are a tropical plain, crisscrossed by many rivers and shrouded by forests of dense trees and shrubs (*matas*). The prevalence of trees, almost always in sight, contrasted markedly with the pampas and the Great Plains. The llanos are bounded to the north and west by the Andes and to the south by the Amazonian jungle. Depending on the definition used, the llanos of Venezuela cover between 237,000 and 300,000 square kilometers, or up to 30 percent of the national territory.[7]

Two seasons, a dry summer (*verano*, October-March) and a rainy winter (*invierno*, April-September), divide life in the region. These seasons are extreme and inhospitable. Drought conditions and high temperatures alternate with torrential downpours and mass flooding. The llanos of Venezuela average 1,200 mm (47.28 inches) of rainfall per year, but it all falls within a six-month period. Some areas, such as Guanare and occasionally Barinas, receive up to 2,000 mm (nearly 79 inches) of rainfall annually. Within the llanos, subregional variations exist, but the livestock industry developed throughout the tropical plains.[8]

The Scottish aficionado of equestrian life, Robert B. Cunninghame Graham, rode most of the plains regions of North and South America in the late nineteenth and early twentieth centuries. He left a vivid description of the llanos:

> A very sea of grass and sky, sun-scourged and hostile to mankind. The rivers, full of electric eels, and of caribes, those most ravenous of fish, more terrible than even the great alligators that lie like logs upon the sandbanks or the inert and pulpy rays, with their mortiferous barbed spike, are still more hostile than the land.
>
> Islets of stunted palm-trees break the surface of the plains, as the atolls peep up in the Pacific Ocean and also bear their palms. The sun pours down like molten fire for six months of the year, burning the grass up, forcing the cattle to stray leagues away along the river banks, or in the depths of the thick woods. Then come the rains, and the dry, calcined plains are turned into a muddy lake, on which the whilom centaurs of the dry season paddle long, crank canoes dug from a single log.[9]

The foreboding, fascinating plains of Venezuela hold an important position in the nation's economic and political history. The llanos served as the site of an expanding colonial livestock industry, as the chief battleground during the independence and subsequent civil wars, and as the birthplace of prominent caudillos such as José Antonio Paez. The llanos shaped Venezuela's political destiny. Despite their historical significance, however, the tropical plain and its inhabitants remain enigmas in Venezuelan historiography. Few substantial studies exist of the horsemen, cattle ranches (*hatos*), or geopolitical and economic development of the llanos.[10]

Great Plains from Mexico to Canada

Mexico's ranching frontier actually began during the 1530s in the central valleys and plains of Queretaro, Michoacán, and Guanajuato. Some ranches began with grants of Indian labor (encomiendas) or lands given to the conquerors who accompanied Hernando Cortés on his invasion of the Aztec capital in 1521. Livestock became a significant element of conquest against the fierce Chichimec tribes of northern Mexico. Spanish soldiers drove livestock with them. Mission and presidio sites raised livestock for food and transportation. Wild and domesticated cattle thrived in the arid plains of San Luis Potosí, Sinaloa, and Zacatecas, where the craggy Sierra Maestra ranges crisscrossed the countryside. From the mid-sixteenth century on, a heavy demand for animals from the silver mining boom fueled north plains ranching.[11]

The Mexican cattle industry required extensive grazing areas, because the native grasses were sparser and less nourishing than in the bountiful Río de la Plata. Water could also be scarce, especially during hot summer months when thirsty cattle strayed widely. But aside from the construction of natural fences out of cactus to protect farmlands, the landscape was little changed by man. The harsh environment, and the Spanish cultural and legal bias, contributed to the growth of large estates in northern New Spain. Great livestock haciendas came to dominate Chihuahua, Coahuila, Durango, and Tamaulipas, and persisted into the twentieth century.[12]

Across the Río Grande, the mountains leveled into the humid coastal plain along the Gulf of Mexico to the east and the brush country of south Texas. Traveling north and west of the brush country, one rose to the high, dry plains (the Llano Estacado) of west Texas and the Panhandle. During his explorations in 1541, Francisco Vásquez de Coronado described the lands that became Arizona and New Mexico as "these deserts." Desert imagery would remain associated with the Great Plains.[13]

The mighty barrier of the Rockies rose along the western flank of the Great Plains all the way from Texas to Canada. The American Great Plains, better watered than northern Mexico, provided good grasses and a greater variety of plant life. In the hot southern plains, ranchers learned to use river valleys for precious water and to protect man and livestock against occasional freezing "blue northers" that swept down from Canada.

In southern Wyoming, the plains change character and climate. The northern plains gave rise to the myth of the "Great American Desert," where early settlers feared that livestock could never winter. But the dry winters cured the grass, and livestock proved capable of surviving all but the harshest winter weather. As the desert myth faded, cattle ranchers and then sheepherders and farmers forged westward across the Ninety-eighth Meridian.

Cattle ranching in western Canada actually began in the Fraser River valley of British Columbia. Americans trailed herds up the Okanagan Trail from Oregon to the mining areas of the Fraser in the 1860s. Ranching declined thereafter, except for brief market spurts fueled by the Canadian Pacific Railway in 1883 and the Klondyke gold strike of 1898. The foothills and plains east of the Rockies in Alberta became the great open-range ranching area of Canada.[14]

Crossing the Canadian border in eastern Montana takes one into the Cypress Hills region on the Saskatchewan-Alberta boundary. These heavily wooded hills offered adequate water, with rainfall of fifteen to nineteen inches a year, and a number of sizable rivers, such as the White Mud and Strong Current Creek. Coulees, or narrow valleys, gave protection here as they did in the American Southwest. According to John Macoun, writing in 1882, the best prairie pastures were "those near Turtle Mountain, Moose Mountain, Wood Mountain, the Cypress Hills, the valley of the South Saskatchewan and its tributaries, Tail Creek, and along the eastern base of the mountains for forty miles north of Bow River."[15]

Moving west along the Forty-ninth Parallel, the hills flatten into the famed "short grass country" of northern Montana and southern Alberta. "Prairie wool," a nutritious blend of blue grama, June, spear, bluejoint, and other grasses, provided ample winter feed for cattle. Warm, dry Chinook winds would melt away winter snow and cure the grasses on the stalk. Before their extermination in the 1870s, buffalo grazed all winter on these grasses. Ranchers assumed that cattle could also forage the plains and survive the winter.[16]

Alberta ranchers also occupied the foothills on the eastern slope of the Canadian Rockies, from the Montana border 240 miles north to the Red Deer River. Mary Ella Inderwick, a rancher's wife, described the countryside near the North Fork Ranch in a letter written in 1884. "We are in the foothills—no plains here—but the most glorious ranges of hills and rolling prairie—which all seems so near that one starts to ride to a certain land mark but finds oneself still no nearer at the end of an hour." She reported being able to see rooftops twenty-two miles away.[17]

Hazards of Plains Life

Despite its rich grasses and fortuitous Chinook winds, the Canadian prairie was no paradise. Riding along the Montana-Alberta border in 1881, Duncan McEachran reported a number of natural hazards. Gopher holes pocked the plains and downed many a horse and rider. McEachran judged the holes "very dangerous to horses unaccustomed to them." Prairie-bred mounts learned to avoid the holes. He also complained of attacks from ravenous "bulldog-flies" and mosquitoes. The former, bigger than a bee, "makes a large hole in the skin, and the blood flows freely from it. These flies are very pertinacious, and the poor horses become frantic under their torment." Such pests plagued riders in all plains areas, particularly during the hot summer months.[18]

Similar complaints abound among travelers who crossed the Argentine pampa. Animal burrows infested the plains and caused falls and injuries to man and mount. Charles Darwin observed that "the holes caused by this animal [the *vizcacha*, the pampa's version of a prairie dog] yearly cause the death of many of the gauchos." This considerable danger and other hazards of ranch work prompted gauchos to develop work games. Many such games tested the surefootedness of mounts and the reflexes and agility of riders (see chapter 8).[19]

Cowboys in the United States suffered similar discomforts endemic to work on the range. Seventeen-year-old William Easley Jackson helped trail cattle from eastern Oregon to Cheyenne in the summer of 1876. He complained of choking alkali dust and giant mosquitoes near the Snake River. Greenhead flies "nearly set the horses crazy." In 1882 Jack Porter drove cattle from Wyoming to Oregon. He recorded another plague of the plains: "About noon that day we encountered what in that country were called 'Mormon crickets' [likely locusts or grasshoppers]. They migrate in untold millions. Every blade of grass was gone, having been devoured by this army of big, dark-brown crickets, each as large as a small mouse. We could see that every bit of brush was thick with these destroying pests. The farther we went, the more dense were their numbers, and our horses and cattle tramped on and killed millions of them."[20]

The tropical climate of the llanos made infection and disease constant threats to riders and their animals. Travelers found themselves under constant attack by what Karl Sachs, a German physician, termed "monstrous armies of insects." He found that "the feeling of solitude and forlornness that in these desert plains overwhelms the traveler who moves completely alone, is difficult to paint." The many rivers held their own dangers. Voracious piranhas, large crocodiles, and electric eels infested the tropical streams.[21]

In reality, then, plains regions did hold considerable dangers. But cowboys seem to have enjoyed the challenges presented by the natural environment in which they worked. To those adapted to them, the plains held their own peculiar charm and beauty. But to outsiders, the plains more often represented a dangerous, forbidding desert. Both positive and negative images became attached to all the plains regions of the Americas.

Conflicting Images: Desert and Garden

Despite vastly different climates and natural features, perceptions of the Venezuelan llanos have been very similar to those of the Argentine pampas. Many view the tropical plain as a virtually untapped font of abundance. Writing in 1875, Manuel Tejera painted a glowing portrait of the llanos, "the immense plains where, without any work by man, livestock multiply, grazing on the abundant grass." He waxed eloquent about the region's "picturesque variety of plants," the "majestic silence of the forests," and the "prodigious vegetation." Some believed that the natural bounty of the llanos, as on the pampas of Argentina, killed initiative by permitting a comfortable life without toil.[22]

Many observers held fast to the vision of the underpopulated llanos as the key to Venezuela's future greatness. Agustín Codazzi, a French geographer, estimated in 1841 that the llanos, with only 390,000 people, could support a population of six million. About three decades later, Luis Alfonso (an apologist for Antonio Guzmán Blanco, who ruled intermittently as dictator from 1870 to 1888) stressed that in view of "the fertility of the land, its vast extension, varied climates," and other advantages, Venezuela needed only capital, roads, and labor to prosper.[23]

In neighboring Colombia, the llanos of Casanare, cut off by the Andes from the rest of the country, remained a backward, static frontier into the twentieth century. But successive Colombian administrations, suffering from an "El

Dorado complex," continued to idealize the llanos as the locus for future growth and riches.[24]

In contrast, other politicians and thinkers conceived of the llanos as bleak, backward, unchanging, and unchangeable. They emphasized the vile, extreme climate, unhealthy for man and beast. The region suffered from repeated, devastating epidemics. Wet-season rains periodically exceeded the norm and flooded vast stretches of the llanos. Rómulo Gallegos, whose writings strongly molded Venezuelan perceptions of the llanos, found many negative elements in the plains. But in his romantic optimism, he hoped that the obstacles could be overcome. In *Cantaclaro*, a novel published in 1934, he has a dying man utter the following lament: "But we're in a completely savage desert! The desert! The enemy against which we should first fight! The cause of all our problems."[25]

The role of the llanos in the nation's political and military history constitutes yet another element of its negative image. Fierce llanero cavalrymen turned the tide of battle during the savage independence wars against the Spanish. Thereafter, the llanos continued to serve as the theater of countless military engagements. Ambitious caudillos erupted from the llanos to keep Venezuela in turmoil. To Venezuelans, the llanos came to represent political disruption and anarchy. As the writer and geographer Antonio Arraiz mused cryptically, "The llano is the enemy and the explanation of Venezuela."[26]

The Magic of the Pampas

Like Antonio Arraiz in Venezuela, the Argentine thinker Ezequiel Martínez Estrada believed in the tellurical power of the pampas. He expresses the mystical forces of the plains in his brooding, masterful, existential *X-Ray of the Pampa*: "The vastness of the horizon, which always looks the same as we advance, as if the whole plain moved along with us, gives one the impression of something illusory in this rude reality of open country. Here prairie is expanse, and expanse seems to be nothing more than the unfolding of the infinite within, a colloquy of the traveler with God. Only the knowledge that one is traveling, fatigue, and the longing to arrive give scale to this expanse seemingly without measure. It is the pampa, the land where man is alone, like an abstract being that will begin anew the story of the species—or conclude it."[27]

The pampas of the Río de la Plata stood as a hostile, forbidding barrier to

European settlement. Spaniards had to make two determined attempts before the backwater settlement of Buenos Aires could be established in Argentina. Compared with the human and mineral riches of Upper Peru and Mexico, the Río de la Plata seemed singularly unappealing for conquistadors bent on New World glory and wealth. And once they acquired horses, the many Indian tribes of the plains became even more formidable opponents to Spanish expansion.

The image of a desert persisted long after the vast plains had been explored and become better known to Europeans. In reality, the humid pampa, radiating out in a semicircle from the Atlantic coast, had nothing in common with a true desert, except for its flatness and sparse population. The dry pampa bridged the humid coastal plain, the western Andean foothills, and the stony Patagonian plains south of the Río Negro. It constituted a geographical and cultural desert. Argentines refer to the incorporation of the dry pampa into the national patrimony as the "conquest of the desert."

Argentine intellectuals and politicians developed views of the pampas similar to those expressed in Venezuela toward the llanos. Domingo F. Sarmiento best expressed Argentina's perceived struggle between "civilization and barbarism." He viewed the plains as the bastion of barbarism. The pampas sheltered disruptive caudillos who stifled progress. Yet he found the strength and skill of the gaucho strangely compelling. Argentine political development was the struggle between caudillos and gauchos of the backward pampa and civilizing, Europeanizing leaders of Buenos Aires. Only by pacifying the plains and repopulating it with "civilized" European immigrants would Argentina enjoy progress and prosperity.[28]

Positive images of the pampa also developed alongside such disparaging views. Observers expressed amazement at the prodigious livestock wealth of the plains. Ironically, some considered the Argentine plains to be too rich: the natural bounty of the region was seen as the root cause of the gaucho's perceived indolence. Henry Marie Brackenridge noted that in Uruguay in 1817 "horses [were] so cheap and abundant that the best [could] be had for only a few dollars." Cattle remained so plentiful in Buenos Aires province through mid-century that meat was not even sold in some areas. Anyone with a lasso could find his own dinner. After consuming a few delicacies, the gaucho left the remainder of the carcass for scavengers.[29]

The modernizing liberal elites of the nineteenth century viewed the pampa as an area of great potential owing to its natural abundance. But the rich land needed better people—white people. The primitive mestizo population of the plains held back progress. Several administrations hatched a variety of colonization schemes to populate and cultivate the frontier. Argentine leaders, including Juan Bautista Alberdi, Sarmiento, and Julio A. Roca, all believed that large numbers of European immigrants could almost magically turn the desert into a garden. According to liberal dogma, sturdy European yeomen would push aside the racially and culturally inferior Argentine rural natives and regenerate the nation economically and socially. Unfortunately for the immigrants and for the nation, very few success stories emerged from these quixotic dreams of agricultural paradise.[30]

Like Brazil, Argentina continues to view its vast hinterland as the key to future national greatness. Brazil in 1964 made such faith a matter of public policy by moving its national capital from coastal Rio de Janeiro to the new city of Brasilia in the backlands. Likewise, in 1987 Argentina decided to move its national capital from the megalopolis of Buenos Aires to the Patagonian "desert." In both cases, progress has been equated with frontier expansion.

Chile's Southern Frontier

The history and imagery of Chile's southern frontier are much like those of the Argentine pampas. Both Argentines and Chileans faced indigenous populations that were too strong militarily to be defeated and dislodged until the late nineteenth century. The white perception of the frontier as a barbarous region derived in part from the continued presence of these "savages." The Araucanians held fast to the lands south of the Bío Bío River and launched devastating attacks on white and mestizo settlements well into the nineteenth century. Chilean officials conceded the south to the Araucanians until nearly the twentieth century. Official policy encouraged Chile's growing surplus of landless labor to cross the Andes and settle in the vacant lands of Argentina's Patagonia.[31]

Like the Argentines, Chilean elites viewed their land as perhaps overly abundant. Landowners complained that the benign climate and fertile land permitted the shiftless rural population to subsist with little or no labor. To the jaundiced elite eye, the rural poor enjoyed a secure life of fiestas and merriment. They worked only long enough to earn a few coins to be squandered at the next celebration.[32]

Also like their neighbors to the east, Chile's landed elite nurtured great hopes that European immigrants would improve the nation racially and culturally. They deprecated the abilities of natives (*criollos*) and looked to racially superior European immigrants. Chile succeeded in attracting substantial numbers of Germans to the southern frontier, where they prospered as farmers and sheep ranchers. But immigration did not insure national greatness on either side of the Andes.[33]

The Great American Desert

The contradictory portrayal of the American West as a garden and as the "Great American Desert" parallels the Latin American cases. In general, the desert image arose because of the West's sparse population and lack of "civilization." But the term also held topographical significance. In fact, Walter Prescott Webb aroused a storm of controversy by asserting that "the heart of the West is a desert, unqualified and absolute." Webb continued, "Once we recognize the desert as the major force in the American West, we are able to understand its history." The dry Southwest had stood as a barrier to Spanish expansion for centuries. The Ninety-eighth Meridian stood for decades as an invisible but ominous barrier to the occupation and settlement of the West.[34]

An image of a desert or wasteland also developed for western Canada. Henry Youle Hind and John Palliser both mounted expeditions to explore the Canadian West in 1857. Their reports fostered the negative desert images. Hind first applied the name "Great American Desert" to the Canadian prairies, and Palliser's reports later reinforced the image. Because of the lack of rainfall, conventional wisdom held that the prairies of southern Saskatchewan and Alberta could not be farmed. A huge area came to be called "Palliser's Triangle," thought to be unsuitable for settlement. The region was bounded on the east by the Souris River in the Turtle Mountains and on the south by the Forty-ninth Parallel. It extended westward to Calgary and north to Saskatoon. Ironically, both men also stressed the fertility of large areas, but it was the desert imagery that stuck.[35]

In his report of 1882, John Macoun flatly asserted that the Cypress Hills region was unsuitable for agriculture. Ranchers with large holdings used the same argument to fend off the subdivision of their lands for farming. Only the great fear of American expansionism from the south pushed the Canadian government to survey its uninviting plains territories. (Chilean migration into Patagonia likewise spurred Argentina's concern with populating its far southern frontier.)[36]

But garden myths accompanied these desert images. The boosterism, optimism, and expansionism that pervaded the American West also invaded western Canada. A glowing countermyth to Palliser's Triangle quickly developed. Utopian poetry and prose lauded the richness and opportunity that awaited immigrants to the region. An 1883 pamphlet described the "nice prairie, covered with beautiful grass, and dotted here and there with little poplar forests which gives the whole a very romantic appearance." The settlers, continued the pamphlet, "look forward to a very happy and contented future." Such idealized descriptions convinced many. In the early twentieth century, thousands of American dryland farmers turned their ambitions and energies northward to the "Last Best West"—the Canadian prairies.[37]

Unfortunately for the optimistic new settlers, the image of the Canadian prairie utopia shattered as quickly as it arose. Beset by the harsh realities of chilling winters and inconstant rainfall, prairie farmers faced ruin. By World War I, the great dryland farming boom had bust. Thousands of disillusioned homesteaders returned to the United States. Palliser's desert seemed to have gained its revenge. Not until the later development of suitable irrigation technology was the desert finally overcome, in myth and reality. Today wheat farming is big business on the Canadian prairies.[38]

Though geographically varied and separated by great distances, the plains frontiers of the Americas evoked similar hopes and fears. "El Dorado" and the "desert" coexisted in the minds of many. Cattle regions represented backwardness, violence, obstacles to "progress," the antithesis of "civilization." Simultaneously, however, they represented hope and the potential for future greatness. Furthermore, cattle frontiers served as boundary or transitional regions where different nations or cultures fought and shared. In *Wolf Willow*, Wallace Stegner captures the essence of such areas: "Frontiers are lines where one body of law stops and another body of law begins. Partly by reason of that difference of basic law, and from the moment the boundary is drawn, they also become lines of cultural division as real for many kinds of human activity as the ecological boundaries between woods and plains, plains and mountains, or mountains and deserts. Likewise they have their inevitable corollaries. They create their own varieties of lawbreakers, smugglers particularly, and they provide for the guilty and the hunted the institution of sanctuary." In such plains frontiers, the cowboys of the Americas lived, worked, played, and died.[39]

CHAPTER 5

In the Saddle

Ranch Work

Working cattle was the cowboy's main job. As we have seen, the livestock industry grew out of roots in wild-cattle hunting. As ranching evolved, a number of specialized tasks developed on ranches in North and South America. Roundups (in Spanish, *rodeos*) became the central event in the ranch work cycle. Cattle had to be trailed from one place to another. Wild horses had to be broken to saddle. Cowboys in different countries developed subtle variations for these generic ranch chores, but a strong Hispanic stamp remained throughout the Americas.

Roundup

At first glance, roundup looked and sounded much the same everywhere: cattle, horses, riders, dust, and noise. Robert Ker Porter watched a Venezuelan roundup in 1832. He was awed by the "almost incredible looking mass of animation and dust, where I beheld thus co-mingled 12,000 head of noble cattle." The British diplomat recalled the impressive sight of a "multitudinous gathering of heads, and horns; bellowing, lowing, and a mingled melancholy crying, set forth by bulls, cows, calves, and oxen."[1]

Roundups consisted of several stages of action. First, riders gathered at a central point, often from great distances. Each large ranch sent a team of riders. Ranchers had to hire extra riders, paid by the day, to work alongside the year-round hands. Once rounded up, cattle had to be sorted by owner for branding and earmarks (the *aparte*). Bulls had to be castrated and often dehorned. Castrated bulls received no medical treatment, so infection and maggot infestations were commonplace among animals on the tropical plain. Other chores arose, as shown by Isaac Holton's description of a rodeo on the Colombian llanos in 1853: "Now begins the business of the day. What calf has not his ear-mark? What youngster of two months has not his little brand on his cheek? What yearling not branded for life in his side? A lazo on his head, another on his heels. A fire burning by the division fence, and the irons are hot. Here is a calf with a sack of morbid growth. A spatula of wood is whittled out with a machete; fifty maggots of all sizes are dislodged from the cavity, and it is filled with the first dry, soft absorbent substance at hand."[2]

Whether in Venezuela or the United States, certain rules of etiquette guided roundups. For example, a rider from one ranch never cut in front of a hand from another ranch while cutting an animal out from the herd. Teamwork was important, with hands covering for one another when an animal broke and ran from the herd. Cowboys rode special cutting horses, held in reserve, during the aparte. In such close quarters, the end of the roundup offered workers an excellent opportunity to show their stuff. Horseback competition between rival ranches, in conjunction with a general fiesta, usually marked the completion of the roundup.[3]

Argentine roundups differed little from those on the llanos. The only notable distinction lay in how the llanero handled a particularly obnoxious animal. Llaneros and Mexican vaqueros would "tail" an animal (*colear*): a rider grabbed the tail of a fleeing bull, veered to throw it off balance, and tumbled it to the ground. Gauchos did not use this technique to any great extent.[4]

Gaucho techniques of roundup and branding (*hierra* or *yerra*) changed little during the nineteenth century. In his fine novel *Don Segundo Sombra*, Ricardo Güiraldes provides a memorable description of the gaucho at work during a rodeo:

> With their old wild instinct flaring they began to mass and to feel out the weakest spot in the circle around them. First they milled from the middle toward the sides; then they seemed to come to an understanding and stampeded with irresistible speed and determination toward a single point. The scrimmage was terrific. The bulls, blind with rage, charged straight ahead, horns lowered. The calves leaped into the chaos, stiff-legged and with tails up. The others rushed about bewildered, charging wherever they could. The men shouted; ponchos whirled in the air; whips cracked on leather. Collisions and falls reached their height; at times horse, rider and bull rolled to the ground together in one mad maze.[5]

Wild-cattle hunts represented the first type of roundup held in Chile, as in other livestock regions of South America. These *rebusques* took huasos into wooded areas where horses found it difficult to work. As a result, ranchers also employed foot peons and dogs when working cattle in the woods. As clear claims to land and animals became established, wild-cattle hunts disappeared. On Chilean *fundos*, or ranches, hands worked tame cattle much as their counterparts did elsewhere.[6]

Once ranches ran tame rather than feral stock, the biggest Chilean rodeos came during springtime to locate and mark newborn calves. Huasos found themselves very busy with roundups as spring came each September. Thomas Sutcliffe, who lived in Chile from 1822 to 1839, observed rodeos at a number of Chilean ranches. As elsewhere, hands dehorned and castrated bulls, marked calves, and branded animals that needed it. "The animals when set at liberty, are so enraged, that they run about bellowing with pain, and attack such as are near them, to the no small diversion of the bystanders." About Christmastime, mature animals were again rounded up for slaughter. Chileans made use of most parts of the animal. Hides and horns went to foreign merchants for export. Dried meat, fat, and suet went to local markets. Like llaneros and vaqueros, huasos ate dried beef. According to Sutcliffe, dried beef could also be roasted, boiled, or combined with vegetables into stews.[7]

Like cowboys everywhere, huasos worked cattle skillfully with their ropes. Sutcliffe described the Chilean lasso and its use: "The lasso is a strip of green hide of considerable length, and made pliable, some are plaited, at one end there is a running noose, the other is fastened to the girth of the saddle; few Chilians [*sic*] travel without their lasso, in the use of which they are uncommonly expert; in fact they ought to be so, for when children their amusement is the ensnaring of cats, dogs, and even poultry, with the lassito. The lasso has often been used in warfare, and many a Spaniard has been dragged from the ranks, or gun, dismounted by the intrepid huassos [*sic*]."[8]

As in South America, Mexican hands from a number of different outfits worked under the direction of a rodeo judge. During Mexican roundups, vaqueros would sweep the brush in a crescent-shaped line, herding cattle toward a central location. The rodeo judge, or *juez de campo*, protected the interests of the large hacendados. As with other resources in Latin America, land and cattle accrued to the rich through careful control of the legal machinery. Numerous regulations originally controlled who could harvest wild livestock. Subsequent rules dictated who could hold roundups where and when. Many roundup techniques of the Mexican vaqueros passed directly to the American cowboy.[9]

In terms of technique, rodeos in Mexico changed little from colonial days to the early twentieth century. Equipment did change, however. Most vaqueros in Mexico dropped the use of lances or spears (*picas* and *garrochas*), which dated from early colonial wild-cattle hunts. In California, however, lances remained in use as late as the 1880s. But the lasso increasingly became the tool of choice in handling cattle. Vaqueros still applied large brands, cut earmarks, and castrated bulls. The old practice of tailing remained common as a work technique. It also became a popular if dangerous equestrian game. Frederic Remington vividly described a Mexican roundup of the 1880s:

> In the morning we could see from the ranch-house a great semicircle of gray on the yellow plains. It was the thousands of cattle coming to the *rodeo*. In an hour more we could plainly see the cattle, and behind them the *vaqueros* dashing about, waving their *serapes*. Gradually, they converged on the *rodeo* ground, and, enveloped in a great cloud of dust and with hollow bellowings, like the low pedals of a great organ, they began to mill, or turn about a common centre, until gradually quieted by the enveloping cloud of horsemen.
>
> You see a figure dash about at full speed through an apparently impenetrable mass of cattle; the stock becomes uneasy and moves about, gradually beginning the milling process, but the men select the cattle bearing their brand, and course them through the herd; all becomes confusion, and the cattle simply seek to escape from the ever-recurring horsemen. Here one sees the matchless horsemanship of the punchers. Their little ponies, trained to the business, respond to the slightest pressure.
>
> The process of "tailing" is indulged in, although it is a dangerous practice for the man, and reprehensible from its brutality to the cattle. A man will pursue a bull at top speed, will reach over and grasp the tail of the animal, bring it to his saddle, throw his right leg over the tail, and swing his horse suddenly to the left, which throws the bull rolling over and over.[10]

Anglo ranchers and cowboys adopted the organization of the Hispanic rodeo, Spanish conventions for brands and marks, and the concept of a stockmen's association. Regional or statewide stockmen's or livestock associations adjudicated the proceedings, just as the Mexican *Mesta* had during colonial times. In colonial Mexico an *alcalde de Mesta* directed the rodeo; after Mexican independence, the official became known as a *juez de campo*. In the United States, a superintendent replaced the Mexican judge in governing roundup conduct. The bylaws and activities of many stockmen's organizations strongly resembled those of the Mesta. Livestock associations furthered the interests of big outfits, just as the Mexican Mesta had represented the most powerful hacendados.[11]

The Anglo cowboy also adopted the vaquero's lasso and modified his way of tossing it. The lasso was the cowboy's main tool for working cattle. Anglos also wielded quirts (a corruption of *cuarta de cordón*, meaning horsewhip) to control their horses. But Anglo cowboys did not use lances, spears, or hocking blades on cattle, although they might use sticks to prod the animals. Nor did cowboys in the United States tail bulls, except for fun.[12]

As in Latin America, general roundups could be large-scale affairs. Spring roundups came in April or May, depending on how far north the range was located. A roundup held in May 1880 in Wyoming included 150 riders and 1,200 work horses from eighteen outfits. On the first day, the hands gathered between five and six thousand head. The logistics of such a vast operation were considerable. Cowmen moved toward more structured labor organization as the livestock industry evolved.[13]

Livestock associations divided the range into roundup districts, using rivers and creeks as dividing lines. Given the considerable logistics of a big roundup, preparations began weeks in advance. Men from the various outfits gathered at a predetermined point and prepared for the intense sixteen- to twenty-hour workdays. Cowboys had to be more stubborn and persistent than the cattle they hunted. They faced ravines, bogs, thickets, prairie dog towns, and alkali flats. All hiding places had to be scoured and every animal driven to the rendezvous.[14]

At the rendezvous, thousands of cattle had to be kept under control. Night guards, working two- to four-hour shifts, slowly circled and sang to their bovine charges. A nighthawk kept watch over the horses. Stampedes could happen by day or, worse, by night. The semiwild Longhorns, trailed northward from Texas, were particularly prone to stampeding. Having assembled the herd, cowboys began cutting out the stock by outfit to be branded and otherwise treated. Cattle on western ranges usually got modest medical attention, uncommon in Latin America.[15]

Records from the Spur Ranch in northwest Texas indicate that roundups absorbed one-fifth of the ranch labor required for the entire year. Extra hands came on board April 1. Equipment repair and other preparation occupied the men until the action began. Roundup superintendents checked to see that hands observed the regulations of the Northwest Texas Stock Raisers Association. Depending on terrain and visibility, riders rode anywhere from a hundred yards to half a mile apart. Reps (representatives) of other ranches attended the cutting out of strays. On big outfits like the Spur, the roundup took months. After three months, the ranch took a six- to eight-week break to rest horses and riders. Working cattle during the very hot summer months also caused them to lose too much weight. Range work resumed in September and continued through mid-December.[16]

The vaquero passed along his methods and equipment to the American cowboy, who in turn carried them north to the Canadian ranges. But a good bit of "homegrown" technique developed in Alberta as well. Alberta's first roundup occurred in the summer of 1879, around Fort Macleod in southern Alberta. Sixteen riders gathered some five to six hundred head, not a very auspicious beginning for Alberta's livestock industry. Some ranchers gave up and moved their herds back south to Montana. But others held on, and roundups grew rapidly in size through the 1880s.[17]

The Canadian ranch calendar resembled that of the northern American ranges. Fred Ings worked his first roundup at the Bar U Ranche in the spring of 1884. The first general roundup on the Alberta range came in that same year. "We adopted pretty much the same system as was carried on across the border," recalled Ings. "Our roundups were community affairs." A general roundup to brand and castrate calves took place each spring. Smaller fall sweeps followed in September to collect late calves and remove spring calves from their mothers for weaning. Mature animals were taken from the range for slaughter in the fall. For district and general roundups, a range boss presided, as in the United States.[18]

Mrs. Lynch-Stauton of Pincher Creek described the frantic roundup routine: "The cowboy's life was a strenuous one while on the round-up; nothing but eat, sleep and ride, ride, ride from start to finish; but through it all he was the most happy-go-lucky individual living, always joking or 'swapping yarns' or 'kidding' someone who had a 'bad actor' to 'wrangle' with in the chilly morning."[19]

In its issue of July 1, 1882, the *Fort Macleod Gazette* expressed hope for "a strong and compact Cattle Association such as is in existence in Montana." Such a group quickly arose. The Western Stock Association directed roundups and otherwise safeguarded the interests of ranchers. Canadian lease laws favored very large operations. As in Latin American, extensive outfits dominated the Alberta range.[20]

George Lane, for example, bought the Bar U in 1904 for $220,000 (Canadian). The ranch included some eighteen hundred acres of deeded and leased land. About five thousand cattle and one thousand horses grazed its ranges. With a spirited program of Shorthorn breeding, Lane increased the herd to twenty-five thousand cattle. His cowboys branded up to eight thousand animals during the spring roundup.[21]

By 1885 roundups on the Macleod range had increased greatly over the meager return in 1879. One hundred cowboys, five hundred mounts, and fifteen chuck wagons gathered in May. Jim Dunlop, from the Cochrane Ranche at Kootenay Lakes, served as roundup captain. The riders gathered some sixty thousand head. The operation proved so big as to be unwieldy. Alberta ranchers took up the practice of district roundups to keep operations more manageable. The districts included Fort Macleod, Pincher Creek, Willow Creek, High River, Medicine Hat, Red Deer River, Cypress Hills, and Whitemud River.[22]

Broncobustin'

Contrary to myth, not all cowboys were highly skilled horsemen. Most experienced hands could ride reasonably well. But in every cowboy culture, the broncobuster who broke wild horses to the saddle stood apart from and above his fellows. His special expertise in taming horses earned him esteem from his peers and higher wages from his employers.

Technique varied and moderated over time. When wild horses roamed freely over the Latin American ranges, riders quickly broke animals to the saddle. But many horses suffered injuries as a result, a matter of little importance given the abundance of animals. But as the feral animals disappeared, and as blooded stock appeared from Europe, techniques became slower and gentler. More expensive, harder-to-replace animals could not be subjected to the harsh treatment accorded the sturdy old creole mounts.

The prestige of Segundo Sombra in the novel by Ricardo Güiraldes comes from his status as a domador, or broncobuster. A domador roped a wild horse, sometimes tightening the lasso to cut off the animal's breath. Thus weakened, the horse fell to the ground, where he was blindfolded. The domador forced bridle and bit on the animal. The horse was then snubbed to a post, mounted, and turned loose. Gauchos only half-broke mounts by the standards of most horsemen. The animals remained difficult to handle, but most gauchos could handle a half-wild mount. Gauchos marked horses that had been ridden by trimming their manes and tails.[23]

Harsh gaucho methods frequently injured horses. The Argentine dictator Juan Manuel de Rosas owned a number of ranches in the province of Buenos Aires. At a taming session at his San Martín Ranch in 1846, riders killed seven of the seventy-five horses. Horses were so inexpensive and plentiful that no one concerned himself with such mortality; the ranch manager simply salvaged the horsehides. Rosas paid his salaried broncobusters 50 percent more than an ordinary peon. But most work was done by itinerant tamers who rode from ranch to ranch, working by the day.[24]

According to Ramón Paez, llaneros employed methods very similar to those on the Argentine pampas. They sometimes put a new hand to the test by giving him a wild horse to ride. If thrown, the new man lost face; if successful, he proved his worth as a good worker. As on the pampas, riders relied on crude strength and brutality more than finesse.[25]

Sir Edward Sullivan observed a llanero taming technique used during the mid-nineteenth century. Akin to the tailing of bulls, the practice was anything but gentle. "An active man and a good horseman will jump on a wild horse without bridle or saddle, armed with nothing but his spurs, and gallop across the plain kicking the poor beast until he begins to flag, when he slips off, and catching hold of the tail gives the horse a heavy fall. A few falls of this kind will tame the wildest horse, and convince him that the thing upon his back is his master."[26]

Llaneros used strenuous, seemingly brutal practices to tame their horses. But they apparently gave their mounts better general care than did the gauchos. In the 1870s Karl Sachs noted that llaneros watered and fed their mounts before tending to their own needs. After a hard day on roundup, riders would unsaddle and bathe their horses. There are various reasons for this better care. The disruptions of war cut sharply into the horse population of the llanos; as a result, mounts were not as cheap and plentiful as they were on the Argentine plains. Second, a host of insects and diseases infested the llanos. These pests posed dangers to man and horse. Caring for one's horse helped keep him alive longer.[27]

Vaqueros developed a number of taming techniques, none very gentle to the animals. David Woodman recounted the method used on mustangs by Texas vaqueros in the 1830s. "By starving, preventing them from taking any repose, and continually keeping them moving, they make them gentle by degrees, and finally break them to submit to the saddle and bridle."[28]

As in Argentina, the relative abundance of horses in California influenced their treatment. A German visitor to California in 1842 expressed shock at the indifferent and brutal treatment that vaqueros gave their mounts: "The barbarous Californians look upon the horse as a useful commodity which is of little value and easily replaced." Europeans, accustomed to scarce, expensive horses, often expressed shock at the cavalier treatment accorded to mounts in the Americas.[29]

Like other Latin American horsemen, vaqueros never broke or rode mares. Riding a mare was considered unmanly. Stallions would be tied, haltered, blindfolded, and saddled, as in Argentina. But gauchos might consider the horse sufficiently broken after a day's work; the vaquero spent several days taming a mount. Tamers (*amansadores*) let the horse fight and tire himself at the end of a long rope for an hour or so. Blindfolded again, the horse next found a rider on his back. Removing the blindfold, the tamer, sometimes tied to the saddle, would ride for a couple of hours. He might continue using the blindfold when mounting and dismounting to avoid being kicked. The initial taming sessions continued for five or six days.[30]

Mexican and Californio broncobusters earned top wages, as did their counterparts elsewhere. In the late nineteenth century, a good hand in California might earn twelve dollars a month. The tamer could command twenty dollars a month. Itinerant pairs of men would ride a circuit of ranches each year. Good work meant an invitation to return to work with the next year's crop of colts.[31]

Horse breakers continued to draw higher wages into the twentieth century. According to J. Frank Dobie, vaqueros in Texas earned twenty-five to thirty dollars per month plus food in 1931. Special skills, such as taming or cooking, brought a premium of at least five dollars per month. But ranchers usually paid Anglo hands ten dollars a month more than they paid vaqueros, regardless of skills.[32]

Broncobusting took its toll on riders as well as on horses. In the American West, men who "snapped broncs" did not have long careers, but smarter "peelers" developed their own special techniques. William Henry Sears rode for the Moore and Powers Ranch, twenty miles east of Las Animas, Colorado, in 1876. The hands there used a novel and wily method of horse taming: "I had my share of breaking wild bronchos while on this ranch. Always we took the wild horses to a large sand bar opposite old Fort Wise and there these bronchos were broken. It did not take long for they were soon worn out from bucking in the deep sand."[33]

Ross Santee's description of broncobusting shows further evidence of the Anglo cowboy's indebtedness to the vaquero: "Each bronc was roped, an' after he choked down, a hackamore [from the Spanish *jáquima*] was put on his head. Then he was tied outside with a long rope, so's he could move around a lot. An' most of them, after they'd fought the ropes an' throwed themselves a time or so, would begin to quiet down. Specially, as soon as their noses got sore from pullin' on the ropes."[34]

Vaqueros passed along their prejudice against taming mares to Texas cowboys. J. Frank Dobie notes that Frederic Remington rode a mare when he went to Kansas in March 1883. "The one he rode was a dun mare from Texas that would not have been ridden by any self-respecting range man in Texas—solely because she was a mare." Higher prices for mounts and orders from ranchers gradually eroded this prejudice among Anglo cowboys.[35]

L. A. Huffman watched a tamer work in 1907. The rider used "just a plain, ordinary, single-rigged cow-saddle, bridle, and lariat, spurs, quirt, and some short pieces of grass rope for the cross-hobbling." Once snubbed and hobbled, the horse felt the weight of the forty-pound saddle for the first time. The rider twisted the horse's ear to distract him as he mounted the animal for the first time. Several bucking sessions were required to bring the horse under man's dominion.[36]

Cowboys from the United States rode north to Canada during the late 1880s. The terrible blizzards of 1885–1886 and the expansion of the Alberta ranges made opportunities in Canada more attractive. Fred Ings recalled that "most of our best riders came from the States and they taught us all we know of cattle lore." His description of horse taming in Alberta in 1884 shows that the vaquero's methods likely traveled through the United States all the way to Canada. Tamers would catch the horses "by the front foot with the rope and by a twist throw them, and while they were down put on the hackamore and blindfold them, then let them up. A blinded horse will usually stand when held without too much fuss till the saddle is on. One rides with a hackamore which is a braided rawhide halter with the headstall fairly closely fitting and the nosepiece adjustable so that pulling on the shanks smothers a horse down, cutting off his wind and making him possible to control."[37]

Bert Sheppard, of Longview, Alberta, stressed some of the differences between "real" horse taming and rodeo bronc riding.

The old unwritten code was that a horse should not be beaten over the head or spurred in the shoulder. Whereas the Rodeo rider receives marks of merit for spurring in the shoulders, the broncho-buster [sic] stood a pretty good chance of getting "fired" if caught doing it. Everything in front of the cinch was supposed to belong to the horse.

Horse breaking consists of encouraging a horse to do the right thing and discouraging him from doing the wrong. When a horse decided to buck he was discouraged while bucking by whipping him with a shot loaded quirt. A top rider would whip him every jump until he quit and then either pet him or leave him alone. The easier he rode his horse and the more rein he gave him the better rider he was considered.[38]

Sheppard also pointed up the hazards suffered by the broncobuster, who might face six or eight horses in a day: "He was in constant danger of being kicked when pulling up the cinch. Sore horses would bite and chase a man out of the corral. If a horse started in to buck before the rider was on, it was sometimes necessary to hang and rattle with only one stirrup till he quit. There was no whistle in ten seconds, no pick-up men and no Boy Scouts to run out and help him if he got his wind knocked out. The horse might start the ball rolling either by bucking, falling over backwards or stampeding. These riders had to be masters of every situation that arose and they came out on top most of the time."[39]

According to one observer, Canadian cowboys treated their horses well. "Cowboys who own their mounts almost 'baby' them with kindness." Some ranch foremen preferred not to hire hands who brought their own mounts. The foremen believed that the men did not ride their own animals hard enough to do the strenuous work required on the range. Of course, this practice also tied the worker to the ranch by making him dependent on the outfit for his mounts.[40]

Trail Drives

Perhaps the most storied event in cowboy popular culture is the trail drive. Edward Charles "Teddy Blue" Abbott titled his cowboy memoirs *We Pointed Them North*. In the United States, monumental drives moved thousands of head at a time from Texas to Great Plains railheads. Edward Piper made perhaps the first northern drive when he moved a herd from Texas to Ohio in 1846. Beginning in 1866 and 1867, large numbers of drives continued until railroads pushed their way into the Southwest by the mid-1880s. Some six to seven hundred thousand animals moved north during 1871 alone. The quarantine against Texas cattle enacted by Kansas in 1884 checked the large northern drives. By then the northern plains were reasonably well stocked. The final blow to the trail drives came when railroads pushed trunk lines southward. Trailing northward continued on a reduced basis until about 1895.[41]

Trail bosses used much the same system from the Río Grande to the Canadian border. Sources vary as to how many men were needed on a cattle drive. Most of the discrepancy is due to the nature and size of the herd. Texas Longhorns required more men than tamer, less formidable breeds. Figures range from eight to twenty hands to trail a herd of 2,000 to 3,000. Philip Ashton Rollins estimated one man per 250 to 350 head. All crews included a cook, and some added an assistant foreman. A horse wrangler (generally a young boy) handled the six to eight mounts needed for each man.[42]

If we visualize the herd as having a head (point) and feet (drag), then swing men watched the "shoulders" of the herd and flank men the "hips." Riders bringing up the drag got the full benefit of the herd's dust. Drives from Texas began in early spring, when new grass had pushed up but before runoffs had swollen rivers. On northern ranges, drives had to be completed before autumn snowfalls. Crews did well to move a herd twelve to sixteen miles a day. A slower pace, perhaps ten to twelve miles per day, permitted animals to graze and gain some weight enroute. But the drive cost the owner of the herd about five hundred dollars per month, so there was no dawdling. Cowboys supplied their own gear and earned twenty-five to forty dollars per month.[43]

Long drives also had to be made on Latin American ranges. Llaneros faced major trail drives at least twice a year. As noted above, floods alternated with droughts in the climatic extremes of the llanos. During the dry season, riders herded animals from the high northern llanos south to the Apure River. The animals had to be moved back north by May or June before the onset of floods during the wet season.[44]

Faced with navigating animals through the many watercourses of a tropical plain, llaneros became skilled at getting cattle to cross rivers. Unlike many cowboys, llaneros were as a rule excellent swimmers. Brute force often moved the lead animals into the water; the herd instinct prompted the remainder to follow. But if cattle began milling in the water, many could drown. Other dangers abounded. The tropical rivers held legions of electric eels, alligators, piranha, and other dangerous fish and reptiles.[45]

Cowboys elsewhere feared river crossings, because they generally could not swim. Larry McMurtry well captures the terror of a young hand's first river crossing in *Lonesome Dove*. One hapless youth dies after falling into a nest of water moccasins. Swollen rivers might delay a herd for days and result in injured and and lost animals. Cowboys had to ride into the center of a milling herd to straighten out the leaders. According to Joseph G. McCoy, the lack of sizable rivers was a distinct advantage of the Chisholm Trail.[46]

The vast distances of the pampas of the Río de la Plata dictated many long drives. The drover (*tropero* or *resero*) possessed specialized skills and commanded higher wages. In Uruguay, drovers acted as buying agents for meat processing plants. They then trailed the animals to market. Although ranchers earned lower prices for their cattle when selling to the tropero, they also avoided the expense and hazards of driving the animals.[47]

Descriptions of Argentine trail drives sound much like those of the American West. Two gauchos rode point, while others guided the flanks and brought up the rear. An orderly herd might cover ten to twelve miles during the first four to five hours of the morning. (Gauchos worried less about animal weight loss on the trail than American cowboys, because Argentine cattle generally were marketed for dried meat and hides, not beef.) Before noon, riders changed mounts and let the cattle rest and graze for an hour. Resuming the drive, the trail boss would try to find well-watered pasture a few hours before sunset. Generally, each thousand head of wild cattle required five riders. Drovers could handle tame herds with fewer men. Two other men or boys worked as horse wranglers, caring for the many spare mounts needed on drives.[48]

Cowboys on a drive faced other dangers and obstacles in addition to river crossings. Stampedes posed a grave threat to the herd and its keepers. A witness to an Idaho stampede in 1889 reported the grisly details. The stampede killed 341 cattle, two horses, and one cowboy. Several men suffered broken legs. The dead cowboy "was literally mangled to sausage meat. His horse was little better, and mine was crushed into a bloody mass. I found that I could not get up, for my leg was broken just below the thigh."[49]

Bad weather could always threaten a drive. Wallace Stegner gives an evocative description of a Canadian cowboy's day on the trail when overtaken by cold weather: "By day the labor and the cold and the stiffness of many hours in the saddle, the bawling of calves, the crackle and crunch of hoofs and wheels, the reluctant herded movement of two or three hundred cows and calves and six dozen horses, all of whom stopped at every patch of grass blown bare and had to be whacked into moving again. By night the patient circling ride around the herd, the exposure to stars and space and the eloquent speech of the wolves, and finally the crowded sleep."[50]

Horses could step into gopher holes and throw their riders. A foot tangled in a stirrup meant death or injury as the cowboy was dragged across the ground. An excellent vaquero in Arizona, Eli Lucero, met his death this way. Richard Deane, a Mounted Police officer, offered an understated opinion on the rigors of trail driving. "For the benefit of those who have not tried it may I say that driving refractory cattle on a tired horse is very poor fun."[51]

Jerome Harper, a Virginian transplanted to British Columbia, completed what is surely one of the most remarkable drives of all time. Gold strikes lured him and his brother Thaddeus first to California and then north to British Columbia. They found supplying miners to be more lucrative than digging for gold. In the early 1860s, they began trailing cattle into Canada from Oregon. Thaddeus died in 1870. Six years later Jerome gathered a herd of twelve hundred cattle and determined to drive them to San Francisco. Aided by eight or nine riders, he moved the animals south, the largest herd ever to travel the Okanagan Trail. Moving ten or twelve miles a day, it took them eighteen months to reach San Francisco. The *British Colonist* of February 5, 1878, reported that "the cattle are large and well grown beeves, rolling in fat, and have been sold at seventy dollars per head." Alas, Harper's financial skills did not match his trail savvy. A decade after completing the monumental drive, he was bankrupt.[52]

Saddle-Sore

In spite of the hardships and dangers, trail drives, broncobusting, and roundups offered excitement. They also provided a chance to show off riding and roping skills to other cowboys. But most of a cowboy's life consisted of hard, routine chores that required hours alone in the saddle. The diaries of H. M. Hatfield reveal the ranch work calendar in Alberta during the mid-1890s.[53]

Spring plowing began in March and continued through May. Once fields were ready, Hatfield planted rye and wheat. Animals also needed attention, as branding took place in April and May. Hatfield also spayed the heifers in May. By late May and early June, it was spring roundup time. July found Hatfield back in the fields, cutting hay and rye. He mixed pleasure with practicality, shooting ducks and geese for the larder during the hunting season in August and September. Late September and early October brought Hatfield together with his neighbors for the fall roundup. One final, smaller roundup was held each year in November. During the winter months, Hatfield earned some extra cash from wolf and coyote bounties.

The work calendar for ranches from Montana to Texas generally resembled the regimen followed by Hatfield. Winter layoffs left many cowboys without work. The lucky few who had jobs during the winter faced difficult chores. John Baumann recorded his winter discontent on a Texas ranch during the 1880s: "We have nothing before us but the long dreary winter months, which will be spent in cheerless dug-outs, line-riding, repairing fences and corrals, killing wolves, and turning the heavy drift of starving cattle, which must inevitably take place, as much as possible off our range."[54]

Of course, spring work began earlier in the south, and fall roundups began earlier in the northern ranges. In springtime hands had to mend fences and "ride bog," that is, free animals trapped in bogs created by spring rains and runoff. Water holes had to be cleaned. Cowboys enjoyed the big spring roundup, but then had to face summer haying. After the disastrous winter of 1885–1886, most ranchers began growing hay for winter feeding. Hands dispensed some medical care to animals, such as treating them for screwworms on the southern ranges. As fall freshened the air, ranchers joined for another roundup to cut out animals destined for market. Most cowboys lost their paychecks during the winter months. Ranchers kept only a skeleton crew to handle repairs, routine chores, and the exigencies of bad weather.[55]

Regardless of weather, animals needed tending. And the worse the weather, the greater the need. For those few hands lucky enough to have winter work, the chores mounted. James C. Dahlman, a Texan who worked on the western Nebraska range, recalled that "those kept during the winter months chopped and hauled logs, corral poles, posts; they built barns, houses, ice-houses, corrals, or anything the foreman ordered done. The Texas Puncher was always sighing for spring."[56]

Once fencing became common, hands had to ride fence year-round. On the Spur Ranch, line riders covered up to thirty miles a day from their lonely line camps. Range riding, more interesting work, occupied other hands in any season. Cowboys checked for predators, strangers, sick and injured animals. Blizzards could sweep in and kill men and animals on the northern Great Plains. On the southern ranges, "blue northers" (aptly named for the color of the threatening sky) would bring freezing temperatures and high winds. Cowboys had to find drifting cattle and try to turn them from fences, ravines, and other obstacles. Otherwise herds would stack up and perish in the cold.[57]

Plains life was harsh. Natural assaults came from lightning, fires, floods, hail, snow, and tornadoes. Disease, suicide, and hunger took other lives. A Texas cowboy song warned against the hardships of the cold, northern ranges.

Ranch work *throughout the Americas pitted men on horseback against large herds of cattle and the vagaries of nature. Depending on terrain and season, cowboys faced choking dust, swollen rivers, driving rainstorms, and howling blizzards. But through it all, cattle had to be tended. Few men have labored under such harsh, variable conditions for so little pay.*

From the dry pampas *of Argentina to the "Great American Desert," cowboys chased and herded cattle. This dusty roping scene from the Matador Ranch in Texas in 1905 contrasts sharply with the rose-tinted, romantic picture of cowboy life in popular mythology. (Erwin E. Smith Collection, Amon Carter Museum, Fort Worth)*

River crossings *always posed danger, particularly to cowboys who could not swim. If cattle began milling and were swept downstream, men and animals could be lost (pp. 79–80). (Drawing by A. R. Waud,* Harper's Weekly, *October 19, 1867)*

In the Hawaiian Islands, *conditions demanded that the paniolo work cattle around water (p. 45). Cattle had to be transported by small boat from land to awaiting steamers. Cowboys tied the animals' horns to the gunwales and then hoisted them aboard the steamer with a sling, as shown in this photograph of the 1920s or 1930s. (Bishop Museum, Honolulu)*

Llaneros of Colombia and Venezuela *faced seasonal water hazards. Crisscrossed by rivers, much of the llanos became inundated annually from April to September (p. 58). Unlike many cowboys elsewhere, llaneros had to be expert swimmers and boatmen. But like cowboys elsewhere, they wielded long lassos that were indispensable in handling cattle. (From Ramón Paez,* Wild Scenes in South America, *New York, 1862)*

Tailing bulls *was a dangerous work technique practiced by both llaneros and vaqueros (pp. 71, 131–32). It also became a favorite sport to exhibit one's bravery, strength, and skill. This is one of many examples of how cowboys blurred the lines between work and play.* (Above: *drawing by César Prieto, 1904.* Below: *drawing by Frederic Remington,* Harper's Monthly, *March 1894, courtesy of Yale University Library)*

The cowboy's morning *began with a predawn breakfast. Hands then saddled their mounts and dispersed over the range to perform a variety of tasks. Note the leather leggings, the tall sombreros, and the charro-style jackets of these riders in northern Mexico. Although many vaqueros considered firearms unmanly, Frederic Remington depicted these vaqueros armed with both revolvers and rifles.* (Harper's Monthly, *December 1893, courtesy of Yale University Library)*

Without horses, *there could be no cowboys. But horses had to be tamed before they could be ridden. In every cowboy culture, a broncobuster enjoyed special prestige and higher pay. C. A. Kendrick took this dramatic photograph in 1904. (Prints and Photographs Division, Library of Congress)*

In Remington's *1903 oil painting* His First Lesson, *the horse shows his obvious terror and aversion to his new relationship to man. A skilled broncobuster quickly established dominance over the horse (pp. 76–77). Riding wild, bucking horses is one of the cowboy work skills that carried over into popular culture via the rodeo (pp. 142–43). (Amon Carter Museum, Fort Worth, 1961. 231)*

A corral kept *a wild horse from running across the plains. But the close quarters could also spell danger to cowboys trying to subdue a stubborn animal. Claud Jeffers, photographed in 1908 on the Matador Ranch in Texas, demonstrates the roping skill that was a necessary part of broncobusting. Technique varied from country to country, but the Mexican vaquero influenced how cowboys in the United States tamed their broncos. (Erwin E. Smith Collection, Amon Carter Museum, Fort Worth)*

Handling cattle,
especially wild bulls or Longhorns, took courage and strength in man and mount. The Mexican vaquero, as illustrated by Frederic Remington (facing page), used his multipurpose serape *to haze cattle. The vaquero's saddle included a strong, large horn used to snub the rope against a pulling bull. Like the vaquero, the Chilean* huaso *dressed in a poncho and faced wild or semiwild cattle. (*Opposite: Harper's Monthly, March 1894, courtesy of Yale University Library. Right: Carpenter Collection, Prints and Photographs Division, Library of Congress)

Seasonal roundup and branding *required extra manpower and long days in the saddle. Sorting and branding cattle on the open range required cooperation between different ranches. It also provided an opportunity for the unscrupulous to enlarge their herds at their neighbors' expense. Roundup customs and techniques were passed from Mexico to the United States. As with bronco-busting, corrals assisted cowboys during branding. (Prints and Photographs Division, Library of Congress)*

From Argentina to Alberta, *we find remarkably similar descriptions of the busy branding season. Cowboys everywhere used ropes, a branding iron, a hot fire, and a sharp knife for ear marks and castration. The gauchos pictured at right are placing a ring in a bull's nose. The Canadian branding scene photographed by S. A. Smyth (below) looks much like activity in the United States. (Right: Argentine postcard, author's collection. Below: Glenbow Archives, Calgary)*

Ranch workers *everywhere depended on the rope as the foremost tool in controlling cattle (pp. 85–86). Mexico's vaquero gained a well-deserved reputation for roping expertise. This "Toro" English china plate by Allerton and Sons (1850s) shows Latin American horsemen pitted against wild bulls (center) and horses (around the rim). The tropical scenery would suggest a location in the llanos, but horsemen throughout the Americas performed similar riding and roping activities. (Ex collection of Petra Williams, courtesy of the Library of Congress)*

BRANDING CALVES, SOUTHERN ALBERTA.

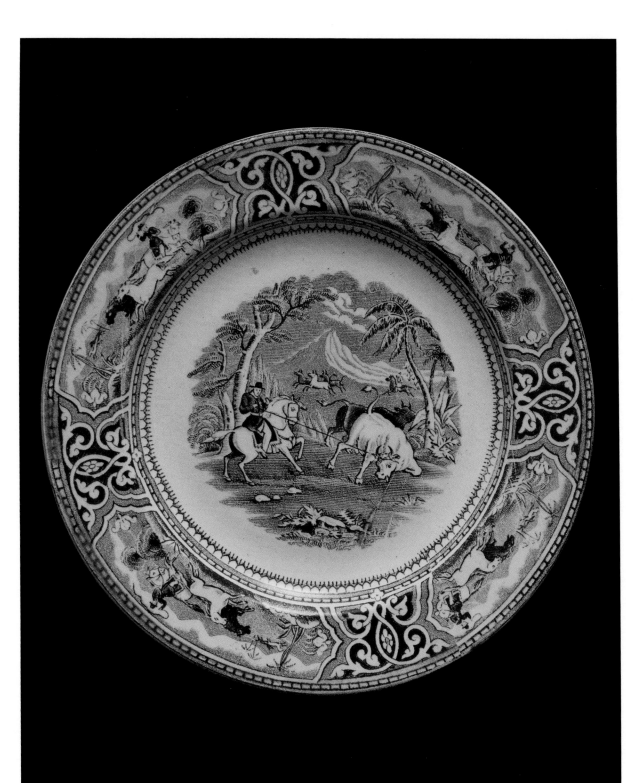

Wives and daughters *on small ranches had to pitch in with whatever chores were needed. However, cowboy work was not considered ladylike in any culture, so women's roles on the cattle frontier were restricted. O. T. Davis took this photograph in 1894 on a San Luis Valley cattle ranch in Colorado. (Courtesy of Colorado Historical Society)*

The political economy *of ranching pointed inevitably to the death of cattle. Wild-cattle hunters killed animals for their hides and tallow and left the meat to rot. Later, as first salted and then chilled meat became important market commodities, more of the cow was utilized. Killing, skinning, and cutting up animals was not work for the squeamish, as shown by these photographs taken on the LS Ranch in Texas in 1908. (Erwin E. Smith Collection, Amon Carter Museum, Fort Worth)*

By the late nineteenth century, *changing technology and rising market values for cattle stimulated better care. Infections and disease no longer went untreated. Cattlemen everywhere began treating their animals on the range and at the ranch. This photograph of about 1915 shows cattle being dipped to kill ticks on the Circle Ranche in Alberta. (Glenbow Archives, Calgary)*

Remington's famous oil painting The Fall of the Cowboy *(1895) captures the end of open-range ranch life in dark, brooding colors. Barbed wire cut ranch labor needs and altered the nature of cowboy work (pp. 178–80). The wild, free-riding cowboy of old passed quickly from the pages of history to fiction and popular culture (pp. 190–91). (Amon Carter Museum, Fort Worth, 1961. 230)*

But stay home here in Texas
Where they work the year around
And where you'll not get consumption
From sleeping on the ground.

Montana is too cold for me,
And the winters are too long,
Before the round-ups have begun,
Your money is all gone.[58]

But working cattle in the brush country of south Texas held its own hazards. Concealed in a thicket, a big Longhorn bull could rush a rider before the
cowboy had time to react. Throwing ropes in thick brush required special
techniques and care. A hand and his mount could be dragged into cactus or
brush by a roped animal. Thorns and branches could quickly poke out an eye.[59]

Winters along the eastern slope of the Canadian Rockies are not as harsh
as one might think. But the Canadian cowboy got his fill of winter riding.
Duncan McEachran pointed out the importance of getting men on the range
after a winter storm. Animals faced the menace of freezing and starvation.
Men faced the additional threat of snow blindness. "Much therefore, depends
on the activity and interest of the cowboys, not during, but immediately after
a storm. Sometimes a bunch of cattle are hemmed in by deep snow in the
coulees, which require a path to be tramped down by the man for himself and
horse. Many a cow and calf if driven in, sheltered and fed for a few days would
live and do well, but unassisted they die."[60]

John Macoun, another Alberta rancher, explained why cattle and snow did
not mix well. "As cattle use the nose instead of the hoof to clear away snow,
they cannot support themselves when the snow gets too deep." Thus, in Canada, cowboys had to perform one of the most hated of chores—putting up
hay. If snow became too deep, then hay had to be put out for the stock—cold,
unpopular work. Men made repeated, tedious trips hauling hay. If painful
snow blindness struck, a man had to spend several days in a darkened room,
eyes bandaged.[61]

Cowboys in any temperate zone, whether the Argentine pampa or the Canadian plains, faced the danger of freezing weather. Wallace Stegner graphi-
cally described the rigors of a Saskatchewan winter:

Icy nights, days when a bitter wind lashed and stung the face with a dry
sand of snow, mornings when the crust flashed up a glare so blinding that
they rode with eyes closed to slits and looked at the world through

their eyelashes. There was one afternoon when the whole world was overwhelmed under a white freezing fog, when horses, cattle, clothes, wagon, grew a fur of hoar frost and the herd they had gathered had to be held together in spooky white darkness mainly by ear.

On bright days they were all nearly blind, in spite of painting their cheekbones with charcoal and riding with hats pulled clear down; if they could see to work at all, they worked with tears leaking through swollen and smarting lids. Their faces grew black with sun and glare, their skin and lips cracked as crisp as the skin of a fried fish, and yet they froze.[62]

Extremely cold weather was unusual but not unheard of on the Argentine pampas. The annual ranch work calendar included most of the same chores performed on North American ranges. Traditional open-range ranching began to give way to fenced, diversified livestock operations during the 1870s. Roundups, branding, castration, and dehorning still required additional hands. The abundance of wild livestock on the pampa made it possible for many gauchos to exist without regular employment. Ranchers had to pay top wages, especially after agriculture began competing for labor, in order to attract workers during roundup. The landed elite also used legal constraints to force the independent gauchos into regular labor.[63]

On modern estancias, foot peons took care of the haying, building of fences, and orchard work. Some gauchos yielded to the pressures of change and accepted work as foot peons. But many steadfastly refused any labor that could not be done on horseback. By the latter decades of the nineteenth century, most Argentine estancieros kept sheep as well as cattle on their ranges. Many gauchos disliked herding sheep, and all preferred beef to mutton. Others learned to work sheep as well as cattle. Women took part in shearing, one of the few jobs open to them in the livestock economy outside of domestic chores. European immigrants increasingly occupied positions on the diversified ranches. On the modern ranch, the horsemanship and roping skills of the gaucho became less important than a willingness to perform a wide range of jobs, including farming and other footwork.[64]

Cowboying was work for young men. Long hours in the saddle, falls, and inclement weather all took a toll on the health of ranch hands. John R. Craig, of the Oxley Ranche in Alberta, summed up the Canadian cowboy's average day, but his description could fit a hand working virtually any range from Calgary to Santiago: "The cowboy is in the saddle twelve to fourteen hours on the stretch, with a bite from hand to mouth, caught at odd intervals, as his only sustenance."[65]

Lariats, McCartys, and Other Ropes

One cannot imagine the cowboy without a horse and a rope. But the type of rope and the manner of using it varied widely. In South America, cowboys braided ropes from rawhide or horsehair. The llanero had a distinctive roping style. He braided the end of the lariat into the tail of his horse—a tactic that took its toll in horsehair. But llaneros used dexterity and balance, not brute force, against a lassoed animal. Llaneros used this expedient because their lightweight, tropical saddles did not offer sufficient bulk or strength to secure the rope.[66]

Sir Edward Sullivan marveled at the success of this roping style in his travel notes, first published in 1852.

> I could never believe this till I saw it. It always struck me that it would either pull the horse's tail out by the root, or else throw him down; and so it would, but the horses become so cunning and so fond of the sport, that the moment the lasso leaves the hand of the rider, instead of stopping short, as I always imagined was the method, they gallop off at a slight tangent as fast as they can, when if the lasso is round the leg, the slightest jerk brings the bull to the ground. So little actual force and so much knack is there in it, that many men will throw bull after bull with a mere jerk from the shoulder, without laying any strain whatever on the horse. Great misapprehension exists as to the distance the South Americans throw the lasso; seven or eight paces is a good long cast, and four or five not a bad average.[67]

Concerned that the wild cattle herds would be decimated, the ranchers' organization (Mesta) in New Spain banned the hamstringing of cattle in 1574. It outlawed the use of lances and hocking knives on pain of a twenty-peso fine or one hundred lashes. These restrictions promoted the greater use of the lasso by vaqueros hunting wild cattle. Until the late eighteenth century, the vaquero, like the llanero, tied the lariat to the horse's tail. But the development of heavier, more substantial saddles changed this technique. Vaqueros began wrapping the end of the rope around the horn of their considerable saddles. This wrapping technique, called *dar la vuelta* (take a turn), passed over to Anglo cowboys, who corrupted the Spanish term into "dally" or "dally welter." Vaqueros and the cowboys who copied the practice could slip the rope against the saddle horn and gain leverage against a roped animal. But faulty technique could be hazardous. A thumb caught between the lariat and saddle horn might be amputated by the whizzing rope.[68]

Vaqueros skillfully braided long reatas from four rawhide strips. They could make much of their equipment from leather. They also wove horsehair into a fine rope called a *mecate*. (Anglos corrupted that Spanish term into "McCarty.") Lariats in California ran from 65 to 110 feet in length and about five-eighths of an inch in diameter. In the Texas brush country, vaqueros used shorter ropes that did not become entangled in the underbrush. Vaqueros threw a variety of loops, according to the task at hand. A figure eight would bring down a running animal. The *piale*, an underhand toss, caught the animal's hind legs as it stepped into the noose. The *mangana*, an overhand throw, opened to catch the animal's forefeet.[69]

In addition to rawhide and horsehair ropes, vaqueros used the tough, stringy fiber of the maguey plant to make ropes. (The same versatile plant is used to make a popular alcoholic beverage called *mescal*.) Because maguey fiber stiffens in damp weather, vaqueros used it only on dry ranges. Sisal, from the leaves of the agave plant, ran a distant third to rawhide and maguey as material for ropes.[70]

The vaqueros who sailed to Hawaii in the 1830s to train ranch hands also transmitted their skills in rope making and throwing. Thus, the Hawaiian cowboy (paniolo) became a "dally man." Clyde "Kindy" Sproat, a cowboy from North Kohala, explained the rationale for dally roping (*hawili*). Because it was dangerous to tie the rope fast to the saddle when facing a heavy animal, such as a wild bull, the paniolo wrapped the rope (kaula 'ili) a few turns around the saddle horn "and let it slide along and smoke da' pommel!"[71]

Like the paniolo, Texans and other Anglo cowboys benefited from the vaquero's expertise with the rope. Some Anglo cowboys, particularly in the West and Northwest, became dally men too. Others tied long ropes securely to the saddle. Texas cowboys worked the brush country with short ropes. They often tied them securely to the broad, squat horn of their double-cinch saddles. We know less than we would like about early roping techniques, but Texas cowboys after the Civil War used a variety of catches, including the pitch, slip, heeling, backhand slip, and forefooting. By the late 1860s, cowboys had developed the hoolihan, in which the roper swings the loop only once above his head before letting fly. This fast throw is useful for catching horses by the head in a corral. The Anglo cowboy's debt to the vaquero remains clear in roping technique. The backhand forefooting catch, for example, is the vaquero's mangana.[72]

Some Anglo cowboys learned to make rawhide lariats and horsehair Mc-Cartys. They also used maguey ropes from Mexico. But the importation of so-called Manila hemp made ropes of that fiber the most common in the American West. Three-strand Manila hemp ropes, produced by the Plymouth Cordage Company in Massachusetts, became the cowboy's favorite by the late nineteenth century. Purchased in large rolls, the rope was simply cut to needed length to replace limp, worn-out lariats. Once stretched and conditioned with tallow and paraffin, the rope was ready for action.[73]

The Argentine gaucho, like some Anglo cowboys, tied the lasso to his saddle. Gauchos used a comparatively short rope, about twelve yards in length, for working cattle in corrals. On the open pampas, gauchos wielded ropes twenty yards long. Gauchos carefully cut a single piece of cowhide into strips and braided it into a strong lasso. A small iron ring was often attached to form the noose. Gauchos began practicing with the rope as youngsters. As one British visitor recalled, "The natives are extremely expert in using the lazo; it is their earliest toy in childhood; and to lazo cats, dogs, and sheep, is the delight of children."[74]

Canadian cowboys had access to the same range of ropes and roping techniques as did their American counterparts. Cowboys had strong opinions about what equipment worked best. Fred Ings favored rawhide over hemp ropes. In the 1880s, he recalled, cowboys "used strong light rawhide ropes more exact on the throw than the coarser hemp ones commonly used today" (about 1938). But the cheapness and ready availability of manufactured hemp ropes made them the standard on both Canadian and U. S. ranges.[75]

Tall in the Saddle

Roping technique is linked to another indispensable cowboy tool, the saddle. The type of saddle he used partially determined how a cowboy used his lasso. The llanero's light saddle, suited to the tropical heat and rain, offered no place to anchor a rope, so the llanero tied his lariat to his horse's tail. The sturdy saddles developed in Mexico and the American West provided a secure anchor for a rope. Some cowboys tied the rope to the saddle horn; others, the dally men, levered the rope with the horn to help them with their roping.

The construction of saddles, lariats, and other riding gear varied across North and South America. Most Latin American cowboys could make part or all of their gear from rawhide. Few cowboys in the United States and Canada developed these leather-working skills. They depended on their nations' more advanced manufacturing economies to provide machined saddles, bridles, and ropes. As Frederic Remington noted, "Vaqueros make their own saddles and reatas; only the iron saddle-rings, the rifles, and the knives come from the patron, and where he gets them God alone knows, and the puncher never cares." Philip Ashton Rollins adds that "the American ranchmen's saddles were built by professional manufacturers and not, as commonly in Mexico, by the cowboys themselves."[76]

Gauchos of the Río de la Plata used a flat saddle (*recado*) that consisted of seven or more different layers. The saddle was comfortable, well adapted to the flat pampas, and the parts served as a bed at night. William MacCann described how the gaucho put together his saddle in the mid-nineteenth century. Sheepskin became available to the gaucho as Argentine ranchers began importing and raising sheep as early as the 1820s. Note that even the self-sufficient gaucho used textiles imported from England.

> First a large sheepskin placed on the horse, then a woollen rug neatly folded, which serves the rider for a blanket; on this was laid a covering of untanned dry hide for the purpose of keeping off the rain; next came a woollen quilt made for such purposes in Yorkshire, with long tassels hanging from the corners: this was carefully folded, and on it was laid a piece of leather, sufficiently large to protect the whole from damp or rain, its ends and sides were neatly stamped with an ornamental border: these coverings answer to the English saddle cloth. Then came what may be termed the saddle-tree, from which the stirrups are suspended, and made of strong leather and wood, forming the basis of a flat seat, although curved a little to suit the back of the horse. The entire of this furniture was secured by a large girth of raw hide, twelve or fourteen inches wide. The saddle is covered, for the sake of ease and comfort, also to serve for a pillow at night, with a sheep-skin, having the wool on . . . ; upon this is placed a flat covering, somewhat similar to the fringed woollen mats laid at drawingroom doors in England, and over that a piece of thin soft leather, forming the seat of the rider; the whole is again secured to the horse by an ornamental leather girth.[77]

Gauchos used tiny round wooden stirrups. Usually riding barefoot or wearing open-toed soft boots, they inserted only the big toe into the stirrups. Years of riding in this fashion enlarged and deformed the big toes. Bowlegged, with deformed toes, the gaucho found walking difficult, not to mention undignified. The Anglo-Argentine writer William Henry Hudson described the gaucho on foot who "waddles in his walk; his hands feel for the reins; his toes turn inwards like a duck's." But galloping across the plains on his soft, comfortable saddle, the gaucho was a centaur to be reckoned with.[78]

Chilean huasos also used voluminous, multilayered saddles. Riders in Chile and Argentina wore large spurs, made of silver for the rich and of iron for the poor. But the huaso attached very large stirrups in place of the small wooden toe rings favored by the gaucho. Sir Francis Bond Head, who rode across the pampas several times in the 1820s, contrasted equipment used by huasos and gauchos: "The spurs of the peons [in Chile] were bad, and their stirrups the most heavy, awkward things imaginable. They were cut out of solid wood, and were altogether different from the neat little triangle which just holds the great toe of the gaucho of the Pampas."[79]

Like gauchos, llaneros used toe stirrups so that they could dismount quickly in case a horse stumbled. But in place of the flat, plump gaucho saddle, the llanero's had a high-backed, wedge-shaped seat. Robert B. Cunninghame Graham, always an expert witness on matters of horsemanship, described the llanero saddle as "a sort of compromise between the Argentine 'recao' and the high peaked, high cantled saddle of the Mexicans. That is to say it has a horn, usually made of brass, but more for ornament than use. The cantle is almost as high as the cantle of the Western cowboy's saddle. The stirrups are small, and made to be used either barefooted, or with the alpargatas [sandals] that the Llaneros all affect. Underneath the stirrups is a wedge-shaped prolongation to make it hang more steadily."[80]

Recall that two horse cultures developed in New Spain. The charro tradition of the rich and the vaquero tradition of the poor working cowhand grew side by side. Differences between these two traditions were reflected in the equipment the riders used. *La silla vaquera*, the early vaquero saddle, consisted of a rather crude, light, rawhide-covered wooden tree, a small horn, and large wooden stirrups. The whole affair was lashed together with thongs and held in place by a single bellyband. Frederic Remington recorded rather unsympathetic observations of the vaquero saddle used in Mexico: "The Mexican punchers all use the 'ring bit,' and it is a fearful contrivance. Their saddle-trees are very short, and straight and quite as shapeless as a 'sawbuck pack-saddle.' The horn is as big as a dinner plate, and taken altogether it is inferior to the California tree. It is very hard on horses' backs, and not at all comfortable for a rider who is not accustomed to it."[81]

La silla charra, the heavy, richly ornamented saddle of the wealthy, included finely tooled leather and silver trim. Scalloped silver rosettes (*conchos*) held in place the many leather thongs used to tie things to the saddle. Silver chains and coins decorated the breastband that kept the saddle from slipping backwards. Ostentation and power radiated from the charro saddle.[82]

Simple, functional vaquero equipment lacked such rich design and materials. Gradually, vaqueros developed a more comfortable, serviceable saddle by adding a leather covering with built-in saddlebags. The so-called *mochila* saddle was more comfortable than the traditional hard, rawhide model. During the brief days of the Pony Express, riders used this rig. The mochila, filled with mail, could be moved quickly from one saddled mount to the next. For work in the brush country, vaqueros added *tapaderas*, leather coverings that protected the feet by hanging over and below the stirrups. "Taps" also prevented the foot from sliding all the way through the stirrup. A vaquero riding with tapaderas could not get his foot hung in the stirrup and be dragged by his horse.[83]

Saddle makers in the United States gradually made changes in the original Mexican saddles. The western stock saddle went through decades of evolution and variation. The Mother Hubbard, for example, appeared during the late 1860s. It resembled the mochila except that the covering could not be removed. The placement and number of cinches changed. "Single-fire" rigs with just one cinch traced their lineage most directly to the vaquero saddle. Jim Redfern described the types of saddles he saw on a trail drive from Oregon to Wyoming in 1885: "All but one of the saddles I noticed were rim-fire rigs, that is, having both front and rear cinches, as is true of Texas, Montana, and Wyoming rigs. One, however, was a center-fire or so-called Spanish rig, being a single cinch with the cinch well in the middle of the saddle. This rig was common in Oregon and California."[84]

Writing in 1891, Theodore Dodge summarized the variety of North American saddles that had developed in a few short decades. The cowboy

rides what is well known as the cowboy's saddle, or Brazos tree. It is adapted from the old Spanish saddle—is, in fact, almost similar—and differs sensibly from the Mexican. The line of its seat from cantle to horn, viewed sidewise, is a semicircle; there is no flat place to sit on. This shape gives the cowboy, seen from the side, all but as perpendicular a seat in the saddle as the old knight in armour. There are, of course, other saddles in use. The Texas saddle has a much flatter seat than the Brazos tree; the Cheyenne saddle a still flatter one with a high cantle and a different cut of pommel arch and bearing; and some individuals may ride any peculiar saddle. But all must have the horn and high cantle. In no other tree would the cowboy be at home or fit for service.[85]

The vaquero saddle also became transformed in Hawaii. The paniolo put his special stamp on the mochila saddle imported from Mexico in the 1830s. Hawaiians, like the llaneros, kept their saddle (*noho lio*) very light, perhaps for the same reason—rainy, tropical climates. Because the paniolo was a dally man, the saddle had a substantial, strong horn, but it remained lighter than the Mexican equivalent. Hawaiians added a distinctive island touch to the mochila, which they called the *lala*: they tooled the leather covering with richly embellished floral designs. The paniolo saddle also retained the Mexican tapaderas. Short, bucket-shaped "bull-dog taps" offered protection when working in rough brush country. The eight- to twelve-inch-long "mule-ear taps," closer to the original Mexican model, offered protection and an eye-catching flourish.[86]

Burt Sheppard of Longview, Alberta, recalled the old double-rigged saddles used by Canadian cowboys during the late nineteenth century. Many old-time saddles were built on "White River trees."

The cantle boards of these trees were fairly high and sloped back with the top of the cantle beveled back. The bars were thinner than those in the present-day saddles. Occasionally a tree would break across the bars. The forks were fairly high and sloped ahead a little. Also, the horn was high enough so that the hand could hook around it solidly when climbing on a bronc. The old saddles had very little leather in the seat and were built to tip a rider into the middle of the saddle.

In the old stock saddles, the thin bars and light seat covering allowed a rider to get close down to his horse. Most of them were built with a three-quarter loop seat; that is, the stirrup leathers looped through the seat and there was a hand hold under the fork with which to pick the saddle up. Where the modern saddles have a rounded up seat, the old saddles were more flat just behind the stirrup leather loops. This was important as the edge of the seat at this point would catch a rider's leg whenever a horse twisted and gave him a chance to shift to the right position.[87]

Saddle styles varied over time and from region to region. Cowboys everywhere adapted their equipment to the terrain, climate, and tasks at hand. But the Spanish stamp remains clear, in ropes, saddles, and technique, all the way north to the United States and Canada. Likewise, ranch work calendars retained similar chores regardless of where cowboys labored.

Cowboys performed their work on ranches owned by others. They were by definition employees. Ranchers owned the land, paid the cowboy's wages, and often furnished part of his equipment. In the next chapter we will examine the relationship between cowboys and ranchers. It could be a close bond, but significant differences created a considerable social distance between them. These differences were particularly dramatic in the highly stratified societies of Latin America.

CHAPTER 6

Ranchers and Cowboys

The relationship between ranch owners and their employees varied widely. In Latin America absentee ownership and large estates were the rule. Ranch owners might visit their estates for a few weeks of vacation, but a resident manager (mayordomo) ran the ranch on a daily basis. Cowboys in both North and South America generally lacked significant opportunity for upward mobility. Others owned or controlled the land. Given meager, seasonal wages and other limitations, few cowboys could expect to become small ranchers in their own right.

Ranch Labor Relations

Ranchers who resided on and ran their outfits sometimes developed close, quasifamilial ties with the permanent hands. These favored cowboys could live at the ranch year-round. Most went unpaid during the winter months, but stayed on with room at the bunkhouse and board. Others had to hunt wild game to survive. Cowboys often found themselves "riding the grub line," drifting from ranch to ranch, perhaps chopping wood for a meal, several months out of the year.[1]

Cowboying was strenuous, young man's work. Once a hand became injured or too old to ride the range, he often found himself unemployed. In some cases, old cowboys worked as cooks or horse wranglers. Ranching and cowboying were cherished ways of life. Often strong bonds developed between cowmen and their loyal hands, particularly over their common concern for animals. But ranching also was a business. And ranchers for the most part treated their hands, particularly seasonal workers, as hired help, not as family.[2]

The employer-employee relationship strongly favored the rancher over the cowboy. Most ranching regions enjoyed a relative labor surplus. Despite this demographic and economic reality, we find ranchers everywhere complaining about being short-handed. But most ranchers could find sufficient manpower, except at the height of the roundup season. Repressive legal and military pressures did drive some gauchos and llaneros away from settled ranching areas, thereby precipitating temporary labor shortages. Farmers, faced with more labor-intensive work, did have problems finding enough workers during planting and harvest times. For example, farmers in southern Uruguay had to pay higher wages for scarce labor. But ranchers in the livestock regions of northern Uruguay found labor cheap and plentiful.[3]

Chilean landowners seldom experienced labor shortages. The colonial landed elite kept ranches as much for the prestige of landowning as for the income they derived. Chilean rural workers suffered from long periods of unemployment and from lack of access to land. A marginal society of rural vagabonds developed—Chilean huasos who found work only during roundup. Unemployment and underemployment haunted Chilean rural workers well into the twentieth century.[4]

The Chilean elite tried to keep the number of persons living on their holdings to a minimum. John Miers observed in 1825 that "upon a grazing estate the proprietor seldom permits many persons to reside." Traditional Argentine ranchers similarly restricted their ranch populations. More people meant more danger of livestock theft. Some estancieros even forbade workers to have families on the ranch. Only trusted senior employees, such as the ranch manager, enjoyed the company of a family.[5]

Ever compliant to the demands of the powerful Agricultural Society, the Chilean government performed an extraordinary act of discrimination in 1874. A land law passed in that year excluded Chilean nationals from buying land on the southern frontier. The government provided this exclusion so that landowners in the central valley of Chile would not lose their surplus labor. Chilean nationals remained ineligible to own lands on the southern frontier until 1898.[6]

Politically powerful Argentine estancieros likewise controlled the nation's legal and political apparatus. A myriad of laws restrained the gaucho's movements and economic options, contributing to the end of his traditional way of life. Seasonal employment needs meant that gauchos went without cash wages for long periods. But until well into the nineteenth century, they enjoyed the possibility of hunting wild cattle and ostriches to earn money. The abundance of the pampa made life less precarious for the gaucho than for the huaso.[7]

Latin American ranchers availed themselves of another labor pool—slaves. Contrary to assertions by Arnold Strickon, repeated by Alistair Hennessy, ranchers throughout South America used slave and forced labor. Debt peonage and various types of working papers were common means of compulsion. Slaves remained in bondage through legal subterfuge for decades after abolition in Argentina. The dictator Rosas employed slaves on his estancias through the 1840s. On at least one of his ranches, slaves comprised a majority of the workers.[8]

Slaves worked throughout the llanos of Venezuela as well. In 1791 some 180 slaves lived on or near sixteen ranches in Tucupido. The same records list only 10 resident free peons, so most ranchers relied on slave labor. On his visit to the llanos in 1799, Alexander von Humboldt described the ranch workers of the llanos. "These Mulattoes, who are known by the name of *Peones Llaneros*, are partly freed men and partly slaves." Despite abolition, slaves remained in the llanos after independence came to Venezuela. In 1831 the province of Apure included 193 slaves. But eight years later Apure had only 158, Barcelona 941, and Barinas 1,458. The llanos moved steadily away from slave labor, although more than 11,000 still lived in Venezuela in 1858.[9]

But the end of slavery did not mean the end of repressive labor control on the llanos. Rural workers, lacking legal protection, found themselves in conditions that one authority called worse than slavery. Writing in 1896, William E. Curtis described the pathetic condition of rural labor: "While the laws of peonage have never existed in Venezuela, the relation between the planter and his laborers, particularly in the interior of the country, is equivalent to this form of slavery, and it is tolerated by both classes as the natural consequence of the difference in their wealth and social position." These comments are directed toward plantation labor, such as on the vast cacao estates on the coast. But rural workers throughout Latin America suffered from generally declining prospects during the nineteenth century. Latin American elites prospered at the expense of the rural masses.[10]

Fortunately for Anglo cowboys in the United States and Canada, those two countries did not have the draconian rural labor laws of Latin America. But ranchers in the United States generally enjoyed labor surpluses as well. Records for the Spur Ranch indicate that the manager had difficulty securing enough hands only once between 1885 and 1909. The same records show the marked seasonality of cowboy employment. During the late nineteenth century, only one-third to one-half as many hands worked from December through March as from April to November. Nearly two-thirds worked only one season or just part of a season at the ranch. Those without work survived on handouts and odd jobs. The prudent passed the winter by living frugally off their meager savings.[11]

Because hands were easy to replace, ranchers exercised considerable control over their labor force. At the Spur Ranch, creditors used the ranch manager to pressure cowboys for payment of debts. The ranch decreed prohibition from 1885 to 1890. Hands might be fired for perceived insubordination or on suspicion of theft or being "not truthful." The more economically rational ranching became, the more businesslike and less familial were relations between ranch management and labor.[12]

Ranchers on the sparsely populated Alberta frontier did experience occasional shortages of skilled cowboys. In the early days of ranching in the 1870s, few men could be found with the necessary horsemanship and knowledge of animals, grasses, and weather. In 1883 John Craig complained that "first-class experienced cowboys are not plentiful." On the other hand, he found "imitations" in great abundance.[13]

The early small ranches employed one or two men per one hundred cattle. Mrs. Duthie, a Pincher Creek ranch wife, recalled that their bunkhouse usually held about five hands and a cook. The Canadian lease laws encouraged large ranches at the expense of smaller operations. The big outfits hired fewer men in proportion to the number of cattle; a large ranch needed only one hand per thousand head.[14]

Montana cowboys quickly filled the bill, and by the mid-1880s Alberta ranchers had more hands. John D. Higinbotham recalled that from 1884 to 1887, herds were trailed from as far south as Texas up to Alberta. Released at the end of the drive, the cowboys found themselves out of work. "For a time the country was overrun with unemployed punchers and broncho-busters." Alberta ranchers generally found sufficient manpower to keep pace with the expanding livestock industry.[15]

"Remittance men" came from England to make their fortunes in the West. The term derived from the money they were sent for their maintenance by families in Great Britain. Few experienced any great success on the frontier. As open-range ranching declined in the United States, cowboys pushed north looking for work. Not until World War I did Canadian ranchers again face labor shortages. Most British hands did not return to Alberta after the war.

The Alberta ranges became increasingly populated by hands from the United States, but the livestock industry was already in decline.[16]

Seasonal Work

Sharp seasonal swings in ranch employment almost insured that hands could not accumulate savings or depend on a steady income. In Uruguay, for example, lack of rural employment and lack of access to land forced mass migration to the capital city of Montevideo. Rural-to-urban migration is the dominating demographic movement of twentieth-century Latin America. The result has been the proliferating slums that ring virtually every major urban center.[17]

Throughout the nineteenth century, ranch workers in Latin America lived a nomadic existence. Few had permanent abodes, and those who did occupied adobe hovels. If wages rose, the increase did not keep pace with rising food costs. In rural Latin America, we rarely find cases of a hard-working ranch hand earning enough to buy land and become a rancher himself. Entrenched landed elites monopolized access to land then, as they do today.[18]

Few cowboys in the United States or Alberta managed any degree of upward mobility. But their chances were greater than those of their Latin American counterparts. Most cowboys accumulated nothing beyond the clothes on their back and a saddle. Many cowboys in the United States did not even own their own horses; they rode mounts furnished by the outfit. As one observer rightly noted, "How can a man be expected to save money enough for a start in life when he gets only $40 or $50 per month, and is obliged to live idle nearly half the year at that?"[19]

Some western ranchers did provide means for hands to improve their lot. During the early days on the Texas range, cowboys sometimes branded calves on shares, which netted them one of every four animals branded. With this incentive, some became stockowners in their own right. Charlie Siringo reports that some ranchers let hands graze a few animals on their land for a small fee. This arrangement permitted a cowboy to start a herd of his own.[20]

Canadian cowboys enjoyed similar opportunities. George Lane, for example, worked his way up from cowboy to ranch foreman. He purchased two Alberta ranches, the Flying E in 1892 and the YT spread on the Little Bow River a few years later. Expanding his operations through a partnership, he controlled some thirty thousand head of cattle by the early twentieth century.

Other provident cowboys achieved similar success. John Ware and Herb Miller became ranchers near Macleod. But as with most success stories of the Henry Ford and Andrew Carnegie genre, these are exceptions that prove the rule of infrequent upward mobility.[21]

According to a Miss Shaw, quoted in the London *Times* of October 21, 1898, the Canadian West offered ample opportunity: "Any man having earned enough money to buy a cow may turn her loose upon the public range. Upon branding her calf in the following spring, he will be the possessor of two animals instead of one, and may continue while he works for wages to add to the number of his herd, until such time as he sees a chance of making profit enough to justify the establishment of a separate homestead."[22]

Miss Shaw's optimism caused her to overlook a few unavoidable facts. Without a bull in addition to one cow, offspring were unlikely. The land lease laws of Canada promoted large operations at the expense of small ranchers. Finally, the seasonality and generally low wages of ranch work made it unlikely that many cowboys could save enough to make the considerable investment needed to start a ranch. The most a cowboy could hope for was a position as a ranch foreman or manager, at double to triple the wages earned by the average hand.

Seasonality, low wages, and lack of rural labor organization kept cowboys at a subsistence level. The diary of James C. Shaw reveals the problem of winter layoffs and how a cowboy might cope. Shaw worked for six weeks in Wyoming during fall roundup in 1879. Laid off on Christmas Day, he received permission from the rancher to hunt wild game until spring. When springtime came, Shaw found work on the Laramie River for thirty dollars per month.[23]

The *Kansas Cowboy* estimated in 1885 that "the boys only get work three or four months in the year" on the northern ranges of Montana. Canadian cowboys also faced a bleak winter. John R. Craig noted that after the fall roundup "there was not employment for them [the hands] until the following spring, and although they had been in recent good wages—$45 to $50 a month and board for the summer—they are 'broke.'" Men in these circumstances did odd jobs, "rode the grub line" getting handouts at different ranches, or existed on wild game and "slow elk" (poached beef).[24]

On a few occasions, cowboys tried to unite to improve their lot. In 1886 about eighty cowboys banded together to form the Northern New Mexico Small Cattlemen and Cowboys' Union. Among the group's resolutions was that "the working season of the average cowboy is only about five months, and we think it nothing but justice that the cowmen should give us living wages the year around." The union also established a wage scale, based upon experience.[25]

This and other attempts at cowboy unionizing failed. Well-organized and powerful stockmen's associations responded by blacklisting cowboys who were active in union movements and by using strikebreakers. Union organizers differed little from rustlers in the eyes of the big rancher: both threatened his power and his wealth. Rural workers similarly failed in their organizational attempts in Uruguay, Argentina, and Chile. Striking sheep shearers in Patagonia were gunned down by the Argentine army.[26]

Cowboy unionization failed for the same reasons that cowboy wages remained generally low. Ranchers generally enjoyed a labor surplus, and striking hands could easily be replaced. The political climate of the nineteenth century was militantly antiworker. Both rural and urban workers often found themselves the victims of government-sponsored strikebreakers and violence. Moreover, the dispersed and migratory nature of the ranch workforce made meeting and organization difficult. For many hands, cowboying was a way of life, not a job. They focused their attention on tending animals, with little concern for economic advancement. Finally, cowboys everywhere exhibited an independent, self-reliant streak that militated against collective action.[27]

Low Wages

In the employer-employee relationship of rancher and cowboy, the rancher held nearly all the cards. Ranchers paid top money for breeding bulls and bottom dollar for cowboys. Wages for ranch workers were uniformly low throughout the Americas. What deceives some observers is that daily wages during the busy roundup season might be quite high by local standards. But we must remember that hands earned these good wages for a very short time. They went unemployed or worked for much lower monthly wages for most of the year.[28]

The landed elite in Chile went to extraordinary lengths to keep wages down—indeed to avoid paying money wages at all. The rural labor surplus meant that in Chile, "fiesta labor" could be hired for roundup or for the agricultural harvest (*mingaço*). Fiesta laborers received no wages, only a grand fiesta with food, drink, and dance. By the 1850s cash wages became more common, a paltry fifteen to twenty cents per day being the going rate. Chileans migrated to Peru and later to southern Argentina (Patagonia) in search of employment. Only the privileged few *inquilinos de a caballo* (mounted tenants) enjoyed a more stable position in society. They received a hectare (2.47 acres) for planting, as well as grazing lands for a dozen animals.[29]

Chile followed the Latin American trend of worsening rural conditions in the nineteenth century. After 1860 agricultural wages in the central valley fell farther and farther behind the cost of basic necessities. Tenants found themselves beset with more onerous requirements. Wages in the south of Chile remained too low for rural workers to purchase meat.[30]

Argentine and Uruguayan rural laborers fared better than the Chilean huasos and farm workers. In the mid-nineteenth century, a rural peon in Uruguay earned eight to twelve pesos per month. A *capataz* (foreman) earned the very respectable wage of sixteen pesos per month. Uruguayan ranchers complained of unfair competition from southern Brazil, where ex-slaves were paid no more than five pesos per month.[31]

But by 1878 the Uruguayan immigration office reported that a labor surplus had pushed wages "far below" the level of earlier years. An influx of Italian immigrants and the diligent persecution of "vagrants" had swelled the rural labor pool. A few ranchers had also begun fencing their land, which further reduced their labor needs. Real monthly wages continued to fall through the early twentieth century, reaching a low point of about five pesos. Gauchos in Uruguay faced a bleak world of shrinking employment opportunities and falling wages.[32]

Argentine gauchos did not suffer as dramatic a decline in wages as their Uruguayan neighbors. But they faced similarly reduced employment opportunities as changing ranch technology cut the need for their labors. From 1888 to 1895 real rural wages dropped in Buenos Aires province from a high of 20.4 to 5.6 gold pesos per month. Wages did not approach their 1888 level until 1911–1912. Agricultural demand during the Boer War and World War I pushed wages steadily upward in the early twentieth century, but prices for food and other necessities rose more quickly. The gaucho could no longer find wild cattle for a free meal, so his beef consumption was greatly reduced during the nineteenth century.[33]

Mexican vaqueros, like their South American counterparts, often found themselves in debt. In New Mexico, for example, debt peonage was already common by 1800. It persisted through the nineteenth century in Mexico. Frederic Remington noted that vaqueros "are mostly *peoned*, or in hopeless debt to their *patrons*, who go after any man who deserts the range and bring him back by force." Through the early twentieth century, vaqueros earned the equivalent of eight to twelve dollars per month. Vaqueros in Texas faced wage discrimination from Anglo ranchers. The Scott and Byler outfit, for example, paid their Anglo hands twenty dollars per month, but reduced the wage to ten to twelve dollars for vaqueros. Only the highly skilled vaquero broncobuster could aspire to higher wages; he might earn twenty dollars per month.[34]

We have more complete wage data for cowboys in the United States and Canada. The accompanying tables summarize representative wages in the two countries. Canadian wages are for cowboys in Alberta; for the United States, the state or territory from which the data come is indicated. More experienced hands naturally earned higher wages than novices. As in Latin America, wages rose during the busy seasons of spring and fall roundup.

As table 2 shows, the neophyte hand earned little more in 1904 than he had thirty years earlier. As elsewhere, special skills and more experience meant higher wages. H. B. C. Benton earned top wages of $75 per month in 1882 to break horses for the Sand Creek Land and Cattle Company in Idaho. Cooks also commanded higher wages, earning from $70 to $90 per month during the 1880s, compared with $30 for a beginning hand. Daily wages from the 1860s through 1885 ranged from about $1.50 to $2. Wages also varied depending on whether the ranch provided "keep" (room and board).[35]

Twentieth-century cowboys fared no better economically. Ranch work continued to hold its appeal as a way of life, but ranch wages lagged far behind those in other sectors of the economy. Writing in the *Wall Street Journal* of June 10, 1981, William E. Blundell noted that "the days of the cowboy are marked by danger, drudgery, and low pay." Cowboy wages averaged $500 per month, without room and board. Not much had changed in a century.

The earnings of Canadian cowboys generally paralleled those of cowboys in the United States (see table 3). The heady agricultural demands of World War I pushed cowboy wages upward. And as elsewhere, except for a privileged few permanent hands, most cowboys worked as migrant laborers. The account books of Harry Denning illustrate one Canadian cowboy's wanderings. Among other odd jobs, he earned $2 castrating colts in June 1908. In March and May 1909, he did the same thing at different ranches. He made $12.30 breaking horses in July. From January through April 1910, he worked for J. W. Ings and made $40 per month. In May 1910 he earned $4 castrating colts. In July he worked fighting a fire and made $29. At various times, he also worked at a mill, on farms haying and threshing, and on a road crew. Clearly, a cowboy had to be willing to take whatever work was available.[36]

For cowboys everywhere, no work generally meant no pay. Ralph Clifton

Table 2. Representative Ranch Wages, United States, 1870–1909

Year(s)	Cowboy (U.S. $ per month)	Foreman (U.S. $ per month)	State/Territory
1870s	25	—	Kansas
1872	20	—	Texas
1879	35	—	Wyoming
1880s	25–40	50–90	—
1880	30–75	—	Wyoming
1881	35–75	75	Wyoming
1882	30–75	—	Wyoming
1883	30–75	—	Wyoming
1884	30–50	—	Wyoming
1885	25–50	125	Texas, Wyoming
1886	25–50	—	Wyoming
1887	30–40	—	Wyoming
1888	30–40	—	Wyoming
1889	35–40	150	Wyoming
1890	30–45	125–150	Texas
1891	25–40	—	Wyoming
1892	25–30	—	Wyoming
1893	30	—	Wyoming
1904	30	—	Texas
1909	37	—	Texas

Sources: Joseph G. McCoy, *Cattle Trails of the West and Southwest* (1874; repr., N.p.: Readex Microprint, 1966), p. 369; John K. Rollinson, *Wyoming Cattle Trails: History of the Migration of Oregon-raised Herds to Mid-western Markets* (Caldwell, Idaho: Caxton Printers, 1948), p. 338; Philip Ashton Rollins, *The Cowboy: An Unconventional History of Civilization on the Old-Time Range* (1922; repr., Albuquerque: University of New Mexico Press, 1979), p. 208; N. R. Davis, "Cash Book, 1878–81" and "Journal No. 2, 1884–1888," (MSS., Western Range Cattle Industry Study, Colorado Heritage Center, Denver); Fred Hesse, "Papers of Fred Hesse, manager of Powder River Cattle Company, 1880–1896, and owner after 1882 of the '28' Ranch" (microfilm, reel 2, Western Range Cattle Industry Study, Colorado Heritage Center, Denver); William C. Holden, *The Espuela Land and Cattle Company: A Study of a Foreign-Owned Ranch in Texas* (Austin: Texas State Historical Association, 1970), p. 117.

**Table 3.
Representative Ranch Wages,
Alberta, Canada, 1881–1915**

Year	Cowboy (Canadian $ per month)
1881	20
1883	45–110
1885	40–50
1887	40
1891–92	30–100
1904	20–30
1905	20–35
1906	25–40
1910	30–40
1912	35
1914	70
1915	70

Sources: David H. Breen, "The Ranching Frontier in Canada, 1875–1905," in Lewis G. Thomas, ed., *The Prairie West to 1905: A Canadian Sourcebook* (Toronto: Oxford University Press, 1975), p. 231; Walrond Cattle Ranche (MS., Glenbow Archive, Calgary, M 264), p. 11; Cochrane Ranche, "Letter Book" (MS., Glenbow Archive, Calgary, M 234), pp. 83, 147, 210, 234, 256; Kenneth Coppock, "Another Came West," *Canadian Cattlemen* 1:4 (March 1939):157, 177; Breen, *The Canadian Prairie West and the Ranching Frontier, 1874–1924* (Toronto: University of Toronto Press, 1983), p. 270; Ralph Clifton Coppock, "Leger [*sic*], 1904–18" (MS., Glenbow Archive, Calgary, BR, C 785, Box 1), 1:10, 45–46, 66; Harry Denning, "Account Book, Lineham, Alberta, 1908–1954" (photocopy, Glenbow Archive, Calgary, BR D 411A), pp. 9, 12–13.

Coppock worked as a cowboy for $25 per month in Alberta from July through September 1905. But he got hurt on August 29 and missed more than a week's work. Those days were deducted from his pay. A "stove up" cowboy, one who had been hurt too seriously to continue working on horseback, faced bleak prospects. He might land a job as a cook. Otherwise, he had to make do with charity and odd jobs.[37]

Rancher Control of Land and Politics

Latifundia, large estates that dominate the countryside, have long been major problems in much of Latin America. Today land remains concentrated in a few hands in many Latin American nations. A large sector of the rural population has always lacked access to land for grazing or agriculture. In the late 1970s, for example, 60 percent of rural Mexican households were landless or near landless. The figure stood at 66 percent for Colombia and 70 percent for Brazil.[38]

Ranching helped to perpetuate latifundia because ranchers took an extensive approach to livestock raising: more animals meant more land. The high social status and great political power of landowners insured that public policies would further their interests. Cowboys in Latin America owned no land and lacked the resources and opportunity to accumulate any.

Chile is among the extreme cases of a latifundia-dominated society. Traditionally, an elite few controlled the best lands in the central valley near Santiago. They also exercised juridical and police functions on and around their estates. Ranchers, not the central government, maintained rural social control during the eighteenth century.[39]

During the latter half of the nineteenth century, some subdivision of agricultural lands took place. But most often, the resulting *minifundia* (tiny plots) could not support a farm family, much less provide room for grazing animals. The old rural social order of a wealthy few dominating the poor masses remained. Benjamín Vicuña MacKenna noted in 1866 that large ranches persisted. "The farms are usually very large, frequently comprising several thousand acres, and herds of cattle five, ten, or twenty thousand in number are pastured on the elevated plains and tended by the rough huasos, till the period of their slaughter arrives." Absentee ownership on such large estates represented the norm.[40]

Military action during the early 1880s finally defeated the fierce Araucanians on the southern Chilean frontier. But as new lands became available for settlement on the frontier, Chile (like Argentina) promoted land concentration with public policy. High down payments effectively excluded the poor from purchasing the newly opened lands. As we will see below, other policies aimed at promoting immigration discriminated against the native-born poor, including the huaso.[41]

Beginning in 1838, the rural oligarchy organized to voice its political interests through an Agricultural Society. Refounded in 1856 and again in 1869, the society remains an important political lobby group in Chilean society. In the late nineteenth century, ranchers pushed successfully for import taxes on beef. This protectionism against cheaper, better-quality Argentine beef lasted through World War I. The Chilean urban worker and middle class subsidized the landed elite by paying higher prices for domestic meat. For rural Chileans, as for the huaso, beef remained a luxury beyond reach.[42]

The twentieth century witnessed a rise both in land concentration and in the gulf between Chile's landed oligarchy and rural masses. By 1924 fewer than 3 percent of the farms in the fertile central valley controlled 80 percent of the agricultural lands. Beholden to the landed patron, the rural poor—huasos, sharecroppers, migrant workers, squatters—delivered their votes and their labor to enrich and empower him further. Residing in palatial estates in Santiago, the oligarchs maintained a firm grasp on the land and the landless. Not until the frustrated attempts at land reform under Salvador Allende (1970–1973) were the oligarchs challenged. His overthrow and death removed for a time threats to Chilean elite power.[43]

Across the Andes in the Banda Oriental (Uruguay), similar circumstances obtained. Spanish colonial policy promoted land concentration and the marginalization of the gaucho. Rich, landed families—the Viana, de la Quadra, and others—came to dominate the countryside and, after independence, the country. Justices of the peace, obedient to landed interests, wielded civil and military authority in the countryside. Ranchers organized the Uruguayan Rural Association to promote their policy interests at the national level.[44]

The process continued, aided by technology and subservient politicians and police, during the nineteenth century. Fencing, too expensive for small ranchers, offered the rich another means of grabbing land. The nation's rural code, first issued in 1876 and modified three years later, insured the legal domination of the rural oligarchy and the submission of the gaucho. As in Chile, marginalized rural workers sometimes labored for food alone. Many Uruguayan cowboys owned nothing more than a saddle. The social reform programs brought to Uruguay early in the twentieth century by President José Batlle y Ordóñez (1903–1907 and 1911–1915) did nothing to improve life for the gaucho. Land, and therefore power, remained in the hands of a few.[45]

In Argentina, rich in land and poor in population, much the same story unfolded. Colonial and national policies encouraged the few to control the vast plains. Occasional meager efforts at land reform were defeated by the power of the oligarchy. The Argentine provinces also used legal repression, in the form of rural codes, to subjugate the gaucho. As in Uruguay, rural justices of the peace did the bidding of the landed elite. Controlled access to land inhibited the growth of a stable rural middle class. The countryside was largely populated by wandering gauchos, migrant farm workers, and transient sharecroppers.[46]

Like the landed elites of Chile and Uruguay, Argentine estancieros organized. The Argentine Rural Society, formed in 1866, and the Jockey Club, organized in 1882, epitomized the ranchers' political power and social status. Ironically, the *Annals* of the Argentine Rural Society, the official organ of the landed oligarchy, lamented the very social conditions that the elite had largely created. "Unfortunately, in Argentina an intermediate class between the rustic campesino, totally lacking education, and the urban resident, horrified by the camp [countryside], does not exist."[47]

The last great expansion of the cattle ranching frontier in Argentina came with the defeat of the pampas Indians by General Julio A. Roca in 1879–1880. But once again, land was delivered in huge chunks to speculators and Roca's political clique. The government distributed land taken from the Indians in units of forty thousand hectares. Land fraud accompanied the transactions, as was the norm in Argentine public land management.[48]

Great estates (hatos) also developed on the Venezuelan llanos during the early eighteenth century. By about 1750, thirty families owned forty ranches that covered 219 square leagues. About three hundred thousand cattle grazed on these estates. Absentee ownership became more common over time, as the wealthy congregated in Caracas, away from the heat and humidity of the plains. But unlike their counterparts in Uruguay, Argentina, and Chile, the ranchers did not run the country. The great coastal cacao plantations gave the planters a dominant role in policy making. Far from the seat of power in Caracas and economically marginal, the ranchers of the llanos often found public policy detrimental to their interests. Discriminatory taxation and lack of infrastructural development held back the economic development of the llanos through the twentieth century.[49]

Independence speeded land concentration in Venezuela as it did elsewhere in Latin America. For example, a compensation law for war veterans gave them land grants in 1823. Llaneros valued cattle, not land, and communal grazing rights were well established on the plains. A wealthy few, including General José Antonio Paez, separated the llanero soldiers from their holdings for a pittance. Once more the rich got richer. Paez promoted the interests of the landed, including access to water and grasslands, and sought to punish landless trespassers—the llaneros. Politicians and caudillos, whether liberal or conservative, continued the process of land concentration.[50]

The caudillo José Gregorio Monagas distributed land to his followers in 1848. But more than half of the land went to ten concessions. Political favoritism and nepotism shaped public policy in Venezuela as elsewhere in Latin America. Successive Venezuelan constitutions enacted between 1811 and 1914 reaffirmed the rights of the landed elite. Economic power meant political domination. The power exercised by the coastal planters redounded to the benefit of plains latifundia holders as well. Llanos cowboys, like their fellows elsewhere, remained landless migrant workers.[51]

Mexico's landowners established the first association in the Western Hemisphere to promote ranching interests. In 1529 town councilmen in Mexico City organized the Mesta, patterned on a powerful organization of sheep ranchers in Spain. The stockmen's group promulgated its first codes in 1537 and added more stringent rules governing rural social life in 1574. For example, *castas* (nonwhites) were forbidden from owning horses. Ranchers provided mounts for these early vaqueros.[52]

The Mexican Mesta did not gain the power and prestige of its Spanish predecessor. But it reinforced the power and autonomy of the Mexican landed elite in both agricultural and livestock regions. The organization set conditions for labor, wages, and brand registration, and assessed penalties for infractions. The Mesta appointed many important rural officials, including those who presided over roundups and who prosecuted rustlers and other accused criminals. As a public official recorded in 1594, ranching and agriculture were "in the hands of the rich and of those possessing Indians under the *encomienda* system" (royal grants of Indian labor made to Spaniards in the New World). Recent studies have shown that latifundia were not universal in Mexico. But in the northern grazing areas, the large haciendas described by François Chevalier dominated into the twentieth century.[53]

Ranchers in northern Mexico utilized a wide range of mechanisms to control land and labor. The powerful Sánchez Navarro clan purchased strategic lands in Coahuila and thereby dominated rivers in the northern part of the state. They then leased water rights to others. Debt peonage was more prevalent on northern estates than in central and southern Mexico. In fact, even missionaries used debts to control their workers. The company store (*tienda de raya*) helped to perpetuate worker debt. Peons who fled were usually recaptured, at least on the Sánchez Navarro latifundio. In New Mexico in the early nineteenth century, a small clique of fifteen to twenty families controlled society. Intermarriage and business cooperation helped to perpetuate elite control.[54]

When independence came to Mexico, the Sánchez Navarros owned some eight hundred thousand acres. But another Coahuila hacendado, the Marquis of Aguayo, owned fifteen million acres and about 213,000 cattle. The Sánchez Navarro family eventually accumulated lands equal in size to the state of West Virginia. Yet traditional, often backward agricultural and ranching techniques rendered much of the vast holdings fallow. Even profit-minded ranchers, like the Sánchez Navarros, often worked their huge estates conservatively and inefficiently.[55]

The power of Mexico's landed elite continued unabated despite major political change and turmoil. Frederic Remington described the rural social order under the dictatorship of Porfirio Díaz in the 1890s: "In the haciendas of old Mexico one will find the law and custom of the feudal days. All the laws of Mexico are in protection of the land-owner. The master is without restraint, and the man lives dependent on his caprice. The *patrón* of Bavicora, for instance, leases land to a Mexican, and it is one of the arrangements that he shall drive the ranch coach to Chihuahua when it goes. All lessees of land are obliged to follow the *patrón* to war." Even the great upheaval of the Mexican Revolution only replaced one elite with another. Vaqueros remained landless marginals in rural society.[56]

Latifundia were less institutionalized through law in the American West. On the contrary, law and political sentiment were biased in favor of smaller family farms. Many ranchers scratched out a meager living with small herds and crude accommodations. But many huge ranches developed from Texas northward. By the end of the nineteenth century, Richard King had accumulated some 1.27 million acres in his south Texas ranch. He employed 300 vaqueros who worked 65,000 cattle and 10,000 horses. John Chisum's well named " Rancho Grande" stood on the west Texas–New Mexico border. In a single season before Chisum died in 1884, his cowboys branded 18,000 calves. Charles Goodnight's outfit in the Texas Panhandle covered some 700,000 acres in 1883.[57]

Large outfits also developed on the northern plains. In 1884 in Montana, ten companies owned 90 percent of the livestock in the area of Fort Benton. The Swan Land and Cattle Company, owned by Scottish investors, came to control 600,000 acres in Nebraska and Wyoming. Speculators and large ranchers committed land fraud to add to their holdings. For example, the Desert Land Act of 1877 and the Timber and Stone Act the following year offered easy pickings to the unscrupulous. The theoretical limit of 640 acres under these acts could be exceeded by the wily. By selecting alternate sections of land, a buyer could effectively double the grazing range he controlled. Illegal fencing of public lands offered another means of extending one's holdings. Up to 95 percent of the final titles under the Desert Land Act probably were fraudulent.[58]

Like ranchers in Latin America, those in the United States banded together to further their economic interests. In many parts of the West, stock-men's associations effectively ruled territories and states. Cattlemen in Wyoming organized the Wyoming Stock Growers' Association in 1873. By the 1880s the group controlled roundups around the territory. However, the association did permit nonmembers to participate in the association roundups. Colorado stockmen organized in 1872. As with similar organizations representing other industries, the largest ranches dominated the proceedings and set policy. The associations governed all areas of ranching: roundups, grazing on public and Indian lands, and brand registration. As the ranchers' political voice, the groups lobbied strenuously and often successfully to promote the cattle industry over farming and sheep ranching.[59]

Eastern and foreign consortia invested in western livestock with a vengeance during the early 1880s. Thereafter stock associations often appeared to serve as mouthpieces for foreign "cattle barons." These large corporate ranches were precursors of the powerful agribusiness interests that came to dominate twentieth-century farm policy. Large outfits often considered small ranchers no better than or different from rustlers. In the early days of the cattle industry, strong figures such as Charles Goodnight ruled their ranches with paternalism and autocracy. The stock associations codified, organized, and generalized rules of the range that increased the distance between cowboys and ranchers.[60]

Canadian ranchers organized for similar reasons—to cooperate in solving common, far-flung range problems and to voice a political agenda. Eleven ranchers around Macleod organized in 1883 into an association. In 1890 ranchers formed a province-wide organization, the Alberta Stock Growers' Association, which became the Western Stock Grower's Association two years later. Issues ranging from combating rustlers and wolves to lobbying about import and export policies came before such groups.[61]

Canadian ranchers enjoyed several practical advantages over their counterparts to the south. Indian "pacification" preceded the cattle frontier in Canada. Canadian ranchers did not have to mount private armies of their own cowboys, as did ranchers in the United States and Latin America. The Mounted Police had largely established the rule of law and subdued the Indian population before livestock raising reached Alberta. "Flying patrols" of Mounties watched for strangers on the range, persecuted rustlers, and visited ranches regularly. The South-Western Stock Association, headquartered in Macleod, offered rewards to assist the Mounted Police with frontier law enforcement. The association announced in 1883 that it would pay one hundred dollars for information leading to the conviction of anyone who killed cattle, stole horses, or set fire to the range.[62]

Canadian lease laws favored large ranchers over small ones. In 1884, ten companies controlled two-thirds of the stocked land in southwest Alberta. Four—the Cochrane, Walrond, Oxley, and North-West Cattle Company ranches—controlled almost half the land. The Cochrane Ranche leased 189,000 acres, the Oxley and Walrond 180,000 acres each. As in the United States, speculators profited from the leasing arrangement. Their activities further reduced opportunities for small operators.[63]

Unlike the many self-made men of the ranching frontier in the United States, Canada's ranchers were ready-made gentlemen. Most came from eastern Canada or England, complete with upper-class tastes and conservative politics to match. As one observer noted in 1911, Canada's ranchers "are hardly of the traditional bronco-busting, raw-punching sort. They are Englishmen of the country class." The ranching elite mixed and married with the urban upper crust at the Ranchman's Club in Calgary, founded in 1891.[64]

Until the tide of national politics turned against them, the conservative ranching elite of Alberta boasted an impressive record of successful lobbying. Land leases, particularly choice, well-watered range, went to large ranching companies. Tariffs favored the beef exporters. The stock raisers succeeded for about twenty years in keeping out competition from ranchers and farmers in the United States. The threat of sheepmen was met by requiring special grazing permits granted through the Ministry of the Interior. The Canadian ranching frontier offered the cowboy a measure of civility and comfort, but few cowhands could aspire to gather a herd and obtain leases themselves.[65]

CHAPTER 7

Home on the Range

Ranch Life

R anches from Alberta to the Argentine pampas shared similar characteristics. Diet, housing, and pastimes tended to be simple and straight-forward. Ranchers and hands everywhere enjoyed eating beef, although cooking methods varied a bit. If ranch hands generally lived in primitive shacks, small ranchers did not enjoy deluxe accommodations either. Wealthy ranchers built true palaces in country and city, but most hands saw these ornate and sometimes garish structures only from afar.

During the busy season, ranches were little more than places to catch a quick meal and bed down at the end of the workday. But the ranch also represented the most important social institution on the cattle frontier. The bunkhouse could be the scene of card games, practical jokes, tall tales, and occasional fights. During their free time, cowboys entertained themselves as best they could. Singing was commonplace among cowboys everywhere, and because the cowboys themselves often wrote the lyrics, the songs reveal a good deal about their values and character.

Fresh and Dried Beef

W ith so few amenities on the range, it is not surprising that the cowboy diet was spartan and limited. Given his choice, the cowboy ate beef several times a day. Robert B. Cunninghame Graham noted that beef was "the staple, almost the only food of the llanero." Since the tropical climate made it impossible to preserve fresh meat, the llanero consumed dried beef much more often. Exploring the llanos in the late eighteenth century, Alexander von Humboldt noted of the inhabitants that "their food is meat dried in the air, and a little salted; and of this even their horses sometimes eat." If freshly killed beef was available, it was spitted and roasted by an open fire. Llaneros prized the kidney, liver, and ribs.[1]

George Flinter visited the llanos during the stormy independence wars and described the llanero method of cooking beef: "The general way of preparing the meat, is by cutting it up in large pieces of ten or twelve pounds each, and putting it on a huge wooden spit, and placing between every two pieces of meat, pieces of the heart, the liver, and large lumps of suet, this they call entreverado; they roast it before an immense wood fire." Lacking wood, llaneros used cow dung for the fire. They sometimes hunted tigers, using dogs to track the quarry. The tiger meat was either sold or eaten.[2]

In the Río de la Plata, gauchos used a similar method to prepare an *asado* by roasting a side of beef ribs on small metal spits. Beef, washed down with highly caffeinic mate tea, constituted their favorite meal. Diners simply sliced off a chunk of meat with a long knife, the only utensil used for eating. The temperate climate of the pampa permitted gauchos to carry fresh meat with them for a few days. They simply tied a few pieces to the saddle and cooked it briefly whenever and wherever hunger overtook them. Denied wood as fuel on the largely treeless pampa, the gaucho used dung or dried bones to build a fire. Wild cattle abounded on parts of the pampa through the mid-nineteenth century. Unmindful of waste, gauchos would rope and kill a cow only to consume some choice morsel and leave the remainder to rot. Gauchos favored the tongue and what they called *matambre*, the meat between the ribs and hide.[3]

For special occasions, gauchos and huasos prepared a delicacy called *carne con cuero* (literally, meat with a hide). Chilean cooks stuffed a calf with a variety of foods, wrapped it in a cowhide, and slow-cooked it by a fire. Like gauchos, huasos used only long knives to eat meat. The Argentine version often omitted the stuffing, but the hide still held in the juices and flavor. Vaqueros cooked a similar dish using only the head of a freshly killed yearling. Wrapped in hide and a wet gunnysack, the head was buried in a shallow hole. It cooked slowly all night under a roaring fire. The meat, brains, and tongue provided a delectable repast the next day.[4]

The gaucho enjoyed easy access to fresh beef well into the nineteenth century. But the Chilean huaso, like the llanero, often had to eat dried beef (*tasajo* or *charqui*, hence jerky). For them, fresh meat of any kind was a rare luxury. Then, too, the tough, rangy creole cattle that dominated the Chilean range until the 1870s were better suited for dried than fresh meat. John Miers visited Chile in 1819 and reported favorably on the jerky that "requires no salt, and will keep sweet many years if preserved in dry places." But it is worth remembering that slaves in Brazil and Cuba constituted by far the biggest markets for dried meat. That should leave little question about its palatability compared with other foods.[5]

Vaqueros also liked beef. A *Scribner's Magazine* correspondent in Mexico in 1912 found vaqueros carrying fresh beef on their saddles as did the gauchos. "They sat gracefully astride mules, with their *serapes* (blankets) wound closely about them, each with a chunk of raw beef, bleeding and uncovered, dangling from his saddle. Starting for the mountains just at nightfall, with the raw freshly killed beef dripping blood from the saddle, the *maleta* [saddle bags] filled with cold *tortillas* (bread) and *frijoles* (beans) and tobacco, and the little tin cup covered with dirt and dust dangling from the saddle strings."[6]

Vaqueros and Anglos in south Texas made and ate beef jerky as well. German immigrants to such towns as Fredericksberg and New Braunfels continue to produce jerky in large, savory, sweet chunks. The export of dried beef along with hides and tallow represented a major part of the pre-Anglo economy of California well into the nineteenth century. An average carcass might yield about two hundred pounds of meat suitable for *carne seca* (jerky).[7]

Like his Latin American counterparts, the American cowboy liked beef and lots of it. Steaks, fried well-done in a cast iron skillet, ranked high. Other beef cuts and parts went into the legendary "son-of-a-bitch" stew. Cooks preferred to have meat and parts from an unweaned calf. To the choicest meat, they added sweetbreads, marrow gut from between the two stomachs, kidneys, heart, liver, and tongue. Brains and flour thickened the mix, and onions and chilis sometimes added flavor. This was cowboy cuisine at its finest.[8]

But profit-minded ranchers and trail bosses did not always provide a bounty of fresh beef. Granville Stuart, a noted Montana rancher and politician, recorded that cowboys on the trail ate corn meal, sorghum molasses, beans, salt, and bacon. Game, including deer or, while they lasted, buffalo, might add meat to the regimen. Practical considerations entered in. Jack Porter recalled that on a trail drive in the early 1880s, the hands ate smoked rather than fresh meat. The waste of meat common on the Argentine pampa found less favor in the American West. As one cowboy remarked, "We could not keep ourselves in fresh meat like a cow outfit does on a roundup for the reason that we had a smaller crew than the average roundup uses, and we had no visitors to drop in for a meal. Another reason was that our animals were of large size, and with the weather so very hot, meat would not have kept fresh."[9]

Hot Coffee and Mate

Along with plenty of meat, cowboys wanted a hot drink with caffeine. Gauchos, huasos, and much of the population of the Southern Cone had an addiction to mate. Mate is a tea made from the highly caffeinic leaves of the *Ilex paraguariensis*, a plant related to holly. Grown in Paraguay and the rest of the Paraná River basin, mate has long been a favorite beverage of the region's Indian population. The Spanish adopted the drink, and its popularity continues. Chileans sometimes take their mate with a bit of sugar in the morning; Argentines tend to favor it straight.[10]

For huasos and gauchos, however, mate represented far more than an invigorating beverage. Ritual and proper equipment are tied inextricably to the consumption of the tea. Mate is sipped through a metal tube (*bombilla*), sometimes embellished with ornate silver- and goldwork. The tube has a strainer at one end that is inserted into a small, hollowed-out gourd (also called a mate) filled with tea leaves and hot water. The liquid is replenished with more hot water as the gourd empties. Fresh leaves are added as needed. Mate is consumed communally if at all possible. Gauchos and huasos would imbibe a few sips and pass the gourd to the next person. Many workers, rural and urban, still drink mate with every meal and at breaks throughout the day.[11]

Outside the Southern Cone, coffee is the Latin American beverage of choice. Many nations of Latin America, notably Brazil and Colombia, grow coffee. Llaneros drank their coffee sweetened with raw sugar. According to one source, coffee was more important to the llanero than mate to the gaucho and as important as *coca* leaves to the Bolivian Indian. "Give the llanero bad liquor, bad tobacco, or bad food, but never bad coffee." In town, llaneros might take their coffee with milk (*cafe con leche*). Oddly, milk was rarely used in any of the cattle regions of North or South America.[12]

In the American West, the brand name Arbuckle was synonymous with coffee. Cowhands drank copious quantities of strong black coffee, brewed in three- to five-gallon pots, with every meal. *Arbuckle* became a derogatory term for a greenhorn hand, who was supposedly obtained with stamps given away with cans of coffee.[13]

Before the Arbuckle brothers of Pittsburgh developed their special roasting and coating techniques, ranchers had to roast their own coffee. Canadian ranchers did likewise. The supply list from the Cochrane Ranche in Alberta for February 21, 1885, was as follows:

Ranch life *held little of the glamour and excitement popularized in cowboy novels and B Western movies. Cowboys ate simple food and lived in simple housing. They rarely owned more than they could pack in their saddlebags. Cowboys everywhere shared a taste for beef, tobacco, alcohol, and a strong, caffeinic beverage, coffee, mate, or tea. Small ranchers often shared the rustic, spartan existence of working cowboys. But wealthy cowmen spared no expense in showing off and enjoying luxuries that they could purchase and bring to the cattle frontier.*

The Argentine gaucho *probably ate more beef than anyone else in the world. With wild cattle roaming the pampas until the mid-nineteenth century, gauchos could rope and kill a cow for nothing more than a single meal. Gauchos used a metal spit, called an* asador, *to slow-roast a side of ribs next to an open fire (p. 112). An entire sheep or goat could be spitted and roasted in this same fashion. Gauchos cut and consumed their* asado, *or beef roast, using only the long, sword-like* facón. *(Argentine postcard, author's collection)*

Cowboys seldom ate *meals seated at a table. On a cattle drive or at work on the range, they sat on whatever was available, including the ground. Unlike their Latin American counterparts, cowboys in the United States and Hawaii sometimes dined with tin plates and cups. The paniolo, Hawaii's cowboy, also showed his Hispanic roots in his musical instruments, the guitar and the ukulele (p. 127). Music served as a favorite recreation and a form of cultural expression and memory in all cowboy cultures. This photograph dates from the mid-twentieth century. (National Archives, Washington, D.C.)*

Like the gaucho, *the Venezuelan llanero and Chilean huaso cooked meat with an asador. Independence wars of the early nineteenth century devastated the llanos livestock industry, however, so the llanero could not feast on beef as readily as the gaucho. Llaneros and huasos also ate beef jerky, a rarity on the Argentine plains (p. 112). César Prieto sketched this scene in 1904. (Author's collection)*

Thanks to the chuckwagon *and the availability of canned goods, American cowboys ate a more varied diet than those in Latin America (pp. 113, 116). The Argentine gaucho, for example, subsisted mainly on beef and mate (pp. 117, 120). The chuckwagon, with its cast iron kettles, Dutch oven, and three- to five-gallon coffeepot, even provided such luxuries as sugar. Inventive and adaptive, ranch cooks, such as this one on the JA Ranch in Texas in 1907, created their own special cuisine from the basics of beef, beans, and bread. (Erwin E. Smith Collection, Amon Carter Museum, Fort Worth)*

While riding the range, *a cowboy's lunch consisted of some dried beef, dried fruit, some sourdough biscuits, and perhaps a cup of coffee if he carried a pot in his saddlebags. Meals at camp or at the bunkhouse offered greater variety and abundance. Cowboys also enjoyed the sociability of mealtime, a chance for conversation, a practical joke, and maybe a song or two. The photograph below was taken around 1900 at the Peñasco Cattle Company ranch camp in south-central New Mexico. The cowboys above were photographed in Colorado in 1884. (*Above: courtesy of Colorado Historical Society. *Below:* Rio Grande Historical Collections, New Mexico State University Library*)

C. M. Russell's *pan-oramic* Cowboy Camp during the Roundup *(oil on canvas, 1887) highlights the joyous bustle of the busiest time in the ranch calendar (pp. 71–73). General roundups brought together cowboys from far and wide for several weeks at a time. Besides working together, cowboys enjoyed friendly roping and riding competition and gambling. (Amon Carter Museum, Fort Worth, 1961. 186)*

The tropical llanos *dictated that dwellings be designed for hot, humid weather (pp. 118–19). Even ranchers (hateros) who owned land showed little ostentation in their dwellings. A thatched roof, open, airy design, and the inevitable dog marked the traditional llanero dwelling, as shown in the watercolor below by an unknown artist of the mid-nineteenth century. (Prints and Photographs Division, Library of Congress)*

Cowboy housing *and diet were typically spartan. The Chilean huaso, like the rural poor in general, lived in a simple hut. Depending on local materials, the hut might be thatched or adobe. Whatever family life a cowboy might enjoy depended on whether he owned a small parcel of land where he could build a modest house. Most Latin American cowboys owned no land or house. They lived in bunkhouses when employed at a ranch and otherwise slept outside. (Drawing by Kiltietz, 1827)*

Mexican ranch buildings *often included wide covered patios as refuge against the blazing sun. Mexican ranch architecture, with its adobe-chinked logs and red tile roofs, carried over into the American Southwest. As elsewhere in Latin America, the* casa grande *(big house) of the rancher featured comforts and spaciousness not found in the humble shelter allotted to vaqueros. (Drawing by Frederic Remington,* Harper's Monthly, *March 1894, courtesy of Yale University Library)*

Line shacks, *far removed from the main ranch houses, were homes to cowboys in the United States and Canada for months on end. These shacks could be crude, dank adobe or sod huts built into the side of a hill. They offered few amenities or improvements, other than the traditional horseshoe over the door for good luck (pp. 119–20). Cowboys passed the time reading labels on cans, singing songs, telling tall tales, or having their hair cut. This shack served as the original headquarters of the Matador Ranch in Texas during the 1880s. (Erwin E. Smith Collection, Amon Carter Museum, Fort Worth)*

Gaucho huts *and even the dwellings of many landowners in Argentina and Uruguay remained primitive well into the nineteenth century. Adobe walls and thatched roofs were common, as seen in this painting by Emeric Essex Vidal from the 1820s. Cold and damp in winter, hot and bug-infested in summer, these crude lodgings offered* *few creature comforts (pp. 117–18). On the traditional* estancia, *gauchos staked out cattle hides to dry in the sun, then bundled them for export to Europe. (From* Vidal's Views in Buenos Ayres and Monte Video, *London, 1820, Yale Collection of Western Americana, Beinecke Rare Book and Manuscript Library)*

Larger ranches *featured substantial dwellings, corrals, and better outbuildings (pp. 117–18). Members of the Argentine landed elite built city mansions as well as massive, castle-like ranch estates. Working ranches in the United States often blended European luxury with western rusticity. The photograph above shows the 101 Ranch headquarters in Oklahoma in 1903; below, the Greene Cattle Company headquarters in Hereford, Arizona, 1910. Few working hands in any country, however, could aspire to own a large spread and comfortable ranch house. (Prints and Photographs Division, Library of Congress)*

Wealthier Alberta ranchers *replicated the lifestyles of the English gentry. Canadian lease law favored large ranches, such as the Upper Walrond Ranche in Alberta, shown here around 1893. The Rocky Mountains formed a protective barrier from winter harshness in western Canada. (Glenbow Archives, Calgary)*

Open-range ranching *became a thing of the past in the United States after the great winter losses of 1885 and 1886. Barbed wire and wooden fences stretched across the plains. Windmills dotted the landscape. New breeds of cattle, Hereford and others, pushed the hardy old Longhorns into the pages of folklore and history. This photograph shows the JA Ranch in Colorado in 1904. (Prints and Photographs Division, Library of Congress)*

20 Sacks best flour	30 lbs [?] raisins
10 " Coffee sugar	3 Boxes Price's Baking Powder
2 " Oatmeal	100 lbs Rice
2 " Cornmeal	200 " coarse salt
500 lbs Bacon	100 " table "
500 " Beans (small white)	25 " Corn starch
500 " [?] apples	50 " [?] soda
6 Boxes dried prunes	10 Gals. Vinegar
200 lbs green coffee	20 lbs Mustard
20 " best green tea (small [?])	6 " Cinnamon (grd)
6 Cases Leaf Lard (360 lbs)	5 " Allspice
15 Boxes canned Corn	20 " Pepper (whole)
10 " " Tomatoes	1 " Ginger (ground)
3 " Electric soap	10 Gals. best syrup
1 " Candles (about 20 lbs)	

W. F. Cochrane ordered supplies for six months at a time. "If you have some good, plain pickles, say cucumbers, you might put in 2 or 3 gals, but no expensive bottled stuff like Chow-chow," he added. Note that the list includes ten sacks of coffee sugar and two hundred pounds of green coffee; obviously, the Cochrane Ranche did its own roasting. The list also offers an honest look at the ranch hand diet in general. Clearly, meat, other than bacon, was supplied from the ranch itself.[14]

More Grub

Beyond a penchant for beef, caffeinic drink, tobacco, and alcohol, cowboys differed widely in their tastes. Diets showed strong regional variations. As the supply list from the Cochrane Ranche indicates, Canadian cowboys ate canned vegetables and lots of beans. An anonymous source from the early twentieth century describes a diet of bacon, beans, canned goods, and wild fowl. Syrups and stewed prunes usually served as dessert. On the trail, canned tomatoes helped to quench thirst. Philip Ashton Rollins notes that acidic tomato juice counteracted alkali dust inhaled by men on the trail. In Canada and less frequently in the United States, hands might drink tea instead of coffee.[15]

Fred Ings described how Canadian hands began their day during roundup in the 1880s: "Breakfast at daybreak was eaten in the mess tent, a hot substantial meal of meat, potatoes, bread, jam, with strong black coffee. Our dishes were tin and we ate sitting around on bed rolls or a box if one was handy, or on the ground. Before we were through, the tinkle of a bell told us the night wrangler was near with the saddle horses."[16]

A meal at a roundup in the United States during the 1880s closely resembled that described by Ings—canned fruit, bacon, beans, fresh meat, dried fruit, soda biscuits, tea, and coffee. The hand riding out overnight without a pack horse rolled the bare necessities into his slicker: "frying-pan, some flour, bacon, coffee, salt, and, as a substitute for yeast, either a bottle of sour dough or a can of baking-powder."[17]

The diet of the American cowboy was similar to that of his Canadian counterpart. Unlike the Latin American cowboy, North American ranch hands had access to processed foods, notably canned fruits and vegetables. The basic lunch and supper included beef, bacon (termed "overland trout"), lots of biscuits, beans, coffee, and dried prunes, apricots, or peaches. Breakfast might include eggs or salt pork. Cowboys preferred sourdough biscuits to those made with buttermilk or baking powder. Ranch cooks used the versatile Dutch oven to bake biscuits. One source attributes the often bowed legs and lean physique of the cowboy to his calcium- and calorie-deficient diet, although long hours on horseback likely were the major cause.[18]

Ironically, milk played virtually no role in the ranch diet in North or South America. Canned condensed milk might be used for cooking in North America, but never for drinking. A number of practical considerations militated against milk. First, cowboys hated any footwork, including milking cows. Second, storage and spoilage presented major problems. Third, it was no easy feat to milk wild cattle.

Joseph G. McCoy noted that "in camp, on the trail, on the ranch in Texas, with their countless thousands of cattle, milk and butter are almost unknown, not even milk or cream for the coffee is had." With his usual condescension toward ranch workers, he attributed the lack to "pure shiftlessness and the lack of energy." Theodore Roosevelt also remarked on the absence of milk: "Most ranchmen at that time [the early 1880s] never had milk. I knew more than one ranch with ten thousand head of cattle where there was not a cow that could be milked."[19]

On his visit to the Venezuelan llanos in 1876 and 1877, Karl Sachs found no milk for coffee. Ranchers did produce and sell cheese (*queso de mano*), but not butter. Ramón Paez likewise complained about having to take his coffee black. The typical llanos ranch house reminded him of "a bee-hive of vast proportions, naturally suggesting the idea of a 'land of milk and honey.' Unfortunately neither of these could be obtained either for love or money, although the woods and pastures of the estate abounded in both the creatures that produced them. So we were compelled to resort to our reserved stock of *papelón* [raw sugar] to sweeten our coffee, and to its own delicious natural aroma in the place of milk."[20]

Instead of the biscuits favored by Canadian and American cowboys, llaneros ate *arepas*, or corncakes. Much thicker and harder than the Mexican corn tortilla, white- and yellow-corn arepas remain very popular in Venezuela today. Beans were as much a mainstay on the llanos as on the Great Plains. In the United States, cowboys preferred red beans. In Latin America, the choice might well be black beans. Llanos cuisine did develop dishes in addition to the staples of meat, beans, coffee, and corncakes. *Sancocho*, for example, is a tasty stew of meat or chicken and vegetables. The numerous rivers of the tropical plain also yielded a variety of fish. In fact, llaneros had to be expert swimmers and boatmen, because of the annual floods that swept the lowland plains. These skills were not generally shared by other cowboy types.[21]

The gaucho had the most limited of all cowboy diets. Beef, mate, tobacco, and nothing more nourished gauchos for months at a time. Gauchos shared the disdain for milk found in plains regions elsewhere. But, unlike his counterparts, the gaucho also refused vegetables. Bread remained scarce on the pampas until the arrival of European farmers late in the nineteenth century. One British visitor in the early 1820s remarked that gauchos viewed vegetables "with eyes of ridicule" and considered a man who would eat them "as little superior to the beasts of the field."[22]

Cattle Skulls, Bunkhouses, and Line Shacks

Ranch hands did not expect much in the way of housing, nor did they get much. When riding the range, cowboys slept under the stars, with only a tarpaulin or poncho for protection. Throughout Latin America, hands and small ranchers lived in rustic adobe shacks. Only the wealthiest ranchers constructed palatial manors on their vast estates, and these they occupied only on infrequent visits to the ranch from their city dwellings.

Ranch houses where families lived sometimes showed more attention to creature comforts. In ranch country, most women were wives or daughters of ranchers. Many ranchers discouraged hands from marrying. Some Argentine landowners even forbade women and children from living on their estates. Ranchers sometimes looked at women as dangerous distractions and sources of discord among their men. Many domestic tasks assigned to women in the nineteenth century simply went undone. Except for shearing sheep, women seldom found employment on ranches. Many ranch wives rode horses, however. As one Canadian ranch wife indicated, "I verily believe that if I did not ride, they [the hands] would have nothing to do with me."[23]

Foreign visitors often expressed shock at the modest dwellings of South American ranchers who owned thousands of head of cattle. John Mawe visited the Banda Oriental (now Uruguay) in 1804. He described the thatch-and-mud houses as "wretched." Furniture consisted of "a few skulls of horses." Charles Darwin stayed at the estancia of Juan Fuentes, near Maldonado, Uruguay, in 1833. He expressed surprise that a rancher who had so many cattle and workers lived in such crude accommodations. "After witnessing the rude wealth displayed in the number of cattle, men, and horses, Don Juan's miserable house was quite curious. The floor consisted of hardened mud, and the windows were without glass; the furniture of the sitting-room boasted only a few of the roughest chairs and stools, with a couple of tables. The supper, although several strangers were present, consisted of two huge piles, one of roast beef, the other of boiled, with some pieces of pumpkin: besides the latter there was no other vegetable, and not even a morsel of bread."[24]

By the late nineteenth century, some health officials began to worry about the primitive housing that sheltered the rural poor in Argentina and Uruguay. Some attributed high levels of rural disease to the adobe shacks. Infested with insects and vermin, the huts were damp and dank in winter and hot and stuffy in summer. Still, rural workers probably fared no worse than urban workers of the time, who found themselves stuffed into insalubrious tenements in Buenos Aires. Descriptions of housing on the pampa remain uniformly negative through the twentieth century.[25]

Venezuelan hateros (ranch owners) and ranch hands also lived a primitive existence throughout the nineteenth century. Like their counterparts in the Río de la Plata, they used animal skulls and skins to construct rudimentary furniture. For example, a crocodile skull might serve as a chair. A British diplomat described the ranch of General José Antonio Paez, one of Venezuela's independence heroes. His hato differed "in no respect from those of the humbler plainsmen, than in size—occupying one side of a strongly palisaded square court of large dimensions." The Paez home did have brick floors, a rarity on the llanos. It also had a tile roof instead of the normal palm thatch. Openings between the roof and rafters permitted welcome air flow, but also gave entrance to "scorpions, centipedes, tarantulas, and hundreds of other nasty noxious reptiles."[26]

Ranch hands generally slept under a thatched roof set on four poles. Men slept in hammocks to receive whatever breeze might blow and to keep away from crawling insects and reptiles. Away from the hato, men might sling a hammock between two trees or simply sleep on the ground.[27]

Primitive housing and the tropical environment presented llaneros with serious health hazards. Cuts or bites on man or beast became infected easily. In his autobiography, General Paez recounts cutting his hand on the reins. The wound attracted flies and as a consequence became infected with worms. Epidemics swept the plains with disconcerting regularity. A plague of "black vomit" (yellow fever) swept over the llanos in 1865. Equally dangerous and morbid diseases struck cattle and horses. An epidemic in 1843 killed off virtually all semiwild cattle that remained on the plains after the predations of the independence and civil wars.[28]

In 1879 officials reported a "fever" epidemic (probably yellow fever) in Ortíz, a town in Guárico. The "principal families of the town are suffering," noted José Yaría Grateral, a local official. Dr. Eulogio Velásquez recorded the sad progress of the disease. During the week of August 17, 1879, 133 new cases of fever appeared; 6 persons died. The following week brought another 70 cases. By the end of September, 233 persons were sick; 14 died during the last two weeks of the month.[29]

Llanos housing remained primitive into the twentieth century. Some ranchers added fences to protect food crops grown in a garden: yucca, bananas, beans, corn, potatoes. Varieties of palm trees furnished roofing material that could last for decades. The tree roots could be eaten in a salad and the sap used as a sweetener or fermented into wine. Palm seeds could be processed into soap and used as a condiment.[30]

Frontier housing on the Great Plains offered few amenities. Two-room sod huts, often dug into a hillside, provided shelter for many. In the Southwest, adobe served in place of sod. Buffalo-skull seats and doors and beds made of hide graced many dwellings. In areas with adequate timber, frontiersmen built log cabins, chinking the logs with mud and moss. With the westward expansion of railroads, more refined building materials became available. But small ranches and bunkhouses continued to be cold and drafty in winter and hot in summer.[31]

Early Great Plains ranches shared another characteristic with Argentine estancias: many ranch houses had few cultivated plants growing nearby. According to Philip Ashton Rollins, at most ranches "there was no fencing, for there was no field of grain or hay, no patch of vegetables, no garden of flowers." Charles Darwin, Alexander Caldcleugh, and other visitors remarked the absence of vegetables in the rural Argentine diet. For cowboys in the United States, vegetables "grew in cans." In Argentina, gauchos seldom consumed anything other than mate and meat.[32]

Ranch housing in Alberta resembled that of the northern Great Plains. But more Canadian homesteads included a barn, a building that did not grace many American ranches until after the mid-1880s. Duncan McEachran described Alberta ranches of the early 1880s as "consisting usually of a small log house, with stable for eight to ten horses, corrals or fenced enclosures for branding, feeding and preserving hay for winter use."[33]

Fred Ings described a bunkhouse of about the same vintage. Such buildings were made "of round spruce logs chinked with clay, roofed with poles and sod. They seldom had a floor and were sparsely furnished with rude bunks made of poles, hand made tables and benches. The stove pipe stuck through the roof. Sometimes in the summer the cooking was done on an open fire outside. Spruce boughs or dry grass served as mattresses though frequently bed rolls had to be spread on the dirt floor."[34]

Of course, the abodes of wealthy ranchers everywhere did not contain such humble furnishings. J. J. Young described the stone mansion at the Cochrane Ranche in 1902, "with its green lawns, beautiful flower beds, and vines and rose bushes, and furnished as it is with all the refinement that wealth and taste can suggest—with its fine reception hall, its open fire places, its pictures, its flowers, its trained servants from the Old Country, its pianola interpreting Chopin's music with the skill of a virtuoso and even a mocking bird in the conservatory." Regardless of country, the few who controlled large sections of range land lived well.[35]

Ranch Fun and Frolic

Lack of money and opportunity meant that cowboys could not always avail themselves of the popular vices of the day: gambling, drinking, and "fallen" women. In many cases, they had to invent their own fun. Practical jokes and other humorous outlets were popular with cowboys from Buenos Aires to Calgary. Writing of life on the Midway Ranche in Alberta, Fred Ings recalled that "the cowboys used to have great fun—always up to some prank. A tethered horse at night might have his saddle reversed, particularly if its rider was paying court to some girl. A horse and buggy left standing would be found seemingly intact, but with the horse on one side of the fence and the buggy on the other." The famous "snipe hunts," popular in the United States too, left the victim afoot far from help with nothing but a candle and a bag for comfort.[36]

Vaqueros and American cowboys also played practical jokes. Putting unlikely or uncomfortable objects in a cowboy's bedroll or boots was popular. At spring roundup, kangaroo courts might be held. Goading a coworker's horse, just as the man was occupied with lighting a cigarette or other task, provided great entertainment. The cook became a favorite target of pranksters. Two Hispanic teenagers named Aguirre decided to scare the cook at their Red Rock, Arizona, ranch. Hiding in the kitchen, they made moaning noises and tugged on his apron from behind. The cook ran right through the screen door to escape from the "ghost." Vaqueros also loved roping one another from ambush.[37]

Some outside observers judged cowboys by their behavior in front of strangers. To the outsider they often appeared taciturn in the extreme, but among themselves, cowboys passed long hours exchanging jokes and tall tales. For example, William T. Hornaday misread cowboy character during his visit to cowcamps in 1886. "I never saw elsewhere in this country a set of men that were so careful in the avoidance of sarcasm and smart sayings likely to give offense. They are severely matter-of-fact in everything, and very little given to joking. Indeed, where every man carries a six-shooter, jokes are not safe things to handle, unless they are of mighty small calibre. Any joke, no matter how old and rusty, if pointed at a cowboy, is liable to go off, and kill the very man that 'didn't know it was loaded.' "[38]

Gauchos of Argentina likewise exhibited a coolness and quietness toward strangers. Their common response to the questions of a prying outsider was "Who knows?" Cowboys shared their own peculiar values. Outsiders often had difficulty seeing and understanding the real cowboy culture.[39]

Cowboys of Canada and the United States shared one pastime that set them apart from their Latin American counterparts—reading. Few Latin American ranch workers could read or write. Literacy was rare in rural society in general. But Northern Hemisphere cowboys, especially those posted at lonely line shacks, read voraciously. Even labels on cans of food became the objects of intense study. Cowboys turned reading into yet another game. They memorized the food labels and held contests to see who could recite them without error. At the bunkhouse, reading occupied the brief time between dinner and bedtime. Philip Ashton Rollins described the typical ranch library as "composed of a patent-medicine almanac, a well-thumbed catalogue of a mail-order house, several catalogues of saddle makers, and, finally, fragments of newspapers from widely scattered localities and of vintage dates."[40]

Singing Cowboys

If reading was limited to the North American ranges, music of varying quality and musicians of varying talent could be found in cattle country everywhere. In fact, a good deal of cowboy folklore has been preserved and perpetuated through song. Charlie Seemann of the Country Music Foundation estimates that three-fourths of original cowboy songs began as verses composed by working cowboys. These poems sometimes found their way into print, often in western newspapers or stockmen's publications. When set to traditional folk tunes, the poems evolved into cowboy songs. Lyrics offer helpful clues about cowboy life and material culture. Range songs cover the gamut of cowboy life: lost love, horses, hazards of the trail. The lyrics often contain a heavy dose of fatalism and nostalgia.[41]

A guitar, or some variant, is associated with cowboy music from Argentina to Alberta. Gauchos adapted their music to the frontier by using local materials to fashion a guitar-like instrument. Guitars did grace the bunkhouses of many ranches in the United States. On the trail, however, instruments had to fit into the saddle bags. This limited options to the harmonica, jew's harp, and an occasional fiddle. The guitar became strongly associated with the cowboy during the rise of the singing-film cowboys of the 1930s and 1940s.[42]

John Baumann reported on the role of music on the Texas range in 1887. "The younger hands are whiling away the time 'whittling' and 'plug chawing,' drawling out yarns of love and sport and singing ribald songs, until someone strikes up the favorite wail, 'Oh, bury me not on the lone prairie, Where the coyotes howl and the winds blow free.'"[43]

The heyday of cowboy life in the United States passed quickly, and, not surprisingly, a longing for bygone days suffuses many cowboy tunes. One American song of unknown authorship wistfully asks, "Make me a cowboy again for a day."

Thunder of hoofs on the range as you ride,
Hissing of iron and sizzling of hide,
Bellows of cattle and snort of cayuse,
Longhorns from Texas as wild as the deuce.
Mid-nite stampedes and milling of herds,
Yells of the Cow-men too angry for words,
Right in the thick of it all would I stay,
Make me a Cowboy again for a day.

Under the star-studded Canopy vast,
Camp-fire and coffee and comfort at last,
Bacon that sizzles and crisps in the pan,
After the round-up smells good to a man.
Stories of ranchers and rustlers retold,
Over the Pipe as the embers grow cold,
Those are the times that old memories play,
Make me a Cowboy again for a day.[44]

It is worth recalling the utilitarian origin and purpose of other cowboy songs—to soothe restless cattle at night. Steady, low, melodious tunes helped to keep cattle from starting at unexpected sounds. Night riders sang, usually unaccompanied, to their bovine charges. When they ran out of tunes, cowboys put together a miscellany of words and music, mixing the sacred and the profane. Popular cowboy songs generated innumerable variations, as different singers forgot or altered the words.

Accounts of horse-races, unflattering opinions of the cattle, strings of profanity, the voluminous text on the labels of coffee and condensed milk-cans, mere humming sounds, alike and with seemingly deep religious fervor, were poured on many a night into the appreciative ears of an audience with cloven hoofs.

This serenading was done partly to hold the cattle under the compelling spell of the human voice, and partly to disabuse from the mind of any fearsome member of the herd suspicion that either a puncher's silhouette against the sky-line or else the noise of his moving pony might represent a snooping dragon.[45]

Many B Western movies have starred singing cowboys, such as Gene Autry, Roy Rogers, and the Sons of the Pioneers. But in reality, cowboys did not burst into song every ten minutes. Quiet conversation, not songs around the campfire, commonly marked the end of the day. William G. Johnson, who worked as a cowboy during the 1880s, recalled that "there was no singing or playing the fiddle around the campfire as the story writers and the movies would have you believe." After a hard day in the saddle during roundup, men did not burst into song; they played poker. "There is little else but hard work in the life of a cowpuncher," Johnson concluded.[46]

Some puritanical spirits "sanitized" latter-day versions of many cowboy songs. John A. Lomax, for example, altered lyrics to remove profane references in his famous anthology *Cowboy Songs*, issued in 1910. Likewise, many commentators discreetly omitted mention of prostitutes on the frontier. Myth making has long been a part of the cowboy culture.[47]

Spanish words worked their way into some cowboy songs, particularly from the southern ranges. Like the Anglo cowboy's general working vocabulary, some of his lyrics showed Hispanic influences. But old Scottish and English melodies also contributed to the mix. Some songs are adaptations of earlier compositions. "The Dying Cowboy" ("Bury Me Not on the Lone Prairie") is a rewrite of an old sailor's song called "The Ocean Burial," first published in 1839. Songs reveal much of the realities of the cowboy's life, including his salty language. Cowboys added their own verses to popular tunes, so that some songs have literally hundreds of known verses. This version of "The Old Chisholm Trail" tells of cowboy adventures and vicissitudes on a trail drive:

> Oh, I had a ten dollar hoss and a forty dollar saddle,
> And I started up the trail just apunchin' Texas cattle.
>
> When I hit the saddle I give a little yell,
> The tail cattle broke and the leaders went to hell.
>
> I don't give a damn if they never do stop;
> Cause I'm gonna ride like an eight-day clock.
>
> We rounded up the herd and put 'em on the cars,
> And that was the last of the Old Two Bars.
>
> When I got to the boss and tried to draw my roll,
> He had me figured out nine dollars in the hole.
>
> I'll sell my outfit as soon as I can
> And I wouldn't punch cows for no damned man.[48]

In some cowboy cultures, especially that of the gaucho, the folk singer became an esteemed figure. Called a *payador*, the wandering singer of gaucho tunes could always find shelter and a drink in exchange for his songs. Gauchos played a small guitar-like instrument called the *charango*. The sound box, topped by five courses of double strings, was made from the carapace of an armadillo. Many songs carried political overtones, but the pain of love is perhaps the most common theme. A wide variety of song types and dances developed. Rural dances included the *estilo*, *milonga*, *zamba*, *gato*, *chacarera*, *malambo*, *vidala*, and *vidalita*. The Spanish heritage comes through clearly in gaucho music and in Argentine folk dances.[49]

The gaucho's competitiveness, so evident in his equestrian games, spilled over into his music. A favorite type of entertainment was a singing duel, the *payada de contrapunto*. (A somewhat more recent song type called the *cifra* also features word duels.) Two singers improvised, tossing insulting verses back and forth. In these lively exchanges, musical combat could end with the clash of knives. A rustic guitar usually hung from the tavern wall so that patrons could play and sing.[50]

Gaucho humor surfaces in many songs. For example, note this musical advice to a woman:

> Don't marry an old man
> Because of money,
> The money goes
> But the old man stays.[51]

Fatalism marks music of the pampas, as it does that of other cowboy regions.

> Riches are for naught
> Knowledge is too,
> Death reaches all
> And to earth we go.[52]

Argentine composers began incorporating themes from gaucho folk music and *gauchesco* writers into their works in the late nineteenth century. *El rancho abandonado* (The abandoned ranch), composed by Alberto Williams in 1890, is among the first to show influences from gaucho music. Juan José Castro drew upon the famous Hernández poem for his cantata *Martín Fierro*. Alberto Ginastera includes stanzas from *Martín Fierro* in his ballet *Estancia*. His *Obertura sobre el Fausto criollo* takes inspiration from the famous and funny gauchesco poem *Fausto*, by Estanislao del Campo. Francisco A. Hargreaves, Arturo Berutti, Julián Aguirre, Constantino Gaito, Felipe Boero, and other Argentine composers also incorporate folk traditions and literature from the pampa into their compositions.[53]

Like gauchos, llaneros enjoyed music as part of their lively folk culture. Laborers on the llanos devised work songs for a wide range of chores. On a trail drive, the point man and the drag man sang verses back and forth. Llaneros, like other cowboys, recognized that music helped to soothe and tame cattle. They sang melancholy tunes called *yaravis* to quiet the cattle. Workmen called milk cows by singing songs incorporating the animals' names.[54]

Music on the tropical plains reflected llanero values, material culture, and humor. Colombian llaneros sang *galerones*, musical tales filled with heroism and romance. A typical melody of the plains, called a *tono* or *tonada llanero*, might treat any subject of interest to the llanero. Verses from the plains often mixed humorous references to love and food. Clearly, these fundamental drives preoccupied llaneros.

For the chicken, corn,	Para la gallina el maíz
For the goose, fish,	para la ganza el pescao
And pretty girls	y las mujeres bonitas
For the love-struck man.	para el hombre enamorrao.
To be good, a woman	Una mujer pa' ser buena
should have two things:	dos cosas debe tener
Much desire to work	muchas ganas pa' el trabajo
and very little to eat.	y muy pocas de comer.[55]

Like the gaucho, the llanero prized the ability to improvise songs. Karl Sachs reported that some llaneros were masters of improvisation. "For this reason llanero singing enjoys great celebrity in the country."[56]

As in Argentina, Venezuelan composers drew upon folk tunes. Juan Bautista Plaza set to music the text of llanero poems of Luis Barrios Cruz. Such creole music often resounded with a heady nationalism. The *joropo*, a jig-like dance in six-eight time, is the typical dance of the llanos. Plaza made the joropo the basis for his composition called *Fuga criolla* (Creole fugue).[57]

The vaquero is most associated with the typical Mexican *corrido*. These folk songs have eight-syllable lines, with the second and fourth lines rhymed. Regional variations are legion. For example, the Huasteca variant often includes cowboy yells (*gritos de vaquero*). Many corridos celebrate the daring deeds of outlaw heroes. The ballads of Gregorio Cortés and Joaquín Murieta are perhaps the best known. Other corridos recall the feats of famous Mexican bandits, such as Heraclio Bernal, the "Thunderbolt of Sinaloa." Bernal attained Robin Hood status among the Mexican poor for defying the officials of Porfirio Díaz's dictatorship. Vaqueros and the rest of Mexico's rural poor commemorated those who rose above their humble origins to challenge and flaunt authority.[58]

Other vaquero songs dealt with the realities of ranch life. "Mi caballo bayo" recalls a vaquero who loved his cutting horse too much to sell him at any price. Vaqueros of the King Ranch in Texas sang "El toro moro" to eulogize a particularly fierce bull.[59]

Vaqueros who sailed to Hawaii in the 1830s to train the paniolo doubtless carried guitars with them, but Hawaiians quickly put their distinctive stamp on guitar playing. They developed a unique style of slack-key guitar music called *kiho'alu*. The guitar is tuned so that the open strings produce a chord. What we now call the Hawaiian guitar style developed during the 1890s as the forerunner of the country music sound produced with slide- and steel-guitar styles. The craft of guitar making developed on the islands. Craftsmen use native and imported woods and local shells in their beautifully styled instruments. The ukulele typifies Hawaiian music even more than the guitar. But this quintessential island instrument also has Iberian roots: it evolved from the Portuguese *braguiha* introduced to Hawaii in the 1870s.[60]

Many Hawaiian songs celebrate persons, places, or events associated with ranching in the islands. But unlike cowboys in most other cultures, the paniolo usually did not compose songs. Hawaiian singers developed a vocal style, yodeling, that is often associated with cowboy music. But Hawaiian music included yodeling in the 1890s, whereas the technique did not appear in cowboy music on the mainland until Jimmy Rogers popularized it in the 1920s. "Cattle Call" (first recorded in 1935 by Tex Owens and popularized by Eddie Arnold in 1955) is one of the best-known cowboy yodeling tunes.[61]

Music served as an important pastime for cowboys from Argentina to Texas to Hawaii. Much cowboy music developed out of the work situation of singing to cattle. As we will see in the next chapter, other work activities carried over into cowboy fun. Cowboys blurred the boundaries between work and play—as long as they could remain on horseback.

CHAPTER 8

Horsin' 'Round

Equestrian Fun and Games

Cowboys, regardless of their national origins, lived to ride. Most of the cowboy's favorite games and pastimes were equestrian contests. Using Allen Guttmann's typology, we find that cowboys often engaged in games (organized forms of play) and contests (competitive games). They also enjoyed showing off their individual horsemanship and courage in a number of spectacular and dangerous ways. As with work methods and equipment, we find the Spanish influence reaching throughout North and South America. But in their games, as in their work lives, cowboys of the Americas also exhibited considerable diversity.[1]

The Spanish Heritage

Many cowboy cultures evolved from a blending of the Spanish heritage of the conquistadors and pre-existing Indian cultures. The common Hispanic element is evident in equipment, work routines, the use of the lasso, and similar equestrian contests. From Mexico, equestrian games moved northward into the American Southwest. The "all-American sport" of rodeo carries a clear Hispanic stamp.[2]

The Spanish transplanted their equestrian attitudes, practices, and equipment from Iberia to Latin America. For example, the Spanish prejudice against riding mares extended to the New World. In areas where horses were abundant, as in Argentina, gauchos would never ride a mare; it was an unmanly thing to do. In colonial Chile, the shortage of mounts forced huasos to ride mares. But as horses became more plentiful, huasos reasserted the macho prerogative of not riding mares. In both Argentina and Chile, mares served only as work and draft animals.[3]

Specific equestrian practices as well as attitudes crossed the Atlantic with the Spanish. *La sortija* (the ring race) entertained crowds and riders into the twentieth century. The roots of the game extend back to sixteenth-century Spain and likely to Moorish origins. Riders in Chile and Argentina, armed with foot-long wooden lances, galloped toward a tiny golden ring dangling from a slender thread. The rider who successfully skewered the ring won it as a prize. He would then present it to a woman he wished to impress. Vaqueros in Mexico and the American Southwest also enjoyed the ring race.[4]

The *juego de cañas*, jousting with canes, was an Arabian contest that crossed the Atlantic with the Spanish. Each contestant threw a cane at his opponent while riding full tilt towards him. The goal was to catch the opponent's cane in midair and to avoid being hit by it. This aristocratic contest came to Mexico with the Spanish conquerors and appeared in Chile by 1663.[5]

Of course, Spain held no monopoly on equestrian contests; similar practices appeared in the antebellum American South. The southern fixation on medieval chivalry extended to replicating a tamer version of a jousting tournament, which rose to great popularity in the 1840s in Virginia. Riders used eleven-foot-long lances to spear a series of rings ranging in diameter from a half-inch to two inches. The rings dangled from supports spaced twenty-five to thirty yards apart. A rider would cover the hundred-yard course in about ten seconds, skewering as many of the elusive rings as possible. Such contests are still held in some parts of the South.[6]

Frontier Work and Survival Skills

While some games were Spanish imports, others grew out of the survival skills necessary to exist on the vast plains frontiers of the New World. These often dangerous contests tested the strength and courage of man and mount. Both had to be strong, even in the face of charging wild bulls, in order to work and survive. Many games developed out of the work routines of the American plains.

One dangerous (and therefore highly esteemed) gaucho survival game was *pialar*. The word means to lasso an animal by the legs, and that is exactly what happened. A single horseman galloped down a gauntlet of gauchos who all twirled lassos. As the rider sped past, the men in the gauntlet lassoed his horse's legs and threw the animal abruptly to the ground. The gaucho sought to land on his feet after the tumble, with the horse's reins still in hand. This activity, like many others, grew out of skills necessary to survival on the vast, solitary plains of Argentina. The pampa was honeycombed with animal bur-rows that frequently tripped even the most sure-footed mount. A solitary gaucho who lost his mount on the frontier stood little chance of survival.[7]

Chilean huasos trained their mounts to stop suddenly without throwing the rider. The horses would skid quickly to a stop by dropping onto their haunches. Appropriately called *sentada* (sitting down), this skill could well save the rider and mount from injury or death in an emergency. Likewise, Mexican vaqueros engaged in a contest called *rayar* (literally, to draw a line), in which two riders galloped from opposite directions toward a line drawn in the dirt. Each pulled his horse into a slide, as in the Chilean sentada. The player whose horse stopped nearest the *raya*, or line, was declared the winner.[8]

Man versus Beast

Many contests pitted cowboys against cattle in rec-reational versions of ranch work life. Cowboy com-petition in the American West quickly developed into tournaments and then rodeos, with prizes, rankings, and professional performers. Professionalization of rodeo in the 1930s largely broke the links between rodeo performances and working cowboys. The *Denver Republican* recorded the excitement of a tournament in September 1887 at Montrose, Colorado:

> The cowboys' tournament in which roping from the ground, from the saddle, heading and heeling, riding bucking bronchos, etc., afforded much sport, but well nigh terminated fatally. One of the cowboys was riding a bucking broncho when the animal made a dash towards where the ladies were seated and could not be checked before he struck Mrs. James A. Ladd, who was thrown violently to the ground beneath the animal's hoofs. The horse struck the lady with its front feet on her chest and pinioned her to the earth for a second or two, but he was quickly grasped by one or two gentlemen who stood near the lady and prevented from trampling her to death. Every lady on the grounds screamed and one or two fainted.[9]

In 1893 Calgary witnessed its first cowboy tournament that awarded prizes to contestants. Winners of the six-hundred-yard horse race and of the roping competition received saddles worth seventy-five dollars. George Lane, a rancher from High River, arranged the contests at the Calgary midsummer fair. In 1912 Calgary would commence its famous "Stampede," one of the world's great rodeo extravaganzas.[10]

Like the American cowboy, the gaucho enjoyed pitting his strength against wild steers. Gauchos jumped onto the backs of wild steers and horses. The steer might be ridden about for awhile and then dispatched with a knife thrust into the throat. Much like modern rodeo bull riders, the llanero tied a stout rope around the bull's girth just behind the front legs. Using the rope as a handhold, the llanero would ride the wild bull to exhaustion or until he was thrown. The Mexican version of bull riding resembled that of the llanero. After mounting a lassoed bull, the vaquero would hang on for dear life and ride the animal to submission—or until he was thrown or injured.[11]

Contests between man and bull had many variants. Colear (tailing the bull) dates from early colonial times. Llaneros first performed the feat in pairs. One rider would gallop up behind the bull, grasp the tail, and twist the animal off balance. Before the bull could recover, the other rider jumped down and deftly castrated the hapless animal. Here again, work skills become stylized into a recreational pastime. In later versions, riders simply tumbled the bulls without adding the insult of castration.[12]

Sir Edward Sullivan and Ramón Paez both described the popular practice of tailing in mid-nineteenth-century Venezuela:

> The colleador, mounted on a good horse that knows his business, gallops close up to the bull, when catching hold of the tail he clenches it under his knee, and the horse darting off at right angles pulls the bull's legs from under him, and he comes to the ground with crashing force. This art of throwing bulls by the tail is all knack, and the slightest men generally make the best colleadors. They say that, as in bull fighting, there is a certain fascination in the danger, and though many lose their lives every year, it is a favourite sport amongst the wild riders of the plains; and the reputation of being the best colleador of a district, ensures the happy possessor the admiration of his comrades and the prettiest partners at the fandangos. An expert colleador will by himself throw and brand fifty wild cattle on a day.[13]

The rider first gallops close to the rear of the bull, and seizing his tail with one hand, gives it a turn or two around his wrist to prevent its slipping. When thus prepared, he urges his horse forward, until the heads of the two animals are on a "dead-heat;" then quickly turning in an oblique direction, and exerting all his strength, he pulls the bull toward him, and does not relinquish his hold until he perceives that the enemy is tottering, when he is easily overthrown from the great impetus imparted by their rapid pace. Some men are so dexterous that they can colear with both hands at the same time.

If too powerful resistance is offered at the outset by the bull, as is sometimes the case, the rider still clings to the tail of his adversary, and throwing himself off his horse while at full speed, the impetus combined with his weight and strength never fail in bringing the bull like a fallen giant to the ground; then the man quickly drawing the tail between the hind legs, awaits the arrival of his companions to assist in securing the prize.[14]

The *coleada* was another work skill that became great recreation for the llanero. By excelling at such equestrian feats, political caudillos could win respect among plainsmen. José Antonio Paez, the Venezuelan political strongman, would tail bulls; Juan Manuel de Rosas, the Argentine dictator, would run the gauntlet to perform the dangerous pialar. Both caudillos won adherents among the llaneros and gauchos with daring, skilled horsemanship. In late 1827 a British diplomat watched Paez tail a bull and daringly jump on its back. Unfortunately for the caudillo, the bull "took revenge with his horns in the fleshy part of the Chief's person," and Paez was unable to ride for some time. As the Briton noted, on the llanos "the play is dangerous and often both horse and man get gored to death."[15]

James W. Wells watched vaqueiros tail bulls in northern Brazil in 1886. The rider, "dashing alongside a galloping bull, seizes its outstretched tail with his hand, and lo! the astonished animal is capsized on the ground." Vaqueros in Mexico and old California also enjoyed tailing bulls and became very adept at it. Horsemen would pursue a herd of wild bulls. The toss was made by passing the bull's tail under one's right leg, turning it round the pommel of the saddle, then wheeling one's mount sharply away. With this type of leverage, even youngsters could fell large bulls. As with the chicken race (see below), cowboys of the American West learned tailing from the vaquero. However, it never reached the popularity that it maintained among vaqueros and llaneros.[16]

Grizzly bears offered an attractive adversary to the California vaquero looking for thrills. Spotting a grizzly, several riders would lasso him by neck and feet. Choking off his air to subdue him, the vaqueros then trailed him back to a village to be pitted in battle against a wild bull. Along the way, they would take turns riding in front of the bear and provoking a charge. Anglo cowboys in the mountain states of Colorado, Wyoming, and Montana also roped grizzlies for fun. California fiestas often featured bull and bear fights, in which the grizzly usually killed several bulls before being gored mortally.[17]

Ostrich Hunting

Hunting provided cowboys with entertainment and meat. But for the Argentine gaucho, hunting also contributed an important source of income. Gauchos stalked wild cattle and horses for their hides, and rheas (ostriches of the pampa) for their feathers, prized in European fashion markets. A favorite weapon well adapted to the flat, grassy plains was the bolas or boleadoras, which the gaucho acquired from the pampas Indians who preceded him. Bolas, called *las tres Marías* (the three Marys) by gauchos, consisted of one, two, or more commonly three stout rawhide thongs of up to ten or twelve feet in length. The thongs were bound together at one end and tipped with leather-covered stones or metal balls at the other. The balls varied in size according to the size of the animal being hunted. This weapon proved its worth over centuries of use on the pampas, and gauchos found it particularly well suited for hunting ostriches.[18]

Gauchos developed different bolas to use against cattle and ostriches. Thomas Jefferson Page described the types used during the mid-nineteenth century: "The bolas are of two kinds: that used for catching cattle consists of three wooden balls, or stones, about three inches in diameter, covered with raw hide, each joined to the other in a common centre by a thong of the same of about three feet in length. The other is of two balls, smaller, and is used to catch ostriches. The gaucho holds the smallest ball in his right hand, and, giving the other two a rapidly whirling movement, throws them with great velocity and unerring aim at the legs of the animal; and the more he struggles to extricate himself, the more he becomes entangled."[19]

William MacCann, who crossed the pampas in the early 1850s, described gaucho tactics during an ostrich hunt: "Hunting ostriches is a favourite sport. When a hunting-party is formed, it is customary to move in a circular form, gradually closing in upon the birds until they become alarmed, and seek safety in flight; the hunters then give chase, and when within proper distance throw the bolas at their legs, and so bring them to the ground."[20]

Such hunts, or *boleadas*, had considerable economic importance, because gauchos could sell ostrich feathers for export to the merchant at the local pulpería. But beyond that, the hunt became a festive occasion. Dozens of riders might gather from miles around to participate. Gauchos sometimes set range fires to drive the ostriches out of brushy areas into the open where the bolas could do their work. Naturally, this practice did nothing to endear them to ranchers who lost livestock and grazing lands to the fires.[21]

The Argentine ranching elite and their political representatives wanted to deprive the gaucho of his ability to subsist independently. Hunting provided income that helped the gaucho maintain his economic independence. The ranching elite, often faced with labor shortages, wished to coerce gauchos into working as subservient peons on the large estancias of the pampa. Argentine officials, at the request of the landed elite, repeatedly forbade boleadas and other gaucho pastimes in an ultimately successful attempt to extirpate the unruly social group from society.[22]

Courage in Man and Mount

Argentine gauchos and Chilean huasos enjoyed another dangerous contest called "crowding horses." Two riders sharply spurred their horses in an attempt to crowd or push the other in a specified direction or toward a marked point. In a variation, two riders galloped down a narrow track and tried to push each other's mounts off the track as they raced. In the 1860s a visitor to Chile watched identical races between huasos who tried to knock each other off the track. According to one French observer, almost all pastimes in the Chilean countryside were on horseback.[23]

George A. Peabody, a Massachusetts sportsman on a hunt in South America, watched Argentine gauchos race in 1859. "The track is of a certain width, & if one of the horses is able to crowd the other off the acknowledged track, he wins the race: they accordingly run down the course, each horse pushing with all his might, & it is frequently not the fastest, but the best trained and strongest horse that wins."[24]

Vaqueros enjoyed a horseback game of tag called *juego de la vara* (rod game). Riders arranged themselves in a circle with their mounts facing the center. A vaquero outside the circle would thrust a wooden rod into the outstretched hand of another man and quickly ride around the circle. The player in possession of the rod galloped in pursuit. The pursued rider dashed for an opening in the circle. If he was caught, the man with the rod beat him over the head and shoulders, a painful penalty for the slow rider. Riders continued the games of pursuit, beating, and riding for hours.[25]

Many contests required great stamina in the gaucho's mount (which he referred to as his *pingo*). In the *cinchada*, two horses were fastened together tail-to-tail with stout rawhide lassos tied to the saddles. The rider who could pull the other backward past a mark won this equestrian tug-of-war. This contest grew out of the need for mounts strong enough to pull against a wild, lassoed steer. More dangerous and macho than the cinchada was *pechando*, or "breasting." Two mounted gauchos faced each other over a distance of up to 220 yards. At a signal, they galloped at top speed directly toward one another. The concussion of the head-on crash usually tumbled one or both riders (and often their mounts) to the ground. Recovering and remounting, the combatants quickly charged again until stopped by exhaustion or serious injury. Chilean huasos also battled with their mounts until one dropped from exhaustion.[26]

Mexican vaqueros performed dangerous combat similar to breasting. Samuel C. Reid, Jr., described the event during the fiesta of San Juan in Mexico in the mid-nineteenth century:

Men and boys of all ages, sizes, and conditions are mounted on the best and most gaily caparisoned steeds they can procure, and parade the streets in holiday attire. Whooping and yelling like Indians, they dash through the streets in large parties, charging upon and riding down every thing that impedes their progress. Single horsemen sometimes meet in full career, and as it is disgraceful to give the road on such occasions, they ride directly upon one another, and the consequence is, that the weakest horse or the most unskillful rider is dashed to the ground, while the victor rides on in triumph, rewarded for his gallantry and skill by bright smiles from the balconies above. Occasionally large rival parties meet in the narrow streets, and then a scene of wild confusion ensues. Like madmen, they yell and rush together; and when the horses are not overthrown by the shock, they grasp each other by the neck or waist, and attempt to drag their antagonist from the saddle to the ground. Wo to the awkward or unskillful rider who places his foot in the stirrup on the festival of San Juan![27]

Chilean horsemen practiced a hazardous form of equestrian combat not unlike the gaucho's cinchada tug-of-war. But in the Chilean version, rawhide thongs bound together riders instead of horses. Despite its name, *tirar al gallo* or *tiro al gallo* (rooster shoot), this contest did not actually involve a bird. (The Mexican "chicken race" described below uses birds.) A rawhide thong was lashed to the right wrists of two mounted contestants. At a signal the bound men began to race. The race continued until one man pulled the other from the saddle, to the applause of the spectators. Strength and agility were necessary to keep one's seat and win the contest.[28]

Other Chilean contests challenged the strength and courage of huasos and their mounts. In the *topeadura* or *topeo*, riders positioned their horses side-by-side, with the animals' heads over a railing. The object was to push the opponent's horse beyond the end of the railing or to unseat the opponent. By the eighteenth century, violence had spread from the contests to spectators. The disorder, fighting, and drunkenness that accompanied horse races and other equestrian contests became a serious problem to colonial authorities. Officials eventually introduced regulations to maintain order.[29]

In cowboy mythology, a horseman usually shows special affection for his mount. The famous horse-and-rider duos of the Western movies, such as Roy Rogers and Trigger, perpetuate this notion. But cowboys needed a fresh, strong mount for strenuous ranch work, so they rode a number of different animals. In fact, most cowboys didn't even own their own mounts. Ranchers generally supplied working horses for their hands. But American cowboys were unlikely to mistreat their mounts, since ranchers would not countenance destruction of valuable property.[30]

Argentine gauchos, on the other hand, routinely maltreated their horses. If a mount was injured or even killed in a drunken contest, the rider simply abandoned him and got a fresh mount. Vast herds of wild horses roamed the pampas during the eighteenth century, and a rider could quickly and easily enlarge his herd (*tropilla*) with the toss of a lasso. Owing to their great abundance, horses cost next to nothing until the mid-nineteenth century. Even the humblest gaucho maintained a string of perhaps a dozen animals, matched by color if possible.[31]

One North American visitor to the pampa in the mid-nineteenth century rebuked a gaucho for such cruelty to horses. The gaucho replied laughingly, "Why do you pity him? He is worth but three dollars." Gauchos wasted little time in gentling these disposable mounts. They controlled their half-wild horses with large, vicious spurs. A horse that could not withstand the quick, brutal taming process, or such strenuous contests as breasting, represented a risk to the gaucho whose life depended on a strong mount and his own skills and reflexes.[32]

Cowboys everywhere shared many superstitions concerning their horses. The color of a horse was important to a cowboy. Vaqueros, for instance, retained a Spanish prejudice, perhaps traceable to Arab roots, against spotted or yellow mounts. Vaqueros preferred dark-colored animals, chestnuts, blacks, and grays.[33]

Vaqueros in turn passed their superstitions along to Anglo cowboys. Many cowboys in the United States believed that paints (also called pintos by old-timers) did not make good cutting horses. They considered solid-colored mounts to be better work animals. Cowboys preferred darker horses and avoided pintos, palominos, and Appaloosas. Interestingly, the Nez Perce Indians of the Pacific Northwest bred Appaloosas and believed them superior as war-horses.[34]

Jack Porter reported that these color preferences extended to the northern ranges of the United States. He helped trail a herd from Oregon to Wyoming in 1883. "A rangeman," recalled Porter, "would rarely ever buy a horse for his cavvy [band of saddle horses, from the Spanish *caballada*] unless it was a 'straight-colored' one, so that was the reason our cavvy, like most all others, was composed of bays, browns, grays, sorrels, blacks, whites, and roans."[35]

South American cowboys also developed superstitions and preferences about the color of horses. Llaneros believed that white or silver-gray (*rucio*) horses were better swimmers. In the tropical plains, subject to seasonal flooding and crisscrossed with rivers, swimming was a necessary and important skill for man and horse. But mounts with four white hooves were to be avoided because they were weak. Argentine gauchos liked roan mounts and tried to gather a matched herd.[36]

Of Ducks and Roosters

Pato (duck), in which riders fought for possession of a duck stuffed in a hide, was actually a cross-country free-for-all on horseback. The wild game found adherents from the early seventeenth century in both Argentina and Chile. William Henry Hudson well described the game as played in the 1840s:

Pato means duck; and to play the game a duck or fowl, or, as was usually the case, some larger domestic bird—turkey, gosling, or moscovy duck— was killed and sewn up in a piece of stout raw hide, forming a somewhat shapeless ball, twice as big as a football, and provided with four loops or handles of strong twisted raw hide made of a convenient size to be grasped by a man's hand. A great point was to have the ball and handles so strongly made that three or four powerful men could take hold and tug until they dragged each other to the ground without anything giving way.

On the appearance of the man on the ground carrying the duck the others would give chase; and by-and-by he would be overtaken, and the ball wrested from his hand; the victor in his turn would be pursued, and when overtaken there would perhaps be a scuffle or scrimmage, as in football, only the strugglers would be first on horseback before dragging each other to the earth. Occasionally when this happened a couple of hot-headed players, angry at being hurt or worsted, would draw their weapons against each other in order to find who was in the right, or to prove which was the better man. But fight or no fight, some one would get the duck and carry it away to be chased again. Leagues of ground would be gone over by the players in this way, and at last some one, luckier or better mounted than his fellows, would get the duck and successfully run the gauntlet of the people scattered about the plain, and make good his escape.

To the gauchos of the plains, who took to the back of a horse from childhood, almost as spontaneously as a parasite to the animal on which it feeds, the Pato was the game of games, and in their country as much as cricket and football and golf together to the inhabitants of this island [Britain]. Nor could there have been any better game for men whose existence, or whose success in life, depended so much on their horsemanship; and whose chief glory it is to be able to stick on under difficulties, and, when sticking on was impossible, to fall off gracefully and, like a cat, on their feet.[37]

Riders would range for miles across the pampa, fighting over the duck, scattering livestock, destroying fences, and wreaking havoc. Like ostrich hunts, pato attracted the ire of ranchers and government officials because of livestock loss and property damage. Spanish colonial and later Argentine national officials banned the contests at least six times between 1799 and 1899. But pato's popularity persisted as long as the gaucho roamed.[38]

In Chile, the game became a traditional event on June 24, the Feast of San Juan. The same rambunctious air that characterized gaucho play infused the huaso version of pato. The contests became so scandalous that in 1748 the Church requested that it be regulated. "Horse races held in all the streets more resembled bacchanal feasts." By the late eighteenth century, the government had passed rules governing most horseback contests. Officials banned pato in 1768, following the death of a participant. A five-hundred-peso fine was assessed to those who practiced the proscribed game. In both Chile and Argentina, elite rulers exercised social control over the rural masses by regulating and even prohibiting their pastimes.[39]

Vaqueros in Mexico and the American Southwest developed their own version of a game similar to the pato of southern South America. The chicken race (*correr el gallo*) used an unfortunate rooster, duck, or chicken. The fowl was tied to a tree or more commonly buried up to its neck in the ground. Horsemen galloped after the bird. Whoever succeeded in grabbing it then became the object of pursuit. Sometimes riders followed a set course. If the vaquero with the chicken crossed the finish line without being caught, he kept the fowl as a prize. As in pato, the racers rode miles cross-country and pulled one another off their mounts. As with pato in Chile, the Mexican chicken race was often held on San Juan's feast day. The victor presented the prize to a women he wished to impress, and fandango street dancing often followed.[40]

So much of the American cowboy's equipment, language, and work habits comes from the Mexican vaquero that it is not surprising to see games carry over north of the border. By 1888 the chicken race had made its way north to Gunnison, Colorado. At a fair held in that town, five cowboys competed in a "chicken pulling" after other horse races had been concluded.[41]

Another contest passed from the Mexican vaquero to the Anglo cowboy was called "picking up." The object was to pluck from the ground a small coin, handkerchief, arrow, or even a potato, at a full gallop. Texas Rangers, Indians, and Hispanics competed at picking up in San Antonio in 1844. Contests were also part of the first Texas State Fair in 1852. California vaqueros competed often, including at the 1891 Tournament of Roses in Pasadena (well before football became the main event). Wild West shows also featured vaquero riders performing this impressive feat.[42]

Argentine gauchos had their own variation of the showy and useful skill of plucking up objects at a gallop. Gauchos would disassemble their multilayered saddles while galloping across the pampa. Each pad and piece would be dropped to the ground until the gaucho rode bareback. On a return pass, the rider would pick up each piece in reverse order and reassemble the saddle at a full gallop. Of course, loss of balance during the pick up or assembly meant a nasty head-first fall.[43]

Gauchos and llaneros liked to compete against each other one-on-one, but some solo exhibitions permitted an individual to show off his equestrian prowess. Gauchos placed a bar across a corral gate just above a horse's head. As a participant galloped up to the bar, he would jump out of the saddle, over the bar, and land on his mount's back on the other side. Timing, coordination, and strength spelled the difference between a spectacular leap and a dusty fall. In a variant, called the *maroma*, a bar was placed high above a corral gate. A gaucho stood on top of the bar and leaped onto the back of a wild horse as it raced underneath out of the corral. The rider would stay with the wild horse until the animal was exhausted or tamed. Llaneros added a novel twist to this show of courage and coordination: they dropped onto the running horse backwards. Using the animal's tail as a bridle, they would then gallop wildly about.[44]

At least one cowboy in the American West practiced a variant of the maroma. Tom Horn, a renowned Arizona Indian scout, performed the dangerous stunt in the 1880s. He would hang by his hands from a corral gate crossbar and drop onto the back of a passing mustang. Taking on his foe bareback and in open country, Horn would ride the animal into submission. It seems likely that Horn made up his own version of this trick. We have no other evidence of its performance outside of the Río de la Plata and the llanos.[45]

Vaqueros had their own feats of daring. In the aptly named *paso de la muerte* (ride of death), a brave Mexican vaquero rode alongside a wild horse. He then jumped onto the wild animal and rode it bareback until it was tamed. This daring exhibition likely developed from an old means of capturing and taming wild horses at the same time. In a less dangerous game, riders placed a coin under each knee and pressed them to the saddle. They then galloped around an obstacle course, jumping and weaving around hurdles. The goal was to maintain one's seat so well that the coins remained in place at the end of the course.[46]

Foot Races

Cowboys in both North and South America were single-mindedly equestrian and avoided footwork at all costs. But cowboys in the United States differed in one area of recreation: they would engage in footraces for fun, whereas most Latin American cowboys considered walking, much less running, beneath their dignity. Cowhands from different American ranches competed against one another. These contests involved strategy as much as speed because the course would be littered with sagebrush, rabbit holes, ravines, and animal skeletons. Cowboys from the host ranch, being more familiar with the rugged terrain, usually won. Bets always rode on the ranch favorites. Other contests involving strength and speed, popular on the American frontier, likewise did not appear in South America. Some cowboys also competed in the popular and strenuous nineteenth-century jumping contests (including the high jump, broad jump, and hop, step, and jump).[47]

It was not only his disdain for pedestrians that kept the gaucho from running in footraces. He suffered from an additional physiological handicap: his legs became badly bowed from a lifetime in the saddle, and his big toes became enlarged and deformed into talon-like claws from clutching small wooden stirrups. Thus, gauchos often could walk only with great difficulty; running was completely out of the question. The only foot contest that appealed to the gaucho was the knife duel.[48]

Work as Play

Some commentators have drawn a sharp contrast between play, as purposeless activity done for its own sake, and work. Johan Huizinga and Michael Novak have depicted work as virtually antithetical to the freedom and playfulness supposedly embodied in sport. If cowboy recreation is any guide, this ideological position is seriously flawed.[49]

Gauchos, vaqueros, and llaneros certainly did not recognize stark distinctions between work and play. As long as they could be on horseback, they were content. Putative distinctions between work and play blurred. Mounted labor included strong elements of play, and dangerous, vigorous equestrian contests employed "real-life" skills necessary to frontier survival and work.

In the 1840s Hudson described the playfulness of a gaucho confronting a steer. The rider might "leap lightly onto its back, stick his spurs in its sides, and, using the flat of his long knife as a whip, pretend to be riding a race, yelling with fiendish glee." Observers of the busy roundup season verify that gauchos enjoyed the activity greatly. They readily mixed pleasure with work, as long as they could remain on horseback. Don Segundo, the protagonist in the gaucho novel by Ricardo Güiraldes, emphatically linked the gaucho to his horse: "A gaucho on foot is fit for nothing but the manure pile."[50]

Llaneros resisted attempts to organize and "rationalize" ranch work because it reduced the sportive value of their labors. They transformed the work skill of tailing a bull into a game, as did the Mexican vaqueros and Brazilian vaqueiros. Whenever possible, cowboys combined work with play on horseback.[51]

From the pampas and llanos to the Alberta prairies, riding for work or pleasure was the joyful essence of cowboy life. A Mrs. Duthie, a ranch wife at Pincher Creek, Alberta, found the same love of the equestrian life in Canadian cowboys. "Cowboys never play baseball," she observed. "Their sport and recreation like their work was always around the corral, breaking, riding horses."[52]

Vaqueros in California mixed work and play during the *matanza*, the slaughter of wild cattle for their hides. The grounds where the slaughter took place naturally attracted hordes of scavengers, from flies to buzzards and coyotes. But the carcasses also lured grizzly bears. Vaqueros would hold the matanza under the light of the moon in order to rope scavenging bears. In 1835 eleven vaqueros roped some forty grizzlies. They later matched the most vicious bears against wild bulls.[53]

For the vaquero in Mexico or Texas, the lasso served equally well as an instrument of work and play. Mexican ranch children, like little boys on the Argentine pampas, learned to rope chickens and dogs at a very early age. During his visit to Mexico, Frederic Remington observed that vaqueros would rope anything. "Men have become as expert in dodging the rope as the vaqueros are in throwing it," the artist noted. Vaqueros would even sit in ambush to rope an unsuspecting victim. By the late nineteenth century, roping contests in Texas were commonplace. One contest, held in San Antonio at the state fair in 1888, featured vaqueros as well as performers from Buffalo Bill's Wild West Show.[54]

Competition among cowboys of different ranches often accompanied round-ups in the American West. Contests on the range became associated with holidays, notably the Fourth of July, and gradually rodeos came into being. To the consternation of the American cowboys, an Englishman won the bronc-riding competition at Deer Trail, Colorado, on July 4, 1899: "The Englishman rode with hands free and kept plying his whip constantly. There was a frightful mixup of cowboy and horse, but [Emilnie] Gardenshire refused to be unseated. For fifteen minutes, the bay bucked, pawed, and jumped from side to side, then amid cheers, the mighty [horse named] Blizzard succumbed, and Gardenshire rode him around the circle at a gentle gallop. It was a magnificent piece of horsemanship, and the suit of clothes [the prize], together with the title 'Champion Bronco Buster of the Plains,' went to the lad from the Milliron ranch."[55]

"Civilizing" Cowboy Games

Foreign visitors and the Argentine ruling elite looked with disfavor on the gaucho's life and habits. To the "civilized" eye, his backwardness and violence held back the nation politically and socially. But it is worth noting that many gaucho "vices" afflicted the gentry of the American South. There social critics berated the excessive fondness for horse racing, cockfighting, gambling, and drinking—pastimes that were equally popular throughout Latin America.[56]

But very different sociopolitical contexts marked the American South and Argentina. In the Old South, the gentry largely monopolized the leisure activities of hunting, horse racing, and cockfights. As Benjamin Rader observed, the gentry "always sought to restrict participation to members of their own class." In contrast, these were lower-class pursuits among gauchos on the Argentine pampa. In North America, the elite exercised its power to limit participation in such contests; Latin American elites labored mightily to eliminate or control the same practices.[57]

During the course of the nineteenth century, many wild, dangerous equestrian contests became transformed and "civilized." In South America, modernizing politicians successfully altered or eliminated many vestiges of gaucho and huaso life. The transformation of gaucho games into organized sport offers one of the clearest examples of this process. Similar forces provoked changes across the Andes in Chile.

By the 1890s the gaucho's frenetic, sometimes fatal pato contest had been tamed and institutionalized into a more subdued, organized sport. Rules were written and leagues formed under the auspices of the Argentine Pato Federation. In the new version of pato, two four-man teams competed on a field 90 yards wide and 230 yards long. Players had to carry a six-handled leather ball with arm outstretched so that opponents could try to snatch it. Tossing the ball into a net suspended on a nine-foot pole earned a point. The federation also managed a handicapping system, like that of polo. Such modernization changed pato from a participant folk contest into an elite spectator sport, for the edification of gentlemen and ladies of Buenos Aires.[58]

Writing in the early 1920s, Captain J. Macnie remarked the disappearance of many old gaucho equestrian practices. No riders now performed the daring and dangerous maroma, dropping from a gate rail onto the back of a wild bull. The pialar, in which ropers tripped a galloping horse and its rider, had likewise faded into the past. Macnie found that the ranch peon on the modern estancia could not "sit a really bad horse"; he had lost the finely honed riding skills that allowed his gaucho predecessor to stay on virtually any mount. The same forces overtook venerable, dangerous huaso games. Little of the old daring and skill remained by the early twentieth century. Stylized rodeos and "gentrified" precision exercises patronized by the Chilean elite supplanted rough-and-tumble folk festivities.[59]

In place of the old gaucho contests, Macnie saw spectator sports for the leisure class. Bartolomé Gutiérrez and some traditionalists expressed nostalgia for the old gaucho games, but the elite of Buenos Aires imported polo from Europe, along with other English and French cultural artifacts. (Polo was also popular among Anglophile ranchers in Calgary.) Many Argentine polo players gained worldwide reputations. The Jockey Club, Tortugas, Mar del Plata, Colonel Suárez, and North Santa Fe were the foremost of many teams organized throughout the country. The Cup of the Americas competition between the United States and Argentina began in 1928. The Americans won the first two meetings, but Argentina won the cup five successive times between 1936 and 1969.[60]

The elite of Buenos Aires, flush with new wealth from booming beef and cereal exports, took to heavy gambling on horse races and other sporting events. During the 1890s, Argentines spent a half-billion pesos on gambling—one fifth of the total value of the country's exports for the period. The Hurlingham Club of Buenos Aires was a self-conscious replication of its famous English namesake. The elite membership could watch or participate in polo, tennis, golf, cricket, and fox hunting. During the twentieth century, Argentine races and horses gained fame. Arturo A (the winningest horse in South American history), Old Man, Macon, and Yatasto became known to fans around the world. The elite met at such races as the Gran Premio Carlos Pellegrini, the Gran Premio Nacional, and the Gran Premio Jockey Club, which became world renowned.[61]

One of the foremost symbols of elite cultural hegemony, the opulent Jockey Club, was founded in 1881. That organization provided an exclusive meeting place for the highest elite circles. The club sponsored thoroughbred horse races and brought the high culture of the turf to Buenos Aires. The racetrack generated such huge profits that by the early twentieth century the Jockey Club was searching for worthy charities. In this way, the club served the same function of social discrimination as jockey clubs of the antebellum American South and elsewhere.[62]

As in North America, rodeo became increasingly popular in the twentieth century. Rodeo performers began making the rounds to Buenos Aires, Rosario, and other major cities, entertaining urban crowds of people who had never sat a horse. In 1909 the Sociedad Sportiva Argentina (Argentine Sport Society) announced a rodeo competition. The winners were to travel to the United States to compete against rodeo riders from several countries. Rodeo, with lots of traditional huaso trappings, also remains popular in Chile.[63]

In yet another sign of change, bicycles became as commonplace on the pampas as horses. Small towns cheered bicycle racers at the central plaza instead of the wild gaucho riders of yesteryear. By 1899 cycling clubs had spread to many small towns on the pampa. Fierce local rivalries developed between neighboring villages. Some towns even built velodromes. In short, by the turn of the century, the elite expurgation of the gaucho's "barbarism" appeared complete. A new, rich, Europeanized, "civilized" Argentina faced the twentieth century with pride and confidence.[64]

Across the Andes to the west, the Chilean landed elite took similar steps to control their rural masses. By 1920 rich Chilean landowners had organized soccer leagues and established playing fields on their estates. One goal was to provide a more constructive use of leisure time to curtail excessive gambling and drinking among their workers. But the landowners also sought to create in the rural lower class a sense of solidarity, loyalty, and identification with the hacienda. As in Argentina, elite cultural hegemony involved imposed change and efforts to establish lower-class complicity with the cultural values of the dominant class. Organized sport is one means of creating bonds across class lines that attenuate potentially explosive class conflict.[65]

Of course, horse racing and other competition among cowboys did not die out completely. Huasos continued to gather on Sundays and holidays to race horses. In the 1930s George McBride watched huasos compete in the traditional topeo, where mounts pushed against each other along a log rail. Occasionally, competition—usually accompanied by drink—turned violent, and knife fights resulted.[66]

The Canadian ranching frontier exhibited little of the wild violence and disorder that characterize other cowboy haunts of the Americas. On the Canadian frontier, "civilization" preceded settlement. The Royal Canadian

Mounted Police maintained a level of law and order uncommon in other frontier regions. Canadian cowboy fun quickly came under legal regulation. Long, five-mile races had become very popular. Police at Fort Calgary in Alberta prohibited Sunday horse races in September 1883, but races continued on other days. Mrs. Alfred Wilson, a Pincher Creek pioneer, recalls many afternoon horse races that drew riders from all over the province. Contests on July 1, Dominion Day, were particularly popular.[67]

Traditional British sports, including polo, cricket, soccer, and rugby, also found their adherents in Alberta. The first polo match in North America was staged in 1884 by smaller ranchers from the area of Pincher Creek. By 1886 ranchers were engaging in hunts across the Alberta hills and plains. But concessions had to be made to the local environment: the ranchers chased coyotes instead of foxes.[68]

From Folk Games to Spectacles

In the United States, organized rodeos and Wild West shows appeared even before the closing of the open range brought an end to traditional cowboy life. But it was the mass market for popular culture, not the "civilizing" efforts of a political elite, that wrought changes in cowboy play. Local boosters, anxious to cash in on the mass appeal of cowboy culture, developed spectacles such as the Cheyenne Frontier Days, first held in 1897. The following year Wyoming promoters combined it with the famous cowboy extravaganza, Buffalo Bill Cody's Wild West Show. Progressively, the games and contests of working cowboys gave way to trained, professional rodeo riders, Wild West show actors, and circus performers. Ties to the leisure-time activities of working cowhands on the range largely disappeared.[69]

William F. Cody's famous show started in his hometown of North Platte, Nebraska. In 1882 he convinced the town to sponsor an "Old Glory Blowout" each Fourth of July. Events included the rodeo competition and horseback exhibitions that provided the germ for his world-famous show. Like pulp novels and later B Western movies, Buffalo Bill's show promoted the simple formulas of good versus evil, of civilization against barbarism. Two famous performers were Hispanic cowboys from San Antonio. "Champion Vaquero Rider" Antonio Esquivel performed off and on from 1883 to 1905. Another vaquero, José "Mexican Joe" Berrara, performed rope tricks. The show fur-

The line between work and play *was often blurred on the cattle frontier (p. 141). Single-mindedly equestrian, cowboys enjoyed showing off their riding skill and courage in a variety of mounted games and contests. But cowboys also had fun afoot. They enjoyed music, dancing, gambling, drinking, and sometimes fighting. Theirs was a rough-and-tumble life lived with gusto.*

Taming a wild horse *was both work and fun. Mexico's first vaqueros, Indian novices at Spanish missions, became excellent riders and ropers (pp. 20–22). Blessed with an abundance of horses, Latin American cowboys wasted little time being* gentle: *they broke horses quickly and brutally (pp. 75–77). But as horses became more expensive and ranchers extended their power and control, cowboys had to use less violent means to tame ranch mounts. (From José Cisneros,* Riders Across the Centuries, *© 1984 by Texas Western Press of the University of Texas at El Paso)*

Cowboys of the American West adopted *Mexican riding equipment and techniques (p. 44). Like the vaquero, the cowboy enjoyed showing his stuff on the back of a bad horse. A man new to the outfit would likely have to prove himself to his peers on the back of a lively mount. Frederic Remington painted* The Cowboy *in 1902. (Opposite:* Amon Carter Museum, Fort Worth, 1961. 382)

Horse races, *often accompanied by heavy betting, provided entertainment through the Americas. Cowboys liked competing against other riders as much as challenging a wild horse. Argentine gauchos and Chilean huasos developed variations on the race, such as "crowding," in which riders tried to push one another's horses off the track (p. 134). Vaqueros and gauchos also ran their horses into each other in an attempt to knock the other rider to the ground (p. 135). (*Below: illustration by Emeric Essex Vidal, from* Picturesque Illustrations of Buenos Ayres and Montevideo, *London, 1820, Edward E. Ayer Collection, Newberry Library, Chicago)*

Hunting was *a popular activity for both recreation and profit. California vaqueros hunted down grizzly bears, lassoed them, and pitted them against wild bulls (pp. 132–33). Some* cowboys in the American West emulated this risky pastime. C. M. Russell captured the action in his 1916 oil painting *Loops and Swift Horses Are Surer Than Lead.* *The clothing, facial features, and saddles of the two ro-pers indicate that Russell was depicting vaqueros. (Amon Carter Museum, Fort Worth, 1961. 180)*

Argentine gauchos
hunted ostriches for their feathers, downing the fleet birds with a toss of the bolas, as depicted by Emeric Essex Vidal. To the consternation of ranchers, gauchos would set fire to the pampas in order to chase ostriches into the open (pp. 133–34). (From Picturesque Illustrations of Buenos Ayres and Montevideo, *London, 1820, Edward E. Ayer Collection, Newberry Library, Chicago)*

There seemed *to be no limits on cowboy inventiveness with a rope. Like vaqueros and other Latin American riders, American cowboys would try to rope anything, as C. M. Russell shows in his 1904 oil painting* Roping a Wolf. *The rider in the middle wears the woolly sheepskin chaps popular in colder, northern plains areas like Montana. (Amon Carter Museum, Fort Worth, 1961. 183)*

The ring race *is one of several horseback games that Mexican vaqueros passed over to the American cowboy. It can be traced to medieval Spain and is likely of Moorish origin (p. 129). Anglo and Hispanic cowboys in the Southwest tried to skewer tiny dangling rings with a short lance. John Wheeler is shown here competing in Emma, Texas, around 1905–1915. (Erwin E. Smith Collection, Amon Carter Museum, Fort Worth)*

Vaqueros and Anglo cowboys *swapped tall tales and ghost stories around the campfire. Superstitious vaqueros, like those depicted by Frederic Remington, enjoyed frightening tales of spirits and buried treasure (pp. 40, 121, 227). Erwin E. Smith photographed a storytelling session at the LS Ranch in Texas in 1908.* (Below: Harper's Monthly, February 1894, courtesy of Yale University Library. Opposite: *Erwin E. Smith Collection, Amon Carter Museum, Fort Worth)*

Gambling *in all shapes and forms was a favorite cowboy pastime. Medieval Spaniards played cards with relish, and the passion carried over to the New World (pp. 154–55). As ranchers tightened their control over ranch hands, some outfits forbade card playing and alcohol on the premises. These cowboys took time out for a game of hearts at the Three Circle Ranch in Texas, around 1901–1910. (Erwin E. Smith Collection, Amon Carter Museum, Fort Worth)*

Cowboys in Canada
*and the United States
also enjoyed reading, a
pleasure seldom shared
by the mostly illiterate
cowboys of Latin America
(pp. 121–22). Food
cans, old catalogues and
newspapers—anything
with print attracted the
cowboy's eye. Note that
some of these Canadian
cowboys, photographed at
the Bar U Ranch in Al-
berta in the early 1900s,
wear warm sheepskin
chaps. (Glenbow Archives,
Calgary)*

Cowboys liked music,
*and their songs provide
insight into their values.
Guitars and smaller
stringed instruments
could be found throughout
Latin America, Hawaii,
and the United States
(pp. 122–27). American
cowboys might play the
harmonica. The Mexican
dance band depicted by
Frederic Remington added
violins and a harp. (Har-
per's* Monthly, *December
1893, courtesy of Yale
University Library)*

Dances, *such as the Chilean* zamacueca, *the Venezuelan* joropo, *and square dancing in the United States, became important elements of national folklore (pp. 125–26). Given the short supply of women on the cattle frontier, cowboys sometimes had to put up with each other as dance partners. (Above: drawing by César Prieto, author's collection. Below: Henry Worrall,* Dance House in Abilene, *from Joseph G. McCoy,* Historic Sketches of the Cattle Trade in the West and Southwest, *Kansas City, 1874)*

After months *on the trail or range, in the company of only men, cowboys often visited prostitutes in town. C. M. Russell's watercolor* Just a Little Pleasure *(1898) shows a happily drunken cowboy with one of the "soiled doves" of the West. After a quick sexual encounter and perhaps a bath, the cowboy returned to work, with nothing but a hangover, a grin, and an empty wallet to show for his visit (pp. 155–57). (Amon Carter Museum, Fort Worth, 1961. 285)*

Wild behavior, *often liquor-induced, gave rise to many negative appraisals of cowboy character (pp. 45–46). Letting off steam at the end of a long cattle drive, cowboys "on a tear" in town caused quite a commotion. In this 1886 illustration by R. F. Zogbaum entitled* Painting the Town Red, *the cowboy at the left is terrorizing a Chinese man. Hispanics and blacks often suffered similar harassment and discrimination at the hands of Anglos (pp. 165–68). (*Harper's Weekly, *October 16, 1886)*

Western saloons, *Mexican* cantinas, *and Argentine* pulperías *attracted a large clientele, including cowboys. Depending on the country, cowboys drank gin, rum, whiskey, beer, and other alcoholic beverages (pp. 152–54) The cowboy's seeming propensity for binge drinking and disruptive behavior provoked condemnation by civic reformers and other detractors. Erwin E. Smith photographed this saloon in Old Tascosa, Texas, in 1908. (Erwin E. Smith Collection, Amon Carter Museum, Fort Worth)*

Cowboy violence *has been overblown by pulp novelists and low-budget movie directors. But some of this reputation is deserved (pp. 149–51). Argentine gauchos sometimes engaged in knife fighting for fun. Regrettably, combatants often went beyond the supposed goal of these duels—marking an opponent's face—to inflict serious injury or death. This obviously staged photograph of about 1900 depicts authentic knife-fighting technique. Gauchos wrapped a poncho around one arm as a shield or trailed the poncho on the ground to trip their opponent. Vaqueros, huasos, and llaneros also carried knives (pp. 37–38, 150, 213) (Carpenter Collection, Prints and Photographs Division, Library of Congress)*

ther internationalized by adding riders dressed as Argentine gauchos: spectacles had supplanted traditional folk contests.[70]

The transition from "the age of folk games to the age of spectators" occurred in many cultures but under very different historical conditions. In Argentina, the ruling elite eradicated or tamed the playful, if violent, participatory contests of the gaucho as unwanted vestiges of a barbaric past. They replaced these traditional practices with organized, civilized pato, and imported polo and thoroughbred racing in keeping with their desire to recreate European civilization. Professional rodeo in the United States strayed from its roots in Mexican and Anglo-American ranch work and play. Organized equestrian sport in Argentina and Chile bore little relevance to the substance of rural folk traditions. The new equestrian sports signaled the definitive victory of modernizing, urban elites over the rural masses.[71]

CHAPTER 9

Hellin' 'Round

Drinking, Gambling, and Other Fun

Cowboys worked and played on horseback, but they also pursued other forms of recreation afoot. Besides the practical jokes and singing that occupied some leisure time in all plains areas, more vigorous and sometimes violent diversions—such as drinking, gambling, and fighting—were also widespread. The choice of liquor, games of chance, and weapons varied from country to country, but the exuberant and often disorderly spirit of these pastimes was the same everywhere, much to the chagrin of townfolk.

Saloon Life

Based on observations in the saloons of western cowtowns, journalists formed their judgments of cowboys as wild and drunken. The Cheyenne *Daily Leader* berated cowboys in 1882 as "foul-mouthed, blasphemous, drunken, lecherous, utterly corrupt." The paper found their behavior in town particularly reprehensible because there "liquor has the ascendancy over them." Relatively comfortable taverns, rich with gossip and news, held more attraction for writers than did the hot, dusty plains. Some journalists in the West received a whiskey allowance in addition to their wages. It is not surprising that writers spent more time in the saloon than in the saddle.[1]

Similarly, European travelers on the Argentine pampa saw gauchos lounging, drinking, gambling, and fighting at pulperías. These general stores-cum-taverns dotted the plains and occupied many street corners in Argentine towns. Similar small establishments operated all over Latin America. Outsiders formed unflattering estimates of gaucho character. One mid-nineteenth century visitor opined that "gambling is the moving spirit of existence and enjoyment in the real gaucho. Indeed the veritable camp gaucho is a sort of loafer, hanging about pulperías . . . drinking caña and gin, now and then ripping up somebody with his knife after a dispute of the most insignificant nature."[2]

Viewing cowboys and gauchos in taverns, rather than at work in the saddle, many observers reached biased conclusions about their character and way of life. For most cowhands, idling and drinking at public houses represented only a small, if highly visible, part of their lives. Like other elements of cowboy life, the time spent "hellin' 'round town" became exaggerated and romanticized.

But on the Argentine pampa, it cannot be denied that pulperías encouraged hard drinking, gambling, and fighting. In *Don Segundo Sombra*, Ricardo Güiraldes describes a typical country tavern of the pampa: "It was a single building, rectangular-shaped; the taproom was an open room on the right with benches where we sat side by side like swallows on a wire. The storekeeper handed out the drinks through a heavy iron grating that caged him in with tiers of brightly labeled bottles, flasks, and jugs of every kind. Skin sacks of mate leaf, demijohns of liquor, different-shaped barrels, saddles, blankets, horse pads, lassos, covered the floor."[3]

As sites of predominantly male activity, taverns provided a logical showcase for exhibitions of machismo. The camaraderie between men can be misinterpreted. For example, Lionel Tiger's notion of "male bonding" is based on faulty historical and biological evidence. He argues unconvincingly that male primates establish bonds with one another that are unique to their sex. "Treating" or "buying drinks for the house" did represent a means of temporarily uniting a group of drinking men. It was a gross breach of barroom etiquette to refuse a proffered drink. In the United States one could sometimes get away with substituting coffee for liquor. Toasting, calls of "bottoms up," provided another communal activity that brought drinkers together in a brief, shared moment. Recent research on alcoholism has shown a correlation between participation in masculine activities and problem drinking in the United States. The cultural links between manliness and the consumption of alcohol appear to be pervasive and enduring.[4]

But the rosy glow induced by friendly social drinking often turned to the vivid red of violence: saloons earned their reputations as places of fighting and death. Temporary bonds of communal drinking often gave way to competition and conflict. Rousing, furniture-smashing fistfights ("dog fights") were largely creations of the Western movies, however; cowboys disdained fisticuffs. As one old-timer remarked, "If the Lord had intended me to fight like a dog, He'd a-give me longer teeth and claws." But a cowboy did not hesitate to fight with a knife and "manstopper" (gun). The mining frontier apparently rivaled the cattle frontier for boisterous behavior. Elliott West found high levels of homicide in saloons of Rocky Mountain mining towns.[5]

Some cattle-country saloons became infamous. Violence at the original Bucket of Blood Saloon, owned by Shorty Young in Havre, Montana, led cowboys to apply the term to any tough whiskey mill. Drunken rowdiness was commonplace. A Canadian cowboy visiting Havre in 1906 watched two cowboys ride their horses into the Dew Drop Inn; they "claimed they thought it was a modern feed barn." Such frontier "country clubs" generally offered drink, gossip, and gambling. At "hurdy-gurdy" houses, lonesome cowboys could spend time with the house women for a dollar per dance.[6]

Like saloons of the Old West, Argentine pulperías became justifiably famous for fights. Some men went looking for trouble, and drink only heightened the likelihood of conflict. Gauchos skillfully wielded deadly *facónes*, or sword-like knives, which they preferred long after firearms had reached Argentina. With a degree of Freudian hyperbole, Argentine philosopher Ezequiel Martínez Estrada explained the significance of the facón. The knife, he wrote, is "not part of the costume but part of the body itself. It pertains more to the man than to his apparel, more to his character than to his social status. He who shows his knife when there is no need for it commits an indecent act."[7]

Like other Latin American horsemen (except the llanero), the gaucho disdained firearms. Real men fought with knives. Superstitious gauchos believed that some men could not be wounded with firearms. They called such invincible men *retobados* (literally, wily or cunning). Vaqueros also rejected guns as unmanly. While the frequency of gunfights in the Old West has been inflated by pulp novelists and B movies, Anglo cowboys often did carry sidearms. Canadian cowboys carried guns far less often than American cowboys. Henry Caven recalled that in Canada "there was none of the Wild West gunman stuff that the movies portray about early American west days."[8]

The traditional goal of gaucho knife duels was simply to mark an opponent's face. But drunken fights often went far beyond the rituals of dueling. An Argentine rancher suggested in 1856 (with some exaggeration) that 99 percent of homicides, injuries, and disorders occurred at pulperías. Police and justice of the peace records are full of cases in which knife duels ended in wounding or death. The perpetrator usually fled to other, more remote areas of the frontier.[9]

Pulperías in Chile gained similar reputations as havens for drunkenness and violence. Colonial authorities in the early seventeenth century declared the humble taverns to be "dens of drunkenness, where Indians, Negroes and other castes exchange stolen goods for liquor." In 1635 Governor Francisco Laso de la Vega decreed a thirty-peso fine for any "pulpero audacious enough to sell wine to any Indian, Negro or mulatto, male or female." Tavern owners were forbidden to purchase chickens, food, and small game because Indians "destroyed and robbed the farms and ranches and cattle of all types and took them to sell to said pulperos." But the problem of pulperías did not go away. More than a century later, in 1748, a Chilean bishop complained that men sold their horses, spurs and even the clothes off their backs to purchase liquor. Even allowing for the racial and class biases adhering in such elite views, it is clear that pulperías maintained an active clientele from the colonial period forward.[10]

William B. Taylor found the same volatile mix of machismo, drink, and violence in taverns of colonial Mexico frequented by the lower classes. Arguments and contests of dominance often spawned fights. During the late colonial period in Mexico City, patrons battled one another in lower-class bars. In 1798, 45 percent of all arrests in the city were alcohol-related. In the Mexican countryside or capital, refusal of a drink could be taken as a serious affront to manly honor and precipitate a fight.[11]

Just north of the Mexican border, alcohol-related violence at a barroom helped to doom the western saloon. In the Texas town of Richmond (just southwest of Houston) stood the nondescript Brahma Bull and Red Hot Bar. In 1889 drunken patrons violently beat a man named David Nation. The victim and his wife, Carrie Nation, subsequently moved to Kansas. Carrie Nation's bar-smashing crusade in Kansas spearheaded the ultimately successful drive for national prohibition. In 1920 the Eighteenth Amendment officially ended the heyday of the western saloon.[12]

Barroom violence did not stem from mere physiological changes induced by alcohol. While alcohol impairs sensorimotor capabilities, it does not necessarily act as a disinhibiting agent, nor does it necessarily suspend moral judgment. Rather, social conventions influence drunken comportment, just as they do the behavior of sober persons. David G. Mandelbaum points out that cultural expectations regulate emotional as well as physiological reactions to liquor. A link exists between increased aggression and the consumption of alcohol, but even that relationship is not simply a matter of physiology. Men who drink distilled spirits show higher levels of aggression than those who consume beer. But so do men given a placebo who *think* that they are consuming a distilled beverage.[13]

Violence and lack of accountability for one's actions are part of a set of "time-out" norms when social conventions are suspended. In the case of the saloon culture, the time-out norms represent the values and behaviors of an exaggerated machismo. The killing of a gaucho in a drunken duel was considered to be a *desgracia*—an unfortunate accident. In the eyes of his peers, the killer deserved sympathy not blame. In a sense, alcohol is used as a convenient excuse to escape the restrictive conventions of society and to embrace other norms of the saloon culture. These norms, different from the conventions of proper society outside the tavern, shaped the actions of drinking men. Assertive and domineering machismo, verbal and physical aggression, and gambling with abandon were part of the saloon cultures of North and South America, despite different cultural heritages.[14]

Anglo-American cowboys carried the cultural baggage of a Protestant work ethic that revered and rewarded hard work and distrusted idleness. Nevertheless, Americans drank prodigiously during the colonial period. Rum and homemade whiskey were especially popular for slaking thirst in the eighteenth century. Drinking probably increased in the nineteenth century, and alcohol became one of the many targets of religiously motivated social reformers.[15]

Like sailors home from the sea, cowboys engaged in spree drinking when the rare opportunity presented itself. The end of a long trail drive or of the roundup and branding season provided two such opportunities. But drinking bouts were separated by long dry periods. Liquor was often unavailable outside of towns, and some ranchers insisted on sobriety on the ranch. Teddy Blue Abbott relates the story of one rancher who offered his foreman a hundred head of cattle to stay sober for a year. American social critics identified vagrancy, idleness, and tavern-going as vices associated with the "unworthy" poor. While spree drinking was pardoned, if not entirely condoned, no working cowboy or vaquero could afford (in monetary or social terms) to idle away very much time at the cantina.[16]

In the Spanish Roman Catholic heritage, excessive drinking was condemned and the epithet "drunkard" was an extreme insult. But ritualized drunkenness in connection with festivals was permissible. According to one observer, "Feast days are strictly kept by the gauchos in their own peculiar way," which meant accompanied by much drinking. But the great number of

Catholic feast days provided many more opportunities for acceptable drunkenness than the sparse Protestant religious calendar and the seasonal ranch work schedule. During his long, repressive dictatorship as governor of Buenos Aires province (and de facto ruler of Argentina), Juan Manual de Rosas issued decrees to eliminate some of the many holidays that served as excuses for drinking and idleness.[17]

One minor difference between the drinking behavior of various cowboys was in the type of liquor consumed. Gauchos drank caña or gin at the pulpería. Caña, the favorite, was a type of rum distilled from sugarcane juice. The juice of palm trees could also be processed into an alcoholic drink. Pulperos sold other beverages. One late nineteenth-century visitor to the pampa recalled a pulpería where "vermouth, absinthe, squarefaced gin, Carlon, and *vino seco* stand in a row, with a barrel of Brazilian caña, on the top of which the *pulpero* ostentatiously parades his pistol and his knife." [18]

For the Venezuelan llanero, *aguardiente*, a fiery rum, held a favored position. But the tropical llanos yielded a range of alcoholic beverages, including *guarapo*, made from sugar cane. Palm wine and *chicha*, a beverage fermented from maize like the *pulque* of Mexico, could also be found. The remoteness of the llanos meant that imported drink was less common than in either the American West or Argentina.[19]

Drinking found its way into folk poems of the Venezuelan plains. For example:

Me gusta un trago de ron	I like a drink of rum
mas que muchacha bonita,	more than a pretty girl,
porque el ron siempre me quita	because rum always
las penas del corazón.	stops my heartache.
El aguardiente de caña	Rum
es de tanta fortaleza	is so strong that
que lo echan pa la barriga	you pour it in your belly
y se va pa la cabeza.	and it goes to your head.[20]

In the American West, cowboys favored whiskey—bourbon, rye, or corn—which they generically termed "bitters." Texas cowboys referred to whiskey as "Kansas sheep-dip" in honor of the cowtowns where they quaffed drinks at the end of a trail drive. Cowboys called very strong whiskey a "Brigham Young cocktail"; as the saying went, "One sip and you're a confirmed polygamist." Other colloquial names for liquor included tornado juice, coffin varnish, mountain dew, redeye, red ink, snake poison, and tanglefoot. Beer enjoyed great popularity toward the end of the nineteenth century as breweries moved into the West.[21]

The Gambling Passion

Balzac opined that "the gambling passion lurks at the bottom of every heart." Gambling appears to have been epidemic among cowboys everywhere, like drinking, love of riding, and competitive machismo. Tavern keepers were more than happy to host games of chance. Card games played on cattle frontiers traced their roots to Europe. Latin America's cowboys came by their penchant for gambling honestly: Spain may have been the card-playing capital of medieval Europe. Soldiers, sailors, and even clerics played cards enthusiastically. Canasta, a variant of rummy, held many adherents. That popular game, and many others, traveled from Spain to Spanish America with the conquistadors.[22]

Games of chance remained very popular in Spanish America, despite various and repeated prohibitions. Regional favorites appeared. In Mexico both men and women of all classes patronized *salas*, or gambling halls. Women often worked as dealers. Spanish monte, played like short faro, was the most popular card game of Mexico. Chileans enjoyed cards and a variety of dice games. Betting accompanied horse races and other equestrian games of the Venezuelan llaneros, Chilean huasos, and Argentine gauchos. In Argentina, William MacCann noted that at the pulperías, the gauchos' "chief amusement is card-playing, and they are confirmed gamblers." On the pampa, however, the most popular card game was *truco*. Played with a forty-card deck, it included a good bit of clever signaling and witty table talk. Verbal sparring played an important role in the game. In some cases, players also sang verses back and forth as part of the game.[23]

The dandified Mississippi riverboat gambler is the most colorful representative of western gaming. But every saloon included a number of busy card tables. One Denver pioneer wrote in an 1859 letter that "there is more drinking and gambling here in one day than in Kansas City in six—in fact about one-half of the population do nothing else but drink whiskey and play cards."

But by 1872, Kansas City, the "Cowboy Capital," offered a range of lavish saloons famed for gambling—the Crystal Palace, Alhambra, Lady Gay, Alamo, and Lone Star. Gamblers enjoyed the hospitality of the Gold Room in Cheyenne and the Bull's Head in Abilene.[24]

Cowboys liked the simplicity and clarity of poker, especially draw and stud. Faro and monte also found favor with many gamblers. Cowboys distrusted complicated gambling machinery or fancy card games, just as they distrusted other artifacts of eastern culture. Many cowboys lost their hard-earned wages to more skillful gamblers at saloon tables. Cheating in many guises was commonplace. A "card mechanic" might "jump the cut" and deal himself an especially good hand. "Buying chips" came to mean jumping into a fight— evidence of the close relationship between gambling and fighting.[25]

Many ranchers prohibited gambling at the home place, so sprees in town came as a welcome relief. Cowboys played poker each evening by the roundup camp fire, if the roundup boss permitted it. The *Kansas Cowboy* recorded in 1885 that "gambling in cow camps is an evil which is commencing to attract the attention of thinking stockmen." Texas stockmen prohibited card playing during roundup. R. G. Head, manager of the Prairie Cattle Company, bluntly warned his cowboys about gambling in 1885: "So if you feel like you cannot live without gambling, be man enough to say so, get what is due you and go to town, or some place, where you can gamble unmolested. You cannot play cards in camp during the working season and do your work properly at the same time. It will not be tolerated, and any employee knowingly violating this rule will be subject to discharge."[26]

Gambling and drinking did not seem to be as widespread among Canadian cowboys as among their American counterparts. But Duncan McEachran, a generally reliable witness, compared Alberta cowboys of the 1880s with sailors in that they worked hard but would then "blow it in," drinking and gambling in town. On the other hand, "George," a Montana cowboy who went to Alberta, described the two regions as very different. In Montana, he said, "when I would get into a town I wanted to have a good time. I usually took a few drinks, and sometimes got into a game of poker, and generally left town 'broke.'" In contrast, he found neither gambling nor whiskey readily available in Alberta, and he actually saved some of his wages there.[27]

Gambling, particularly combined with drinking, raised the specter of violence. A verse from the old song "The Cowboy's Lament" warned of the perils of gambling and drink:

It was once in the saddle I used to go dashing,
Once in the saddle I used to go gay;
First to the dram house, then to the card house,
Got shot in the breast, I am dying today.[28]

Card playing concerned many ranchers and reformers in North and South America. But gauchos enjoyed many other types of gambling activities on the Argentine pampas. As Thomas Hutchinson commented, "Gambling is their life, soul, and very existence." Gauchos enjoyed playing *taba* as much as cards. In this ancestor of modern dice games, players throw the anklebone (talus or astragalus) of cattle or horses. The outcome of the throw, heads or tails, determines the winner. Chilean huasos also played taba. Cowboys everywhere participated in and bet on equestrian contests. By sponsoring a horse race, ostrich hunt, or similar event, a tavern keeper could draw patrons from great distances on the pampa.[29]

Everywhere in Latin America, a cockfight (riña de gallos) would draw a large, boisterous crowd. In cities and throughout the countryside, raising and fighting cocks absorbed the energy and attention of multitudes. Municipal governments often licensed and taxed the fights and supervised the construction of special arenas. This was the case in Santiago. Visiting the Chilean capital in 1838, Captain Allen F. Gardiner recalled that on Sunday "from first dawn of daylight we were disturbed by the shrill crowing of the numerous cocks." The first two fights of the day began at 11 a.m. On the Venezuelan llanos, a good fight could draw a crowd of two to three hundred. Matched for combat by weight, the ferocious birds usually gave spectators their money's worth.[30]

Soiled Doves of the Plains

Frontier taverns offered many activities to attract customers and generate additional profits. Prostitution provided a natural adjunct to liquor and gambling. Richard Erdoes notes that "Westerners divided women into two categories—good ones and bad ones." The preponderance of males in frontier regions dictated that most men, especially poor, working cowboys, socialized only with "bad ones." One commentator estimated that there were six to ten men per woman on the American ranching frontier. The ratio was probably even more extreme in Latin America.[31]

Because of the lack of women, prostitutes found many doors open to them. Alfred Doten, a Virginia City newspaperman, wrote a revealing journal entry in 1870. At a benefit ball held to aid Benito Juárez and the Mexican liberals, "the women were principally whores, although there were some decent women among them." The "fallen angels," "soiled doves," or "calico queens" of the West graced most cowtowns, despite city ordinances and the determined efforts of civic and religious reformers.[32]

In Abilene reformers did make a largely successful effort to exclude prostitutes in 1870. The term "red light district" supposedly originated in one of the foremost cowtowns, Dodge City. As the *Rocky Mountain News* lamented in 1889, saloons "were the most fruitful source for breeding and feeding prostitution." While some sanitized memoirs of life in the Old West discreetly omit this element of cowboy life, others are more forthright. Teddy Blue Abbott devotes an entire chapter of his memoirs to the cowboy's relationship with prostitutes. Some, such as Cattle Annie, with her heart of gold, became legends in their own right. Besides prostitutes, saloons employed "hurdy-gurdy" girls who danced with patrons and brought them drinks—for a price.[33]

Demographic imbalance between the sexes also characterized Canadian ranching country. Albertans, except for the puritanical, attached little stigma to a cowboy's visit to a "sporting house." There were simply few unmarried women available other than prostitutes. The town of Lethbridge had its special section of brothels on "The Point." This spit of land, jutting out into Oldman Coulee to the west of town, drew cowboys, miners, and settlers like a magnet. Madams reportedly liked cowboys as customers, because men of the range tended to spend money a bit more freely than other workers.[34]

As in all frontier regions, women were in short supply on the Argentine pampa. The demands of ranch work as well as powerful negative pressures from the landed elite condemned most gauchos to enforced bachelorhood or, at best, serial concubinage. Some ranchers discouraged or even prohibited women from living on the ranch. Women were thought to arouse jealousy and fighting among the men. Gauchos lived mobile lives because of the requirements of ranch work and the desire to escape military conscription. With little hope of owning land, gauchos had few opportunities for a stable home life. Prostitutes often provided their only female companionship.[35]

If the local population near a pulpería did not suffice to warrant resident prostitutes, an itinerant madam and her charges probably serviced the area. The arrival of such an entourage in a high-wheeled oxcart signaled the beginning of an impromptu fiesta that quickly drew gauchos from far and wide.

Setting up small tents for the clients and women, the madam sold candles of varying lengths that measured the time allotted to each patron. Because of the lack of employment opportunities for women in the countryside, many moved to towns and worked as prostitutes. Most towns regulated the business and required periodic health inspections. With a nod to social propriety, some municipalities prohibited solicitation on the street.[36]

CHAPTER 10

Cowboys and Indians

Frontier Race Relations

Cowboy life was not all wild times and fun. Cattle frontiers were regions of racial mixing and tension. In general, white Europeans came into violent conflict with Amerindians as explorers, ranchers, miners, trappers, and others sought to extract wealth from the frontier. Blacks, through the institution of slavery, also became part of the cattle culture. Frontier democracy is a myth—the livestock industry developed clear, discriminatory color lines. As in society at large, whites imposed their will and rule on nonwhites.

Indian-white conflict persisted for several centuries in some areas of Latin America. Cowboys were not the only horsemen in plains regions of the Americas. In both North and South America, the horse developed major cultural significance for many tribes. The horse extended the political and military influence of many Indian groups, reshaped their values, and increased their means of economic survival. Thanks to the animals brought to the United States by Spanish explorers, Plains Indians gained access to horses. The Kiowa and Missouri adapted to the horse, and other tribes followed suit. The Apaches, Sioux, and Comanches of the North American plains became skilled horsemen and therefore formidable enemies. The Maluches and Araucanians in Chile and several groups on the Argentine pampas also became skilled horsemen. By the eighteenth century, the Snakes, Blackfeet, Piegans, and other tribes of the Canadian prairies were mounted. "The horse very early became the prime objective in inter-tribal raiding," observed Wallace Stegner. "Horse-stealing became one of the most honorable of Indian activities." This cultural value, along with a taste for horseflesh, put Indians in direct conflict with whites, to whom horse stealing was a crime deserving of summary capital punishment.[1]

As European conquerors and settlers fanned out from coastal settlements to exploit frontier riches, they began to battle and mix with indigenous groups. In Latin America, mestizo cowboys more often than not served as the "shock troops" in these cultural conflicts. Blacks, first as slaves and runaways, and later as freedmen, added to the cultural and genetic mix of frontier regions. Convicts exiled from Portugal, runaway slaves, and other rootless wanderers populated the Brazilian backlands. One-sixth of the inhabitants of sixteenth-century New Spain may have been vagrants. White urban elites came to view plains regions as bastions of dangerous nonwhite criminals who threatened their power and competed for frontier wealth.[2]

Frontier regions thus gave rise to populations usually comprising a mix of Spanish, Indians, and blacks. Gauchos and llaneros had a similar ethnic makeup, but local differences altered the proportions. In Venezuela, the greater number of runaway slaves who escaped from coastal plantations probably made the black element on the llanos stronger. Estimates for Venezuela in the early nineteenth century place the white population (Spaniards and creoles, or American-born Spaniards) at about 20 to 25 percent of the total, with castas (nonwhite lower classes), slaves, and Indians comprising the balance.[3]

Amerindian Influences

Indigenous cultures strongly influenced frontier life in Latin America. For example, the "marriage" ritual of some pampas Indians included the stylized abduction of the future bride by the bridegroom. With the marriage consummated, the families of the parties negotiated appropriate economic exchanges. Rural lower- and even middle-class mestizos in Argentina adopted this ritual of abduction, followed by familial sanction and acceptance.[4]

Other borrowings from indigenous cultures on the pampa include the gaucho's use of the bolas and his taste for mate tea. Indians had developed the bolas even before the advent of horses on the plains, but in the hands of a horseman it became a deadly weapon of hunt or battle. Mate, the caffeine-rich tea of the Río de la Plata, had been widely used by Indians from upper Peru south. The gaucho needed little beyond mate, beef, and some acrid tobacco for subsistence.[5]

Elements of gaucho dress and speech exhibit indigenous roots. The ubiquitous poncho and chiripá owe their origins to pampas Indians. Linguistic evidence offers another measure of Indian influence in the social formation of plainsmen. The vocabularies of the llanero, gaucho, and huaso are rich with indigenous terminology. Gaucho words such as *bagual* (horse), *ñandú* (ostrich), and ombú (a typical plains tree), as well as many other plant names, originated in Amerindian tongues. Contributions come from Quechua, Guaraní, Pampa, Pehuelche, Charrúa, and other cultures of the Southern Cone.[6]

A perusal of *Vocabulario del hato*, compiled by José Antonio de Armas Chitty, reveals the extent of indigenous contributions to the everyday speech of the llaneros. We find words of Taino, Nahuatl, Quechua, Caribe, and Guaraní origin. And for Chile, René León Echaiz lists words in the huaso vocabulary of Quechua or Mapuche origin.[7]

In the cases of Argentina and Chile, cultural contact extended over the Andes. A description of a Maluche horseman in 1838 in southern Chile could apply equally to a gaucho of the Uruguayan or Argentine pampa. The Indian appeared in "a dark coloured poncho, and seated with bare legs upon a rude kind of saddletree above and beneath which a couple of sheepskins were strapped, his great toes alone being thrust into the tiny wooden stirrups. A red fillet or head-band . . . worn around the forehead confined in part his long black hair." The sole differences between the gaucho and the huaso might be the former's more brightly colored poncho, matted beard, and small-brimmed hat.[8]

Competition for Frontier Resources

Cowboys fighting marauding Indians has long been the stuff of pulp novels and B Western movies. But economic conflict over natural resources—salt, cattle, and horses—provoked several centuries of serious and nearly continual Indian-Spanish conflict in the lower Río de la Plata. Indeed, Spanish settlement in the region began most inauspiciously. Indians killed one early explorer, Juan Díaz de Solís, in 1516. Formidable attacks in 1536 wiped out the humble village that Pedro de Mendoza had established at Buenos Aires.

Wild livestock quickly became the prime frontier resource in colonial Río de la Plata. Feral horses and cattle numbered in the millions. By the early eighteenth century, Indians had developed a flourishing livestock trade. They moved animals from the Argentine plains to Chilean mountain valleys. Livestock bounty drew new tribes to the pampa, notably the fierce Araucanians of Chile, by 1725. They emulated pre-existing tribes—Puelches who roamed the south pampa to the Río Negro, Tehuelches in northern Patagonia, Pehuenches who controlled critical Andean mountain passes, Ranqueles in San Luis and Mendoza, Pampas, and others—in rounding up herds of cattle and trailing them to Chile. The herds of horses and cattle supplied most daily necessities, including beef, mare's meat, and leather for building *toldos* (rude huts) and making clothing. The busy cattle traffic brought Indians into conflict with gauchos who also hunted the wild beasts.[9]

The Spanish need for salt created further conflict. Essential to food preservation and to the processing of salted beef, the commodity brought Spaniards into contact and competition with plains Indians. Annual expeditions from the city of Buenos Aires (re-established in 1580) to the salt beds at Salinas Grandes began by 1730. The expeditions moved deep into Indian territory in heavily armed convoys. The expansion of cattle hunting and ranching across the Río Salado created further tensions: Spanish livestock drove off game animals used for food by the Indians. As in the American West, the expansion of settlement into "vacant" Indian lands and the destruction of resources needed by Indians triggered violent retaliation.[10]

Faced with stout, successful Indian opposition, Spanish officials sporadically took the offensive. The principal Spanish tactic was to field itinerant patrols. The city of Santa Fe sent out patrols in 1712. But the poorly trained and ill-equipped troops proved a weak deterrent to Indian raiders. The town council of Buenos Aires created companies of *blandengues* (gaucho cavalrymen) to patrol the countryside. The first three units, formed in 1752, were "La Valerosa," based near Mercedes, "La Invencible," at Salto, and "La Conquistadora," near Magdalena. Each consisted of fifty men plus officers. But once again, the skill of the mounted Indians and the vastness of the pampas rendered the blandengues ineffectual. The units disappeared by 1766.[11]

Chilean colonial officials faced similar difficulties in their efforts to subdue the fierce Araucanians. The Indians became much more skillful horsemen than the Spanish soldiers and repeatedly defeated the cavalrymen in battle. In 1566 they forced the Spanish to abandon two forts at Arauco and Cañete and gained 360 horses in the bargain. By the early seventeenth century, the Spanish adopted the tactic of the *maloca*, scorched-earth raids that destroyed Indian crops and villages. The Spanish also enslaved Araucanians for labor. As in Argentina, frontier troops were often criminals or the rural poor impressed into service. Ill-fed and poorly supported, they offered little impediment to speedy, mounted Indian raiders.[12]

The failure of Chilean and Argentine frontier defense points up the inherent problem of rural conflict between the elite and the masses. Forced recruits saw little incentive to serve. Soldiers faced harsh treatment, abysmal conditions, and late or nonexistent pay. Why should they trade a largely self-sufficient existence as wild-cattle hunters for the privations and dangers of military life? Gauchos and huasos saw little reason for defending the economic interests of the same landed elite that outlawed their access to wild livestock. Frontiersmen were economic competitors and political enemies of the landed elite.[13]

Efforts to enlist gauchos against Indians fared no better during and after the independence wars with Spain beginning in 1810. The new Argentine government re-established blandengue units in December 1816. Military patrols were ordered into the countryside "to recruit vagrants and deserters"—that is, gauchos—for frontier military service. The new leadership faced the same dilemma as had colonial officials. Gauchos were not inclined to fight Indians to defend the interests of the landed elite. As a result, Argentine officials faced Indian incursions with a shortage of troops until the latter decades of the nineteenth century.[14]

Red, White, Black, and Brown Cowboys

The frontier represents a melange of many races and cultures. The precise proportions of indigenous, Spanish, mixed, and black influences are difficult to gauge. As we have seen, white Europeans did not expunge all elements of nonwhite cultures on the frontier. Hispanic influence can be traced throughout Latin America and, via the Mexican vaquero, to the United States and thence to Canada. Various commentators stress the primacy of Hispanic, native American, and other influences on the frontier and elsewhere in society. Heated passions, fueled by a variety of ideologies, color the debate. In Argentina, adherents of Hispanism have prevailed in downplaying indigenous cultural contributions. Elite leaders have sought to project an image of a white, European population. Chile and Mexico, on the other hand, have enshrined the Araucanians and Aztecs, respectively, as heroic, mythologized ancestors. In any case, plains regions of Latin America came closer to the reality of a racial melting pot than most areas where the term has been applied.[15]

By the nineteenth century, most descriptions of plainsmen in South America commented on their nonwhite appearance. Visiting Uruguay in 1804, John Mawe noted that Paraguayan Indian children were brought to Uruguay to be raised as peons. That practice infused Guaraní blood into Uruguayan rural society. Mawe described the peons as being of an "honest and harmless race," but criticized their "excessive propensity to gambling." Sir Francis Bond Head, who crossed the pampas of Argentina in the 1820s, found the rural population to be of "all colors, black, white and red." A British diplomat found llaneros in the early 1830s to be "wild looking men of various hues, from downright black to bright mahogany. Each well mounted, lanced, and belted to which hung a long straight Toledo [sword]." Toward the end of the nineteenth century, William Curtis described horsemen in Brazil as "low caste, halfbreed Brazilians and Indians."[16]

Frontier Racial Conflict

Racial mixing and cultural borrowing notwithstanding, mestizo plainsmen clearly distinguished themselves from Indians. Gauchos referred to themselves as "Christians" and to Indians as "savages" or "infidels." The distinction was more cultural and racial than religious. On occasion, however, repression by central governments could push gauchos to cross the frontier line and live with Indians. The Spanish in the Río de la Plata and Chile and the Portuguese in São Paulo carried out slaving expeditions against the Indians. The Spanish in Chile launched raids against the Indians (called malocas or *campeadas*) from the late sixteenth century through the seventeenth. Bandeirantes of São Paulo made Indian slaving the mainstay of their existence. This set the tone for racial antagonism that kept Europeans and Indians warring for several centuries.[17]

Eighteenth-century Capuchin priests in the llanos described their Indian charges in unflattering terms as barbarous, irreligious, polygynous, spiteful, and drunken. A report of 1745 complained that the Indians were "very lazy, slothful, and indolent, much given to idleness, and great lovers of liberty, like the wild beasts of the forest." Similar descriptions of mestizo plainsmen abound.[18]

Racial distinctions and prejudice took on even stronger political overtones during the independence and civil wars of the early nineteenth century. White elites, whether Spanish colonizers or creole patriots, feared the nonwhite masses. Neither side wanted a social revolution. Both needed nonwhites as cannon fodder and labor. Both strenuously avoided granting nonwhites any real measure of political power or economic progress.

The racial element of the independence wars emerges clearly on the llanos. Mestizo and black cavalrymen from the plains, led by regional caudillos, battled the forces of the creole elite in Caracas. José Tomás Boves, the wily and terrible Spanish Army officer, ably manipulated racial hatreds to rally llaneros behind his standard. It took the prowess of a llanero caudillo, José Antonio Paez, to swing the fierce cavalrymen of the llanos to the patriot cause.[19]

Forceful military leaders like Boves and Paez could command the respect of llaneros and draw them into military service. But the llanero in general held little esteem for military superiors. A couplet in llanero dialect records this sentiment:

Amigo, no he dió a la guerra	Friend, I didn't go to war
ni siquiera soy sordao.	and wasn't even a soldier.
No me diga General	Don't call me General
porque yo a naide he robao.	because I've robbed nobody.[20]

Argentina's elite leadership in Buenos Aires despised and feared the provincial masses, calling them *cabecitas negras* (little black heads). To the centralizing elite, the masses in the interior provinces, mounted and armed as *montoneros*, provided the basis of popular and military support for disruptive caudillos. Racism pervaded and shaped elite policies toward labor, immigration, and other matters throughout the nineteenth century. And the topic of race relations, particularly concerning the Indian population, remains taboo in Argentina today.[21]

"Greasers"

Vaqueros of northern Mexico faced double discrimination. First they suffered social and legal disadvantages because of their status as castas (nonwhites) in a highly stratified Spanish colonial society. After the United States warred successfully to annex northern Mexico in 1845, vaqueros suffered new forms of Anglo racism, discrimination, and derision. These negative forces have continued into the twentieth century.

In the borderlands of Mexico and the United States, Anglos stereotyped "greasers." During the 1840s the notion of "Anglo-Saxons" as a race became current in the United States. Armed with a sense of racial superiority, Americans found all sorts of negative characteristics in nonwhite people. Nineteenth-century writings by Richard Henry Dana, Francis Parkman, Clarence King, and others depicted Hispanics as lazy, thieving, untrustworthy, and incompetent. These negative images attached themselves to vaqueros in California, the Southwest, and Texas.[22]

William Whelan, a stationmaster in Arizona, routinely noted the arrival of greasers in his diary from 1869 to 1872. Joseph G. McCoy's viewpoint typified Anglo-American attitudes of the past century: "The 'Greasers' are the result of Spanish, Indian and negro miscegenation, and as a class are unenterprising, energy-less and decidedly at a stand-still so far as progress, enlightenment, civilization, education, or religion is concerned." Cowboys also applied the derogatory term *chili-eaters* to Hispanics.[23]

Writing for *Harper's New Monthly Magazine* in 1891, Colonel Theodore A. Dodge, a self-styled authority on horsemen, painted a disdainful, racist stereotype of the vaquero and an equally romanticized picture of the Anglo cowboy:

> The vaquero is generally a peon, and as lazy, shiftless, and unreliable a vagabond as all men held to involuntary servitude are wont to be. He is essentially a low down fellow in his habits and instinct. Anything is grub to him which is not poison, and he will thrive on offal which no human being except a starving savage will touch.
>
> In his ways the vaquero is a sort of tinsel imitation of a Mexican gentleman, and very cheap tinsel at that. Our cowboy is independent, and quite sufficient unto himself. Everything not cowboy is tenderfoot, cumbering the ground, and of no use in the world's economy except as a consumer of beef. He has as long an array of manly qualities as any fellow living, and, despite many rough-and-tumble traits, compels our honest admiration. Not only this, but the percentage of American cowboys who are not pretty decent fellows is small. One cannot claim so much for the vaquero in question, though the term vaquero covers great territory and class, and applies to the just and unjust alike.[24]

The western white population exhibited the blatant racism of the nineteenth century against "Meskins," "blacks," and "Injuns." Racially mixed persons, referred to as "half-breeds" in the United States and Canada, also suffered social stigma. Vaqueros earned only one-third to one-half the wage of white cowboys; some Anglo ranchers preferred to hire vaqueros to save money. Despite their reputation as superior ropers and horsebreakers, vaqueros seldom rose above the common cowboy ranks to become foremen or trail bosses. Even the King Ranch of Texas, famous for using mostly *Kineños* (vaquero ranch hands), hired only Anglos as foremen.[25]

The law also weighed more heavily on the vaquero than on his Anglo counterparts. The predations of the Texas Rangers against Mexicans during the Mexican War and against Mexican-Americans north of the border are well documented. Happy in their work as agents of Manifest Destiny, Texas Rangers crossed the Mexican border with impunity. They worked assiduously on behalf of powerful Texas ranching interests to the detriment of Hispanics on both sides of the border.[26]

Frontier saloons segregated customers by both class and race, a circumstance not unique to the cattle frontier. Prices charged for beverages effectively segregated western saloons by social class. Denver saloons charged from five to twenty-five cents for a mug of beer. Cowboys and others with little money gathered at the cheap saloons. Cattlemen, buyers, and other businessmen gathered at fancier bars in hotels. Racial segregation excluded Chinese, discriminated against Hispanics, and isolated blacks in separate establishments. The same class and racial divisions that cut through society in general also obtained in western whiskey mills.[27]

Despite racial prejudice, vaqueros worked on ranches throughout the West and Northwest. In 1837 Philip Edwards drove cattle from California north to Oregon with the help of California vaqueros. Eastern Oregon ranchers employed Mexican-American cowboys during the late nineteenth and early twentieth centuries. In 1869 Juan Redón and six vaqueros drove three thousand head of cattle belonging to John Devine into Oregon. They established the first ranch in eastern Oregon's Harney County. Redón continued to work as Devine's foreman on what was at the time Oregon's largest ranch. Devine himself wore hacendado garb. The terrible winter of 1888 put Devine out of business, so Redón hired on as cattle superintendent for the Miller and Lux outfit (Pacific Livestock Company). Other Oregon ranchers, including Peter French and Dick Anderson, also hired Mexican cowboys. Vaqueros comprised up to half of the cowhands on many large ranches in the area until the big operations disappeared in the 1920s and 1930s.[28]

Black Cowboys in the American West

Black slaves tended cattle during the early days of ranching (the 1830s and 1840s) on the south Texas coast. Anglo settlers in Texas brought their slaves with them from their home states in the South. At the time of statehood in 1845, Texas had an estimated 100,000 whites and 35,000 slaves. On the eve of the Civil War in 1861, the state had 430,000 whites and 182,000 slaves. After the Civil War, ranches east of the Trinity River often had all-black crews. West of the Nueces River, ranchers used vaqueros more than black cowboys. Far fewer blacks populated the northern ranges. Censuses for Montana counted only 183 blacks in 1870 and 346 in 1880.[29]

The long trail drives north from Texas between 1866 and 1895 employed about 63 percent white cowhands, 25 percent black, and 12 percent Mexican or Mexican-American. About 5,000 black cowhands helped trail herds from Texas. By another estimate, Hispanics and blacks each comprised about one-seventh of the total cowboy population. Black cowboys, invariably referred to by such names as "Nigger John," faced social discrimination but less economic discrimination than vaqueros. Like an aging white hand, a good black cowboy might be rewarded with the job of cook after his riding days were done. Black wages generally matched those of white cowboys, and they received pay increases with experience. On the other hand, blacks frequently occupied the low-status job of horse wrangler and seldom became foremen.[30]

Blacks faced the same social discrimination and occasional violence on the frontier as they did elsewhere in the United States. In 1878, for example, a trail crew on a drive from Texas to Kansas hired a black cowboy. A racist Anglo named Poll Allen objected to the new man and refused to let him eat or sleep with the rest of the cowboys. Finally, Allen fired shots at the black man and drove him off. Blacks found no more upward social mobility on the frontier than elsewhere in society. Jim Perry worked at the giant XIT Ranch for twenty years. That outfit included seven divisions or ranges by 1900, each requiring a foreman. "If it weren't for my damned old black face," lamented Perry, "I'd have been boss of one of these divisions long ago." Instead he ended his days at the ranch as a cook.[31]

While slavery still existed, however, some odd reverse discrimination could take place. Because of their value as property, slaves were sometimes treated differently. In 1853 Abel "Shanghai" Pierce was breaking horses in Texas, assisted by some black slaves. Someone reportedly ordered that Pierce be given the most dangerous mounts, because "those Negroes are worth a thousand dollars a piece."[32]

A few black cowboys improved their lot and gained some measure of fame. Bill Pickett became famous as a bulldogger for the Miller and Lux 101 Wild West Show during the 1890s. Pickett reputedly would grab a steer by the horns, bite the animal's upper lip, let his hands loose, and down the animal with his teeth. He died as a result of kicks from a horse in 1932, after a long career as a steer wrestler.[33]

Nate Love, a black cowboy born in Ohio, gained fame as one of several self-promoters calling themselves "Deadwood Dick." The moniker became famous through dime novels written by Edward L. Wheeler. Love claimed to have acquired it by winning a roping contest in 1876 in Deadwood, Arizona, and he titled his fanciful memoirs accordingly. But the exceptional cases of Picket and Love hardly outweigh the oppression and ostracism suffered by thousands of their fellow blacks.[34]

Canada's Civilized but Racist West

Racist attitudes in Alberta closely resembled those in the United States, but vaqueros and black cowboys only rarely made their way so far north. The Cochrane Ranche, one of the first in the Calgary area, hired a vaquero as foreman. He worked hard and ably, and even headed a ranch roundup. But Anglo cowboys resented him, despite his knowledge of livestock. The most famous black cowboy of Alberta, an ex-slave called "Nigger John" Ware, first worked as a hand in Texas and Idaho. After hiring on with the Quorn and Bar U ranches, Ware saved up enough money to stock a ranch of his own, which he ran until his death in 1905. In 1933 rancher Fred Ings recalled Ware as having "black skin, but he was all white in spirit, courage and nerve." Albertans named some landmarks after him.[35]

Anglos generally found Indian culture and customs distasteful. Duncan McEachran complained in 1881 that "the practice of selling their daughters is very common among the Indians," often for one to six ponies. He added that in southern Alberta, white men cohabited with squaws "at almost every ranch which we passed." With buffalo herds decimated by 1879, some Indians migrated to Montana, while others sometimes killed cattle for food. McEachran listed the ranchers' major complaints as "stealing by Indians, prairie fires, and mosquitoes." William F. Cochrane recorded a problem with Indians from a reserve near the Cochrane Ranche in 1885. "The boys surprised the Indians after they killed a cow Thursday, but the Indians got away. They had a pack horse with them."[36]

Occasional Indian depredations continued into the early 1890s. The *Macleod Gazette* editorialized against lax policies toward Indians who left the reservations. The paper suggested a pass system to control Indian movements because of the "grave dangers which are threatened through all parts of the country being infested by marauding Indians, who once loose from their reserves, kill cattle, steal, get drunk, and in various other ways prove they are not fit to be trusted abroad." While admitting that a few "bad eggs" caused many problems, the paper insisted on stricter regulations and harsher punishments for killing cattle.[37]

But compared with the American West, where white migration preceded Indian pacification, serious conflict between Indians and whites in Canada was relatively rare. Mounted Police established the rule of law and implemented Indian policy, including reservations and government food subsidies, before the cattle industry began. Canadian Indian policy may not have been as farsighted and just as popular history would have it, but compared with the violence and ruthlessness of American western policy, Canada's was a model of restraint and wisdom.[38]

The Final Indian Wars

Canada, however, did not face a serious "Indian problem" on its cattle frontier. Ranchers complained of occasional livestock losses that they attributed to Indian thefts, but Canadian Indians were segregated on reservations. In the United States, countless movies and pulp novels have sensationalized the Indian wars. Recent scholarship has added much more reliable information about American Indian policy and race relations. But without question, cowboys considered Indians the enemy, and many Indians reciprocated the sentiment.[39]

A story in the *Daily Optic* of Las Vegas, New Mexico, reported that an Indian chief had asked a cavalry general for a cannon. The general refused, saying that the Indians would kill cavalrymen with the weapon. "No want cannon to kill soldiers," the chief replied. "Can kill soldiers with sticks. Want cannon to kill cowboys." Another Las Vegas paper, the *New Mexico Stock Grower*, offered some candid recommendations for Indian policy: "These Indians are brutes and the same attention should be given to them that would be bestowed upon any other brute that can do harm. They should be confined, and a great sigh of relief would go up to heaven from the thousands of pioneer homes of the territories if every red-colored demon of creation was then taken out and shot."[40]

The dynamics of Indian-white relations in Argentina and Chile bear a strong resemblance to events in the United States. An examination of the final Indian wars of Argentina offers a case study of an expanding livestock economy in conflict with a contracting Amerindian world.

General Julio A. Roca launched Argentina's "final offensive" against its Plains Indians at the same time the United States Cavalry was busy opening up the West. Roca brought together for the first time sufficient commitment, materiel, technology, and planning to accomplish what had been talked about for centuries—security against Indian attack. In 1878 he affirmed the need "to break the spirit of the Indian and keep him full of fear and terror of us. That way, instead of thinking to invade us, he will only think of fleeing, seeking his salvation in the depths of the forest." He also ordered villages leveled and *caciques* (chiefs) exiled to Chile along with the *chusma* (a disparaging term for Indian women and children). This repressive policy was meant to destroy Indian morale, like earlier scorched-earth raids practiced by the military in Chile.[41]

In 1883 Roca affirmed somewhat prematurely that "the wild Indians, then, have disappeared, with no danger that they can return." Yet in April of that year a band of fifty braves attacked German immigrant ranchers on the frontier in Buenos Aires province. They killed and mutilated at least eight ranchers, injured others, and stole an estimated three thousand cattle. One newspaper reported that "with the band of Indians went some gauchos." Argentine officials had yet to subdue entirely the Indian or gaucho population.[42]

Chronic manpower shortages plagued military commanders and rendered inoperative strategies that required large numbers of troops. Officials from the colonial period on faced the problem of how to mobilize unwilling gauchos to fight Indians. In terms of class, culture, and economic interests, gauchos had more in common with the "savages" than with the elite leaders giving the orders. Vagrancy laws, passports, and arbitrary conscription antagonized gauchos and hindered frontier settlement. The government held no legitimacy in the eyes of the men who made the best cavalrymen—the gauchos of the plains.[43]

The Argentine military faced a cultural gap between its leadership and its enlisted men. Gaucho troops, accustomed to traditional ways of surviving on the pampa, did not always readily accept army mandates. Any orders involving footwork, such as digging defensive ditches, aroused gaucho ire. They considered such work servile and unmanly, and preferred to leave it to immigrant laborers. (In fact, as we have already seen, a life in the saddle, grasping a small stirrup with the big toe, rendered some gauchos virtually unable to walk.) Nor did gauchos take to firearms; many preferred their traditional boleadoras and facónes.[44]

Even orders about caring for their horses might be met with hostility or indifference on the part of the gauchos. Articles 9 through 14 of the orders issued by Colonel Conrado Villegas in 1876 required that troops care for and groom their mounts. Soldiers were forbidden to ride horses with sore backs. "Without horses there is no calvary," affirmed Villegas. Commanders had to insist on these matters, because gauchos customarily gave their mounts little care, knowing that they could be replaced easily and cheaply. Gauchos could ride anything and so wasted little effort in breaking or training their mounts. Short of manpower, frontier commanders had to make do with immigrant volunteers who could not ride and native troops who abused and injured mounts.[45]

In the final analysis, the major shortcoming of Argentine frontier strategy lay in conceptualization, not in technology, tactics, or military intelligence. The racial and cultural prejudices of Spanish and then creole elites precluded a comprehensive, positive frontier policy. From the days of sixteenth-century slaving expeditions, this policy served negative goals: to exterminate and subjugate—but never to integrate—the Indians of the pampa. The Indians had formulated a sophisticated cattle trade that might well have evolved into economic partnership, not conflict, had the Argentine leadership been so inclined. In Argentina, the American West, and Chile, white expansionists created "frontiers of exclusion" to push aside existing Amerindian cultures.[46]

The intermittent success of treaties placing Indians in military service and directing changes in their activities and lifestyle show that such adaptation was possible. But national elites, from the sixteenth through the nineteenth centuries, conceived the frontier as an uncrossable line dividing the forces of "civilization" and "barbarism." And the gaucho, the elite's most potent force against the Indian, also came to be considered a barbarian, outside the pale of acceptable society. Had accommodation and integration played larger roles than marginalization and extermination in formulating strategy, perhaps the prolonged frontier conflict in Argentina would have taken a different direction.[47]

In both North and South America (Canada excepted), cattle frontiers represented theaters of racial and cultural mixing and conflict. In Latin America, indigenous, black, and mixed-blood cowboys first worked as wild-cattle hunters. Gradually, whites established control over the resources of land, livestock, and water. With the rise of systematic ranching and domesticated stock, nonwhites continued to labor as ranch hands. Amerindians found themselves pushed back and then aside by the expanding livestock industry.

In the United States, the three races labored side by side, but much less mixing occurred than in Latin America. As in Argentina, cowboy mythology largely ignored nonwhite culture and created the pervasive imagery of the Anglo cowboy hero. Plains Indians found their lands taken and their cultures profoundly shaken by white expansion. Canada's cattle industry likewise was dominated by white cowboys. Very few Métis (mestizos) or Indians worked as cowhands on white-owned ranches in Alberta, although stock raising, especially horse breeding, did take place on some reservations.

In the Southern Cone countries of Argentina and Chile, the violent conquest of resistant indigenous cultures did not succeed until the latter decades of the nineteenth century—about the time of the last Indian wars in the United States. In both North and South America, the expansion of the ranching frontier contributed to the decline of Amerindian cultures. In turn, the livestock industry suffered encroachment and then decline in the face of agriculture. Conscripted cowboys in several Latin American nations were instrumental as the cavalrymen who defeated and pushed aside the Plains Indians. But the cowboy himself was going into eclipse. Rapid changes during the late nineteenth century brought traditional cowboy life and open-range ranching to an end in most of the Americas.

CHAPTER 11

Riding into the Sunset

In most countries, the decline of the cowboy followed the pacification of the Indian frontier during the late nineteenth century. But for the Venezuelan and Colombian llanero, decline came much earlier as a result of generalized political violence. Ranching fell off precipitously on the llanos during the independence and civil wars, which lasted from 1810 through the 1850s. The warfare decimated herds, drained manpower, and interrupted market routes. Similar but shorter-lived disruptions affected Chile and Uruguay. We can date the decline of the Mexican vaquero with precision to the violent revolution that swept the nation from 1910 to 1920.

Decline came gradually to the gauchos of Argentina during the latter decades of the nineteenth century. The disastrous winters of 1885–1886 and 1886–1887 marked the beginning of the end of open-range ranching and classic cowboy life in the United States. In Canada a harsh winter in 1907 combined with the rise of dryland farming to push aside ranching and the cowboy. In every case, complex processes hastened the end of traditional cowboy life.

Political Violence, Economic Disruption

The llanos had already begun to decline vis-à-vis coastal plantation agriculture during the late eighteenth century. But the llanero witnessed (and participated in) the near total destruction of Venezuela's livestock economy during the independence wars of 1810–1821. Both patriots and royalists freely appropriated animals for consumption, riding, and draft. Much fighting occurred in the llanos, sparked by the need to have access to livestock, and the region suffered grave devastation. The number of cattle in the Venezuelan llanos fell from about 4.5 million in 1812 to a quarter of a million a decade later. Between 1814 and 1820 on the Colombian llanos of Casanare, the estimated number of cattle dropped from 273,000 to 50,000; of horses, from 30,000 to 4,000.[1]

Independence lessened the llaneros' opportunities for legitimate employment and increased repression from the new ruling elite in Caracas. On the Colombian and Venezuelan plains, livestock numbers and exports dropped as demands by competing armies decimated herds. As a result, the economic fortunes of the llanero went into decline long before those of his counterparts elsewhere in the Americas. Small wonder that many plainsmen in Venezuela and Colombia turned to banditry or joined the marauding army of some local strongman.[2]

Filling the military's heavy demands for livestock was not easy, even for large landowners like José Antonio Paez. Six months before the great patriot victory at Carabobo in June 1821, Simón Bolívar requested that Paez furnish him with 32,000 cattle. Paez replied that losses in transit would require capturing twice that number of bulls. "Where do you suppose I'll find this great number of bulls," asked Paez, "when they're so wild that they wander like tigers in the bush?" The caudillo added, "I would rather fight 74,000 battles than catch 74,000 bulls."[3]

No sooner had independence been won than a new cycle of violence began between competing caudillos, regional strongmen who filled the power vacuum in the the new republic. Civil war became a way of life on the llanos. In July 1878 José María Colina, a local official in Pascua, complained to the president of the state of Guárico: "We find today the department at war, and with a considerable number of troops to support, and with no other resources except livestock with which to sustain said forces." Colina pointed out that "this makes it a little difficult to collect the livestock tax, because livestock owners allege that they cannot at the same time pay the tax and give livestock for the sustenance of the Army, a strong argument on their behalf that civil authority cannot well counter."[4]

The neighboring Colombian llanos faced similar disruptions from nineteenth-century civil wars. Competition for labor from the burgeoning coffee sector drew workers away from the llanos. (The twentieth-century oil boom would have the same effect in Venezuela.) Ranches in the Casanare region of the llanos continued to operate from the colonial period through the twentieth century. But by 1907 the region held only about 150 ranches containing a total of 250,000 cattle and 50,000 horses. Some Colombian ranchers modernized their operations to produce higher-grade beef for local markets. The number of cattle in Colombia grew slowly from about 4.4 million in 1898 to some 6.7 million in 1925. But coffee was king. As in Venezuela, ranching had become a small, backwater segment of the national economy.[5]

The independence wars that swept Chile in 1817 and 1818 had similar negative effects. The livestock and agricultural industries, particularly in the southern part of the nation, suffered. Livestock production during the 1820s fell to less than half of what it had been during the first decade of the century. Taking advantage of the turmoil, Indians in the south pushed the frontier of European settlement back further to the north. Like the llaneros, huasos found themselves fighting as cavalrymen rather than working on ranches. Civil wars in Uruguay during the 1840s also disrupted rural production and uprooted gauchos there.[6]

As in Venezuela and Colombia, ranching became increasingly marginalized in the Chilean economy during the nineteenth century. The Chilean landed elite failed to modernize either ranching or agriculture. As a result, they could not compete against more efficient producers in the United States, Argentina, and Australia. They fought protectionist rearguard actions to keep out superior, cheaper Argentine beef. Controlling national politics, the landed elite kept internal beef prices artificially high to guarantee themselves a good return. The huaso faced shrinking economic prospects and higher food prices as the protected livestock industry failed to compete internationally. Late in the century, the rise of the nitrate industry and copper mining pushed northern Chile to economic prominence and further marginalized the ranching sector.[7]

While independence wars raged throughout Venezuela and Chile, Argentina escaped any direct attack and devastation. Except for short-lived, localized invasions by the British in 1806 and 1807, Argentina suffered only the self-induced pillage of civil war during the nineteenth century. During the fight against the Spanish, the able gaucho cavalry of Martín Güemes held off royalists in the north. The towering Andes protected the west, and unsettled Patagonia buffered the south. The Argentine pampa emerged from the independence period with its livestock richness intact. Wild herds, if somewhat less plentiful than during the eighteenth century, still represented a considerable source of wealth. Many estancieros began to tame the wild cattle and to claim exclusive grazing rights to choice areas of the pampa and ownership of all cattle thereon.[8]

Buffered from the ravages of the independence wars, the livestock industry of the Río de la Plata expanded. British and Argentine investors established new *saladeros*, or meat-drying plants, around Buenos Aires. While José Antonio Paez risked life and limb against the Spanish, Juan Manuel de Rosas commenced his saladero and ranching activities. Independence brought prosperity to the pampa and despair to the llanos.

But like other countries in Spanish America, Argentina experienced civil wars between liberal and conservative political factions. Gauchos became cavalrymen for a wide range of political causes. Moreover, the nation's very prosperity carried with it changes that threatened the gaucho's traditional way of life. The landed elite, masters of a burgeoning livestock industry, instituted repressive measures to control rural labor, always in short supply in the region. They also began husbanding livestock wealth more carefully and asserted control over the land itself. Both of these concepts were alien to the gaucho. Federico Brito Figueroa's conclusion for Venezuela holds equally well for Argentina: "National emancipation reaffirmed the political power of the landowning class."[9]

Political disruptions in Mexico had the same effect on the vaquero as they had on the llanero, huaso, and to a lesser extent the Uruguayan gaucho. For example, during the 1860s fighting between the liberal forces of Benito Juárez and the occupying French armies of Emperor Maximilian destroyed the huge estate of the Sánchez Navarros in Coahuila. By 1864 the ranch was a battlefield. Both sides looted and pillaged livestock and grain. Carlos Sánchez Navarro, a conservative, sided with the imperialist cause of Maximilian. This decision sealed the family's economic doom. Juárez exacted revenge on the family and jailed Sánchez Navarro after defeating and executing Maximilian in 1867.[10]

But even peace in the countryside did not insure a better life for the vaquero and peasantry. The long dictatorship of Porfirio Díaz (1884–1910) greatly increased the socioeconomic distance between the landed and landless in rural Mexico. Díaz offered generous land concessions to foreigners, broke any attempted strikes, and generally reduced rural Mexicans to peonage status. Mexico, like Venezuela, failed to attract significant European immigration. Abysmal rural social conditions offered little incentive to foreigners.[11]

The situation became increasingly dire under Díaz's rule. Farm wages fell 17 percent between 1895 and 1910. Ninety-eight percent of Mexicans were landless by 1910. Many labored as migrants to survive. Skilled cowhands did not suffer the same wage decline as farmhands, but many vaqueros found work only seasonally on the great estates that dominated northern Mexico. Banditry became an alternative form of employment. Bandit leaders, such as Jesús Arriaga ("Chucho el Roto") and Heraclio Bernal, became popular symbols of opposition to the dictatorship.[12]

The violence and disorder of the Mexican Revolution broke forth in 1910. The fighting created tumultuous conditions akin to those suffered by Venezuela a century before. Armies proliferated under Emiliano Zapata, Francisco "Pancho" Villa, Alvaro Obregón, Pascual Orozco, Pablo González, Venustiano Carranza, and other revolutionary chieftains. Orozco stole cattle from northern Mexican estates and sold them in the United States to purchase arms. All of the armies needed mounts, draft animals, and meat. Through forced and voluntary donations of livestock, ranchers lost their herds as armies swept through in advance or retreat. Some owners tried to ship cattle to the United States to avoid seizure, especially by Pancho Villa.[13]

The revolution largely destroyed Mexico's livestock industry. In 1902 an estimated 396,000 cattle roamed the state of Chihuahua. Pillage and disruption cut the number about 75 percent by 1923. Sonora suffered a similar decline from some 261,000 head to 69,000. Durango experienced the greatest loss, from 233,00 to 23,000. Overall, the number of cattle in Mexico dropped 67 percent between 1902 and 1923.[14]

Unemployed vaqueros turned their equestrian skills to service as cavalrymen. But, unlike the new revolutionary elite that emerged during the 1920s, the vaquero and other poor rural Mexicans did not prosper after the wars ended. The Mexican livestock industry gradually recovered, but vaqueros remained exploited, poorly paid, and landless. The revolution failed to overturn the stratified hacienda social order, with powerful landed elites at the top and poor cowhands and peasants at the bottom.[15]

Political violence in Mexico and Venezuela hastened the decline of the cowboy. In Argentina and Uruguay, social changes precipitated by massive immigration and economic diversification into agriculture marginalized the gaucho. The Chilean huaso, already living on the fringes of society, found survival even harder as foreigners received preferential treatment from the government. Changing technology reduced ranch labor needs and curtailed the opportunities of the open range.

Fenced In

Fences, in particular, played a role in marginalizing the cowboy. Forward-looking ranchers began importing wire fencing into the Río de la Plata during the 1850s. By the 1880s barbed wire was commonplace on larger estates. Uruguayan Minister of the Interior Andrés Lamas exempted wire from import duties to encourage its use. Uruguay also exempted fencing from internal taxation (*contribución directa*). Fencing reduced the ranchers' expenses for labor and markedly in-

Cowboy spectacles –
*Wild West shows, circuses,
and rodeos – proliferated
at the end of the
nineteenth century as
authentic cowboy culture
fell into decline. Some of
the early stunt riders and
rodeo performers had
worked as ranch hands.
As time went on, however,
performing cowboys
developed their own career
paths – which seldom
included experience
working cattle on ranches
(p. 210).*

"Buffalo Bill" *Cody's
Wild West Show presented
cowboys from around the
world, including gauchos
and vaqueros, who
performed daring
horseback stunts and rope
and shooting tricks (pp.
146–47). The romanticized
gauchos shown in this
1899 poster wear Cossack-
style hats. Cody's
immensely popular shows
carried cowboy imagery
and excitement from the
West to the eastern United
States and around the
world. (Poster Collection,
Prints and Photographs
Division, Library of
Congress)*

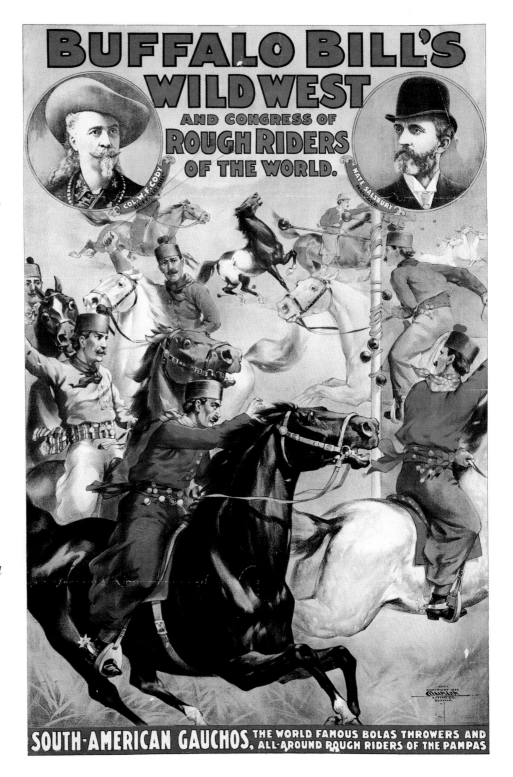

Major Gordon W. "Pawnee Bill" Lillie
organized his "Far East" show in 1888. Annie Oakley was a favorite drawing card. Like Cody, Lillie toured widely throughout the United States and Europe. He and one of his Mexican riders are shown in front of painted show backdrops in Boston in 1906. The exotic costumes, such as the one worn by this Mexican charro, *and special skills of foreign riders made them great hits in North American Wild West shows. Faced with mounting debt, Cody combined his show with Lillie's from 1911 to 1913, when both were forced into bankruptcy. (Prints and Photographs Division, Library of Congress)*

Calgary's famous Stampede *began in 1912 and remains a popular July event. Rodeo continued to gain fans long after Wild West shows disappeared. In the photograph above, taken in 1912, the man on foot wears "woollies," the sheepskin chaps common on northern ranges. The rider on the right is using a saddle with "taps" hanging down over the stirrups, evidence of Mexican influence in North American saddle making (p. 90). At least one Mexican vaquero, Magdaleno Ramos (below), attended the 1912 Stampede. (Glenbow Archives, Calgary)*

In the United States, *rodeo has become the quintessential all-American sport. Rodeos in Pendleton, Oregon, Cheyenne, Wyoming, and elsewhere gained international fame. First held in 1897, Cheyenne's Frontier Days became one of the biggest western spectacles. These early Frontier Days photographs show a rider named Jones challenging Silver City in 1910 (above), and a cowboy named O'Donnell facing Whirlwind the following year (below). (Prints and Photographs Division, Library of Congress)*

O'DONNELL ON WHIRLWIND," CHEYENNE FRONTIER DAYS.

COPYRIGHT, 1911, BY UNION PACIFIC R.R. CO.

County and state fairs *throughout the nation included rodeo competitions, such as the one advertised in this poster of the 1940s. Women found a place in rodeo, just as they had on the frontier. In early rodeos, women competed in what later became men's events, such as saddle bronc riding. In 1919, H. J. Rogner photographed a woman saddle bronc rider taking on Winnemucca in Rawlins, Wyoming (below). (Prints and Photographs Division, Library of Congress)*

Trick riding *at rodeos showed the common heritage and crowd-pleasing showmanship of rodeos and Wild West shows. Riders throughout the Americas delight in showing their skill and courage at dangerous tricks on horseback (pp. 134–41). This rodeo performer was photographed in 1930 by Erwin E. Smith in the Southwest. (Prints and Photographs Division, Library of Congress)*

Beginning in the 1930s, *rodeos reduced women's participation to special events, such as barrel racing (p. 213). But the "cowgirl" remains an important American icon. These women rodeo performers were photographed by Erwin E. Smith somewhere in the Southwest between 1905 and 1915. (Prints and Photographs Division, Library of Congress)*

The Hispanic roots *of American rodeo are well documented (pp. 128, 211), but Mexican vaqueros and charros also enjoyed their rodeos and* charreadas. *Frederic Remington depicted vaqueros arriving at a rodeo at Los Ojos ranch in northern Mexico in 1894 (above). Hispanic cowboys, such as Maclovia Lucero at the LS Ranch in Texas (below), showed their considerable talents, including bulldogging, on both sides of the border.* (Above: Harper's Monthly, *March 1894, courtesy of Yale University Library.* Below: Prints and Photographs Division, Library of Congress)

Argentina's gauchos *enjoyed many spectacular riding games, as the selection of paintings by Florencio Molina Campos (following p. 210) shows. Across the Andes in Chile,* huasos, *dressed in their typical ponchos, developed their own brand of rodeo (pp. 213–14). These huasos are blocking and pushing a steer into a padded mat in an event* called the atajada. *While rodeo professionals competed for cash in the United States, competition in Mexico and Chile remained a hobby of middle- and upper-class amateurs. From Calgary to Santiago, rodeos preserve elements of cowboy culture. (Prints and Photographs Division, Library of Congress)*

creased rural unemployment. It also allowed powerful landowners to deny small ranchers access to the public domain. In this fashion, barbed wire furthered the consolidation of land in the hands of a few families.[16]

Fencing had far-reaching consequences for the gaucho. Thomas Hinchliff noted in 1863 that "a good deal of land is enclosed by wire fence, a modern innovation which greatly annoys the thorough-bred *gauchos* who from time immemorial have been accustomed to gallop by day or night in any direction, and as far as they please."[17]

Literally fenced in, gauchos lost important elements of their traditional lifestyle. Fencing permitted estancieros to control their livestock more strictly than they could on the open range. Wild livestock became scarce on the plains. Free food, hides to sell, and abundant mounts to ride were no longer the rule. Fences prevented gauchos from chasing ostriches freely across the plains. This deprived them of an important source of income from the sale of ostrich feathers. Fencing also made agriculture possible. This economic diversification further marginalized the gaucho, who steadfastly refused to bend his knee and work the soil.[18]

Fencing and windmills appeared in the American West beginning in the mid-1870s. Joseph E. Glidden began marketing barbed wire in the United States in 1875. Besides hiring fewer hands, ranchers could manage the range more efficiently. Breeding control could be maintained. Losses due to theft and straying were reduced. With water pumped by windmills, ranchers could stock the range with more animals than when only surface water was available. In some states, large outfits fenced public lands, thereby cutting off access to smaller ranchers. Finally, fencing, along with the westward and southward extension of railroads, doomed the great cattle drives that once employed tens of thousands of hands in trail crews.[19]

Fencing heralded similar changes on the Alberta ranching frontier. Unlike the American Great Plains, Alberta enjoyed an abundance of trees in the western hills. Wooden fences appeared well in advance of barbed wire. Fred Ings described fence building in the mid-1880s. Hands constructed calf pens and fences from "poles, cut in the hills and sawed into post lengths. The ends of these poles we rested on the ground on a slant; in a hole drilled through them with a two inch auger we inserted a brace, then nailed on thin poles. This made a strong efficient fence."[20]

Barbed wire and farmers followed soon thereafter. In 1906 the superintendent of mines in Calgary reported that "the farmer and his fences are gradually driving the big rancher further and further back, and it is only a question of years when the real ranche will have ceased to exist." Within a year, an extremely harsh winter further reduced the attractiveness of ranching in Alberta.[21]

Ranchers on the llanos brought in wire fencing later and less extensively than their counterparts elsewhere. In Venezuela the first fence on the llanos did not appear until 1890 on El Corozo, a ranch in Guárico. But such advances were the exception, not the rule. Most herds of cattle continued to graze unfettered and semiwild. Llaneros used salt licks and a few tamed animals to help control their herds. Of all the ranching areas of the Americas, the llanos changed the latest and the least.[22]

Farmers and Foreigners

In addition to its other social and economic effects, fencing made it possible for ranching and farming to coexist. Fences kept cattle from trampling and eating crops. But the political assumptions about fencing varied sharply between Anglo-America and Latin America. Traditional Spanish law placed the burden of protecting crops on the farmer. This bias is consistent with the status and power of ranchers in Spanish and Spanish-American society. In 1737, for example, farmers at San Fernando de Bexar (in Texas) complained of "the continuous damage done to their cornfields by the unherded cattle of the missions and of the soldiers and residents of this royal presidio." Farmers faced similar problems in Latin America throughout the colonial and national periods.[23]

English herd laws, in contrast, assigned to cattlemen the responsibility for damage to agriculture. Not surprisingly, law and the political climate favored the expansion of agriculture at the expense of open-range ranching in the United States and Canada. In both societies, the extension of farming represented the coming of "civilization" to the frontier.[24]

Thus, the relationship between farming and ranching frontiers varied widely across the Americas. But nineteenth-century Latin American leaders shared a common goal: to attract immigrant farmers from Europe to diversify their economies and upgrade their racial stock. Argentina and, to a lesser extent, Chile showed success in drawing immigrants; Venezuela and Mexico were less successful. In Chile agriculture had always coexisted with ranching in the fertile central valley around Santiago. A few wealthy landowners controlled both grazing and farmlands. Sharecroppers worked the land, supplemented by migrant labor during the harvest and roundup seasons. The Chilean elite looked down upon the native rural population and worked assiduously to replace it with "superior" immigrant blood. Indeed, Chile may well have been the most Europhile of all Latin American nations during the nineteenth and early twentieth centuries. In his multivolume history of Chile, Francisco Encina applauded the benefits of Chile's "precious gift of European blood."[25]

Chile's leaders viewed European immigrants as a key ingredient in the nation's future greatness. Plans to colonize frontier regions discriminated against native-born Chileans and favored foreigners. Felix de Campo, a Chilean intellectual, wrote in 1904 that "colonization with native-born sons of the country will retard its development." Huasos, like others of the marginal rural poor, collectively called *rotos* (broken ones), had no place in the elite's grand development schemes.[26]

Government officials even evicted Chilean squatters in order to give the land to immigrants. As a result of such policies, the Chilean rural landless ended up working for foreigners in the countryside. Southern Chile became a virtual German colony during the late nineteenth century. Marginalized ranch workers and other landless Chileans migrated over the Andes. Ironically, Chile's discrimination against its rural poor spurred the Chilean settlement of Patagonia. Faced with a growing foreign population on its soil, Argentina took belated interest in developing the southern Patagonian frontier. In 1895 only three hundred of the twenty-four thousand inhabitants of the border territory of Neuquén were Argentine; the remainder were Chileans. In 1914 only 1 percent of Argentines lived in Patagonia. Argentines, remembering that earlier Chilean emigration to Bolivia and Peru had fueled Chilean expansionism, did not wish to see the War of the Pacific (1879) repeated in Patagonia.[27]

Argentina's liberal, modernizing elite displayed a similar scorn for its native gauchos. Many colonization projects sought to populate the plains with European farmers. Europhile leaders believed the immigrants to be racially and culturally superior to Argentina's mixed-blood population. The government created special programs and subsidized trans-Atlantic passage for immigrants. Argentina absorbed 46 percent of all European immigration to Latin America between 1851 and 1924. Thirty-eight percent of the emigrants came from Italy and another 28 percent from Spain.[28]

Many immigrants to Argentina became tenant farmers. But the spread of agriculture did not occur, as Terry Jordan has suggested, because "cattle ranchers retreated before advancing waves of wheat farmers, a retreat which halted only when the ranchers found refuge in lands too dry for the 'sod-busters.'" On the contrary, Argentina's ranchers controlled the spread of agriculture and used it to promote their livestock raising. Farmers were permitted only because ranchers needed someone to raise alfalfa for new hybrid cattle. Agriculture remained subservient to ranching. It became dominant only where cattle and/or sheep ranching was less significant, as in Santa Fe province.[29]

Santa Fe and other Argentine provinces became prosperous agricultural regions through the infusion of European farmers. Unsuitable for raising merino sheep, the lands were not dominated by ranchers. The vast grazing lands of Buenos Aires province remained under the control of the ranching elite. Tenant farmers and immigrant farm workers labored on lands owned by Argentine ranchers. Sharecroppers raised wheat or corn for up to five years. Then they planted alfalfa, moved to another plot, and the rancher turned his hybrid cattle loose to graze on the improved pasture. The upshot was the continued control of land by the few, the further marginalization of the gaucho, and a general lack of upward mobility for rural immigrants.[30]

Like the Chilean and Argentine elites, leaders in Uruguay also endorsed colonization and immigration schemes. Uruguay succeeded in attracting sizable numbers of immigrants, but most remained in the capital of Montevideo. Like the Argentine landed elite, Uruguayan estancieros refused to alter the monopolistic land tenure system. As a result, gauchos and the bulk of rural society remained poor, landless, and marginalized. A few large landholders continued to control access to land, especially in the northern part of the country, thereby limiting economic opportunity. Agriculture did not push aside ranching in Uruguay, but the gaucho still lived a marginal existence.[31]

As in Chile, agriculture played a more important role than ranching in Venezuela's national economy. Coastal planters carried more political weight during the colonial and national periods than did ranchers of the tropical interior plains. During the early eighteenth century, cacao (processed into chocolate), cattle hides, and tobacco ranked as Venezuela's most important exports. But as the century wore on, cacao greatly increased in relative importance. Coffee, indigo (for dye), and cotton production also expanded. Hide exports dropped in significance, even before the devastation of the independence wars. In both the agricultural and livestock sectors, absentee ownership was common. Overseers and slaves worked the estates. Landowners preferred the creature comforts and better climate of Caracas to the rigors of tropical plains life.[32]

As early as the 1820s and 1830s, under General Paez, Venezuela tried to attract European immigrants, but the efforts largely failed. Paez stressed that the nation needed "foreign immigration to furnish the hands with which to cultivate the riches of its fertile territory." But few answered the call, and those who did found frustration, not riches. A Scottish colony failed in the mid-1820s, partly because the settlers knew little about tropical agriculture. Lack of credit, marginal land, haphazard organization, and weak administration also helped doom the project.[33]

Immigrants everywhere faced the threat of xenophobic backlash. Anti-foreign sentiment peaked in Latin America during the early twentieth century. But anti-Semitism raised its ugly head in the llanos town of Coro in September 1831. Dutch Jews from Curaçao, numbering about twenty-two, became the targets of a vicious public campaign. A note addressed to town leaders threatened that Jews would be killed if they did not leave within eight days, "because they have become masters of commerce and finance and worse they bring ridicule to our religion and to the saints of the Church."[34]

A mob attacked Jews in their homes, fired rifle shots into some houses, then fled to the safety of the plains. Another hand-lettered note issued the warning: "Jews!!! The people tell you to go or die." Another threatening note was signed by "sons of the country," who described themselves as "comrades and patriots."[35]

Threats and attacks continued for several months. On October 13 a "Circular to the Jews" warned that "30 neighbors of this city and the countryside are meeting tonight to give you a final warning." Governor Rafael Hermoso appealed to other governors to assist him in providing support and protection for foreigners. Article 218 of the Constitution guaranteed the security of life and property to foreigners, but enforcement was required. "Underpopulated as the country is," warned Hermoso, immigration was vital. But shots rang out again in the Jewish neighborhood during the night of December 23. By February 1832, however, this round of hostilities had died down. Needless to say, such incidents did little to entice foreigners to settle on the llanos. Later attempts to promote immigration also failed. Opportunities in the United States, Argentina, southern Brazil, and Chile offered Europeans too great a comparative advantage.[36]

Immigration failure did not hurt coastal planters, who depended upon slave labor. After independence, coffee and cacao planters become even more important. During the 1830s, for example, cacao and coffee accounted for between 54 and 71 percent of total exports. In 1848–1849, the two crops represented 70 percent of all exports. During the remainder of the nineteenth century, coffee outdistanced cacao. Tobacco and cotton exports practically disappeared, and modern chemistry delivered the coup de grace to indigo dyes. Llaneros engaged in very little farming, other than to raise food crops for local consumption.[37]

"Civilization" Conquers "Barbarism"

The history of the nineteenth century in Latin America is the story of urban elite domination over the rural masses. Modernizing elites throughout the region tried to "civilize" their nations using induced social change (immigration), technology (fencing), and public policy (free trade). Future greatness, in elite eyes, depended on supplanting rustic, "barbarous" cowboy elements with European immigrants. The process as it took place in Argentina illustrates the changes that befell rural society in Latin America.[38]

From the 1820s on, elites ruling from the port city of Buenos Aires waged military and political war against the gaucho population. They passed a plethora of restrictive laws. Internal passports, working papers, military conscription, and vagrancy laws curtailed the movements of gauchos. Elite policy had two main goals: to make the gaucho fight in the frontier militia against another "barbarian" threat—Plains Indians—and to transform him into a docile, obedient ranch peon.[39]

Nineteenth-century administrations, including the long dictatorship of Juan Manuel de Rosas during the 1830s and 1840s, extended the efforts against the gaucho. Beginning with Buenos Aires province in 1865, officials formulated comprehensive rural codes that sounded the death knell for the gaucho way of life. These broad-ranging codes, backed with better-armed and more diligent police and military forces, virtually outlawed the gaucho life.[40]

No area of life went untouched. The ranching elite meant to expunge all relics of the gaucho's alleged barbarism. Some ranchers forced diet changes to save money and improve worker efficiency. The traditional fare of self-service beef and mate around an open fire gave way to cafeteria-style rations. Cecilio López, a landowner in Buenos Aires province, estimated that the changes cut his expenses by 40 percent. López also banned the drinking of mate—a move akin to denying coffee to Texas cowboys—on the grounds that it wasted too much time. New laws forbade the gaucho's traditional homemade boots, crafted from the leg skin of a horse. Ranchers charged that men stole and killed horses simply to make boots. In stripping the gaucho of his traditional dress, diet, and pursuits, the elite made his self-sufficient survival impossible.[41]

By the 1880s gauchos faced few viable options. Ostrich hunting, a means of livelihood and recreation, had been outlawed. Gauchos could labor as sedentary peons, under the thumb of a ranch overseer, who even forced them to perform hated footwork. One commentator painted an unhappy portrait of the transition from gaucho to docile ranch peon: "But the last gaucho has galloped across the far-away horizon of the pampas and into the twilight of history, and Argentina has lost its most characteristic and attractive citizen. His successor is a poor, miserable, underpaid peon who is called a *paisano* [countryman] but never a gaucho."[42]

Gauchos also faced military conscription under penurious conditions. Soldiers encountered harsh corporal punishments, meager and late pay, and few incentives to do anything other than desert. Many did; others avoided service altogether by riding to the remote frontier, beyond the pale of the law. These frontiersmen usually led an outlaw existence to survive. Some of the last groups of gauchos were bands of ostrich hunters and rustlers who killed cattle illegally in remote frontier areas. But by the late nineteenth century, the gaucho, for the most part, had passed from the realm of history into folklore. Similar changes befell his counterparts elsewhere.[43]

Sodbusters and Sheepherders

On the cattle frontier of the United States, cowboys faced swift, abrupt changes arising from a combination of natural and economic conditions. Farmers began pushing against the edges of the cattle kingdom within a few years after the Civil War. In the late 1870s Baylis John Fletcher complained of encroachment in Texas: "Civilization and cattle trailing were not congenial, and we had been greatly annoyed in the settled districts of Texas. Depending entirely on free grass for forage for our cattle and horses, we had constantly come in collision with the farmer, who wanted the grass for their domestic animals."[44]

Cattlemen and cowboys disliked farmers on principle. But a New Mexico rancher, Joe Pankey, summarized some practical objections to farming as well: "Dry farming didn't do the land here no good. Didn't have enough moisture. Farmers plowed up all the native grasses, then walked off and left it, and then the wind got to blowing on it, and kind of swept it off, and all kinds of noxious weeds grew back."[45]

English legal tradition gave the farmer the juridical upper hand. The farmer's westward migration during the latter half of the nineteenth century tipped demography, and hence voting power, in his favor. Barbed wire provided low-cost technology to separate the interests of cowman and agriculturist. The end of the open range was at hand, even before the disastrous winter of 1885–1886 sealed its doom.[46]

Conflict between sheepherders and cattlemen offered a sideshow to rancher-farmer discord. Spurred by equal parts of prejudice and belief in the destructiveness of grazing sheep, cowmen in the United States battled to keep sheep off the range. Race prejudice often entered in, with Anglo cowboys looking down on the predominantly Basque and Hispanic sheepherders. In 1900 the *Denver Republican* discussed (with clear partiality) the differences between cowboys and shepherds.

> The physical and mental differences between the cowboy and the sheep herder are as great as those of their respective callings. From the very nature of his occupation the cowboy is a wild, free being.
>
> He breaks the savage and almost untamable ponies to the saddle, and then rides them. His work is swift and vigorous, and his charges are the great, strong, free bulls and cows that have never known the touch of the human hand. He lives and endures hardships with others of his kind, and his pleasures are as fierce as his work. His is the strenuous life.
>
> The sheep herder, on the other hand, pursues his solitary occupation afoot, his only companion being a dog and the thousands of stupid sheep, which have no individuality, and are maddeningly, monotonously alike. The very loneliness of his occupation has made the herder either a morose and sullen brute or a poetic dreamer, with all the fight worn out of him.[47]

Range wars flared briefly in many parts of the West. Cattle ranchers sometimes resorted to violence to combat the threat of farmers and sheepmen. The famous conflict in 1892 in Johnson County, Wyoming, gained considerable notoriety, but it was not unique. In 1896 cowmen met at the tiny village of Paulina in central Oregon to organize the Crook County Sheep Shooters Association. They and other like-minded ranchers killed thousands of sheep. Some sheepherders also met violent deaths at the hands of cowmen. But like the farmer, the sheepman gradually found an accepted place in the West.[48]

Sheep did not prompt this type of conflict on the Argentine plains. Harmony was possible because the ranchers who already controlled landownership and cattle raising diversified into sheep raising. Cattlemen became sheepmen as well, some as early as the boom in wool prices in the 1850s. English-born ranchers played a leading role in the introduction of sheep to Argentina. By the 1870s most large ranchers devoted part of their lands to sheep. Refrigeration technology added chilled mutton and beef to the nation's list of profitable exports. By 1895 some fifty-three million sheep grazed the pampa in Buenos Aires province.[49]

The introduction of agriculture and sheep raising brought changes to range work everywhere. In the early 1880s many north plains ranchers in the United States still did not put up hay for the winter. Alexander Begg observed in 1882 that "it is the custom in the West not to put up hay or build shelter for stock in winter." A Miles City, Montana, newspaper gave the ranchers' rationale: "The animals quickly learn to 'rustle' through the snow to the sweet hay beneath." This faith in the cattle's ability to survive winters on the plains received a rude shock a few years later.[50]

A drought in Texas during the summer of 1885 was followed by a devastating winter across the southern plains. The following winter was terrible on both the northern and southern ranges. Perhaps 190,000 cattle perished in Montana, and another quarter of a million head in Wyoming, during the winter of 1886–1887. The summer of 1887 was very dry, and overstocking compounded the losses. Following these natural disasters, few ranchers stuck with traditional open-range grazing. Cowboys faced a new and unsavory chore—haying. By the 1890s hay rakes, mowing machines, windmills, and fence-mending and ditching tools took their places with the lariat, branding iron, and saddle. Cowboys still worked in the saddle, but more tasks on the new range required them to join the common folk on foot.[51]

The harsh weather of the mid-1880s delivered the coup de grace to open-range ranching. But changing settlement patterns in many areas, such as Kansas, had already impinged on the cattle frontier. The growing population of Kansas farmers had already lobbied successfully for restrictions on the Texas cattle trade and on open-range grazing before the disastrous winters hit. With the Anglo-American bias on behalf of agriculture, cattlemen were viewed as holding back civilization. Thus, culture, weather, demography, and unwise range practices all combined to eclipse the open-range cattle industry.[52]

Large corporate ranches imposed new work rules that suited the more efficient, rationalized organization of the modern ranch. For example, the large

XIT outfit in the Texas Panhandle issued twenty-three new rules in 1888. Such regulations further reduced the cowboy from free spirit to rural proletarian. Employees at the XIT could not "own any cattle or stock horses on the ranch." So much for starting one's own herd. "The abuse of horses, mules or cattle by any employee will not be tolerated. . . . Employees are not allowed to run mustang, antelope or any kind of game on the Company's horses." So much for hunting. The rules also forbade card playing and alcohol. So much for fun. Rule 20 conveyed management's opinion of western society: "Loafers, 'sweaters' [men who sweated as a result of their great efforts to avoid work], deadbeats, tramps, gamblers, or disreputable persons, must not be entertained at any camp, nor will employees be permitted to give, loan or sell such persons any grain, or provisions of any kind, nor shall such persons be permitted to remain on the Company's land anywhere under any pretext whatever."[53]

Canada's "Last Best West"

Change also came to the Alberta range. But competition between farmers and ranchers in Canada did not break into violence. Once again, the Canadian frontier proved less violent than its counterpart to the south. Disputes generally ended through the judicial process, not in gunplay. But many ranchmen found little to admire in the wave of agricultural immigrants that engulfed them. In 1910 Mounted Police Superintendent Richard Burton Deane received a complaint of horse theft. The victim, an immigrant Mormon farmer from the United States named Roueche, lost two animals to men who worked for him for a few days. The superintendent complained that farmers, "having been too careless and too indolent to take reasonable care of their horses," now showed that "they were too careless and too indolent to make a reasonable attempt to recover their property. The Western prairie is swarming with useless settlers of this calibre."[54]

Potentially violent rancher-farmer altercations did occur. Sam Livingston, a farmer, settled on land near Fish Creek, Alberta, in 1875. In 1885 hands from the large Cochrane Ranche began driving his livestock from lands claimed by the ranch. "For the present," responded Livingston, "I defend my claim as my neighbours do, behind my Winchester." Elected chairman of a farmers' group in April 1885, he proclaimed that farmers "must either fight for our rights or leave the country."[55]

Natural and political phenomena combined in the early years of the twentieth century to push farming onto the western Canadian ranges. The region experienced higher-than-average summer rainfall from 1900 through 1905. This fueled confidence in the potential of dryland farming and helped to erode belief in the desert qualities of Palliser's Triangle. The Liberal government of Canada promoted western settlement. Farmers, many of them emigrants from the United States, pushed confidently into the Canadian West. Most hopes became quickly dashed, however, as rainfall levels returned to normal. A harsh winter in 1906–1907 further dampened farmers' dreams for making it big in the "Last Best West."[56]

Buoyed by strong international markets, Alberta ranchers withstood the agricultural onslaught and expanded their herds. But the harsh winter struck livestock as hard as it did the farmers. In early December 1906 the temperature in Alberta fell to minus 25 to 30 degrees. By February the mercury fell to minus 40, and the bitter cold lasted through March. The diary of H. M. Hatfield recorded the effects of the winter on his ranch near Macleod. "This wind is warranted to bite anything living or dead," he wrote on December 30, 1906. "*Cold a terror*" (December 31). "This is the worst winter I have ever seen" (January 17, 1907). "I wonder if the blamed snow ever will melt" (March 18). "The winter lasted over *26 weeks*" (May 15). Some large ranches lost 80 percent of their herds, but small outfits suffered less.[57]

Despite the harsh winter, Alberta's spring roundup in 1907 was one of the province's biggest. Cowboys collected some 130,000 head. Alberta livestock fared reasonably well in cold weather, because most ranchers had been putting up hay since the 1880s. Fred Ings recalled cutting only enough hay for saddle horses in 1884; cattle rustled for themselves. But most ranchers made provision for heavy snows. Canadian cowboys worked on hay rigs well before it became common for hands in the United States.[58]

Wesley F. Orr, a Calgary rancher, wrote a letter on December 20, 1891, to John Stephenson in Denver. Orr reveals a cautious approach toward winter dangers. "We do occasionally have pretty cold weather but very seldom have much heavy wind when it is very cold so that cattle and horses do well on the ranges all the year. . . . All stock men put up some hay against a storm. Last winter the loss of stock was not over 4 percent."[59]

But the heyday of the cattleman and cowboy was drawing to a close in Alberta, as it had two decades earlier in the United States. In both cases, weather, agricultural immigration, and public policy combined to shake the livestock industry. Vast lands, once leased for grazing, were sold to farmers by the government and by the Canadian Pacific Railway. Dryland farming likewise went into decline. But irrigation technology later revived agriculture on the Canadian prairies. Still later, in the 1970s, oil gave rise to yet another Texas-style boom and bust in the region.[60]

Not all cowboys accepted the passing of the cattle frontier gracefully. A mock will, penned in 1919 by a Saskatchewan cowboy, reveals a bitterness against "sodbusters." The cowboy wished to "create a fund, to be ultimately used for the extermination of that class of vermin, commonly known as farmers." He added a clause three years later: "I leave to each and every *Mossback* my perpetual curse as some reward to them for their labors in destroying the *Open Range*, by means of that most pernicious of all implements, the plow."[61]

The cattle industry in Latin America passed through many phases. The region's cowboys started as wild-cattle hunters in the seventeenth century. The huaso, gaucho, llanero, and vaquero developed their horseback cultures over several centuries. But by the late nineteenth and early twentieth centuries, their accustomed way of life was yielding to pervasive, powerful forces. The rise and fall of cowboy life happened much more swiftly on the Anglo-American ranching frontiers. In the space of a few decades, open-range ranching came and went in Canada and the United States. Free-roaming cattle and cowboys gave way to fenced pastures, dotted with windmills and cattle guards. Yet although the traditional life of the cowboy largely disappeared, in both North and South America, popular mythical and literary images of cowboys took hold even before the real McCoy had ridden off into the sunset.

CHAPTER 12

The Cowboy Rides Again
Myth, Literature, Popular Culture

In some cases, mythical and symbolic attributes became associated with cowboys even before their actual decline during the nineteenth and early twentieth centuries. As the heyday of the historical cowboy passed, his fictional successor was born in literature, drama, and mythology. Film and television further popularized romantic images of the cowboy. In some countries, such as Argentina, Uruguay, and the United States, the cowboy took on national cultural significance.

Literary and symbolic evocations of cowboys often show strong transnational similarities. Cowboys are viewed as representing rugged individualism, unbending principle, frontier spirit, and manly courage. In the United States, politicians from Chester Arthur and Theodore Roosevelt to Henry Kissinger and Ronald Reagan have manipulated cowboy imagery. Roosevelt greatly enjoyed his years among cowboys in the Dakota Badlands: "I do not believe there ever was any life more attractive to a vigorous young fellow than life on a cattle ranch in those days," he wrote. "It was a fine, healthy life, too; it taught a man self-reliance, hardihood, and the value of instant decision."[1]

Cowboy mythology developed in stages from the 1880s on. Much credit for popularizing the cowboy must go to Buffalo Bill Cody's Wild West Show. Cody and his star Buck Taylor, "King of the Cowboys," brought the romanticized, shoot-'em-up horseman to America and Europe. The cowboy shed the image of an uncouth rowdy and became a national hero. The penny press and dime novels, such as Prentiss Ingraham's 1887 potboiler about Buck Taylor, made exciting cowboy stories available to a mass audience. Cowboy literature extolled the virtues of courage, honor, chivalry, individualism, and the triumph of right over wrong. Wild West shows, circuses, films, more pulp novels, radio, and finally television perpetuated cowboy mythology.[2]

The historical cowboy has a strong regional identification with the West, but as a representative of traditional American values, he has become a truly national figure. All Americans have some knowledge of the cowboy hero. Film, fiction, advertising, toys, television, rodeo, and other cultural media perpetuate images and values attributed to the cowboy. Although the level of interest in (and hence marketability of) such images is somewhat cyclical, cowboy culture is a constant factor in American life. Many Americans still believe in the efficacy of what they define as the frontier experience. They yearn for the simpler days when the good guys always defeated the bad. Cowboy films and cowboy politics appeal to this desire for a clear, uncomplicated, black-and-white world. The cowboy has supplanted the sturdy yeoman farmer as the foremost symbol of the nation's mythical past.[3]

During the 1980s the nation experienced an upsurge of interest in the cowboy. Part of the impetus stemmed from the influence of President Reagan, whose verbal imagery and ideology resounded with cowboy cliches. His favorite author was Louis L'Amour. Reagan's first major film role was in the 1940 Western *Santa Fe Trail*, with Errol Flynn. Reagan badly wanted to star in big-budget Westerns after Word War II, but the studios offered him only B movies and other light fare. Four of the ten films he made during the 1950s were Westerns. In 1953 he played a thinly disguised Wyatt Earp in a B Western called, appropriately enough, *Law and Order*. Movie posters announced that "his guns were the only law."[4] Reagan's politics, like those of John Wayne, became intertwined with the mythical world created in B Western movies.

A set of mythical and cinematic qualities attributed to the cowboy looms large in the American psyche. President Reagan skillfully played on the popularity of these qualities and on the public's desire for simple answers to frustrating national and world problems. Reagan looked and acted like a cowboy hero, given to straight talk and seemingly decisive action. He enjoyed strong support across the nation, but particularly in the western states. Michael Rogin, in his fascinating portrait of the right wing in America, refers to Reagan as "the movie cowboy." But Rogin fails to develop the importance of cowboy metaphors in Reagan the politician. Much more revealing are the links made by Michael E. Welsh, who writes that "not since Theodore Roosevelt had a chief executive of the United States attached himself so closely to the myths of the American West."[5]

Other public figures have been important in perpetuating the mythical cowboy. John Wayne embodied the nation's concept of the cowboy hero more than any other single person. The "Duke" never backed down; he talked straight, shot straight, righted wrongs, punished the guilty. Unwavering in his belief in the rightness of his cause, he saw life with a clarity that many Americans admire. "They tell me everything isn't black and white," said Wayne. "Well, I say why the hell not?"[6]

Wayne's own heroes further illustrate the power of the cowboy myth. He admired the swashbuckling bravado of Douglas Fairbanks, Sr., and copied Jack Dempsey's fighting style in developing his own barroom brawl technique for the camera. But Wayne also named Harry Carey and Hoot Gibson, earlier celluloid cowboys, among his heroes: myth begets myth. Again, as in his analysis of Reagan, Michael Rogin fails to identify the significance of cowboy metaphor in Wayne's political beliefs. The Duke's personal and film lives projected a simplistic mix of prejudice and suspicion that were all too typical of the rustic frontier.[7]

Wayne's films often showed that one man, acting righteously, could insure that right triumphed over wrong. His politics became intertwined with his art, and the public—at least the politically conservative public—responded warmly. His 1968 film *The Green Berets* met a well-deserved barrage of criticism, but audiences still packed in to see the Duke fighting the Commies. Wayne depicted the complexities of Southeast Asia in terms that most Americans preferred—good cowboys fighting off the bad Indians. He was not alone in recasting Vietnam into simple, familiar frontier metaphors; policymakers did the same thing.[8]

A similar update of a militaristic cowboy in khakis is embodied in more recent film characters, such as Rambo. Typically, these films feature Lone Ranger figures who take on the "Indians," usually in Southeast Asia. Unlike the outcome of the real Vietnam War, right wins over wrong. This same simplicity of vision, coupled with violence and "super-machismo," is common in popular men's magazines, such as *True, Argosy*, and *Stag*.[9]

Cultural myths often change over time. The images fostered by Frederick Jackson Turner's frontier thesis have branched off in many directions. For example, George Armstrong Custer traditionally represented a courageous tragic hero who sacrificed his life to bring civilization to the American West. But in the aftermath of Vietnam, and with the raised consciousness caused by the New American Indian Movement, Custer has come instead to represent the arrogance and brutality of white exploitation. Custer's "Last Stand" has a different meaning for us than it had for previous generations. However, the cowboy has retained a broad popular appeal regardless of this changing political and cultural context. Even the political and economic disasters that the United States has suffered while under the spell of simple-minded political "cowboyism" have done little to erode the popularity of cowboy mythology or related conservative ideologies. Many Americans retain a taste for a B Western worldview in their movies, reading, and politics.[10]

Not only is cowboy imagery popular, it is pervasive. The cowboy supplanted the hillbilly as the dominant country music persona during the 1930s. Today we speak of country-*and-western* music, a hybrid genre represented by the western swing of Bob Wills, the honky-tonk of Ernest Tubb, and more recently the outlaw music of Willie Nelson, Waylon Jennings, and others centering around Austin, Texas. Cowboy life remains a popular theme in country-and-western songs. Nelson warns, "Mammas, don't let your babies grow up to be cowboys." The lyrics of "My Heroes Have Always Been Cowboys" strike a resonant chord. Tammy Wynette complains humorously that "Cowboys don't shoot straight (like they used to)."[11]

Crossover artists, such as Michael Martin Murphey, produce an interesting mix of old and modern western images. Like many original cowboy songs, Murphey's compositions betray a nostalgia for times past. His "Texas Morning," "Another Cheap Western," and "Geronimo's Cadillac" evoke images of western myth and history. "Cosmic Cowboy" (1973, popularized by the Nitty Gritty Dirt Band) offers the following thoughts:

> But ridin' the range and lookin' strange
> Is where I want to be.
>
> I just wanna be a Cosmic Cowboy.
> I just wanna ride and rope and hoot.
> I just wanna be a Cosmic Cowboy.
> A supernatural country rockin' galoot.
>
> Lone Star sippin' and skinny dippin'
> and steel guitars and stars
> Are just as good as Hollywood
> and them bullshit disco bars.
> I'm gonna buy me a vest and head out west
> my lady and myself.
> When we come to town they're gonna gather 'round
> and just marvel at our health.[12]

But the cowboy rides far beyond the country-and-western range. Many pop artists have recorded songs about cowboys, including Sonny and Cher ("A Cowboy's Work Is Never Done"), John Denver ("Cowboy's Delight" and "The Cowboy and the Lady"), Elton John ("Brown Dirt Cowboy"), Jimmy Buffett ("Cowboy in the Jungle"), and Carly Simon ("Cowtown").

Another popular medium, advertising, uses the cowboy to hype a wide range of products. In the 1930s film cowboys including Tom Mix, Roy Rogers,

Hopalong Cassidy, and the Lone Ranger huckstered breakfast cereals to children. In the 1950s the "Marlboro Man" showed that the cowboy image also appealed to adult males. Similar male-oriented advertisements tie cowboy macho to the use of products such as beer, boots, jeans, cigarettes, chewing tobacco, and pickup trucks.[13]

The cowboy is even being used by the microcomputer industry. Ads by two companies, Compaq and Dell, feature illustrations of cowboy dress and equipment. Dell uses old western prints, one of a train robbery and another of cowboys sitting by a chuck wagon, to emphasize the Americanness of its products. The caption in its ads reads: "You can't get good chili in Taiwan." An ad for Northern Telecom, a communications firm, displays a computer keyboard sticking out of a Pony Express rider's saddle; the caption reads: "The data must go through."[14]

In the military arena, we often find imagery of the Old West. During the Vietnam War, the names of air and ground operations frequently had a frontier flavor—"Prairie," "Sam Houston," "Crazy Horse." The area outside of secured fortresses was known as "Indian Country." John Wayne's famous (unintentional) caricature of the war in *The Green Berets* reduced the conflict to a B Western morality play, but soldiers themselves conceptualized the war in terms of cowboys and Indians.[15]

The Central Intelligence Agency uses the term *cowboy* to refer to paramilitary operatives who destroy enemy targets and commit assassinations if necessary. Ray Cline, past CIA deputy director for intelligence, explained the role of cowboys in 1975: "The Russians had cowboys around everywhere, and that meant we had to get ourselves a lot of cowboys if we wanted to play the game. You've got to have cowboys—the only thing is, you don't let them make policy. You keep them in the ranch house when you don't have a specific project for them."[16]

In short, the cowboy is one of the most potent shorthand cultural symbols in America. The real old-time cowboy is only dimly visible in the new sanitized, politicized, symbolic cowboy. Gene Autry's cowboy commandments well sum up the characteristics of the mythical cowboy in American popular culture: The good cowboy never takes unfair advantage, keeps his word, tells the truth, is gentle with children, the elderly, and animals, is tolerant, helps those in distress, works hard, respects women, his parents, and the law, does not drink or smoke, and is patriotic.[17]

Interestingly, some of today's working cowboys object to the romanticized, commercialized distortions of the cowboy image. Cowhands are reviving traditional skills, such as making tack, and Glen Ohrlin, Slim Critchlow, Van

Holyoak, and a few other singers have kept traditional cowboy music alive. Riders in the Sky, a Nashville group, performs songs in the tradition of the Sons of the Pioneers—"Cowboy Song," "Cowboy Jubilee," and "Cowboy's ABC."[18]

Other westerners continue to compose cowboy verse, the basis for most traditional cowboy songs. Forty or more poets meet annually at Elko, Nevada, for the Cowboy Poetry Gathering. In addition to poetry readings, participants view Western movies, photographs, and handcrafted gear, listen to music, and square dance. The January 1988 meeting included a couple of special events: the premiere of Kim Shelton's film *Cowboy Poets* and the opening of an exhibition on the Hawaiian cowboy at the Northeastern Nevada Museum.[19]

Wallace McRae, Waddie Mitchell, Slim Kite, Everett Brisendine, Ken Trowbridge, Baxter Black, Ernie Fanning, Nyle Henderson, and Melvin Wipple are among today's cowboy poets. Most have experience as cowboys or ranchers. Henderson also breaks horses. Their poems mix nostalgia, humor, and serious concerns about contemporary western problems, such as environmental pollution. Of old-time cowboys, Brisendine writes:

> So tip your hats to these old boys
> If they come ridin' by your way
> They never really die, you know
> They just all smell that way.

Wipple conveys the nostalgia common to many of the cowboy poets:

> Those days are gone forever
> Only one place they're still at
> Is in some old man's memories
> Underneath a greasy hat.[20]

The Rehabilitated Gaucho

The gaucho is more important to Argentina than the cowboy figure is in any other country. A few die-hard gauchos persisted with frontier ostrich hunts, rustling, and banditry after traditional gaucho life had largely disappeared from the pampa. But rail and telegraph lines, wheat- and cornfields, barbed wire fences, and millions of European immigrants changed the plains forever. The individualistic, nomadic gauchos gave way to sedentary, obedient peons who worked on the modern ranches of the pampa, often under immigrant overseers.

By the early twentieth century, however, a new threat faced the Argentine elite. Widespread social and labor unrest, fomented by urban immigrants, rocked the country and challenged their rule. Nationalistic, and sometimes authoritarian, writers responded to this threat by looking for a new political weapon. A romanticized portrait of the gaucho emerged as a counterpoint to immigrant-led demands for socialism, electoral reform, and worker rights.[21]

An essay in a volume of a 1908 census declares the gaucho to be the "native spirit of the Argentine genius." The gaucho is lauded for his "instinct of independence and individuality engendered by the free air of a rural life, and which is the antithesis of the dependent spirit symbolized in city life by socialism."[22]

The elite resurrected and rehabilitated the gaucho as the epitome of Argentine national virtue. Maligned as a barbarian and outlaw a few decades earlier, the new gaucho took on the virtues of obedience, patriotism, honesty, and trustworthiness—attributes rarely attached to him before. The ruling elite manipulated the gaucho as a symbolic weapon against a new and more dangerous foe, the urban immigrant masses.[23]

For many Argentines, the gaucho likewise came to represent the best elements of their national character. Writers, thinkers, and politicians used the gaucho to symbolize *argentinidad*, the essential virtues of Argentine national character. Many intellectuals glorified the gaucho, especially during the era of mass European immigration during the early twentieth century. In his influential book *El payador*, Leopoldo Lugones heralded the gaucho as "the hero and civilizer of the pampa, the prototype of the present-day Argentine." Ricardo Rojas concurred. "We believe, therefore, that what is collectively Argentine and genuinely 'ours' is found in the gaucho as the human prototype of our nationality, and in his struggle against the American desert is the schema of our evolution."[24]

Neighboring Uruguay brought about a similar transformation and rehabilitation of the gaucho. A 1904 school text depicted the gaucho as a free spirit and vassal to no one. True, he led a semisavage life, but he fought valiantly against the Spanish during the independence wars. Debates among Uruguayan, Argentine, and Brazilian writers continued over gaucho character and history. But many intellectuals increasingly identified him as the archetype of Uruguayan national virtue. In 1927 Uruguay constructed a national monument honoring the gaucho.[25]

Thus, myth supersedes history. The gaucho becomes a nationally recognized symbol in Argentina and Uruguay. Residents of modern Buenos Aires, with its chic European shops on Calle Florida, identify with elements of gaucho mythology. As an Argentine intellectual observed, "History is at times falsified or its real meaning is altered under the pretext of strengthening the national spirit."[26]

Proponents of diverse political positions call upon the gaucho as a unifying national symbol. Juan Domingo Perón skillfully manipulated symbols of traditionalism, including the gaucho, to unite disparate factions of his political movement. The neofascist military regime that dominated Argentina from 1976 to 1983 chose a little gaucho with a soccer ball to symbolize the nation during the 1978 World Cup soccer championship.[27]

Faced with nativist attacks, some immigrants also turned to the gaucho as a means of proving their patriotism. Traditionalist groups proliferated, perpetuating gaucho folklore, music, and customs. Immigrants who had never sat a horse often outnumbered native Argentines at such gatherings. By 1914 some two hundred clubs existed in Argentina to honor the memory of the gaucho. Italian immigrants made up the membership of many of the more than fifty groups in Buenos Aires. The clubs sported names evocative of the old days of the wild pampa: "Orphans of the Plain," "Gauchos and Indians," "Pampa Tiger and His Men."[28]

Faced with virulent and sometimes violent xenophobia, immigrants sought to prove their patriotism. Once again, the gaucho served as a convenient symbol for national virtues. Alberto Gerchunoff published *Los gauchos judíos* (The Jewish gauchos) in 1910 to combat intense Argentine anti-Semitism. More recently, Juan Goyechea wrote *Los gauchos vascos* (The Basque gauchos) to reinforce the Basque claim to patriotism.[29]

In addition to political manipulation of the gaucho symbol, many other forces contributed to his growing popularity in the twentieth century. Like other urbanizing, industrializing societies, Argentina faced increasingly complex problems, and many Argentines became wistful for "the good old days." The gaucho, like the American cowboy, became the nostalgic reminder of a better, simpler life in the past. Today, elements of gaucho influence remain evident from cosmopolitan Buenos Aires to the smallest country town. Tourist shops on Calle Florida in Buenos Aires feature gaucho paraphernalia of all types. At the fashionable Estancia restaurant, diners partake of asado, beef cooked in time-honored gaucho fashion on spits leaning over a bed of hot coals.

From business executives to day laborers, Argentines (and Uruguayans) sip hot mate throughout the day. Argentines ask one another to perform a *gauchada*, meaning a favor. People who have never ridden a horse can quote from memory stanza after stanza of *Martín Fierro*, the epic poem of gaucho life by José Hernández.

Regional Symbols

Not all cowboy types achieved the status of national figures; some remain identified with particular regions of the country. This is the case in Brazil, where the vaqueiro is associated with the northeastern sertão (dry plains) and the gaúcho with the southern state of Rio Grande do Sul. Neither cowboy type has played a national role in Brazilian culture. In fact, the mythology surrounding the bandeirantes, slave hunters of colonial São Paulo, looms much larger. Some Brazilians have sought to transform the slave hunter into a national paradigm of democratic frontier spirit and enterprise. Again, myth and nationalism override historical reality.[30]

Mexico's vaquero remains identified with the great north Mexican haciendas and with Spanish California. When Mexico did honor a horseman, it was the elitist charro: a monument to the charro was constructed in 1926. Chileans, by and large, have not taken the huaso to symbolize their national identity. The geographical diversity and shape of Chile, the importance of European immigration, and the dominance of Santiago have militated against a national consensus on identity. Similarly, Canadians of Montreal and Quebec have no cultural identification with the cowboy. He is associated principally with Alberta and, to a lesser extent, other western provinces.[31]

In Venezuela and Colombia, the llanero is associated with the interior tropical plains. Some writers, however, have tried to propel the llanero to national significance as a symbol of independence and valor. As early as the 1860s José María Samper looked to the llanero as a national archetype for Colombia. Manuel Tejera presented similar images of the Venezuelan llanero during the 1870s. The llanero came to epitomize fervent patriotism as a result of his role in the victories over the Spanish, such as the battles at Boyacá in 1819 and at Carabobo in 1821.[32]

Myth making accompanied these efforts to make the llanero a national symbol. In a nationalistic essay written in 1861, the Colombian Samper conveniently forgot to mention that llaneros had upheld Spanish "oppression" by fighting for José Tomás Boves. Llaneros had also served many dictatorial cau-dillos after independence. Samper wrote that "the llanero has never served the cause of oppression nor of any dictatorship. When liberty is in danger, he responds enthusiastically to the first call." He lauded "the shepherd of the immense free herds, rider, bullfighter, celebrated swimmer, fabulous cavalry soldier, poet of the pampas and of savage passions. A gallant artist in his way, the llanero is the union between civilization and barbarism, between society with all its more or less artificial conventions and the imposing solitude of the deserts, where only nature rules with her immortal grandeur and solemn majesty."[33]

As in the United States and Argentina, political conservatives in Venezuela have most often used the cowboy figure for partisan purposes. Laureano Vallenilla Lanz, an apologist for the dictatorship of Juan Vicente Gómez (1908–1935), described the llanero as an important ingredient in Venezuelan national identity. He wrote that "in Venezuela even those of us born in the mountains and the coasts have something of the llanero." He found many national virtues—and flaws—epitomized by the llanero: "The consciousness of personal bravery, pride, egalitarian spirit, gentlemanly hospitality, loyalty as the basis of political morality, the tendency toward rash adventures, and at the same time the organic incapacity to constitute stable governments."[34]

Despite such efforts, the llanero has remained a decidedly regional figure for Venezuela, an outsider in the national consciousness. The tropical plain was an economic backwater, especially when compared to the booming oil province of Zulia and rapidly growing Caracas. Some elements of llanero folk-lore, especially dances and music, appeal to Venezuelans outside of the plains. But few Venezuelans take the llanero as their symbol of national virtue.

Nor has the Chilean huaso attained the cultural significance of the gaucho in Argentina or of the cowboy in the United States. As René Echaiz observed, "It cannot be said that [the huaso] has been or is the complete symbol of Chilean nationality, which includes, in addition to him, worse and better things." Nonetheless, the huaso is among the symbolic figures to which Chil-eans turn in their quest for national identity.[35]

Guillermo Feliú Cruz, for example, argues that the landed elite inculcated in their workers—including the huaso—an intense love of the land and of the nation. Performances of creole music and of the *cueca*, a folk dance identified with the huaso, remain popular. As in Argentina, the Chilean upper class promotes an image of the huaso as obedient, hard-working, patriotic, and loyal. This role model is presented to the Chilean working class in hopes of discouraging them from pressing for labor and social reform.[36]

The Alberta cowboy does not represent Canadian national character to most Canadians. In fact, many Canadians, particularly in the East, resist analogies between the wild and woolly West of the United States and Canada's past. Canadians do not wish their history and culture to be viewed as derivatives of the United States. Even less do they wish for erroneous Hollywood-style cliches to be applied to Canada.[37]

If eastern Canadians reject the cowboy as their archetype, western Canadians also distinguish their cattle culture from that of the United States. Cattle, horses, and cowboys did play an important role in the development of Alberta's livestock industry. American influence was strongest in the "short-grass country," stretching from Macleod east to the Cypress Hills. The American cowboy did bring his knowledge of working cattle and horses (largely derived from the Mexican vaquero) to Canada.[38]

But the western foothills and the area surrounding Calgary exhibited a more decidedly British flavor. Law and order, enforced by the Mounted Police, gave the Canadian frontier a less reckless character than America's Wild West. The strong cultural ties to Great Britain and the corporate nature of ranching also shaped rural society in Alberta. In Calgary and surrounding areas, many people take pride in their cowboy culture, but it is viewed as Canadian, not an import from the United States.[39]

Explaining the Cowboy's Significance

One of the forces that shapes the cowboy's relative cultural significance is the political economy of the nation. If the livestock industry is a leading force in the economy and in policy-making, then the cowboy figure of that country will have enhanced status. If the livestock region is politically and economically marginal at the national level, the cowboy figure will achieve lesser significance.

The landed elite of Buenos Aires province achieved hegemonic control over national politics during the latter half of the nineteenth century. Under Julio A. Roca's leadership, economic elites of the interior provinces were also incorporated. The fact that ranchers controlled the national political machinery made ranching culturally and historically important. As a result, despite the objections of urban sophisticates, the gaucho rose to national importance.

At the other extreme are the cases of Colombia, Venezuela, Brazil, and Canada. Livestock regions in these countries were economically and politically marginal. The livestock economies of the llanos and of the Brazilian campanha (Rio Grande do Sul) failed to adapt to changing world demand for high-grade chilled beef.

The Brazilian northeastern sertão, long the haunt of the vaqueiro, suffered repeated droughts and went into decline in the eighteenth century. The northeastern backlands has remained an economically troubled region ever since. It continues to suffer from the vagaries of the weather, and it experiences continued out-migration as Brazilians flock to the more prosperous cities of the south.

As traditional markets for hides and jerked beef declined in the late nineteenth century, ranchers in southern Brazil and the llanos found their fortunes on the wane. They, as well as Chilean ranchers, did not upgrade beef production and remain competitive in the international chilled beef trade.

In Alberta, the cattle boom was short-lived and always threatened by heady competition on the international market. Protectionism in the United States and a weak internal market also hurt Alberta ranchers. Far from the eastern metropolitan seats of Canadian political power, Alberta ranchers lacked the national political hegemony enjoyed by the Argentine landed elite. The Argentines obtained favorable tariff and land policies, whereas high tariffs hurt the Alberta ranching industry. The western prairies lacked demographic and therefore political clout. In 1911 only 18.4 percent of Canadians lived in the prairies. The rancher lost in policy battles against eastern cities and against farmers. Legislation in favor of farming in the early twentieth century helped precipitate the decline of ranching in Alberta.[40]

In contrast to marginal ranching sectors, robust, expanding agricultural production dominated national policy-making in Brazil, Colombia, and Venezuela. The cacao planters ran Venezuela; coffee planters ran Brazil and Colombia. With indifferent or even destructive national policies, ranchers could do little to improve their economic fortunes. To be sure, both regions included a strong strain of cultural traditionalism and resistance to change. But hostile taxation and export and import policies also weighed heavily on the llanos of Colombia and Venezuela and on the campanha of Rio Grande do Sul.

The political economy argument breaks down for the United States, however. The livestock economy enjoyed a very short boom during the decades after the Civil War. But in national terms, cereals agriculture and the burgeoning industrial base of the Northeast were far more important. The cowboy rose to prominence in the United States because of cultural factors, not the political economy.[41]

White Cowboy Mythology

In his transition from a historical to a cultural and literary figure, the cowboy changed dramatically. One of the prevalent myths in many countries is that all cowboys were white. The surge in black historiography since the 1960s has shown that much black history has been stolen, lost, or forgotten. Black and Hispanic cowboys remained invisible men until quite recently. In the early twentieth century, just as the mythical West was taking shape, many Americans felt intense concern over the future of "the Anglo-Saxon race." Massive immigration from southern and central Europe touched off a resurgent racism that also struck blacks and Hispanics already in the United States.[42]

Racial sentiments pervaded the Old West, and the imagery of a mythical white West became stronger as the twentieth century unfolded. The West retained earlier Anglo prejudices against Amerindians. Recalling his cowboy days of the 1880s, Jim Redfern related the virtues of old-time Anglo punchers. Redfern, like many Anglos of his day, held discriminatory attitudes toward nonwhites. Cowboys, he said "would risk their lives to help a fellow of their sort in need. They would give their last dollar to help a needy man or woman. Their word was gilt-edged; they prided themselves on their reputation of having never defaulted in word or deed when promised. They were all American boys—no mixed blood—all sons of the range, either by birth or adoption, and they were the true American type of cowboy."[43]

Like blacks, Hispanics found little place in western mythology, except as villains at the Alamo. Folk sources record the deeds of a few exceptional nonwhite cowboys, but only one Mexican is honored at the National Cowboy Hall of Fame in Oklahoma City. Ramón Ahumada, born in Sonora in 1868, worked as a ranch foreman for some forty years in Arizona. An expert rider and roper, knowledgeable about brands, and a good tracker, Ahumada impressed his fellow cowmen greatly. But it is the Anglo cowboy whose exploits are most storied and most celebrated.[44]

Another reason for the absence of blacks and Hispanics in cowboy mythology is that winners write history. And mythology grows out of history. Western history in general has been depicted as the victory of Anglo civilization over Indian barbarism. Texas history reflects a bias based on the victory of Anglo immigrants over Mexicans. Anglo-Texans applied terms like "half-breed," "nigger," "redskin," and "greaser" to Hispanics and nonwhites. Anglo-Texan mythology has built up Anglo contributions and often ignored or denigrated pre-existing Hispanic foundations: productive, hard-working Anglo-Saxons supplanted the inferior, indolent "greaser."[45]

Anglos in California also applied negative racial stereotypes to the Hispanic population. But racial mythology in California takes yet another twist. Self-proclaimed californios celebrate their pure Spanish heritage, ignoring the reality that the vast majority of the population of Spanish California was mestizo and Indian. Indians at the many missions were California's first vaqueros. But in California mythology, pure-white Hispanics, later joined by Anglos, forged the greatness of the state.[46]

Argentines have also fostered the myth of a white, pure-Spanish gaucho. Argentines have carefully nurtured a national image predicated on the absence of blacks and the relatively small number of mestizos (particularly in Buenos Aires). John W. White repeated the racial mythology in his dreadful book *Argentina: The Life Story of a Nation* (1942). According to White, the Indian blood of the gaucho was bleached out after a few generations. When lecturing in Argentina in 1983, I was asked, somewhat indignantly, why the dust jacket of my book on the gaucho depicted him as an Indian. Argentines wish to think of themselves and of the gaucho who symbolizes the nation as white. This places them with "superior" Europeans and sets them apart from the black and Indian populations of other Latin American countries.[47]

The Cowboy as a Literary Figure

One might assume that status as a politically significant national figure would insure the cowboy a position in "high" culture. This is not the case. As a literary figure, the cowboy's fortunes have risen or fallen quite independently of his perceived status as a national symbol. Despite the cowboy's cultural significance in the United States, "cowboy" novels and art have decidedly second-class status in the nation's cultural hierarchy. In contrast, gaucho poetry and novels have come to be viewed as the national literature of Argentina.

Without question, American cowboy literature can be faulted for its low birth. The penny press and dime novels of the late nineteenth century had few literary pretensions. Like other products of America's expanding industrial base, they were aimed at an undiscriminating mass market. Purveyors of yellow journalism worried more about increasing circulation than about raising the nation's literary standards. Writers of pulp Westerns, from Ned Buntline to Zane Grey and Max Brand, found a vast and receptive audience.

In their hands, the pulp cowboy lost the negative trappings of an outlaw and renegade and became much more the strong, virtuous hero.[48]

The market for cowboy heroes proved to be international. In 1887 Buffalo Bill Cody packed up his two hundred actors and three hundred head of livestock and sailed to England, where his Wild West Show performed for Queen Victoria's Golden Jubilee. The troupe returned for a four-year tour of the Continent in 1889.[49]

The cowboy became a staple of popular British boys' novels. These potboilers seldom depicted cowboys in negative terms; rather, the cowboy served as a paragon of chivalry. In the hands of British pulp writers, he brought law and order to the American Old West. The British concern for virtue, honesty, and decorous behavior were well represented in this version of the cowboy hero.[50]

Owen Wister's novel *The Virginian* (1902) earned the grudging praise of literary critics. While he lacked verisimilitude as a real cowboy, the Virginian had the makings of an American hero. Wister brought together elements of eastern civility and western roughness and virility that appealed to turn-of-the-century America. According to one literary critic, the Virginian represented "that last pioneer nobleman, roaming a frontier beyond the dominion of a mother culture in the East, representing both its rebellious runaway sons and its most poignant dream of manhood and freedom." With its larger-than-life hero, love story, western landscape (albeit without cows), and occasional violence, *The Virginian* skillfully combined essential elements of the formula Western. Unfortunately, later writers replicated Wister's formula but not his literary skill.[51]

Despite general acclaim, not everyone approved of Wister's novel. Many fanciers of Western literature have complained that it contains very little of the real cowboy, cows, or cowboy life. What Don D. Walker has called the "cow school" of literary criticism is more concerned with authenticity than with artistic merit per se. But those who sought writings about the real cowboy did not have to wait much longer: Andy Adams obliged them in 1903 with *The Log of the Cowboy*.[52]

Since many Anglo cowboys could read and write, firsthand accounts and reminiscences of American cowboys joined the Western literary stream in the United States. (Regrettably, no similar literature, except for folk poems and music, emanated from Latin American cowboys, who were almost always illiterate.) These firsthand accounts add to our understanding of cowboy culture. They have also proved to be popular reading. *The Log of the Cowboy* drew praise when it first appeared. Like others working in the genre, Adams exercised considerable literary license, but his writing had a ring of truth and authenticity that appealed to those who demanded realism in their cowboy literature.[53]

Among the notable cowboy memoirs and autobiographies that preceded Adams's are *A Texas Cow Boy* (1886) by Charlie A. Siringo, *Cow-boy Life in Texas* (1893) by Will James, and *The Story of the Cowboy* (1897) by Emerson Hough. The genre continued well into the twentieth century. More history than reminiscence, *The Cowboy* (1922) by Philip Ashton Rollins stands above most such works in its accuracy. Hough published *North of '36* in 1936, and Teddy Blue Abbott added *We Pointed Them North* three years later. In general, however, these writings are admired more as blends of realism, wit, and folklore than as works of real literary stature.

The market for popular cowboy writing seemed insatiable. Frederick Faust, using the pen name Max Brand, earned the title of "King of the Pulps." In twenty years of writing, he produced 179 books containing an estimated 25 million words. Zane Grey wrote some 85 books. Odd hybrid genres emerged, such as the "ranch romances." Perhaps aimed at drawing women readers into the cowboy market, these books were a "combination of the ever-entertaining Western yarn and the age-old love story." Needless to say, these fanciful tales closely resembled those set in drafty Gothic houses, plunging to new lows in both artistry and authenticity.[54]

Pulp cowboy novels and magazines, forerunners of later comic books, retained a large, mostly male following. *Dime Western, Western Story Magazine, Wild West Weekly*—some two hundred different titles in all—delivered action and adventure for a few cents. The likes of Deadwood Dick, who first rode in 1884 in Beadle's Pocket Library, continued to captivate boys and men who wanted to be boys again. The magazines disappeared, along with B Western movies, in the 1950s, both victims of television's growing appeal. But Louis L'Amour and a few others maintain the pulp tradition—still vigorous after more than a century.[55]

Interspersed with the pulps, however, serious Western novels have appeared. Several writers have treated the cowboy with great artistic skill, among them Eugene Manlove Rhodes, who died in 1934. His better-known works—*West Is West, Once in the Saddle, Good Men and True,* and *Pasó Por Aquí*—are noteworthy in Western fiction. Jack Schaefer's *Shane* (1949) also stands out, although the film version is far more famous than the book.[56]

Works such as Edward Abbey's *Brave Cowboy* (1956), Jack Schaefer's *Monte Walsh* (1963), and Larry McMurtry's *Lonesome Dove* (1985) have been well received. But even the appearance of these skilled latter-day Western writers has done little to raise the esteem accorded cowboy literature. Don D. Walker complains about "the persistence of a sad statistical fact about cowboy novels: out of every hundred written perhaps only one has literary sophistication." McMurtry poked self-deprecating fun at the low status of his own art. During the 1960s he reputedly wore a T-shirt on which was printed "Minor Regional Novelist." Like military music, American cowboy fiction seems destined to second-class citizenship.[57]

Latin America's Literary Cowboys

In contrast to American cowboy literature, *gauchesco* literature has achieved national recognition and appreciation in Argentina. Poems, plays, and novels in this genre focus on the gaucho and sometimes are written in gaucho dialect. *Juan Moreira*, a novel by Eduardo Gutiérrez, appeared in 1879. Based on the life of a famous gaucho outlaw, it is the first significant gaucho novel, although Domingo Sarmiento had treated the gaucho at length in 1845 in *Facundo*, his rambling polemic against the Rosas dictatorship.[58]

Many quaint, romanticized tales of gaucho life, not unlike the pulps dealing with the American cowboy, also appeared in Argentina. But Leopoldo Lugones, Ricardo Rojas, Manuel Gálvez, Benito Lynch, Ezequiel Martínez Estrada, and other leading writers have treated and lauded gaucho themes. In works of fiction, criticism, and social analysis, Argentine writers have turned again and again to the gaucho.[59]

In neighboring Uruguay, a number of outstanding authors have written in the gauchesco genre. A strong, independent gaucho figure appears in novels by Eduardo Acevedo Díaz (*Nativa*, *Grito de gloria*, *Ismael*, and *Soledad*). In the naturalistic works of Javier de Viana, the gaucho has lost his freedom and is reduced to peonage. Among de Viana's many novels are *Facundo imperial*, *Campo*, *Guri*, and *Gaucha*. Carlos Reyles, Justino Zavala Muñiz, and others have contributed to Uruguay's vast fictional literature of gaucho life.[60]

The most important literary work on the gaucho is *Martín Fierro*, a two-part epic poem published by the Argentine poet and politician José Hernández in 1872 and 1879. Hernández recorded the injustices and persecution visited upon the gaucho by unscrupulous officials. He attracted censure from elite critics for writing in gaucho dialect, but the burst of Argentine nationalism in the first decades of the twentieth century brought critical acclaim to *Martín Fierro*. Jorge Luis Borges, the quintessential cosmopolitan, used to enthrall audiences by quoting stanzas of the poem from memory. *Martín Fierro* has become the national poem of Argentina.[61]

Another high-water mark in gaucho literature came in 1926, when Ricardo Güiraldes published his classic novel *Don Segundo Sombra*. This touching tale of a boy learning the ways of gaucho life is still appreciated by readers in Argentina and abroad. Güiraldes sketches a memorable portrait of Segundo Sombra, the gaucho *domador* (broncobuster):

> He was not really so big. What made him seem so, as he appears to me even today, was the sense of power flowing from his body. His chest was enormous and his joints big-boned like those of a horse. His feet were short and high-arched; his hands thick and leathery like the scales of an armadillo. His skin was copper-hued and his eyes slanted slightly toward his temples.
>
> A plain pigskin belt girded his waist. The short blouse was caught up by the bone-handled knife from which swung a rough, plaited quirt, dark with use. His *chiripa* was long and coarse, and a plain black kerchief was knotted around his neck with the ends across his shoulders. He had split his *alpargatas* at the instep to make room for the fleshy foot.[62]

Even Argentines who get no closer to gaucho life than an oversized steak at the Estancia restaurant in Buenos Aires identify with the literature and mythology of the gaucho.

By contrast, *criollismo* (literature celebrating rural life and customs) failed to gain high literary stature in Venezuela or Colombia. Novels of rural life, such as *Peonía* (1890) by Manuel Vicente Romero García and *En éste país* (1910) by Luis Manuel Urbaneja Achelpohl, are generally dismissed as representing regionalism or a passing fad of *costumbrismo*, romanticized descriptions of quaint folk customs and life. The cultural hegemony exercised by Caracas intellectuals, with their North Atlantic orientation, has successfully relegated such literature to regional status.[63]

The shining exception that proves the rule is the widely praised *Doña Bárbara* of Rómulo Gallegos. Venezuelans rightly seized upon it as a national literary treasure. The power, mystery, and superstition of the plains come through in the novel's archetypal characters. Interestingly, Gallegos spent only eight days in the llanos prior to writing the novel, but he was well acquainted with llanero folklore and legends. The author's literary stature translated into political power: he served briefly as his nation's president in 1948.[64]

In both North and South America, the theme of the frontier versus the city became an important cultural and political influence. Like Sarmiento's *Facundo*, the Gallegos novel pits civilization against barbarism. *Doña Bárbara* acknowledges the power of barbarism but celebrates the victory of civilization (personified by Santos Luzardo) over the llanos. "Progress will come to the Plain," says the civilizing hero, "and barbarism will be conquered and retreat. Perhaps we shall not see it, but our blood will sing with the emotion of the ones who do."[65]

The cowboy figures only peripherally in Mexican and Chilean national literature. The vaquero makes an early appearance in American literature in Helen Hunt Jackson's 1884 novel *Ramona*. Other Anglo writers occasionally described Mexican horsemen, often adding romantic, exaggerated flourishes. But Mexican authors have not developed the vaquero in their works. Far more common are literary treatments of Indian peasants as downtrodden figures. Novels of the Mexican Revolution, such as *Los de abajo* by Mariano Azuela, typify this genre. The vaquero remains forgotten in Mexican literature.[66]

Chilean writers have seldom turned to the huaso. To be sure, *costumbrista* writers appeared in late nineteenth-century Chile as they did throughout Latin America. The huaso received mixed treatment at the hands of these authors. Some depicted him in positive terms and emphasized his superb horsemanship; others described a brutish, superstitious, alcoholic, violent figure. But none of the writings treating the huaso gained the critical acclaim of *Don Segundo Sombra* or *Doña Bárbara*.[67]

Rodeos, Stampedes, and Charreadas

In terms of popular culture, professional rodeo and Western films probably have brought the cowboy image to more people than printed media. Rodeo and movie cowboys grew up at about the same time. Both often had ties to Wild West shows or to circus performances of horseback tricks. Some early rodeo and film stars actually had cowboying experience, but by the 1930s few working cowboys appeared in either rodeo or film.

By 1915 major rodeo events had become annual occurrences in Cheyenne,

Salinas, Pendleton (Oregon), and Calgary. The following year, Guy Weadick, a rider and promoter from Wyoming, took rodeo performers to New York. Events became more standardized over the decades.[68]

Most of the rodeos began as a means of promoting tourism and business. Cheyenne boosters launched their Frontier Days in 1897. Businessmen in Pendleton planned their cowboy extravaganza, called a "roundup," in 1910. Their early events included "roping, racing, and relays, by cowboys, Indians and cowgirls; steer roping, maverick races, steer bulldogging, riding bucking horses, steers, bulls, buffaloes, and cows; stagecoach racing, Indian ceremonial and war dances, trick riding, mounted tug of war, the grand parade, and that wonderful finale, the wild horse race." What more could an audience want?[69]

At first, rodeo and Wild West show performers shared some characteristics with the working cowboy. Like the early cowboy, rodeo riders gained unsavory reputations for wildness, fighting, and drunkenness. And like the cowboy, most rodeo riders remained poor. Six-time all-around world champion Larry Mahan teaches a number of rodeo "survival skills," including how to travel without a car, how to borrow clothes, and how to put up with ten men in a motel room.[70]

Later rodeo riders, like other professional athletes, took preprofessional training in schools. Many work their way up during high school and intercollegiate rodeo competition. Ties to work on the range are now largely cultural and nostalgic. Rodeo has generated its own mystique, with a bit of glamour, life on the open road, and the potential of hefty winnings. The rodeo rider's once unsavory reputation has been replaced by an "all-American" image.[71]

Rodeo performers had better luck with unionizing than the cowhands who preceded them. In 1936 rodeo riders organized the Cowboy's Turtle Association, often referred to as "the Union." (The turtle moniker reflected the fact that it had taken the performers a long time to organize.) The group became the Rodeo Cowboys Association in 1945 and the Professional Rodeo Cowboys Association in 1974. Through union lobbying and strikes, rodeo riders improved their working conditions and earnings. They won an important victory over rodeo management in 1955 when their point system and standings became the single measure for naming rodeo world champions. Hawaiian riders formed the Hawaii Rodeo Assocation in 1966. The group presently numbers about 250 members and sanctions eight or nine rodeos per year.[72]

Canadian "stampedes" developed at the same time as early American ro-

The gaucho, *the national symbol of Argentina, has been depicted in important poems (*Martín Fierro*), in novels (*Don Segundo Sombra*), and in countless paintings, songs, and films. One of the gaucho's best-known popularizers was Florencio Molina Campos (1891–1959), whose loving and perceptive caricatures of the gaucho are reproduced in this section. Oddly, the most important medium of diffusion for his art was the commercial calendar. The Alpargatas textile company in Argentina distributed millions of calendars featuring his work in the 1930s and 1940s. In the United States, the Minneapolis Molene Power Implement Corporation commissioned his work for calendars from 1945 to 1955.*

A lone gaucho *rides across the flat, largely treeless pampa. Despite such exaggerations as the horse's huge head and bug eyes, Molina Campos's paintings well illustrate many elements of gaucho work and play. This cowboy, with typical beard and long hair, is cloaked in his poncho and* bomba-chas, *the baggy trousers that the gaucho adopted in the late nineteenth century (p. 35). (Hall of the Horsemen of the Americas, University of Texas, Austin)*

The ring race (la sortija) *found adherents in
both North and South
America (p. 129). Accord-
ing to custom, the winning
gaucho received the small
gold ring as a prize and
gave it to his girlfriend.
These gauchos (opposite,
top) wear the diaper-like*
chiripá, *broad silver-
studded* tirador *(belt),
and, on their feet, spurs
and* botas de potro *made
from the legskin of a colt
(pp. 34–35). (Prints and
Photographs Division, Li-
brary of Congress)*

Daring gauchos *also
played* la maroma *(oppo-
site, bottom). Hanging
from a corral gate, a gaucho dropped onto the back
of a wild horse or bull. He
would ride a horse until
he broke it. Gauchos rode
a bull holding on by their
spurs alone. (Prints and
Photographs Division, Li-
brary of Congress)*

An ostrich hunt (bo-
leada) *provided gauchos
with fun and profit
(pp. 133–34). Whirling
their* bolas *overhead, gauchos chased herds of rheas
across the pampa. After
catching and killing the
large birds, gauchos
gathered the ostrich
feathers for sale to a local
merchant. (Prints and
Photographs Division,
Library of Congress)*

***El pato** (duck) was probably the most famous of all gaucho equestrian games (pp. 137–39). Riders fought for control of a duck sewn into a rawhide bag with several handles. The struggle might take them over miles of plains. Exhausted, sore, and bruised, the gauchos gathered at a rural tavern (pulpería) after the contest to toast the winner. (Prints and Photographs Division, Library of Congress)*

The pulpería *was the social hub of gaucho life. Gauchos could exchange ostrich feathers, cattle hides, and other goods with the tavern owners for liquor, mate, and tobacco (p. 33). Tavern owners protected themselves and their wares with strong iron grates. In this calendar illustration, Molina Campos shows an Italian organ grinder and his monkey entertaining a group of gauchos. (Author's collection)*

Card games, *like* truco, *or other gambling were favorite activities at the pulpería (p. 154). Unfortunately, disputes over cards often generated knife fights. (Prints and Photographs Division, Library of Congress)*

Another gambling game, *la taba (p. 156), was popular among gauchos. Competitors took turns throwing the ankle-bone of a cow or horse. As in a coin toss, a call of heads or tails determined the winner. (Prints and Photographs Division, Library of Congress)*

Cockfights *(riñas de gallo) drew avid fans throughout Latin America long after they had been outlawed. In some cases, large fighting arenas could hold hundreds of specta-tors. Molina Campos depicts a much more mod-est arena. Fans always bet on the outcome of these bloody contests. (Author's collection)*

The gaucho carried *his competitive, combative spirit into his music. In a* payada, *a singing duel, two gauchos traded improvised, often insulting verses (pp. 124–25). If the insults went too far, a knife duel might follow the singing. Many of the more skilled singers or* payadores *were black. (Prints and Photographs Division, Library of Congress)*

Gaucho troubadours *(opposite, bottom) traveled the pampas from tavern to tavern, singing in exchange for food, drink, and a few coins. Like Mexican folksongs (corridos), gaucho songs blended humor and folk beliefs with social and political commentary (pp. 124–25). (Author's collection)*

The nineteenth century *marked the gradual demise of the gaucho's traditional free-ranging lifestyle. The Argentine landed elite, acting through the local* juez de paz *(justice of the peace), restricted the gaucho's freedom with a legal labyrinth (pp. 179, 184–85). (Author's collection)*

Stagecoaches, *essential to travel in the American West, also traversed the Argentine pampas. Passengers bumped along for hours on end and passed the night at dirty, bug-infested post houses along the stagecoach route. (Author's collection)*

Gauchos who broke the law *often ended up in the frontier militia. As skilled riders and fighters, gauchos made good cavalrymen to battle the Indians of the pampa (pp. 171–72). But justices of the peace and military commanders often drafted any gaucho they could find, regardless of the legality of such action. By pitting gauchos against Indians, the landed elite increased its social control over both groups. (Author's collection)*

As on other ranching frontiers, *farming made inroads on the Argentine plains. The arrival of immigrant farmers from Italy, steam-powered threshing machines, and later tractors doomed life on the open range for the gaucho (pp. 181–82). He moved from the realm of history into folklore and popular culture. (Prints and Photographs Division, Library of Congress)*

deos. The first took place in Calgary in 1912, when Guy Weadick promoted the idea of a rodeo to commemorate the good old days. Four leading stockmen, George Lane, Pat Burns, A. E. Cross, and Archie J. McLean, backed the idea with an investment of $100,000 (Canadian). Mexican vaqueros and cowboys from the United States participated along with Canadians. Many realized that the heyday of ranching and the cowboy had already passed. As one journalist noted, the Stampede symbolized "the final wave of the hat in token of farewell."[73]

Like the Pendleton Roundup, the Calgary Stampede mixed historical and mythical images of bygone days. Indians in full regalia, including Sarcees, Blackfeet, and Stoneys, mixed with cowboys, chuck wagons, Mounted Police, and marching bands. Kenneth Coppock exhorted fans in 1938 to dress for the occasion and add to the atmosphere. "An effort is being made to have a larger proportion of Stampede patrons wear big hats during the show to help keep up the spirit of the old West." Nearly every year since 1912, rodeo fans and tourists have flocked to Calgary during the second week of July for a taste of the Wild West that never was in Canada.[74]

Along with big, famous shows like the Stampede, Roundup, and Frontier Days, many smaller events came into being. Amateur rodeos, often during summer holidays, became commonplace throughout the western United States and Canada. Ranchers' roundups for amateurs were held in Alberta from 1916 to 1919. By the 1930s Alberta enjoyed some thirty rodeos per year.[75]

Elizabeth Atwood Lawrence argues that rodeo institutionalized many macho values and attitudes of the Old West. As in the old-time cowboy games, in rodeo man asserts his mastery over wild animals. The cruelty and violence toward animals typical of traditional cowboying is perpetuated in many rodeo events. Rodeo cowboys maintain the same macho toughness, endurance, and stoicism toward pain that traditional working hands admired. Lineal ties have largely disappeared between working hands and rodeo performers, but they share a common subculture and exhibit similar values.[76]

Kristine Fredriksson, in her otherwise fine history of rodeo, ignores its important Hispanic roots. Mary Lou LeCompte has shown that the "all-American sport" of rodeo owes a debt to Mexican equestrian displays and competitions. Early cowboy tournaments or contests in the Southwest often included vaqueros and Anglo cowboys. These contests included ranch work skills. But some events came directly from earlier vaquero and charro practices in Mexico. Prescott, Arizona, held one of the earliest rodeos on the Fourth of July, 1864. The event became annual, and in 1888 a vaquero named Juan Leivas won the prize.[77]

Riding exhibitions in Mexico began during the early days of the conquistadors. To impress their Indian subjects and hone cavalry skills, Spanish gentlemen were required to gather periodically for mounted drills called *alardes*. The riding style used was the jinetea, with short stirrups and neck reining to control the mounts. Gradually these military parades evolved into pleasure rides and exhibitions. Spaniards performed a number of riding feats during the sixteenth century, including the popular ring race (sortija) and jousts with cane poles (juegos de cañas). Over time some of the vaquero's work-related skills from roundup and branding worked their way into charreadas, or upper-class riding contests.[78]

Riding exhibitions retained popularity, particularly on the large haciendas of northern Mexico. After the disruptions of the Mexican Revolution, nostalgic landowners and many city dwellers reinvigorated the charreada. By the 1960s some 365 charro clubs existed in Mexico. Unlike rodeo in the United States, charro riding remains amateur and thus the province of those who can afford to participate for fun, not profit. The National Federation of Charros sponsors events around the country.[79]

Like American and Chilean rodeos and Canadian stampedes, charreadas have a fixed schedule of events in which the riders participate. The festivities open with a parade of gaily dressed men and women into the competition ring. In the *cala de caballo*, the first event, riders perform a complex set of maneuvers. Mounts must back up, turn, sprint, and stop quickly on command. Charreada includes mostly riding and roping events. Charros rope on horseback and on foot. Competitors rope mares by their hind feet (*concuros de peales*) and front feet (*manganas a caballo* and *manganas a pie*). In team roping (*terna*), virtually identical with American rodeo, one rider lassoes the head and the other the hind legs. Competitors also ride bulls and mares bareback. One event that did not pass over to American rodeo is the colear, or bull tailing. In the famous paso de la muerte (ride of death), a rider leaps from his mount onto the back of a wild mare and rides the animal bareback. As a special event, a mounted charro might evade and chase a bull. The startling thing about this feat (*rejonear*) is that the rider controls his mount without using the reins.[80]

Like cowboying, rodeo was originally a male province. Women served as window dressing in the roles of rodeo queen and dance partner. Participation by women in American rodeo has grown steadily. Federally mandated equal opportunity programs for intercollegiate sports and the erosion of sexism have forced changes in rodeo. Currently, in collegiate rodeo, men have five events: bareback riding, saddle-bronc riding, bull riding, steer wrestling, and calf roping. Women compete in barrel racing, goat tying, and breakaway tying. Both men and women can participate in team roping.[81]

Women have a lesser role in Mexican charreada than in American rodeo. In Chilean rodeo, however, they still only serve food, dance, and display typical costumes. During a charreada, a few women participate in the *escaramuza*, precision maneuvers done side-saddle. Women are also featured in the *jarabe tapatio*, typical dances performed as a break in the riding action. They wear a typical outfit called the *china poblana*.[82]

Like the Mexican charreada, Chilean rodeo is a middle- and upper-class pastime, not a profession. Michael Moody has provided a good, recent description of Chilean rodeo. The season runs from September to May. After an opening mass charge toward the audience, the huasos begin a variety of events. The first and most important is an exciting pursuit and blocking exhibition called the *atajada*, in which two riders guide a three-year-old steer toward a padded section of fence that serves as a target. One rider's mount actually turns into the steer, blocking and holding it against the fence. Scores are based on a series of trials; points are awarded for each trial. It is more difficult to block the steer at the hindquarters than at the head, so teams get more points for blocking the animal farther back along its body. Unlike professional rodeo riders in the United States, Chileans receive no cash prizes.[83]

Like the stampedes of Canada and the rodeos of the United States, Chilean events include many activities in addition to the mounted competition. At the closing ceremonies, riders line up and receive good Chilean wine and *empanadas* (meat pies that are also popular in Argentina), almost as in a religious communion. A typical dance, called *la cueca*, is performed during the ceremonies. At the rodeo's end, all partake in grand fiestas, with dancing, music, and more wine and food.[84]

Rodeo riders wear the typical huaso dress, including large spurs and Austrian-style stirrups of carved wood. The spurs now have three- or four-inch rowels, reduced from the six-inch giants of the past century. Each performer also dons a colorful manta (poncho) over his bolero jacket and wears a typical hat with a broad, flat brim. Like the gaucho, the huaso carries a knife (called a *corvo*) tucked through his sash across his back.[85]

Because of the lack of cash prizes, Chilean rodeo performers, like charros, cannot earn a living through competition. Most performers are middle-class Chileans with no background in ranching. As befits the Latin American environment of machismo, woman are denied participation, except as rodeo queens, waitresses, and dance partners. Rodeo in Chile, as elsewhere, is a means of perpetuating nostalgia for bygone days. The Chilean folklorist Tomás Lago asserts that the huaso is a national symbol in Chile, whereas the American cowboy is a regional symbol; I believe the reverse to be true.[86]

Celluloid Cowboys

Rodeos and their equivalents bring together the action and drama of expert horsemanship and the charm and nostalgia of old-time cowboy dress. Film and television have added their own twists to the myth, diffusing the cowboy culture far and wide. As a result, the American cowboy has become a recognizable figure virtually throughout the world.

The iconography of Western films has taken on a life and reality of its own. For many Americans, the cowboy is John Wayne or some other silver-screen favorite. Westerns offer escapism, action, and uncomplicated entertainment. Perhaps one reason that Westerns translate so well into other cultures is their simplicity and predictability; most are mounted morality plays. The success of Westerns does not depend upon innuendo, subtle plots, or complex character development.[87]

Western films, especially the B Westerns, offer several attractions to the viewer. They are invariably action-packed, with lots of horseback chases, runaway stagecoaches, gunfights, and fistfights. Right always prevails. After suffering setbacks and wrongs, the cowboy hero will triumph; justice will be done and civilization will be advanced. Men are men and women are women. The heroine will likely lose her father or other protector and thus be in danger. The hero will solve her problem, save her, and perhaps assume the role of her protector.

A few years ago, I asked some B Western fans, members of the Western Film Preservation Society of North Carolina, what appealed to them in these old films. Their responses are typical. These men, mostly aged forty to sixty-five, admitted to escapism, nostalgia, and the desire to recapture the joys of lost youth as "front-row kids." Many fans appreciate the traditional values and role models projected by the B Westerns: individualism, fair play, honesty, integrity, clean-living. They also applaud the inevitable triumph of right over wrong.[88]

The late Tom Walters, a talented writer and "ex-front-row kid," penned a volume of poems about film. *Seeing in the Dark* captures many memories and sentiments common to B Western fans. In a poem titled "Grade B Westerns," Walters wrote:

> How the grainy gray was colored
> By eager eyes.
> Saturday mornings we lived in the dark:
> The garish posters,
> Hoky poses announced a world of thrills
> At thirty cents.
>
> Ah, the purity of punishment
> Meted by cartidged centaurs
> (Lord, there were guns
> And stallions everywhere)
> Right prevailed among
> Hard-ridden horsehair seats.
>
> In colors all our own, in
> The flickering opalescent light,
> We believed, we believed, we believed . . .[89]

Cowboy films share much of the appeal of cowboy politics. The predictable B Westerns create a mythical, comfortable, black-and-white world. A very few Western films, however, have sought for realism, not escapism. Among the best is *Heartland*, a 1979 film starring Rip Torn. Based on the diary of Eleanor Randall Stewart and funded by a grant from the National Endowment for the Humanities, *Heartland* depicts the bleakness and difficulty of life for small ranchers in Wyoming in 1910. Torn plays Clyde Stuart, a small rancher who scratches out a living along with his wife and one hired hand. Hay runs out during a hard winter, cattle starve, and an infant son dies. The isolation and pain of life for the small rancher and the cowboy are projected with an authenticity and power seldom seen in film.

But as with Western fiction, the mass market thrives on formulas and predictability, not verisimilitude. Different strains of cowboy mythology come together in the movies. Singing cowboys, for example, created a world in which cowhands alternate between strumming the ever-present guitar and chasing after bad men. Ken Maynard made the first singing cowboy film in 1929. He was eclipsed by Gene Autry and Roy Rogers, who made more than ninety films each. Tex Ritter made some sixty films. Jimmy Wakely starred in about thirty films, Eddie Dean and Rex Allen in about twenty each. Like pulp novels and magazines, B Westerns, with or without singing cowboys, enjoyed great popularity until the early 1950s.[90]

After the B Westerns died out, some film stars, including Rogers, Autry, and William Boyd, made the transition to television. New mythical western places were born, such as the Dodge City of "Gunsmoke" and the Ponderosa of the Cartwrights on "Bonanza." Real-life dude ranches provide an opportunity for tourists to experience some elements of genteel ranch life. Television reruns and Western film clubs perpetuate the images. In various guises and media, the Western has maintained a popular following that shows no signs of abating.[91]

Hollywood also took a hand in shaping the film imagery associated with the Canadian West. Eager to expand the popular cowboy film market, filmmakers extended their imagination to western Canada as early as 1910. In that year, the Edison company produced two one-reel Westerns supposedly set in Canada: *The Cowpuncher's Glove* and *Riders of the Plains*. Four stars of silent cowboy films, Hoot Gibson, Ken Maynard, William S. Hart, and Tom Mix, made a dozen Canadian Westerns. Later, Autry and Rogers would add their talents to Hollywood's version of Canada's cowboy past.[92]

According to Pierre Berton, a leading critic of Hollywood's deformation of the Canadian past, the films portrayed a mythic frontier "complete with saloons, gambling, and six-gun violence." Gambling and saloons were outlawed; gunplay was rare. But calls for historical reality seldom fazed filmmakers. Hollywood churned out some 575 films depicting Canadian life and history with varying degrees of error. Even that quintessential western Canadian figure, the Mountie, had his uniform and hat altered to suit Hollywood cowboy film fashion.[93]

The cowboy film genre is generally less well developed and less known in Latin America. But Argentina has a long history of gaucho films. *Noblesa gaucha* (1915) became the most popular silent film in all of Latin America. Directed by Eduardo Martínez de la Pera, Ernesto Gunche, and Humberto Cairo, the film utilized intertitles taken from *Martín Fierro*. As in the Hernández poem, the gaucho is depicted as an oppressed, exploited figure. In 1942 director Lucas Demare drew upon the book by Leopoldo Lugones for his film *Guerra gaucha*. Like B Westerns in the United States, and often with a similar level of artistry and sophistication, gaucho films became immensely popular. Some thirty film studios were operating in Argentina by the 1940s.[94]

Like gauchesco literature, many gaucho films are self-consciously nationalistic and political. In 1968 Leopoldo Torre Nilsson won an award for his film based on *Martín Fierro*. (The first Argentine film based on the famous poem had appeared in 1923.) In 1973 Leonardo Favio directed a well-made film about the gaucho bandit Juan Moreira. Bringing in the appeal of the social bandit, Favio sought to use the film to establish a traditionalist context for Juan Perón's triumphal return from exile. In one scene of Luis Puenzo's 1985 film *The Official Story*, students in a literature class read "Juan Moreira." Art in Argentina is seldom far from politics.[95]

The vaquero is a marginal literary figure in Mexico; nor does he occupy an appreciable role as a character in Mexican film. The charro or *ranchero*, a middle-class rancher, does appear occasionally. He is generally a conservative, religious, traditional figure. As in Argentina, politics often makes its way into art. Fernando de Fuentes used the ranchero in *Allá en el Rancho Grande* to laud traditional sex and social roles. The film presents a comfortable, traditional rural order as a counterpoint to the social changes advocated by President Lázaro Cárdenas (1934–1940).[96]

In political symbolism and artistic creations, the cowboy takes on new attributes in the Americas. His role in politics and literature is minimal in Mexico, Chile, Venezuela, and Canada. In these four countries, ranchers as a political force and ranching as an economic activity occupied marginal positions. But in the United States, Argentina, and Uruguay, the cowboy is of paramount cultural importance. In American politics, advertising, and popular culture, images modeled on the cowboy remain significant and pervasive. Some fifty art works from the National Cowboy Hall of Fame represented the United States at an exhibition in 1987 at the Salon d'Automne in Paris. As we have seen, frontier myth making began even as the historical cowboy was still riding the range. John Dinan's comment about the portrayal of the cowboy in pulp novels and magazines holds for the symbolic cowboy in general. "The pulp cowboy," wrote Dinan, "was neither rancher nor cowpoke; he was a strong-willed, iron-fisted symbol—Uncle Sam in a Stetson and chaps."[97]

In spite of this symbolic importance, music and literature associated with the American cowboy have failed to achieve critical acclaim among the arbiters of culture. In Argentina and Uruguay, however, gaucho literature is the national literature. This is not to deny the many other important types of literature that have emanated from those countries, but it does bespeak the continuing importance and power of gaucho imagery.

CHAPTER 13

Conclusions

We have ridden a long way with the cowboys of the Americas. What have we learned about them, collectively, and as distinctive social groups? The broad outlines of cowboy history are similar in North and South America. In Latin America, cowboys evolved over a period of centuries. In Anglo-America, on the other hand, the cowboy enjoyed a heyday of only a few decades. Except in Canada, most cowboy groups started off as wild-cattle hunters. Often these early activities put the hunters outside the law, so a reputation for living beyond the law attached itself to these early equestrians from the Río de la Plata to the Texas coast.

Hispanic Roots

Hispanic influence predominates in both Latin America and Anglo-America. The influence of the "cowpens" experience of the Carolinas on the western open-range livestock industry is marginal and minimal. The direct inheritance from Spain is the upper-class equestrian culture of the Mexican charro. Similar traditions of the gentleman rider appear elsewhere, notably in Chile. These vestiges are still evident in the stylized riding exhibitions of the Chilean rodeo and the Mexican charreada.[1]

Institutions, such as the ranchers' organization called the Mesta and the hacienda itself, underwent changes from Old Spain to New Spain. But the Mesta and the ranch perpetuated the elite social status and political power associated with landholding. In turn, Anglo ranchers in the United States adapted rules and structures from the Mexican Mesta to Texas and the American Southwest.

But it was the working cowhand, like the vaquero, who developed the real cowboy culture. Cowboys in Latin America modified Spanish equipment, such as the saddle and lariat, for use on the plains of the New World. Through the Mexican vaquero, the Hispanic heritage was passed to Anglo-American cowboys and even to the Hawaiian paniolo.

In Latin America, the Amerindian influence is also very important. It complements and modifies the Hispanic tradition. The gaucho got his most formidable weapon, the bolas, and his favorite beverage, mate, from indigenous cultures. The vocabulary of the gaucho and the llanero is heavily peppered with indigenous terms. By contrast, virtually no indigenous element is detectable in Anglo-American cowboy life outside of Oklahoma. The Anglo-American frontier of exclusion and the reservation system isolated Amerindians from Anglo settlement.

Long- and Short-Lived Cattle Frontiers

The evolution of the livestock industry varied widely from country to country. In Latin America the cowboy's transformation from wild-cattle hunter to salaried ranch worker occurred over several centuries. In Argentina, for example, wild cattle were hunted and slaughtered by Indians and gauchos from the early seventeenth century through the mid-nineteenth. But during the mid-eighteenth century, ranchers began to establish control over livestock, land, water, and labor. The transition from wild-cattle hunting to established open-range ranching had begun.

The history of Anglo-American open-range ranching is ephemeral compared with the Latin American experience. We do find cowpens and slaves herding cattle on foot in the Old South. Cattle raising (as distinguished from cattle ranching) moved westward into the Mississippi Valley with Anglo-American settlers. But when we look at equipment, vocabulary, work technique, and organization, it is clear that the roots of open-range ranching in the United States lie to the south in Mexico, not to the east.

Anglo cowboys—mounted men herding cattle—got their start in Texas hunting wild cattle. They also drove off animals belonging to Spanish ranchers, seemingly with few qualms. In all areas where large numbers of cattle ran wild, cowboys considered them natural resources, free for the taking. This notion of use rights extended across the Americas. But the private property ethic and the assertion of ranchers' exclusive rights to range resources created frontier conflict.

Men working cattle on horseback as salaried hands did not appear in any numbers in the United States until after the Civil War. The great cattle drives north from Texas and the spread of open-range ranching across the Great Plains provided the opportunity for significant numbers of cowboys to work in the United States. From 1870 to 1880 the number of cattle in Colorado increased more than tenfold, from 70,736 to 791,459. The increase in Wyoming was even more dramatic, from 11,130 to 521,213 head. The northward expansion of the cattle industry opened opportunities for cowboys during the 1870s, but fencing, farming, the inhospitable climate, and overgrazing closed off opportunity after 1886.[2]

Anglo cowboys of the United States and Canada thrived for only a couple of decades. In the mid-1880s the livestock industry changed quickly and fundamentally. Fencing, haying, windmills, motorized vehicles, the extension of railroads, the arrival of farmers and sheepherders—all altered the face of the West. Extensive open-range ranching came and went in the American West in the space of a single lifetime.

Canada's golden age of ranching was even briefer. Ex–Mounted Policemen and other pioneer ranchers established modest herds in the mid-1870s. A decade later, large corporate ranches had taken control of the best ranges. By the early twentieth century, the Alberta range was experiencing many of the changes that had hit the American West a little earlier. Farmers, encouraged by government policy and frontier mythology, quickly crowded out the big herds and the cowboys who tended them. The heyday of the Canadian cowboy lasted only from about the mid-1880s until the disastrous winter of 1907.

Frontier Opportunity and Democracy

Was the cattle frontier a place of opportunity for the common man? Not really. For example, the Canadian land lease policy enacted in December 1881 favored large corporate ranches. Since leases were awarded for ranches up to one hundred thousand acres in size, considerable capital investment was required. Large ranchers summarily evicted squatters who had the temerity to graze animals on their holdings. The lease laws and the expenses of ranching meant that few Canadian cowboys had an opportunity to gather a small herd and become ranchers themselves. As in Latin America, a few mighty ranchers controlled the land, animals, and labor. Scholars of the American West have likewise determined that Turner's "safety valve" of frontier opportunity operated in a discriminatory fashion, if at all.[3]

Land policy and the pre-existence of latifundia in Latin America limited rural upward mobility. Argentine officials repeatedly turned over vast grazing lands to the powerful landed elite. Julio A. Roca's final "conquest of the desert" in 1879–1880 is but one example. Roca rewarded about five hundred political associates and friends with some twenty million hectares of land wrested from the Indians.[4]

Everywhere low wages, seasonal employment, and rancher-imposed restrictions kept the cowboy from moving up to the rancher ranks. The Marquis de la Torre issued special "ordinances" regulating the llanos in 1772. These repressive rules were extended into the Ordinances of the Llanos in 1811. The rules sharply curtailed the llaneros' rights and fanned their hatred of the creole independence faction in Caracas. Through identification cards, residency requirements, and vagrancy laws, government officials tried to control and subjugate the llanero. Repressive laws emanating from Buenos Aires afflicted the gaucho throughout the nineteenth century. Gauchos in neighboring Uruguay faced similar laws. Frontier opportunity did not exist for the cowboy. On the contrary, he lived under steadily increasing restrictions.[5]

Throughout Latin America, opportunity for advancement was virtually nonexistent for the rural lower classes. Indians and blacks remained at the bottom of the social ladder. Infrequently an Indian might rise to prominence. But careers such as that of Benito Juárez (a Zapotec who became president of Mexico) only underscore the rarity of such success. Racial discrimination played a role in keeping whites at the top and nonwhites at the bottom, but legal restrictions on cowboys further limited their social mobility.

Neither did the frontier promote democracy or social leveling. To be sure, a small rancher and his one or two hands might develop a familial, egalitarian relationship. But in general the livestock industry replicated and sometimes magnified class distinctions in society at large. Within cattle regions, race, wealth, and culture determined one's standing. Whites looked down on nonwhites, as in society at large, and whites controlled frontier resources, just as they controlled opportunity and assets elsewhere in society. In the Canadian West, racial divisions played a minor role on the cattle frontier, because virtually all ranchers and cowboys were white. But almost no leveling occurred, and a "squirearchy," not unlike that of rural England, became established in Alberta.[6]

The Significance of the Frontier

Frontiers should not be analyzed in isolation from the cultures that give rise to them. Disciples of Frederick Jackson Turner went too far in trying to establish the primacy of frontier forces over European roots in the New World. Particularly in the case of the Canadian ranching frontier, English roots are clearly in evidence. English and Canadian ranchers in Alberta transplanted cultural values to the frontier. Those values and practices changed little in the face of frontier influences. Metropolitan values, notably a respect for law and order, were established as a matter of policy in the Canadian West.[7]

Cattle frontiers might well be viewed as membranes separating indigenous and European cultures. Influences passed in both directions, but the dominant pressure on the membrane was from the European side. White, European values met and mixed with indigenous cultures on plains frontiers. The result was often competition for and conflict over resources of the plains. In Latin America, where white elites avoided manual labor, cowboying was left entirely to mestizos, blacks, and Indians. As in the Old South, slaves tended cattle in most ranching areas of Latin America. Latin American cowboys were generally cultural and racial mestizos; they blended the language, equipment, and values of European and Amerindian cultures. Looked down upon by the white ruling elite, gauchos in turn looked down upon Indians as "savages."[8]

We can properly speak of a Western Hemisphere "cowboy culture," bound together by Hispanic influences, shared values, and similar types of work and play. But there are many differences between the various cowboys of the Americas. The cultural significance attached to individual cowboy types varies widely. Those cowboy types with less cultural significance also appear to be less significant in national historiography. At one extreme are the llanero and the huaso, whose presence is little noted in Venezuelan, Colombian, and Chilean history. National historians have ignored these cowboy figures for many reasons. In Venezuela and to a lesser extent Colombia, hero worship has overridden scholarship. The fixation of Venezuelan scholars on the liberator Simón Bolívar has left many other topics, including the llanero, largely ignored. The Venezuelan historian Germán Carrera Damas has termed this phenomenon the "cult of Bolívar." It has deformed the nation's historiography in much the same way that hagiography has deformed that of other nations.[9]

Historical visibility is related to economic significance. The livestock industry played the central economic role in Argentina until the late nineteenth century. Consequently, the gaucho is a prominent topic for national historians. Ranching played a secondary role in economic development in Colombia, Venezuela, and Chile, all of which have largely ignored their cowboy cultures. Agricultural and, in the last two countries, mineral development overshadowed the livestock economy. But this is only a partial explanation for the attention paid to the cowboy by historians. The ranching industry in the United States was overshadowed by the rise of industry during the same period, yet the cowboy and the frontier loom large in the nation's written history.

There are some encouraging signs that the "forgotten llanos" may yet receive greater attention. José Antonio de Armas Chitty, poet, scholar, and himself a llanero, is presently head of the Academia Nacional de Historia in Venezuela. He has written a number of useful histories of llanos towns and states. Foreign scholars are making their impact felt. Miguel Izard, of the Universidad de Barcelona, Spain, has written many articles, based on archival sources, about the llanero. Robert P. Matthews has written a wellresearched dissertation published in a Spanish edition. For the Colombian llanos, Jane M. Rausch (née Loy), is creating an important body of scholarship.[10]

Frontier Abundance

Turnerian frontier mythology in the United States emphasizes the frontier as a place of opportunity, a social safety valve. For the most part this meant that cowboys had the opportunity to work long hours for low pay. Few enjoyed upward mobility into the ranks of landholders. Laws in several Latin American nations imposed sharp restrictions on cowboys. Yet the "garden" image of plains frontiers as sources of great abundance is widespread.[11]

Taking inspiration from Turner, Walter Prescott Webb and David Potter have focused on frontier abundance as a key historical force. Webb posits the mineral riches and new lands of the Americas as driving forces in a fourcentury economic boom for Europe: New World natural riches created Old World wealth. Potter argues that the resources and open lands of the western frontier helped shape the American character. This made the frontier an important force until industrialization and urbanization opened other avenues to abundance.[12]

Drawing upon Turner, Webb, and Potter, we might argue that differential abundance does account for some differences between Spanish and Anglo frontiers. The Spanish found numerous, readily accessible sources of abundance in Latin America. As Webb has emphasized, precious metals in Mexico and Peru created some private fortunes. More important, the Spanish harnessed massive numbers of Indians to labor for them in a wide range of enterprises. "Red gold" in the form of Amerindian labor sparked the economic boom of colonial Latin America. Black African slaves quickly augmented the labor pool.

More to the point of this book, the Spanish "seeded," often inadvertently, several plains regions with livestock. Within a few decades after initial Spanish exploration, herds of wild cattle and horses flourished on plains from the Río de la Plata to northern Mexico. In terms of gold, silver, labor, and livestock, the Spanish enjoyed tremendous riches in their frontier regions.

On Anglo-American frontiers, sources of abundance were less readily accessible. British North America did not include large concentrations of Amerindians suitable for impressed labor. The Aztec and Incan empires had already organized and concentrated the work force; the Spanish simply took it over. Nothing comparable existed in the British colonies.

Neither did the British settlers find mountains of gold and silver, although they spent considerable time looking. In the original British colonies, stock raising was a small affair, with herds numbering in the dozens or perhaps hundreds. Wild cattle and horses by the millions did not roam the eastern seaboard as they did on the pampas and the llanos. On the western plains, settlers found and quickly exterminated massive herds of bison. The nearest that Anglo-America came to a livestock cornucopia were the substantial herds of wild horses and cattle in Texas.[13]

In sum, frontiers in Latin America offered easily exploitable and readily accessible labor, metals, and livestock. In British North America, the path to riches was much slower and more difficult. Some commentators cursed the abundance of livestock on the the pampas for contributing to what they perceived as gaucho indolence. They believed that some gauchos would not work for wages because they did not have to; wild cattle, horses, and ostriches provided sufficient sustenance and income.

I do not wish to overemphasize these frontier differences to the exclusion of the European cultures that exploited them, however. In medieval Spanish Catholic culture, manual labor carried a stigma. Spanish colonies languished where labor was in short supply. Sharp lines of class, culture, and race stratified Spanish colonial society. The Spanish carried over these prejudices to frontier society, where virtually no leveling took place. From the pampas to the Spanish Borderlands of northern Mexico, the frontier failed to promote democracy.[14]

British culture and the Protestant work ethic accepted, indeed glorified, the dignity of manual labor. In addition, as Marvin Mikesell has emphasized, the British settlers created frontiers of exclusion that sharply divided whites and Amerindians. Despite their racial biases, the Spanish and Portuguese accepted Indian women as sexual partners. To some extent, this created frontiers of inclusion, where a mestizo population blended racial and cultural elements of both conqueror and conquered. But Argentina and Chile created frontiers of exclusion as well, so the distinction between British and Spanish colonies in this respect is not absolute.[15]

It is clear that we must look on both sides of the Atlantic to understand the history of the Americas. Some elements of European culture (such as racial and social stratification) stoutly resisted alteration on the frontier. In other cases (such as the bolas used in South America), existing Amerindian societies contributed entirely new elements to frontier cultures. In still other cases (such as changes in Spanish riding equipment), European transplants were modified according to frontier needs. The role of religion and missions provides another interesting example of European culture in a frontier context.

Religion on the Frontier

As we have seen, missions played an important role in extending the livestock industry in many parts of Latin America. Mission Indians were the first vaqueros of northern Mexico, the American Southwest, Texas, and California. Missions played a role in the modest livestock industry of Spanish Florida. The many Jesuit missions among the Guaraní in central South America flourished until bandeirante slave hunters and the expulsion of the order in 1767 ended their activities. On the llanos, Capuchin missionaries established a number of towns, including Calabozo (1723) and Charallave (1735). A missionary drove livestock into the llanos near Santo Tomás de Guayana in 1726. The Capuchins, and to a lesser extent other orders, introduced stock raising and agriculture to Indians in many parts of the llanos.[16]

In Argentina, however, missions and missionaries played virtually no role on the southern frontier. Regular clergy as well as Franciscans, Dominicans, and Jesuits were active in the north from Tucumán to Córdoba. But the Church never enjoyed the wealth and influence in Argentina that it did in other parts of the Spanish Empire. An English Jesuit, Thomas Falkner, visited the southern pampa during the mid-eighteenth century. But the plains Indians of Argentina retained their religious beliefs and practices throughout the colonial and into the national period. On the Argentine plains, the cross did not accompany the sword in frontier expansion.[17]

Yet in terms of spiritual and moral influence, religion little affected the cowboys of North or South America. Much cowboy fun hardly met the standards of religious morality. Given the lack of Church activity on the pampas, it is not surprising to find that gauchos were ignorant of religious matters. True, they used the term *Christian* to distinguish themselves from the Indians, whom they called *savages*. But these terms denoted cultural, not religious, categories. Latin American cowboys, indeed males in general, seldom entered a church. As a consequence, their lives escaped the usual and useful records of baptism, marriage, and death.[18]

Even where mission activity flourished, cowboys seldom exhibited interest in religion. Contemporary reports from clerics on the llanos are uniformly uncomplimentary concerning llanero morals and behavior. Some missionaries endured attacks by outlaws on the plains. Cowboys in the United States seemingly worried little about theology. As a cattle dealer in Texas observed in 1888, "The average cowboy does not bother himself about religion. The creeds and isms that worry civilization are a sealed book to the ranger, who is distinctively a fatalist."[19]

Superstition, not theology and organized religion, underlay cowboy beliefs everywhere. Llaneros, gauchos, and vaqueros believed in a wide range of supernatural forces. The Devil and other vestiges of Christianity might figure into some superstitions. But the mysteries of nature often had superstitious explanations based on Indian cosmology or on fetishistic beliefs developed by cowboys themselves. Thus, we have an ironic juxtaposition of strong mission activity, directed toward Indian populations, and unchurched cowboys sharing the same frontier.[20]

Shared Cowboy Culture

Cattle frontiers of the Americas differed in fundamental ways, but cowboys everywhere shared key values and characteristics. Cowboys occupied a relatively low status as poorly paid rural workers; few exhibited upward mobility. Indeed, given restrictive laws in South America and debt peonage in Mexico, many Latin American cowboys lacked even geographical mobility.

But cowboys everywhere shared a sense of superiority vis-à-vis pedestrians. Their hallmark of worth was a man's ability in the saddle. With few exceptions, cowboys had to be coerced to labor on foot. The llanero might have to work as a boatman during the seasonal floods on the tropical plains of Venezuela, and Chilean ranchers, favored with surplus rural labor, could require cowboys to perform both mounted and foot labor. But even there, mounted workers enjoyed higher status and more perquisites than those who labored on foot.[21]

It is clear that being in the saddle was the most important thing to any cowboy. Not only did cowboys prefer to work from horseback, they also played on horseback. Cowboys developed a number of ingenious games and exhibitions based on real-life work skills. Cowboys did not separate work and play, but preferred to fuse the two if at all possible. Vaqueros and llaneros would tail bulls. Gauchos would let themselves and their mounts be thrown to the ground in the wild pialar. Both of these pastimes evolved from the work setting into recreation. Cowboys eagerly grabbed any opportunity to compete or show off their equestrian prowess.

Cowboys valued courage and machismo as much as they valued skill in the saddle. In their games, folklore, and daily lives, courage played an important role. Many of their games were dangerous. Those who performed the games well were esteemed for their bravery as well as their skill. A gaucho faced possible trampling whenever he dropped from a corral gate onto the back of a charging bull in the maroma. California vaqueros faced grave danger when they eagerly matched strength and wits with a grizzly bear.

Out of a mixture of necessity and preference, cowboys lived a simple life. They favored a basic diet consisting mainly of a caffeinic beverage (coffee or, for the gaucho, mate) and beef. Even when other food staples, such as fresh vegetables and milk, were available, cowboys scorned them. Punchers in the American West took their few vegetables and milk from cans; gauchos ate neither.

Their vices were equally simple: liquor, tobacco, and an occasional night with a prostitute. Cowboys chewed tobacco or smoked hand-rolled cigarettes or acrid cigars. They were prone to binge drinking, because they might go for long periods without liquor or other recreation. Not surprisingly, arrests in Argentina increased when rural workers received their pay. Arrests for public drunkenness and fighting were common everywhere. Cowboys in the American West gained much of their negative reputation by blowing off steam in town after long months in the saddle.

Cowboys generally lacked the opportunity to marry and raise a family. Part of the reason is simple demographics: cattle frontiers were male domains in which men outnumbered women many times over. An occasional liaison with a prostitute or perhaps nothing more than a drink with a bar girl was all the female companionship available to most ranch hands. In the open market of matrimony, wives went to those with more to offer—ranchers, businessmen, and others.

Most cowboys lived migratory lives. Each ranch employed a small core of permanent hands, but most cowboys worked by the day or by the month. This nomadic existence did not lend itself to the ties of a wife, home, and family, even if enough women had been available.

Myth, Symbol, and Reality

Reality and mythology have became almost inextricably confounded in writings about cowboys everywhere. For example, the well-known book *El llanero* by the Venezuelan Rafael Bolívar Coronado is history colored with myth and literary license. (He wrote it under the pseudonym Daniel Mendoza, one of dozens of pseudonyms he used in many different countries.) The author's fertile imagination and unusual publishing history make it difficult to cite his work on the llanero with confidence.[22]

Other Latin American writers have blended strains of folklore, history, and literary fancy. The Spanish-American respect for men of letters has tended to blur the lines between fictional and nonfictional writing. Style matters much more than accuracy of analysis or documentary foundation. Sarmiento's masterful *Facundo* is a blend of political polemic, fanciful folklore, and rudimentary sociology. Still praised by some for its description of various gaucho types, the book was written in Chile long before Sarmiento crossed the pampas and saw gaucho life firsthand.[23]

Writings about the huaso are also long on historical imagination. Popular culture is accepted as historical reality. A substantial, documented history of the huaso remains to be written. The studies by René Echaiz and Tomás Lago lack archival documentation and offer imprecise definitions of their subject. Likewise, there is a paucity of well-documented studies about the vaquero. The charro has received more attention, and the attributes of charros and vaqueros are frequently mixed and confused.

But it is not only a lack of historical studies that distorts our knowledge of cowboys. The huge volume of fictional and cinematographic works about the cowboy has colored our vision. Many Americans are doubtless convinced that a marshal named Matt Dillon actually maintained law and order in Dodge City. Others believe that Ben Cartwright and his boys once rode the Nevada ranges of the "Ponderosa." International film distribution and modern communications satellites have made the American cowboy a part of world mythology. A surfeit of imagery can be as deceptive as a dearth of materials.[24]

Still in the Saddle

If I were to rate the continuing cultural significance of the cowboy, I would describe his *national* importance as being greatest in Argentina, Uruguay, and the United States. The cowboy is a more regional figure in Mexico, Canada, Chile, Venezuela, Colombia, and Brazil. The vaquero is always associated with the large haciendas of northern Mexico and with Spanish California. The llanero remains typical of the interior tropical plains of Colombia and Venezuela. Brazil's vaqueiro is localized in the northeastern sertão and the gaúcho with the southern campanha of Rio Grande do Sul. The heritage of the Hawaiian cowboy is only now receiving attention. Since 1982 Hawaiians have celebrated a Paniolo Day each October. But so far the cowboy has not played a major role in the knotty problem of Hawaiian identity.

A related but not identical question is the significance of the frontier in a nation's popular consciousness. In general, the cultural importance accorded to the cowboy and to the frontier are equal, because the two are so closely associated. As Silvio Zavala has noted, the northern Mexican frontier is not "the source of the Mexican national type." Mexico never developed a version of the frontier myth. Instead, the pre-Columbian Aztec past became an important national icon. In contrast, both the imagery of the frontier and the cowboy loom large in the United States.[25]

But the garden image of the frontier as a source of future wealth and greatness appears frequently in Latin America. The cowboy holds no special national significance in Peru or Brazil, but both have their own versions of frontier mythology. Fernando Belaúnde Terry, twice president of Peru, laid great stress on opening up the rich Amazonian frontier east of the Andes. Likewise, Brazil's president Jucelino Kubitschek moved the national capital six hundred miles inland to push development and population toward the Amazonian frontier. The Amazon retains a magical, mystical appeal, partially supported by gold strikes and drug traffic. In a parallel move, Argentina is relocating its national capital southward to its largely empty Patagonian frontier.

The persistence and importance of the cowboy culture are all the more amazing given the tiny number of men who actually participated in it. We have better historical counts of cows than of cowboys, but the extensive, seasonal nature of ranching meant that relatively few workers were needed. One estimate places the number of llaneros in 1789 (before the destruction of the independence wars) at only twenty-four thousand. I conservatively estimate the gaucho population of Buenos Aires province in 1869 at only about seventy-nine thousand out of a provincial population of nearly half a million. An estimated thirty-five thousand hands helped drive herds north from Texas from 1866 to 1885. Clearly, demography is a poor indicator of cultural significance.[26]

As distinctive social groups, the cowboys of the Americas are gone, along with the vast herds of semiwild cattle they tended from horseback. Working cowhands are still found in all ranching areas. In the United States, some westerners consciously preserve vestiges of old-time cowboy life. Hands may choose to work in the saddle, although a pickup truck or jeep would be faster and easier. Some make tack to preserve old-time handicrafts. But as with the family farm, the number of working cowhands has dwindled to the point of extinction.

Rapid social change and the complexity of modern social problems will not disappear, however. Alvin Toffler's "future shock" now extends to virtually all societies and to most levels of those societies. Faced with the dilemmas of modernity, people will continue to reach back for the security of a simpler past. Cowboy politics and cowboy culture will remain popular as long as people face a disconcerting present. As a temporary escape to "those thrilling days of yesteryear," a dose of cowboy mythology is healthy and enjoyable. Cowboy myth and history both have a place, but we must try to distinguish between them.

NOTES

1. Introduction

1. See Glenn R. Vernam, *Man on Horseback: The Story of the Mounted Man from the Scythians to the American Cowboy* (Lincoln: University of Nebraska Press, 1964).

2. Herbert Eugene Bolton, "The Epic of Greater America," *American Historical Review* 38:3 (April 1933): 474. On Bolton and his influence, see Lewis Hanke, ed., *Do the Americas Have a Common History?: A Critique of the Bolton Theory* (New York: Knopf, 1964); David J. Weber, "Turner, the Boltonians, and the Borderlands," *American Historical Review* 91:1 (Feb. 1986): 66–81; Bolton, *History of the Americas: A Syllabus with Maps* (1935; repr., Westport, Conn.: Greenwood Press, 1979); and Bolton, *Wider Horizons of American History*, (1939; repr., Notre Dame: University of Notre Dame Press, 1967). Peter d'A Jones does attempt a comparative perspective in *Since Columbus: Pluralism and Poverty in the History of the Americas* (London: Heinemann, 1975).

3. Cecil Robinson, *Mexico and the Hispanic Southwest in American Literature* (Tucson: University of Arizona Press, 1963), pp. 33–68, 164–209; Donald E. Worcester, "The Significance of the Spanish Borderlands to the United States," *Western Historical Quarterly* 7:1 (Jan. 1976): 5–18; David J. Weber, "Mexico's Far Northern Frontier, 1821–1854: Historiography Askew," *Western Historical Quarterly* 7:3 (July 1976): 279–293; Weber, *The Mexican Frontier, 1821–1846: The American Southwest Under Mexico* (Albuquerque: University of New Mexico Press, 1982).

4. Alistair Hennessy, *The Frontier in Latin American History* (Albuquerque: University of New Mexico Press, 1978), p. 144; Isaiah Bowman, *The Pioneer Fringe* (New York: American Geographical Society, 1931), pp. 320–321, 325–326, 329, 342–345; W. L. Schurz, "Conditions Affecting Settlement on the Mato Grosso Highland and in the Gran Chaco," in *Pioneer Settlement: Cooperative Studies by Twenty-Six Authors* (New York: American Geographical Society, 1932), pp. 111–115. On the Colombian llanos, see Jane M. Rausch, *A Tropical Plains Frontier: The Llanos of Colombia, 1531–1831* (Albuquerque: University of New Mexico Press, 1984). On cowboys in Hawaii, see Lynn J. Martin, ed., *Nā Paniolo o Hawai'i* (Honolulu: Honolulu Academy of Arts, 1987).

5. Robert P. Swierenga, "The New Rural History: Defining the Parameters," *Great Plains Quarterly* 1 (Fall 1981): 212–213; Swierenga, "Theoretical Perspectives on the New Rural History: From Environmentalism to Modernization," *Agricultural History* 56:3 (July 1982): 495–496. See also James Gardner and George Adams, eds., *Ordinary People and Everyday Life: Perspectives on the New Social History* (Nashville: American Association for State and Local History, 1983).

6. Quoted in James A. Young and B. Abbott Sparks, *Cattle in the Cold Desert* (Logan: Utah State University Press, 1985), p. 107.

7. David Dary, *Cowboy Culture: A Saga of Five Centuries* (New York: Knopf, 1981), pp. 80, 83.

8. I interchange the terms *horsemen*, *riders*, *ranch hands*, *punchers*, and other near synonyms for stylistic diversity. I am grateful to Graham Knox, of the University of Calgary, for cautioning that the

term *horsemen* would legitimately include indigenous plains riders as well as working cowboys. See Vernam, *Man on Horseback*, and Theodore Dodge, *Riders of Many Lands* (New York: Harper and Brothers, 1894) for discussions of other equestrian groups, such as native Americans, "gentlemen" riders, and cavalrymen.

9. John R. Erickson, *The Modern Cowboy* (Lincoln: University of Nebraska Press, 1981), pp. 4–5, 219.

10. Emilio Daireaux, *Vida y costumbres en el Plata*, 2 vols. (Buenos Aires: Lajouane, 1888), 2:197–202; Edward Larocque Tinker, "The Centaurs of the Americas," in *Centaurs of Many Lands* (London: J. A. Allen, 1964), pp. 50–51. See also Tinker's *Horsemen of the Americas and the Literature They Inspired*, rev. ed. (Austin: University of Texas Press, 1967).

11. Laureano Vallenilla Lanz, *Disgregación e integración* (Caracas: Universal, 1930), p. 175; Otto Jessen, "Cosacos, cowboys, gauchos, boers y otros pueblos a caballo propios de las estepas," *Runa* 5:1–2 (1952): 171–186.

12. A. A. Hayes, quoted in *Harper's Weekly*, Nov. 27, 1880:759. On the problems of defining gauchos as a class or race, see Richard W. Slatta, *Gauchos and the Vanishing Frontier* (Lincoln: University of Nebraska Press, 1983), pp. 15–16.

13. Peter Calvert, *The Concept of Class: An Historical Introduction* (New York: St. Martin's Press, 1982), p. 202; see also pp. 10, 202–209, 216. Ezequiel Martínez Estrada, *Muerte y transfiguración de Martín Fierro: Ensayo de interpretación de la vida argentina*, 2 vols. (Mexico: Fundo de Cultura Económica, 1948), 1:251; William H. Hutchinson, "The Cowboy and the Class Struggle (or, Never Put Marx in the Saddle)," *Arizona and the West* 14 (Winter 1972):321–330; Hutchinson, "The Cowboy and Karl Marx," *Pacific Historian* 20 (Summer 1976):111–122; Don

D. Walker, "The Left Side of the American Ranges: A Marxist View of the Cowboy," in *Clio's Cowboys: Studies in the Historiography of the Cattle Trade* (Lincoln: University of Nebraska Press, 1981), pp. 131–146. Jack Weston, *The Real American Cowboy* (New York: Schocken, 1985) offers strong evidence of rancher-cowboy conflict. I am grateful to William B. Taylor, of the University of Virginia, who in 1980 cautioned me about applying the concept of class to the gaucho.

14. Frederick Jackson Turner, "The Significance of the Frontier in American History," in *The Frontier in American History* (1893; repr., New York: Holt, 1958), pp. 22–24, 30, 35, 37; Ray Allen Billington, *America's Frontier Heritage* (New York: Holt, Rinehart and Winston, 1966); Rodman W. Paul and Richard W. Etulain, eds., *The Frontier and the American West* (Arlington Heights, Ill.: AHM, 1977). Discussions of Turner include Richard Hofstadter and Seymour Martin Lipset, eds., *Turner and the Sociology of the Frontier* (New York: Basic Books, 1968); Ray Allen Billington, ed., *The Frontier Thesis: Valid Interpretation of American History?* (Huntington, N. Y.: Krieger, 1977); Billington, ed., *The American Frontier Thesis: Attack and Defense* (Washington, D. C.: American Historical Association, 1971); Jackson K. Putnam, "The Turner Thesis and the Westward Movement: A Reappraisal," *Western Historical Quarterly* 7:4 (Oct. 1976):377–404; Rodman W. Paul and Michael P. Malone, "Tradition and Challenge in Western Historiography," *Western Historical Quarterly* 16:1 (Jan. 1985):31–38; and William Cronon, "Revisiting the Vanishing Frontier: The Legacy of Frederick Jackson Turner," *Western Historical Quarterly* 18:2 (April 1987):157–176.

15. On the frontier in Canada, see David H. Breen, "The Turner Thesis and

the Canadian West: A Closer Look at the Ranching Frontier," in Lewis H. Thomas, ed., *Essays on Western History in Honour of Lewis Gwynne Thomas* (Edmonton: University of Alberta Press, 1976), pp. 147–156; and Carl Berger, *The Writing of Canadian History: Aspects of English-Canadian Writing, 1900–1970* (Toronto: Oxford University Press, 1976), pp. 174–178. On Hawaii, see Martin, *Paniolo.* For a critique of other frontier studies, see William W. Savage, Jr., and Stephen I. Thompson, eds., "The Comparative Study of the Frontier: An Introduction," in *The Frontier: Comparative Studies,* 2 vols. (Norman: University of Oklahoma Press, 1979), 2:3–24.

16. Hennessy, *Frontier,* pp. 19, 113–114. The classic comparative analysis of Western Hemisphere frontiers is Walter Prescott Webb, *The Great Frontier* (Austin: University of Texas Press, 1979). See also Luis Manuel Urbaneja Achelpohl, "El gaucho y el llanero" (Caracas: Elite, 1926); José Eustaquio Machado, *El gaucho y el llanero* (Caracas: Vargas, 1926); Silvio R. Duncan Baretta and John Markoff, "Civilization and Barbarism: Cattle Frontiers in Latin America," *Comparative Studies in Society and History* 20:4 (Oct. 1978): 587–620; Jane M. Loy, "Horsemen of the Tropics: A Comparative View of the Llaneros in the History of Venezuela and Colombia," *Boletín americanista* 31 (1981): 159–171; Richard W. Slatta, "Gauchos, Llaneros, and Cowboys: Horsemen of the Americas," *Persimmon Hill* 12:4 (1983):8–23; Slatta, "Llaneros and Gauchos: A Comparative View," *Inter-American Review of Bibliography* 35:2 (July 1985):409–421; John Charles Chasteen, "Twilight of the Lances: The Saravia Brothers and Their World" (Ph. D. diss., University of North Carolina, 1988); and Michael S. Cross, ed., *The Turner Thesis and the Canadas: The Debate on the Im-*

pact of the Canadian Environment (Toronto: Copp Clark, 1970).

17. Hennessy, *Frontier,* pp. 13, 17, 27.

18. The leading exponent of the "cowpens" school is Terry Jordan; see his *Trails to Texas: Southern Roots of Western Cattle Ranching* (Lincoln: University of Nebraska Press, 1981) and "The Origin of Anglo-American Cattle Ranching in Texas: A Documentation of Diffusion from the Lower South," *Economic Geography* 45 (January 1969):63–87. For evidence to counter Jordan's theory, see Jack Jackson, *Los Mesteños: Spanish Ranching in Texas, 1721–1821* (College Station: Texas A&M University Press, 1986); David Dary, *Cowboy Culture: A Saga of Five Centuries* (New York: Knopf, 1981); Sandra L. Myres, *The Ranch in Spanish Texas, 1691–1800* (El Paso: Texas Western Press, 1969); J. Frank Dobie, *The Longhorns* (Austin: University of Texas Press, 1980); Young and Sparks, *Cattle in the Cold Desert,* esp. p. 109; Weston, *Real American Cowboy;* Don Worcester, "The Spread of Spanish Horses in the Southwest, 1700–1800," *New Mexico Historical Review* 20:1 (Jan. 1945):1–13; Worcester, "Significance of the Spanish Borderlands"; and James A. Young, "Hay Making: The Mechanical Revolution on the Western Range," *Western Historical Quarterly* 14:3 (July 1983):311.

19. Frederick C. Luebke, "Regionalism and the Great Plains: Problems of Concept and Method," *Western Historical Quarterly* 15:1 (Jan. 1984):29, 38; Donald Worcester, "New West, True West: Interpreting the Region's History," *Western Historical Quarterly* 18:2 (April 1987): 146–150. Useful comparative studies include Marvin W. Mikesell, "Comparative Studies in Frontier History," in Hofstadter and Lipset, *Turner,* pp. 152–171; Howard R. Lamar and Leonard Thompson, eds., *The Frontier in History: North*

America and Southern Africa Compared (New Haven: Yale University Press, 1981); Peter Kolchin, "Comparing American History," in Stanley I. Kutler and Stanley N. Katz, eds., *The Promise of American History: Progress and Prospects* (Baltimore: Johns Hopkins University Press, 1982), pp. 64–81; Magnus Morner et al., "Comparative Approaches to Latin American History," *Latin American Research Review* 17:3 (1982):55–90; and Donald P. Warwich and Samuel Osherson, eds., *Comparative Research Methods* (Englewood Cliffs, N. J.: Prentice-Hall, 1973), esp. pp. 3–88.

20. Donald Denoon, *Settler Capitalism: The Dynamics of Dependent Development in the Southern Hemisphere* (New York: Oxford University Press, 1982), p. 8. I also commend to the reader the comparative essays by John Fogarty (a critique of staple theory), J. C. M. Ogelsby (on national identity), and the late Carl E. Solberg (on land tenure) in D. C. M. Platt and Guido diTella, eds., *Argentina, Australia and Canada: Studies in Comparative Development, 1870–1965* (London: Macmillan, 1985). Richard Hogan offers some theoretical considerations for frontier scholars, although he focuses on urban areas; see "The Frontier as Social Control," *Theory and Society* 14:1 (Jan. 1985):35–51; and "Carnival and Caucus: A Typology for Comparative Frontier History," *Social Science History* 11:2 (Summer 1987):139–168.

21. George M. Fredrickson, "Comparative History," in Michael Kammen, ed., *The Past Before Us: Contemporary Historical Writing in the United States* (Ithaca: Cornell University Press, 1980), pp. 457–459; Philip D. Curtain, "Depth, Span, and Relevance," *American Historical Review* 89:1 (Feb. 1984):8.

22. Bolton quoted in Hanke, *Do the Americas Have a Common History?* p. 46.

Chapter 2. From Wild-Cattle Hunters to Cowboys

1. Robert M. Denhardt, *The Horse of the Americas*, rev. ed. (Norman: University of Oklahoma Press, 1975), pp. 36–42; David Dary, *Cowboy Culture: A Saga of Five Centuries* (New York: Knopf, 1981), pp. 4–6.

2. José de Acosta, *Historia natural y moral de las Indias*, quoted in Benjamin Keen and Mark Wasserman, *A Short History of Latin America*, 3d ed. (Boston: Houghton Mifflin, 1988), p. 89.

3. Dary, *Cowboy Culture*, pp. 7, 17–18.

4. Denhardt, *Horse of the Americas*, pp. 36–42; 92, 160; John E. Rouse, *The Criollo: Spanish Cattle in the Americas* (Norman: University of Oklahoma Press, 1977), p. 46. See also José Matesanz, "Introducción de la ganadería en Nueva España," *Historia Mexicana* 14:4 (1965): 533–544; John J. Johnson, "The Introduction of the Horse into the Western Hemisphere," *Hispanic American Historical Review* 23:4 (Nov. 1943):587–610; and Johnson, "The Spanish Horse in Peru Before 1550," in *Greater America: Essays in Honor of Herbert Eugene Bolton* (Berkeley: University of California Press, 1945), pp. 19–37.

5. Joe A. Akerman, Jr., *Florida Cowman: A History of Florida Cattle Raising* (Kissimmee: Florida Cattlemen's Association, 1976), pp. 1–3, 9–10; Charles Arnade, "Cattle Raising in Spanish Florida, 1513–1763," *Agricultural History* 35:3 (July 1961):116–124; George H. Dacy, *Four Centuries of Florida Ranching* (St. Louis: Britt Printing Co., 1940), p. 14; Rouse, *Criollo*, pp. 46, 74; J. S. Otto and N. E. Anderson, "Cattle Ranching in the Venezuelan Llanos and the Florida Flatwoods: A Problem in Comparative History," *Comparative Studies in Society and History* 28:4 (Oct. 1986):678–683.

6. Caio Prado, Jr., *The Colonial Background of Modern Brazil*, trans. Suzette Macedo (Berkeley: University of California Press, 1971), pp. 219–221, 224–230.

7. Prado, *Colonial Background*, pp. 232–241; Charles G. Lobb, "The Historical Geography of the Cattle Regions along Brazil's Southern Frontier," (Ph. D. diss., University of California, 1970), pp. 33, 36; John Charles Chasteen, "Twilight of the Lances: The Saravia Brothers and Their World" (Ph. D. diss., University of North Carolina, 1988), pp. 111–119, 215–222.

8. Madaline Wallis Nichols, *The Gaucho: Cattle Hunter, Cavalryman, Ideal of Romance* (1942; repr., New York: Gordian Press, 1968), pp. 22–25, 30.

9. Nichols, *Gaucho*, pp. 34–35.

10. On colonial plains life, see Victor M. Ovalles, *El llanero: Estudio sobre su vida, sus costumbres, su carácter y su poesía* (Caracas: Herrera Irigoyen, 1905); Ricardo Rodríguez Molas, *Historia social del gaucho* (Buenos Aires: Marú, 1968); and José Cisneros, *Riders Across the Centuries: Horsemen of the Spanish Borderlands* (El Paso: Texas Western Press, 1984).

11. Tomás Lago, *El huaso* (Santiago: Universidad de Chile, 1953), p. 92; Claudio Gay, *Historia física y política de Chile: Agricultura*, 2 vols. (Paris, 1862, 1865), 1:387–388; Robert M. Denhardt, "The Chilean Horse," *Agricultural History* 24:3 (July 1950):162–163; J. Frank Dobie, Introduction to Frederic Remington, *Pony Tracks* (Norman: University of Oklahoma Press, 1961), pp. xi–xii.

12. Denhardt, "Chilean Horse," pp. 162–163; Gay, *Historia física*, 1: 360, 372–373; Brian Loveman, *Chile: The Legacy of Hispanic Capitalism* (New York: Oxford University Press, 1979), pp. 37, 47.

13. Sandra L. Myres, *The Ranch in Spanish Texas, 1691–1800* (El Paso: Texas Western Press, 1969), pp. 24–25.

14. Quoted in Robert B. Cunninghame Graham, *The Ipane* (London: Fisher and Unwin, 1899), p. 58; Edward Larocque Tinker, *The Horsemen of the Americas and the Literature They Inspired*, 2d ed. (Austin: University of Texas Press, 1967), p. 13.

15. Lobb, "Historical Geography," pp. 45–48; Michael G. Mulhall, *Rio Grande do Sul and Its German Colonies* (London: Longmans, Green, 1873), p. 31; Richard M. Morse, ed., *The Bandeirantes: The Historical Role of the Brazilian Pathfinders* (New York: Knopf, 1965), pp. 22–26.

16. Lobb, "Historical Geography," pp. 45–48; Mulhall, *Rio Grande do Sul*, p. 31.

17. José Carlos Canales, "Rio Grande do Sul in Luso-Spanish Platine Rivalry, 1626–1737" (Ph. D. diss., University of California, 1959), pp. 21–22, 262–263.

18. Lobb, "Historical Geography," pp. 11, 34; Mario Dotta, Duaner Freire, and Nelson Rodríguez, *El Uruguay ganadero: De la explotación primitiva a la crisis actual* (Montevideo: Banda Oriental, 1972), p. 23.

19. Jane M. Rausch, *A Tropical Plains Frontier: The Llanos of Colombia, 1531–1831* (Albuquerque: University of New Mexico Press, 1984), pp. 36–37; Eleazar Córdova-Bello, *Aspectos históricos de la ganadería en el Oriente venezolano y Guayana* (Caracas: Tipografía Remar, 1962), pp. 3–5, 17–18; Julio de Armas, "Nacimiento de la ganadería venezolana," *Revista Shell* 3:11 (June 1954):33–35; Agustín Codazzi, *Venezuela en 1841: Geografía física*, vol. 1 of *Resumen de la geografía de Venezuela* (Caracas: Biblioteca Venezolana de Cultura, 1940), p. 79. Pablo Vila, "La iniciación de la ganadería llanera," in *Visiones geohistóricas de Venezuela* (Caracas: Ministerio de Educación, 1969), p. 281, casts doubt on the importance of the Rodríguez expedition in early

livestock growth. But he concurs that colonization occurred in the llanos during the last third of the sixteenth century.

20. Guillermo Morón, *A History of Venezuela*, trans. John Street (New York: Roy, 1963), pp. 48, 49, 70.

21. Ovalles, *El llanero*, pp. 35–38; request of 1723 in "Diversos," vol. 10, pp. 180–206, Archivo General de la Nación (Caracas); Nora E. Ramirez, "The Vaquero and Ranching in the Southwestern United States, 1600–1970" (Ph. D. diss., Indiana University, 1979), pp. 157–160; Dotta, *Uruguay ganadero*, p. 23.

22. Dary, *Cowboy Culture*, pp. 19, 21.

23. Rodríguez Molas, *Historia social*, pp. 60–65, 114–115, 150; Richard W. Slatta, *Gauchos and the Vanishing Frontier* (Lincoln: University of Nebraska Press, 1983), pp. 34–35. See also Emilio R. Coni, *Historia de las vaquerías del Río de la Plata, 1550–1750* (Buenos Aires: Devenir, 1956); Eduardo Azcuy Ameghino, "Economia y sociedad colonial en el ámbito rural bonaerense," in Mario Rapoport, ed., *Economia e historia: Contribuciones a la historia económica argentina* (Buenos Aires: Editorial Tesis, 1988); Alistair Hennessy, *The Frontier in Latin American History* (Albuquerque: University of New Mexico Press, 1978), pp. 113–114.

24. John P. Robertson and William P. Robertson, *Letters on South America*, 2 vols. (1843; repr., New York: AMS Press, 1971), 1:107.

25. Richard W. Slatta, "Pulperías and Contraband Capitalism in Nineteenth-Century Buenos Aires Province," *The Americas* 38:3 (Jan. 1982):347–362; Adolfo Rodríguez, "Trama y ámbito del comercio de cueros en Venezuela," *Boletín americanista* 31 (1981):188–189, 199.

26. Miguel Izard, "Sin domicilio fijo, senda segura, ni destino conocido: Los llaneros del Apure a finales del período colonial," *Boletín Americanista* 33 (1983):21–33.

27. Jane M. Loy, "The Llanos in Colombian History: Some Implications of a Static Frontier" (Amherst: University of Massachusetts, International Area Studies Program Occasional Papers, 1976); John V. Lombardi, *Venezuela: The Search for Order, the Dream of Progress* (New York: Oxford University Press, 1982), p. 33.

28. Richard L. Vowell, *Campaigns and Cruises in Venezuela and New Granada, and in the Pacific Ocean*, 2 vols. (London: Longman, 1831),2:3.

29. George D. Flinter, *A History of the Revolution of Caracas* (London: Allman, 1819), p. 112.

30. José Antonio de Armas Chitty, *Historia del Guárico, 1807–1974* (San Juan de los Morros: Universidad "Rómulo Gallegos," 1979), p. 202; Angel de Altolaguirrey Duvale, ed., *Relaciones geográficas de la Governación de Venezuela, 1767–68* (Caracas: Edime, 1954), pp. xxiv, 213; Hugo J. Estrada R., "La ganadería en el Estado Apure: Sus problemas y perspectivas," mimeograph (Caracas: Consejo de Bienestar Rural, Oct. 1966), pp. 1–4.

31. Chasteen, "Twilight of the Lances," pp. 215–222; Lobb, "Historical Geography," pp. 137, 140, 151, 156.

32. Teodoro Schneider, *La agricultura en Chile en los últimos cincuenta años* (Santiago: Barcelona, 1904), pp. 64–67. See also George M. McBride, *Chile: Land and Society* (New York: American Geographical Society, 1936).

33. Rouse, *Criollo*, p. 74; Arnade, "Cattle Raising," pp. 118–124; Gary S. Dunbar, "Colonial Carolina Cowpens," *Agricultural History* 35:3 (July 1961): 125–130; Terry G. Jordan, "The Origin of Anglo-American Cattle Ranching in Texas: A Documentation of Diffusion from the Lower South," *Economic Geography* 45:1 (Jan. 1969):74–78, 86; Jordan, "The Origin and Distribution of Open-Range Cattle Ranching," *Social Science Quarterly* 53:1 (June 1972):106; Jordan, *Trails*

to Texas: Southern Roots of Western Cattle Ranching (Lincoln: University of Nebraska Press, 1981), pp. 118–120, 155; Forrest McDonald and Grady McWhiney, "The Antebellum Southern Herdsman: A Reinterpretation," Journal of Southern History 41 (May 1975):147–166; John D. W. Guice, "Cattle Raisers of the Old Southwest: A Reinterpretation," Western Historical Quarterly 8:2 (April 1977): 167–187; Paul C. Henlein, Cattle Kingdom in the Ohio Valley, 1783–1860 (Lexington: University of Kentucky Press, 1959), pp. 16–17.

34. Jack Jackson, Los Mesteños: Spanish Ranching in Texas, 1721–1821 (College Station: Texas A&M University Press, 1986), p. 601; Myres, Ranch in Spanish Texas, pp. 49–50.

35. Myres, Ranch in Spanish Texas, pp. 44–45, 50.

36. J. Frank Dobie, The Longhorns (New York: Grosset and Dunlap, 1941), pp. 20–21; Myres, Ranch in Spanish Texas, p. 19.

37. Jackson, Mesteños, p. 601; Myres, Ranch in Spanish Texas, pp. 49–50; Dobie, Longhorns, pp. 11–12, 27–28.

38. Don Worcester, The Texas Longhorn: Relic of the Past, Asset for the Future (College Station: Texas A&M University Press, 1987), pp. 3, 6, 77.

39. James C. Shaw, "Pioneering in Texas and Wyoming," typescript (Western Range Cattle Industry Study, Colorado Heritage Center, Denver, unpag.); Jordan, "Origin of Anglo-American Cattle Ranching," p. 74; Dary, Cowboy Culture, pp. 147, 170.

40. Dobie, Longhorns, p. 29; Jackson, Mesteños, pp. 588–595; Myres, Ranch in Spanish Texas; Myres, "The Ranching Frontier: Spanish Institutional Backgrounds of Plains Cattle Industry," in Harold M. Hollingsworth and Sandra L. Myres, eds., Essays on the American West (Austin: University of Texas Press, 1969).

41. Slatta, Gauchos, p. 15; Dary, Cowboy Culture, pp. 12–13, 38, 42, 44; Ramirez, "Vaquero," pp. 16–18.

42. Dary, Cowboy Culture, pp. 12, 15; Richard J. Morrisey, "Colonial Agriculture in New Spain," Agricultural History 31:3 (July 1957):27.

43. Richard J. Morrisey, "The Northward Expansion of Cattle Raising in New Spain, 1550–1600," Agricultural History 25:3 (July 1951):119–120; Morrisey, "The Early Range Cattle Industry in Arizona," Agricultural History 24:3 (July 1950):151; Morrisey, "Colonial Agriculture," p. 27; Donald D. Brand, "The Early History of the Range Cattle Industry in Northern Mexico," Agricultural History 35:3 (July 1961):134; L. T. Burcham, "Cattle and Range Forage in California: 1770–1880," Agricultural History 35:3 (July 1961):140, 143; Rouse, Criollo, p. 79. See also George P. Hammond and Agapito Rey, eds., Don Juan de Oñate: Colonizer of New Mexico, 2 vols. (Albuquerque: University of New Mexico Press, 1953).

44. Odie B. Faulk, "Ranching in Spanish Texas," Hispanic American Historical Review 45:2 (May 1965):257, 262; Myres, "Ranching Frontier," pp. 44–48.

45. Jackson, Mesteños, pp. 12, 33.

46. Faulk, "Ranching in Spanish Texas," pp. 264–267; Myres, Ranch in Spanish Texas, pp. 48–50.

47. Ramirez, "Vaquero," pp. 4–5; see also the several biographies of Kino, including Herbert E. Bolton, The American West: The Padre on Horseback (Chicago: Loyola University Press, 1963); and Frank C. Lockwood, With Padre Kino on the Trail (Tucson: University of Arizona Press, 1934).

48. Burcham, "Cattle and Range Forage," p. 140; Ramirez, "Vaquero," pp. 16–18.

49. Ramirez, "Vaquero," pp. 5–6.

50. Morrisey, "Early Range Cattle Industry," pp. 151–152; quotation from Don Worcester, "The Spread of Spanish Horses

in the Southwest, 1700–1800," *New Mexico Historical Review* 20:1 (Jan. 1945):13.

51. Morrisey, "Early Range Cattle Industry," pp. 152–156; Maurice W. Frink, W. Turrentine Jackson, and Agnes Wright Spring, *When Grass Was King* (Boulder: University of Colorado Press, 1956), pp. 35–36.

52. Ramirez, "Vaquero," pp. 16, 22.

53. Lynn J. Martin, ed., *Nā Paniolo o Hawai'i* (Honolulu: Honolulu Academy of Arts, 1987), pp. 18, 21, 27, 31.

54. Ibid., pp. 15, 20–21, 26.

55. Ibid., pp. 6–7, 29, 37, 39, 42, 67, 73–74, 92–93.

56. Joseph Nimmo, Jr., "The American Cow-boy," *Harper's New Monthly Magazine* 73 (Nov. 1886):881–882; Dary, *Cowboy Culture*, pp. 228–229.

57. Sheilagh S. Jameson, "Alberta Cattle Breeds and Early Cattle History" (typescript, Glenbow Archive, Calgary, D 636.081 J 31 A, 1970), p. 1; Thomas R. Weir, *Ranching in the Southern Interior Plateau of British Columbia* (Ottawa: Queen's Printer, 1964), pp. 90–91; C. S. Kingston, "Introduction of Cattle into the Pacific Northwest," *Washington Historical Quarterly* 14:3 (July 1923):163–164, 175, 181.

58. Weir, *Ranching*, pp. 85, 89–91; L. P. Gurchon, "A Brief Summary of the History of the Cattle Industry in British Columbia," *Canadian Cattlemen* 1:3 (Dec. 1938):111.

59. Don C. McGowan, *Grassland Settlers: The Swift Current Region During the Era of the Ranching Frontier* (Saskatoon: Canadian Plains Resource Center, University of Regina, 1975), pp. 83, 86, 95.

60. Simon M. Evans, "The Passing of a Frontier: Ranching in the Canadian West, 1882–1912" (Ph. D. diss., University of Calgary, 1976), pp. 2–3, 33–34, 37; Austin A. Lupton, "Cattle Ranching in Alberta, 1874–1910: Its Evolution and Migration," *Albertan Geographer* 3 (1966–1967):48.

61. Kenneth Coppock, "Early Ranching Days in Canadian West," *Canadian Cattlemen* 1:1 (June 1938):12; David H. Breen, *The Canadian Prairie West and the Ranching Frontier, 1874–1924* (Toronto: University of Toronto Press, 1983), p. 32.

62. Roe quoted in *Canadian Cattlemen* 3:4 (March 1941):527; David H. Breen, "The Turner Thesis and the Canadian West: A Closer Look at the Ranching Frontier," in Lewis H. Thomas, ed., *Essays on Western History in Honour of Lewis Gwynne Thomas* (Edmonton: University of Alberta Press, 1976):152; Paul F. Sharp, *Whoop-Up Country: The Canadian-American West, 1865–1885* (Helena: Historical Society of Montana, 1960), pp. 305–306; Evans, "Passing of a Frontier," pp. 41–42.

Chapter 3. Cowboy Character and Appearance

1. René León Echaiz, *Interpretación histórica del huaso chileno* (Santiago: Editorial Universitaria, 1955), pp. 27–29, 34–36, 39–42, 63.

2. Mario Góngora, *Vagabundaje y sociedad fronteriza en Chile, siglos XVII a XIX* (Santiago: Universidad de Chile, 1966), pp. 33, 40; Arnold J. Bauer, *Chilean Rural Society from the Spanish Conquest to 1930* (Cambridge: Cambridge University Press, 1975), p. 55.

3. George Byam, *Wanderings in Some of the Western Republics of America* (London: John W. Parker, 1850), p. 122.

4. Góngora, *Vagabundaje*, pp. 6–7; Brian Loveman, *Chile: The Legacy of Hispanic Capitalism* (New York: Oxford University Press, 1979), pp. 39–40; Tomás Lago, *El huaso* (Santiago: Universidad de Chile, 1953), p. 9.

5. Lago, *Huaso*, p. 315; Loveman, *Chile*, pp. 39–40.

6. Echaiz, *Interpretación histórica*, pp. 66, 77; Lago, *Huaso*, p. 155.

7. Echaiz, *Interpretación histórica*, pp. 66–68; Lago, *Huaso*, pp. 28, 203; Maria Dundas Graham, *Journal of a Residence in Chile* (1824; repr., New York: Praeger, 1969), p. 189.

8. Thomas Sutcliffe, *Sixteen Years in Chile and Peru from 1822 to 1839* (London: Fisher, Son, 1841), pp. 324–325.

9. Sutcliffe, *Sixteen Years*, pp. 325–326.

10. Richard W. Slatta, *Gauchos and the Vanishing Frontier* (Lincoln: University of Nebraska Press, 1983), pp. 9–10.

11. Charles Darwin, *Journal of Researches into the Geology and Natural History of the Various Countries Visited by H. M. S. Beagle* (1839; facs. ed., New York: Hafner, 1952), p. 48.

12. Ibid., p. 48.

13. Robert Cunninghame Graham, "La Pampa," in John Walker, ed., *The South American Sketches of R. B. Cunninghame Graham* (Norman: University of Oklahoma Press, 1978), p. 26.

14. Slatta, *Gauchos*, pp. 9–16, 31–32, 43.

15. Ibid., pp. 32–34, 108, 114–116.

16. Richard W. Slatta, "Images of Social Banditry on the Argentine Pampa," in Slatta, ed., *Bandidos: The Varieties of Latin American Banditry* (Westport, Conn.: Greenwood Press, 1987), pp. 51–52, 56.

17. Ibid., pp. 57, 62.

18. Ranch workers had limited but potentially significant leverage and autonomy during the colonial period. See Ricardo Salvatore and Jonathan C. Brown, "Trade and Proletarianization in Late Colonial Banda Oriental: Evidence from the Estancia de las Vacas, 1791–1805," *Hispanic American Historical Review* 67:3 (Aug. 1987):431–460.

19. Slatta, *Gauchos*, pp. 74–75.

20. William Henry Webster, *Narrative of a Voyage to the Southern Atlantic Ocean in the Years 1828, 29, 30* (London: Richard Bentley, 1834), pp. 81–82. On gaucho dress, see Fernando Assunção, *El gaucho* (Montevideo: Imprenta Nacional, 1963), pp. 215–238, and Assunção, *Pilchas criollas: Usos y costumbres del gaucho*, rev. ed. (Montevideo: Master Fer, 1979).

21. Comisión de Hacendados del Estado de Buenos Aires, *Antecedentes y fundamentos del proyecto de código rural* (Buenos Aires, 1864), pp. 31, 176, 202; Slatta, *Gauchos*, pp. 73–76.

22. Robert B. Cunninghame Graham, "Los llanos del Apure," in Walker, *South American Sketches*, pp. 275–276.

23. Robert Ker Porter, *Sir Robert Ker Porter's Caracas Diary, 1825–1842: A British Diplomat in a Newborn Nation*, ed. Walter Dupuoy (Caracas: Walter Dupuoy, 1966), pp. 189, 868.

24. Ramón Paez, *Wild Scenes in South America: Or Life in the Llanos of Venezuela* (London: Sampson Low, 1862), p. 33.

25. Paez, *Wild Scenes*, p. 14; Karl Ferdinand Appun, "Los llanos de El Baúl," trans. Federica de Ritter, *Anales de la Universidad Central de Venezuela* 32 (Jan. 1953):212. Appun visited the llanos in 1848.

26. Paez, *Wild Scenes*, pp. 13–14.

27. Robert B. Cunninghame Graham, *José Antonio Paez* (London: Heinemann, 1929), p. 18.

28. Porter, *Diary*, p. 680; Karl Sachs, *De los llanos: Descripción de un viaje de ciencias naturales a Venezuela*, trans. José Izquierda (Caracas and Madrid: Edime, 1955), p. 66; Slatta, *Gauchos*, pp. 74, 184.

29. Eleazar Córdova-Bello, *Aspectos históricos de la ganadería en el Oriente venezolano y Guayana* (Caracas: Tipografía Remar, 1962), pp. 40–41.

30. Paez, *Wild Scenes*, pp. 42–43.

31. Miguel Izard, "Los llaneros del Apure," in Izard, ed., *Marginados, fron-*

terizos, rebeldes y oprimidos, 2 vols. (Barcelona: Ediciones Serbal, 1985), 2:42; Paez, *Wild Scenes*, p. 50.

32. Appun, "Los llanos," p. 212; Sachs, *De los llanos*, p. 88; Pál Rosti, *Memorias de un viaje por América*, trans. Judith Sarosi (Caracas: Universidad Central de Venezuela, 1968), p. 183. Rosti visited the llanos in 1857.

33. Graham, "Los llanos del Apure," in Walker, *South American Sketches*, p. 278.

34. Theodore Roosevelt, *Ranch Life and the Hunting Trail* (1888; fasc. ed., Ann Arbor: University Microfilms, 1966), p. 11.

35. J. Frank Dobie, "Ranch Mexicans," *Survey* 66:3 (May 1, 1931):169–170. Nora E. Ramirez, "The Vaquero and Ranching in the Southwestern United States, 1600–1970" (Ph. D. diss., Indiana University, 1979), pp. 191–193, 199–200, also documents the vaquero's superstitions and fondness for tales of treasure and ghosts.

36. Ramirez, "Vaquero," pp. 180–181; J. Frank Dobie, "The Mexican Vaquero of the Texas Border," *Southwestern Political and Social Science Quarterly* 8:1 (June 1927):3.

37. Ramirez, "Vaquero," pp. 182–183, 264; F. Warner Robinson, "The New Cattle Country," *Scribner's Magazine* 51:2 (Feb. 1912):180.

38. Theodore A. Dodge, "Some American Riders," *Harper's Magazine*, July 1891:211.

39. Robinson, "New Cattle Country," p. 180.

40. Jo Mora, *Californios: The Saga of the Hard-riding Vaqueros, America's First Cowboys* (Garden City: Doubleday, 1949), pp. 17–18.

41. José Cisneros, *Riders across the Centuries: Horsemen of the Spanish Borderlands* (El Paso: Texas Western Press, 1984), p. 192; Mora, *Californios*, p. 99; Ramirez, "Vaquero," p. 100. On the Brazilian vaqueiro, see Peter Rivière, *The Forgotten Frontier: Ranchers of North Brazil* (New York: Holt, Rinehart and Winston, 1972).

42. Ramirez, "Vaquero," pp. 184–186, 198; Slatta, *Gauchos*, p. 118.

43. José Ramón Ballesteros, *Origen y evolución del charro mexicano* (Mexico: Manuel Porrúa, 1972), pp. 17–18; Glen R. Vernam, *Man on Horseback: The Story of the Mounted Man from the Scythians to the American Cowboy* (Lincoln: University of Nebraska Press, 1972), p. 155; Francois Chevalier, *Land and Society in Colonial Mexico*, trans. Alvin Eustis, ed. Lesley Byrd Simpson (Berkeley: University of California Press, 1963), p. 306.

44. Cisneros, *Riders*, pp. 187, 198.

45. Lynn J. Martin, ed., *Nā Paniolo o Hawai'i* (Honolulu: Honolulu Academy of Arts, 1987), pp. 70, 74–75.

46. Ibid., p. 44, 61–62.

47. Ibid., p. 44.

48. Ibid., p. 55; see the paniolo portraits, pp. 64–65.

49. Ibid., p. 39.

50. Quoted in Douglas Branch, *The Cowboy and His Interpreters* (New York: Appleton, 1926), pp. 11–12.

51. Quoted in Clifford P. Westermeier, ed., *Trailing the Cowboy: His Life and Lore as Told by Frontier Journalists* (Caldwell, Idaho: Caxton Printers, 1955), p. 47.

52. Issue of Dec. 13, 1884, quoted in Westermeier, *Trailing the Cowboy*, pp. 46–47.

53. Quoted in John K. Rollinson, *Wyoming Cattle Trails: History of the Migration of Oregon-raised Herds to Mid-western Markets* (Caldwell, Idaho: Caxton Printers, 1948), p. 233.

54. Quoted in Westermeier, *Trailing the Cowboy*, pp. 42–43.

55. John Baumann, "On a Western Ranche," *Fortnightly Review* 47 (April 1, 1887):516; see also Baumann, "Experiences

Cowboys in many countries *became popular culture icons. People around the world immediately recognize the American cowboy and the Argentine gaucho as national symbols. Advertisers cashed in on the cowboy's appeal. Novelists and filmmakers provided countless depictions, many notable only for their ahistorical and unartistic renderings. Working cowhands may be relatively few today, but the cowboy's second life in popular culture shows no signs of waning.*

Dried fruits *were a favorite part of the American cowboy's diet. A California prune company recognized the cowboy as an important market and used his image on their packaging around the turn of the century. (Prints and Photographs Division, Library of Congress)*

Advertisers and popularizers *manipulated and propagated exciting cowboy imagery with little concern for historical reality (pp. 191–92). The 1886 trade card below depicts vaqueros hard at work unloading cattle and hogs on a New York City pier, an unlikely event. A cotton thread company used the Mexican vaquero to convey the strength of its product around 1880. (Prints and Photographs Division, Library of Congress)*

A TEXAS COW BOY OR FIFTEEN YEARS ON THE HURRICANE DECK OF A SPANISH PONY. TAKEN FROM REAL LIFE BY Chas. A. Siringo. AN OLD STOVE UP COW PUNCHER WHO HAS SPENT NEARLY A LIFE TIME ON THE GREAT WESTERN CATTLE RANGES.

Unlike largely illiterate *Latin American riders, some American cowboys left written records of their thoughts and views. The first cowboy autobiography,* A Texas Cow Boy *by Charles A. Siringo, appeared in 1885. The success of his book created a cowboy memoir genre. Some classics emerged, but many such writings hold little historical or literary interest (p. 206). (Yale Collection of Western Americana, Beinecke Rate Book and Manuscript Library)*

Andy Adams *wrote one of the best accounts of life on a cattle drive,* The Log of a Cowboy *(1903). The book mixes fact and fiction, but it offers a lively, unvarnished portrait of cowboy life (p. 205). (Yale Collection of Western Americana, Beinecke Rare Book and Manuscript Library)*

THE LOG OF A COWBOY

BY ANDY ADAMS

The cover of The Quirt and the Spur *by Edgar Rye (1909) portrays a dangerous-looking vaquero, complete with giant sombrero and mustache. Unlike some writers of cowboy tales, Rye had lived in the West around Fort Griffin, Texas. (Yale Collection of Western Americana, Beinecke Rare Book and Manuscript Library)*

Owen Wister's *novel* The Virginian *(p. 205), shown here in the first edition of 1902, quickly gained popular and critical acclaim. Selling fifty thousand copies in merely two months, the book inspired innumerable imitators who seldom matched the Philadelphia lawyer's literary skill. (Yale Collection of Western Americana, Beinecke Rare Book and Manuscript Library)*

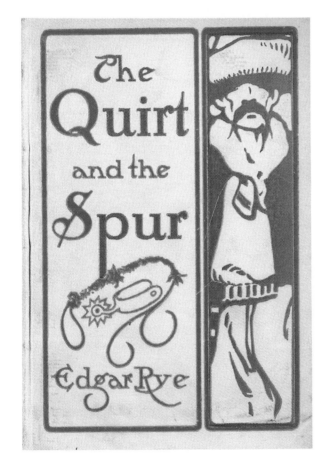

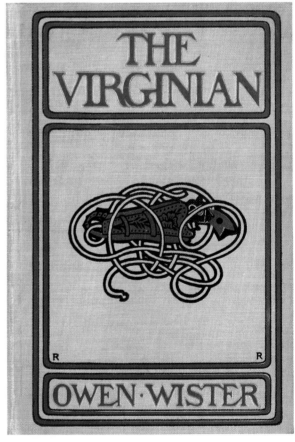

William Roderick "Will" James, *author and illustrator, was photographed in Canada in 1911. Among his books are* Cow Country *(1927), the autobiographical* Lone Cowboy *(1930), and* Cowboys North and South *(1931). He is sometimes confused with W. S. James, whose autobiography,* Cowboy Life in Texas, *was published in 1893. (Glenbow Archives, Calgary)*

The nickel and dime novels of the Beadle publishing house (p. 206), though wildly inaccurate, spread pseudo-cowboy imagery far and wide. *Patent Leather Joe* (1878), *Deadwood Dick* (1884), and other fictitious cowboy heroes meted out justice with a six-gun and saved countless maidens from villains and Indians. (Prints and Photographs Division, Library of Congress)

The gaucho *is an important cultural icon in Argentina and Uruguay. The gaúcho in neighboring Rio Grande do Sul, Brazil, achieved regional significance. Far and away the most important literary work about the gaucho is* Martín Fierro, *a two-part poem by José Hernández (pp. 207–08). Published in the 1870s, the poem captures in the gaucho's own dialect his travails at the hands of corrupt political and military officials.*

Eugene Manlove Rhodes, *shown at right about 1900, wrote a number of fine novels, short stories, and articles about life in the American Southwest (p. 206). Unlike some cowboy writers who used a folksy, ungrammatical style, Rhodes crafted his writing with attention to generally accepted literary standards. Even the title of his best work,* Pasó por Aquí, *shows an appreciation for the Hispanic element of southwestern culture. (Rio Grande Historical Collections, New Mexico State University Library)*

LA VUELTA
DE
MARTIN FIERRO
POR
JOSÉ HERNANDEZ

PRIMERA EDICION, ADORNADA CON DIEZ LAMINAS

SE VENDE EN TODAS LAS LIBRERIAS DE BUENOS AIRES

Depósito central: **LIBRERIA DEL PLATA**, Calle Tacuari, 47

1879

Although only a few *American cowboys became accomplished authors, most enjoyed reading (pp. 121–22). This bronze statue by Grant Kinzer stands outside the library of New Mexico State University in Las Cruces. (Photograph by Tim Blevins, Rio Grande Historical Collections, New Mexico State University Library)*

Cowboy imagery *became important not only in literature but also in politics. Theodore Roosevelt (facing page) relished the reputation he acquired as a rancher in the Dakota Territory and as leader of the famous "Rough Riders" (p. 191). (Prints and Photographs Division, Library of Congress)*

Roosevelt recounted *his adventures in the Dakota Badlands in* Ranch Life and the Hunting Trail *(1888). The future president's recollections, illustrated by Frederic Remington, increased awareness of the cowboy in Eastern establishment circles (p. 191). (Courtesy of Yale University Library)*

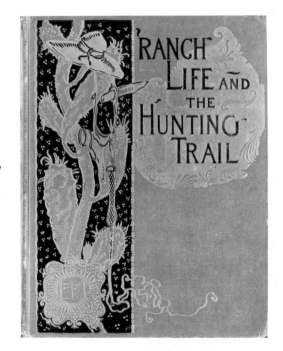

Ronald Reagan *began his acting career as a B Western film cowboy (p. 192). Like his contemporary John Wayne, Reagan blended silverscreen cowboy values and political conservatism. In this scene from* The Bad Man *(1941), a band of Mexicans led by Wallace Beery is about to hang Reagan—a fictional foretaste of his later difficulties with Latin America. The future president's failure to obtain leading roles in big-budget Westerns likely helped move him away from acting toward a political career. (The Bettman Archive)*

THE GREAT TRAIN ROBBERY

WRITTEN BY SCOTT MARBLE

WRESTLING FOR WEALTH.

A DARE-DEVIL COW-BOY TRIUMPHS OVER AN ENORMOUS GRIZZLY.

Like novelists and politicians, *playwrights and film producers capitalized on the cowboy's popularity.* The Great Train Robbery, *a play written by Scott Marble in 1896, included such spectacles as a cowboy wrestling with a bear. The play may have inspired Edwin S. Porter's famous 1903 movie of the same name. That short film created archetypes, including a chase scene and shootout, emulated in the hundreds of cowboy films that followed (pp. 215–16). (Prints and Photographs Division, Library of Congress)*

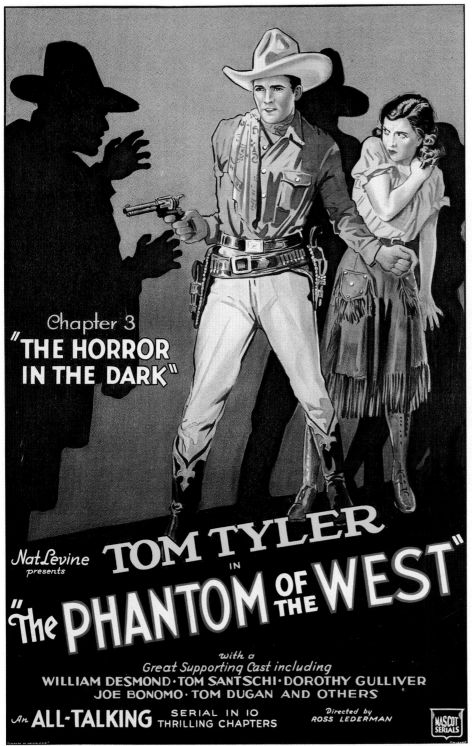

William S. Hart, one of the first cowboy film stars, provided an archetype for later depictions. Hart's cowboy was a strong, silent, moral man who righted wrongs and chilled bad men with his icy stare. He is shown on the facing page in a scene from the 1917 film The Narrow Trail. *(Prints and Photographs Division, Library of Congress)*

B Western movies flourished from the 1920s through the early 1950s. Beginning in the late 1920s, talkies added the exciting sounds of galloping hooves, gunshots, and furniture-smashing fistfights. Tom Tyler, unlike many silent-era stars, made a successful transition to the talkies. The essential Western plot line of a strong, lone hero defeating the forces of evil (after a lengthy chase scene) and winning the girl remained much the same. This poster dates from 1930. *(Poster Collection, Prints and Photographs Division, Library of Congress)*

Argentina became *a major producer of Spanish-language films. Gaucho movies, often based on major literary works, attracted large audiences, just as cowboy movies did in the United States (pp. 216–17). These stills are from* Martín Fierro *(above, 1968, directed by Leopoldo Torre Nilsson), and* La guerra gaucha *(right, 1942, directed by Lucas Demare). (Cinemateca Argentina, Buenos Aires)*

Cowgirls *moved into popular culture via films, rodeos, and Wild West shows. One of the first famous cowgirls was Calamity Jane (Martha Jane Cannary). Her life of cigar smoking, tobacco chewing, hard drinking, and checkered love affairs set her apart from the weak, chaste heroines of the B Westerns. Calamity Jane became a legend in her own time. Larry McMurtry adds to the legend with his fictionalized biography,* Buffalo Girls *(1990). (Prints and Photographs Division, Library of Congress)*

MARIA CONESA

Latin American women *were prevented by machismo from assuming as prominent a role as American cowgirls. We find no equivalents of Annie Oakley or Calamity Jane. Generally depicted in popular culture as weak and retiring, Latin American women served their men loyally and were rewarded with masculine protection. This Mexican belle, Maria Conesa, wears a gay sombrero, a tribute to the staying power of vaquero imagery. (Prints and Photographs Division, Library of Congress)*

The singing cowboy
offered another popular variation in Western films (p. 216): Roy Rogers and the Sons of the Pioneers made many movies together. Rogers also performed with his wife, Dale Evans. Like Roy and Dale, Gene Autry (opposite) successfully moved from movies to television in the 1950s. (Photographs courtesy of the Country Music Foundation, Inc.)

Cowboy music *continued to evolve outside of films, and every variation brought new audiences (p. 194). Bob Wills and His Texas Playboys (above) helped launch Texas swing in the 1940s. During the 1960s Waylon Jennings, Willie Nelson (below), and others created a brand of outlaw cowboy music. (Photographs courtesy of the Country Music Foundation, Inc.)*

By the 1930s, *country music had become country-and-western music as cowboy influence grew (p. 194). Through radio, movies, live performances, sheet music, and finally television, cowboy music spread throughout the nation. The sheet music cover on the facing page shows a cowboy mailing a letter, a subject often depicted in photographs and art. (Music Division, Library of Congress)*

THE LONESOME COWBOY
SONGS of the PLAINS and HILLS
WITH CHORD ACCOMPANIMENTS for UKULELE, TENOR BANJO and GUITAR.
JOHN WHITE
THE LONESOME COWBOY
Net Price $1.00
Compiled by John White George Shackley
M1629 .W58L5 1930
SOLE SELLING AGENTS
F.B. HAVILAND PUB. CO.
NEW YORK.
J.E. DoubleR.Y
VOGEL MUSIC CO., INC.
112 WEST 44th STREET NEW YORK
PUBLISHED BY
GEORGE T. WORTH & CO.
112 W. 44th ST. NEW YORK

Riders in the Sky, *based in Nashville, perform old cowboy music (p. 196), as well as write new songs faithful to the original genre. Like the cowboy poets who gather each year in Nevada, Riders in the Sky help to preserve the cowboy's cultural heritage. (Photograph courtesy of the Country Music Foundation, Inc.)*

American cowboy culture *is celebrated in hundreds of rodeos each year. Popular media perpetuate the lore of the West, as in the 1904 cover of* Sunset *magazine on the facing page. (Prints and Photographs Division, Library of Congress)*

SUNSET

SUNSET MAGAZINE
San Francisco, California

METHFESSEL

JANUARY 1904

THE MAGAZINE OF CALIFORNIA and THE FAR WEST

Going to Sea by Rail — Crossing Great Salt Lake — Stories of Hawaii and Japan

Published by SOUTHERN PACIFIC COMPANY, San Francisco, California.   For Sale by Newsdealers Everywhere

SUNSET PRESS

Argentines celebrate *their gaucho heritage on the "Day of Tradition" each November 10, the birthday of José Hernández. Open-range ranch life may be gone and working cowboys may be few and far between, but the cowboy lives. (Argentine postcard, author's collection)*

EL ARQUETIPO DE NUESTRA NACIONALIDAD
por FELIX J. BERNARD

COZZI A.

Gaucho (año 1850)

10 de Noviembre de 1972 "DIA DE LA TRADICION"

of a Cow-Boy," *Lippincott's Magazine* 38 (Aug. 1886).

56. William Adolph Baillie-Grohman, *Camps in the Rockies* (New York: Scribner's, 1884), p. 344.

57. Joseph G. McCoy, *Cattle Trade of the West and Southwest* (1874; repr., N.p.: Readex Microprint, 1966), p. 10. More cattlemen's views appear in James W. Freeman, ed., *Poetry and Prose of the Live Stock Industry of the United States* (Denver: National Livestock Historical Association, 1905).

58. William Timmons, *Twilight on the Range: Recollections of a Latterday Cowboy* (Austin: University of Texas Press, 1962), pp. 10–11.

59. Lonn Taylor and Ingrid Maar, *The American Cowboy* (Washington, D. C.: Library of Congress, 1983), p. 22.

60. Joseph Nimmo, Jr., "The American Cow-boy," *Harper's New Monthly Magazine* 73 (Nov. 1886):883.

61. David Dary, *Cowboy Culture: A Saga of Five Centuries* (New York: Knopf, 1981), pp. 278–279.

62. Quoted in Wayne H. Goussard, Jr., "Life on the Trail: The 1894 Diary of Perry Eugene Davis," *Colorado Heritage* 1 (1981):28–31.

63. Michael S. Kennedy, ed., *Cowboys and Cattlemen: A Roundup from "Montana, the Magazine of Western History"* (New York: Hastings House, 1964), p. x.

64. Quotations from Florence B. Hughes, "Listening-in at the Old Timer's Hut," *Canadian Cattlemen* 4:1 (June 1941):32.

65. John W. G. MacEwan, *Between the Red and the Rockies* (Toronto: University of Toronto Press, 1952), pp. 149–152; David H. Breen, *The Canadian Prairie West and the Ranching Frontier, 1874–1924* (Toronto: University of Toronto Press, 1983), pp. 25–27, 167–168.

66. John R. Craig, *Ranching with Lords and Commons; or, Twenty Years on the Range* (1903; repr., New York: AMS Press, 1971), p. 86; Thomas quoted in Paul F. Sharp, *Whoop-Up Country: The Canadian-American West, 1865–1885* (Helena: Historical Society of Montana, 1960), p. 72.

67. Duncan McNab McEachran, "A Journey over the Plains from Fort Benton to Bow River and Back," repr. from the *Gazette* (Montreal), Nov. 1881 (Glenbow Archive, Calgary, pamphlet 971.23, M141j), pp. 12–13; Calgary *Herald*, Nov. 12, 1884, quoted in Breen, *Canadian Prairie West*, p. 85.

68. Herbert E. Church, *An Emigrant in the Canadian Northwest* (London: Methuen, 1929), pp. 34–35; Breen, *Canadian Prairie West*, p. 256, n. 60; J. Frank Dobie, *The Longhorns* (New York: Grosset and Dunlap, 1941), p. 125.

69. Calgary *News-Telegram*, Sept. 19, 1912, reproduced in *Alberta Historical Review* 18:1 (Summer 1970):13.

70. Wallace Stegner, *Wolf Willow: A History, a Story, and a Memory of the Last Plains Frontier* (Toronto: Macmillan, 1962), pp. 135–136.

71. Anon., "Memoirs of an Itinerant Cowhand," *Canadian Cattlemen* 5:4 (March 1943):101.

72. Mary Ella Inderwick, "Letter to Alice, May 13, 1884, from North Fork Ranch, Alberta" (Glenbow Archive, Calgary, M 559), pp. 2–3.

73. Monica Hopkins, *Letters from a Lady Rancher* (Calgary: Glenbow Museum, 1981), p. 20.

74. Frank Gilbert Roe, "Remittance Men," *Alberta Historical Review* 2:1 (Jan. 1954):6. For more charitable views of young Englishmen in the Canadian West, see Patrick A. Dunae, *Gentlemen Emigrants: From the British Public Schools to the Canadian Frontier* (Vancouver and Toronto: Douglas and McIntyre, 1981).

Chapter 4. American Plains Frontiers

1. Richard W. Slatta, *Gauchos and the Vanishing Frontier* (Lincoln: University of Nebraska Press, 1983), pp. 18–19.

2. George Catlin, *Episodes from Life Among the Indians and Last Rambles*, ed. Marvin C. Ross (Norman: University of Oklahoma Press, 1959), pp. 129–130.

3. Carl E. Solberg, "A Discriminatory Frontier Land Policy: Chile, 1870–1914," *The Americas* 26:2 (Oct. 1969):115; Brian Loveman, *Chile: The Legacy of Hispanic Capitalism* (New York: Oxford University Press, 1979), pp. 48, 61, 73–74.

4. John Charles Chasteen, "Twilight of the Lances: The Saravia Brothers and Their World" (Ph. D. diss., University of North Carolina, 1988), pp. 215–222; Michael G. Mulhall, *Rio Grande do Sul and Its German Colonies* (London: Longmans, Green, 1873), p. 24. On the colonial history of Rio Grande do Sul, see Oliveira Viana, *O campeador riograndense*, vol. 2 of *Populaçoes meridionais do Brasil* (Rio de Janeiro: Paz e Terra, 1972).

5. Catherine LeGrand, *Frontier Expansion and Peasant Protest in Colombia, 1850–1936* (Albuquerque: University of New Mexico Press, 1986), pp. 8–9. On southern Brazil, see Sergio da Costa Franco, "A campanha," and Paulo Xavier, "A estancia," in *Rio Grande do Sul: Terra e povo* (Porto Alegre: Editora Globo, 1963). For contemporary descriptions of Brazil, see May Frances, *Beyond the Argentine, or, Letters from Brazil* (London: H. W. Allen, 1890), and Charles G. Hamilton, "English-Speaking Travelers in Brazil, 1851–1887," *Hispanic American Historical Review* 40:4 (Nov. 1960):533–547.

6. Alfredo Castellanos, *La cisplatina, la independencia y la república caudillesca, 1820–1838*, vol. 3 of *Historia uruguaya*, 2d ed. (Montevideo: Banda Oriental, 1975), pp. 7, 30–33, 59–64, 82.

7. Juan Iturbe, "Nuestros llanos: Apuntes fisiográficas, biológicas y agropecuarias" (Caracas: La Nación, 1942), pp. 5, 33; John V. Lombardi, *People and Places in Colonial Venezuela* (Bloomington: Indiana University Press, 1976), p. 22. Frederick Gerstacker compares the llanos, pampas, and Great Plains in *Viaje por Venezuela en el año 1868*, trans. Ana María Gathmann (Caracas: Universidad Central de Venezuela, 1968), p. 67.

8. Pablo Vila, *Geografía de Venezuela*, 2d facs. ed. (Caracas: Ministerio de Educación, 1969), pp. 236–239. I have drawn most of my information on the llanos from Venezuelan sources. On the Colombian llanos, see Jane M. Rausch, *A Tropical Plains Frontier: The Llanos of Colombia, 1531–1831* (Albuquerque: University of New Mexico Press, 1984).

9. Robert B. Cunninghame Graham, "The Plains of Venezuela," in *Rodeo* (Garden City: Doubleday, Doran, 1936), p. 46.

10. No work comparable to Rausch's *Tropical Plains Frontier* exists for Venezuela. On llanos historiography, see Richard W. Slatta and Arturo Alvarez D'Armas, "El llanero y el hato venezolano: Aportes bibliográficas," *South Eastern Latin Americanist* 29:2–3 (Sept. 1985): 33–41.

11. Donald D. Brand, "The Early History of the Range Cattle Industry in Northern Mexico," *Agricultural History* 35:3 (July 1961):133.

12. George M. McBride, *The Land Systems of Mexico* (1923; repr., New York: Octagon, 1971), pp. 38, 154.

13. William Eugene Hollon, *The Great American Desert Then and Now* (New York: Oxford University Press, 1966), p. 5.

14. L. P. Guichon, "A Brief Summary of the History of the Cattle Industry in British Columbia," *Canadian Cattlemen* 1:3 (Dec. 1938):111, 138.

15. John Macoun, *Manitoba and the*

Great Northwest (Guelph, Ontario: World Publishing, 1882), p. 255.

16. Sheilagh S. Jameson, "The Era of the Big Ranches: The Romantic Period of Southern Alberta's History" (unpublished MS., Glenbow Archive, Calgary, D 636.081 J31, May 1968), p. 3; reprinted as "Era of the Big Ranches," *Alberta Historical Review* 18:1 (Summer 1970):1–9.

17. Mary Ella Inderwick, "Letter to Alice, May 13, 1884, from North Fork Ranch, Alberta" (Glenbow Archive, Calgary, M 559); reprinted in "A Lady and Her Ranch," *Alberta Historical Review* 15:4 (Autumn 1967):1–9.

18. Duncan McNab McEachran, "A Journey over the Plains from Fort Benton to Bow River and Back" (Glenbow Archive, pamphlet 971.23 M141j, Nov. 1881), pp. 2, 4.

19. Slatta, *Gauchos*, pp. 40, 70.

20. J. Orin Oliphant and C. S. Kingston, eds., "William Easley Jackson's Diary of a Cattle Drive from La Grange, Oregon, to Cheyenne, Wyoming, in 1876," *Agricultural History* 23:4 (Oct. 1949):261, 264; Porter quoted in Jack K. Rollinson, *Wyoming Cattle Trails: History of the Migration of Oregon-raised Herds to Midwestern Markets* (Caldwell, Idaho: Caxton Printers, 1948), pp. 101–102.

21. Karl Sachs, *De los llanos: Descripción de un viaje de ciencias naturales a Venezuela*, trans. José Ezquierdo (Caracas and Madrid: Edime, 1955), pp. 94, 236. On llanos floods and epidemics, see Manuel Landaeta Rosales, *Gran recopilación geográfica, estadística e histórica de Venezuela*, 2 vols. (Caracas: Banco Central de Venezuela, 1963), 2:230–231; and Iturbe, "Nuestros llanos," pp. 25–27.

22. Manual Tejera, *Venezuela pintoresca e ilustrada* (Paris: Librería Española, 1875), p. 247.

23. Agustín Codazzi, *Resumen de la geografía de Venezuela* (Caracas: Ministerio de Educación Nacional, 1940), p. 90; Luis J. Alfonso, *Breve análisis del pasado de Venezuela* (Caracas: Imprenta Nacional, 1872), p. iii.

24. Alistair Hennessy, *The Frontier in Latin American History* (Albuquerque: University of New Mexico Press, 1978), p. 87; Jane M. Loy, "The Llanos in Colombian History: Some Implications of a Static Frontier" (Amherst: University of Massachusetts, International Area Studies Program Occasional Papers, 1976).

25. Rómulo Gallegos, *Cantaclaro* (Caracas: Ministerio de Educación, 1945), p. 246; Gallegos, "Necesidad de valores culturales," in *Una posición de la vida* (Mexico: Humanismo, 1954), pp. 84–85; Marco Aurelio Vila, *Las sequías en Venezuela* (Caracas: Fondo Editorial Común, 1975), pp. 95–129.

26. Quoted in Adolfo Rodríguez, "Los mitos del llano y el llanero en la obra de Rómulo Gallegos" (San Fernando: Cronista del Estado, 1979), p. 5; Laureano Vallenilla Lanz, *Disgregación e integración: Ensayo sobre la formación de la nacionalidad venezolana*, 2 vols. (Caracas: Universal, 1930), 1:66.

27. Ezequiel Martínez Estrada, *X-Ray of the Pampa*, trans. Alain Swietlicki (Austin: University of Texas Press, 1971), pp. 6–7.

28. Domingo F. Sarmiento, *Facundo* (1845), trans. Mrs. Horace (Mary) Mann as *Life in the Argentine Republic in the Days of the Tyrants* (1868; repr., New York: Hafner, 1971). On Sarmiento's views, see Slatta, *Gauchos*, pp. 182–184; and William H. Katra, *Domingo F. Sarmiento: Public Writer (Between 1839 and 1852)* (Tempe: Arizona State University Press, 1985).

29. Henry Marie Brackenridge, *Voyage to South America*, 2 vols. (Baltimore: Cushing and Jewett, 1819), 1:222; Slatta, *Gauchos*, pp. 21–25.

30. On Argentine agriculture, see James

R. Scobie, *Revolution on the Pampas: A Social History of Wheat* (Austin: University of Texas Press, 1964); Slatta, *Gauchos*, pp. 150–160; and David Rock, *Argentina, 1516–1987: From Spanish Colonization to Alfonsín*, 2d ed. (Berkeley: University of California Press, 1987), pp. 135–140.

31. On perceptions of Southern Cone Indians, see Kristine L. Jones, "Nineteenth Century British Travel Accounts of Argentina," *Ethnohistory* 33:2 (1986):195–211.

32. Arnold Bauer, "Chilean Rural Labor in the Nineteenth Century," *American Historical Review* 76:4 (Oct. 1971):1,070.

33. Carl E. Solberg, *Immigration and Nationalism: Argentina and Chile, 1890–1914* (Austin: University of Texas Press, 1970), pp. 139–146. See also Hugo F. Castillo, "Agrarian Structures in a Region of Recent Colonization: La Frontera, Chile, 1850–1920" (Ph. D. diss., University of North Carolina, 1983).

34. Walter Prescott Webb, "The American West, Perpetual Mirage," *Harper's Magazine*, May 1957:26, 29; Hollon, *Great American Desert*, p. 5.

35. R. Douglas Francis, "From Wasteland to Utopia: Changing Images of the Canadian West in the Nineteenth Century," *Great Plains Quarterly* 7:3 (Summer 1987):179–181. See also Francis, "Changing Images of the West," *Journal of Canadian Studies* 17 (Fall 1982):5–19. On conflicting plains imagery in the United States and Canada, see "The Desert and the Garden," part 5 of Brian W. Blouet and Merlin P. Lawson, eds., *Images of the Plains: The Role of Human Nature in Settlement* (Lincoln: University of Nebraska Press, 1975), pp. 125–188.

36. Macoun, *Manitoba*, p. 252.

37. Francis, "Wasteland to Utopia," pp. 187–189; Paul F. Sharp, "The American Farmer and the 'Last Best West,'" *Agricultural History* 21:2 (April 1947): 65–75.

38. Sharp, "American Farmer," pp. 65–75. For more on the Canadian frontier, see Michael S. Cross, ed., *The Turner Thesis and the Canadas: The Debate on the Impact of the Canadian Environment* (Toronto: Copp Clark, 1970).

39. Wallace Stegner, *Wolf Willow: A History, a Story, and a Memory of the Last Plains Frontier* (Toronto: Macmillan, 1962), p. 96.

Chapter 5. In the Saddle

1. Robert Ker Porter, *Sir Robert Ker Porter's Caracas Diary, 1825–1842: A British Diplomat in a Newborn Nation*, ed. Walter Dupuoy (Caracas: Walter Dupuoy, 1966), p. 683.

2. Isaac F. Holton, *New Granada: Twenty Months in the Andes* (New York: Harper and Brothers, 1857), p. 429.

3. Fernando Calzadilla Valdes, *Por los llanos de Apure* (Santiago: Imprenta Universitaria, 1940), pp. 41–42, 46–47; Horacio Cabrera Sifontes, *La Rubiera* (Caracas: N.p., 1972), pp. 81–83; Porter, *Diary*, p. 688. *La Rubiera* is fictionalized history but includes accurate descriptions of llaneros at work in Calabozo, pp. 79–95.

4. Cabrera Sifontes, *La Rubiera*, p. 82; Frederic Remington, *Pony Tracks* (Norman: University of Oklahoma Press, 1961), p. 57.

5. Ricardo Güiraldes, *Don Segundo Sombra: Shadows on the Pampas*, trans. Harriet de Onís (New York: Signet, 1966), p. 126; Richard W. Slatta, *Gauchos and the Vanishing Frontier* (Lincoln: University of Nebraska Press), p. 46.

6. Tomás Lago, *El huaso* (Santiago: Universidad de Chile, 1953), pp. 131–132.

7. Thomas Sutcliffe, *Sixteen Years in Chile and Peru from 1822 to 1839* (London: Fisher, 1841), pp. 326–328.

8. Sutcliffe, *Sixteen Years*, p. 325.

9. Jack Jackson, *Los Mesteños: Spanish*

Ranching in Texas, 1721–1821 (College Station: Texas A&M University Press, 1986), pp. 22–23, 155–157, 161–162, 200.

10. Remington, *Pony Tracks*, pp. 55–57; Sandra L. Myres, *The Ranch in Spanish Texas, 1691–1800* (El Paso: Texas Western Press, 1969), pp. 26–27; Jackson, *Mesteños*, pp. 76–77; Nora E. Ramirez, "The Vaquero and Ranching in the Southwestern United States, 1600–1970" (Ph. D. diss., Indiana University, 1979), p. 31.

11. Myres, *Ranch in Spanish Texas*, p. 20; Ramirez, "Vaquero," pp. 149–150; William H. Dusenberry, *The Mexican Mesta: The Administration of Ranching in Colonial Mexico* (Urbana: University of Illinois Press, 1963), pp. 192–204.

12. David Dary, *Cowboy Culture: A Saga of Five Centuries* (New York: Knopf, 1981), pp. 148–156.

13. James C. Shaw, "Pioneering in Texas and Wyoming" (unpaginated typescript, Western Range Cattle Industry Study, Colorado Historical Society, Colorado Heritage Center, Denver).

14. William T. Hornaday, "The Cowboys of the Northwest," *Cosmopolitan* 2:4 (Dec. 1886):226–227.

15. J. Frank Dobie, *The Longhorns* (New York: Grosset and Dunlap, 1941), pp. 87–106; Hornaday, "Cowboys," p. 227.

16. William C. Holden, *The Espuela Land and Cattle Company: A Study of a Foreign-Owned Ranch in Texas* (Austin: Texas State Historical Association, 1970), pp. 129–133.

17. Kenneth Coppock, "Early Days Ranching in Canadian West," *Canadian Cattlemen* 1:1 (June 1938):12.

18. Charles M. MacInnes, *In the Shadow of the Rockies* (London: Rivingtons, 1930), pp. 213–214; Fred Ings, "Tales from the Midway Ranch" (typescript, Glenbow Archive, Calgary, M 264-f1, 1933), pp. 24–25 (serialized in *Canadian Cattlemen* beginning in 1941); W. F. Stevens, "Livestock and Poultry," in Henry J. Boam, ed., *The*

Prairie Provinces of Canada (London: Sells, 1914), p. 300.

19. Quoted in MacInnes, *Shadow*, p. 217.

20. Newspaper report reprinted in *Alberta Historical Review* 4:3 (Summer 1956):11; MacInnes, *Shadow*, pp. 213–214.

21. Elizabeth (Mrs. George) Lane, "A Brief Sketch of Memories of My Family" (typescript, Glenbow Archive, Calgary, M 652, June 1945), p. 22.

22. Leroy V. Kelly, *The Range Men: The Story of the Ranchers and Indians of Alberta* (1913; repr., New York: Argonaut Press, 1965), pp. 178–179; Coppock, "Early Days," p. 12; Edward Brado, *Cattle Kingdom: Early Ranching in Alberta* (Vancouver: Douglas and McIntyre, 1984), p. 224.

23. Güiraldes, *Don Segundo Sombra*, pp. 174–177; Slatta, *Gauchos*, p. 43; Francis Bond Head, *Rough Notes taken during some Rapid Journeys across the Pampas and among the Andes*, 2d ed. (London: John Murray, 1826), p. 147.

24. Slatta, *Gauchos*, p. 43.

25. Ramón Paez, *Wild Scenes in South America: Or Life in the Llanos of Venezuela* (London: Sampson Low, 1863), p. 76; Victor M. Ovalles, *El llanero: Estudio sobre su vida, sus costumbres, su carácter y su poesía* (Caracas: Herrera Irigoyen, 1905), pp. 48–49; José Antonio Díaz, *El agricultor venezolano o lecciones de agricultura práctica nacional*, 2 vols. (Caracas: Rojas, 1877), 2:xiii–xiv.

26. Edward R. Sullivan, *Rambles and Scrambles in North and South America*, 2d ed. (London: Robert Bentley, 1853), p. 382.

27. Karl Sachs, *De los llanos: Descripción de un viaje de ciencias naturales a Venezuela*, trans. José Izquierdo (Caracas and Madrid: Edime, 1955), p. 88; Calzadilla Valdes, *Por los llanos*, p. 28.

28. Quoted in Dary, *Cowboy Culture*, p. 76.

29. Quoted in Dary, *Cowboy Culture*,

p. 60; J. Frank Dobie, "The Mexican Va-
quero of the Texas Border," *Southwestern
Political and Social Science Quarterly* 8:1
(June 1927):3.

30. Ramirez, "Vaquero," pp. 76–77;
Charles D. Turpin, "The Gaucho as a Romantic and a Realistic Character in Brazilian Prose Fiction" (Ph. D. diss., University of New Mexico, 1976), p. 28.

31. Ramirez, "Vaquero," p. 60.

32. J. Frank Dobie, "Ranch Mexicans,"
Survey 66 (May 1, 1931), p. 169.

33. William Henry Sears, "Notes from a
Cowboy's Diary" (pamphlet, Lawrence,
Kan., n. d., Library of Congress F 596,
S32), p. 3; Emerson Hough, *The Story of
the Cowboy* (New York: Appleton, 1898),
p. 89.

34. Ross Santee, *Cowboy* (1928; repr.,
Lincoln: University of Nebraska Press,
1977), p. 93.

35. J. Frank Dobie, "A Summary Introduction to Frederic Remington," in Remington, *Pony Tracks* (Norman: University
of Oklahoma Press, 1961), pp. xi–xii.

36. L. A. Huffman, "The Last Busting at
the Bow-Gun," *Scribner's Magazine* 42:1
(July 1907):78–79.

37. Fred Ings, "Tales from the Midway Ranch" (typescript, Glenbow Archive,
Calgary, M 264-f1, 1933), p. 12; Ings,
"Roundup Days of the 'Eighties," *Canadian Cattlemen* 1:3 (Dec. 1938):133. See
also Edna Kells, "Pioneer Interviews"
(typescript, Glenbow Archive, Calgary,
D 920 K 29, ca. 1935), p. 131.

38. Bert Sheppard, "Bronco Busters and
Their Saddles of Fifty Years Ago," *Canadian Cattlemen* 1:4 (March 1949):251.

39. Sheppard, "Bronco Busters," p. 251.

40. John David Higinbotham, *When the
West Was Young: Reminiscences of the
Early Canadian West* (Toronto: Ryerson
Press, 1933), p. 204.

41. Douglas Branch, *The Cowboy and
His Interpreters* (New York: Appleton,

1926), pp. 68–69; Peter Watts, *A Dictionary of the Old West, 1850–1900* (New York:
Knopf, 1977), pp. 344–347; Dary, *Cowboy
Culture*, p. 199; Edward Everett Dale,
*The Range Cattle Industry: Ranching on
the Great Plains from 1865 to 1925* (Norman: University of Oklahoma Press, 1960),
pp. 54–55.

42. Watts, *Dictionary*, pp. 344–347;
Holden, *Espuela Land*, p. 147; Philip
Ashton Rollins, *The Cowboy: An Unconventional History of Civilization on the
Old-Time Cattle Range* (1922; repr., Albuquerque: University of New Mexico Press,
1979), p. 258.

43. Dale, *Range Cattle Industry*,
pp. 46–49, 53; Dale, *Cow Country* (Norman: University of Oklahoma Press, 1965),
pp. 35, 45–47; Denis McLoughlin, *Wild
and Woolly: An Encyclopedia of the Old
West* (Garden City: Doubleday, 1975),
p. 522.

44. Sachs, *De los llanos*, pp. 161–162.

45. George D. Flinter, *A History of
the Revolution of Caracas* (London: All-
man, 1819), p. 144; *El cojo llustrado*,
Oct. 15, 1899:681; Robert B. Cunninghame
Graham, *José Antonio Paez* (London:
Heinemann, 1929), pp. 28–29.

46. Larry McMurtry, *Lonesome Dove*
(New York: Simon and Schuster, 1985),
pp. 277–279; *Kansas City Star*, May 4,
1913; Joseph G. McCoy, *Cattle Trade of
the West and Southwest* (1874; repr.,
N.p.: Readex Microprint, 1966), pp.
95–97.

47. José P. Barrán and Benjamín Nahum, *Recuperación y dependencia,
1895–1904*, vol. 3 of *Historia rural del
Uruguay moderno* (Montevideo: Banda
Oriental, 1973), p. 232.

48. Slatta, *Gauchos*, p. 42.

49. Quoted in Westermeier, *Trailing the
Cowboy*, p. 96. J. Frank Dobie vividly de-
scribes the dangers of stampedes in *The
Longhorns*, pp. 87–106.

50. Wallace Stegner, *Wolf Willow: A History, a Story, and a Memory of the Last Plains Frontier* (Toronto: Macmillan, 1962), p. 165.

51. Richard Burton Deane, "A Cattle Drive," in "Reminiscences of a Mounted Police Officer" (MS., Glenbow Archive, Calgary, M 311); Ramirez, "Vaquero," p. 175.

52. John W. G. MacEwan, *Blazing the Old Cattle Trail* (Saskatoon: Western Producer Prairie Books, 1975), pp. 49–55.

53. H. M. Hatfield, "Diaries, 1893–1900" (typescript, Glenbow Archive, Calgary, M 480).

54. John Baumann, "On a Western Ranche, *Fortnightly Review* 47 (April 1, 1887):532.

55. Dary, *Cowboy Culture*, pp. 289–291.

56. James C. Dahlman, "Recollections of Cowboy Life in Western Nebraska," *Nebraska History Magazine* 10 (Oct. 1927):335.

57. Holden, *Espuela Land*, pp. 140–141; Arrell M. Gibson, "Ranching on the Southern Great Plains," *Journal of the West* 6:1 (Jan. 1967): 136, 149; Westermeier, *Trailing the Cowboy*, p. 100.

58. Leland E. Stuart, "Men and Cattle on the Northern Plains, 1860–1887" (Thesis, University of Oregon, 1971), p. 6. On plains hazards, see Craig Miner, *West of Wichita: Settling the High Plains of Kansas, 1865–1890* (Lawrence: University Press of Kansas, 1986), pp. 160–171.

59. Dobie, *Longhorns*, pp. 318–339.

60. Duncan McNab McEachran, *Impressions of Pioneers of Alberta as a Ranching Country, Commencing 1881* (Ormstown, Quebec: published by the author, 1916?), p. 9; Kells, "Pioneer Interviews," pp. 27–28.

61. John Macoun, *Manitoba and the Great Northwest* (Guelph, Ontario: World, 1882), p. 256; Anonymous, "Memoirs of an Itinerant Cowhand," *Canadian Cattlemen* 5:3 (Dec. 1942):101 and 5:4 (March 1943): 148, 152–153, 156–157.

62. Stegner, *Wolf Willow*, p. 152.

63. Slatta, *Gauchos*, pp. 40, 45.

64. Ibid., pp. 62–63, 142–143, 159–161; Barrán and Nahum, *Recuperación*, p. 184.

65. John R. Craig, *Ranching with Lords and Commons; or, Twenty Years on the Range* (1903; repr., New York: AMS Press, 1971), p. 233.

66. Quotation from Robert B. Cunninghame Graham, *Rodeo* (Garden City: Doubleday, Doran, 1936), p. 48; Flinter, *History of the Revolution*, p. 109; Edward Larocque Tinker, *Centaurs of Many Lands* (London: J. A. Allen, 1964), p. 57.

67. Sullivan, *Rambles and Scrambles*, pp. 380–381.

68. Dary, *Cowboy Culture*, p. 21; Vernam, *Man on Horseback*, p. 245; Ramirez, "Vaquero," pp. 95–96; Watts, *Dictionary*, p. 110; Myres, *Ranch in Spanish Texas*, p. 25.

69. Ramirez, "Vaquero," pp. 71–73, 93, 95–96; Dobie, "Mexican Vaquero," pp. 3–6.

70. Dary, *Cowboy Culture*, pp. 154–155.

71. Lynn J. Martin, ed., *Nā Paniolo o Hawai'i* (Honolulu: Honolulu Academy of the Arts, 1987), p. 41.

72. Dary, *Cowboy Culture*, pp. 147–154; Robert H. Fletcher, *Free Grass to Fences: The Montana Cattle Range Story* (New York: University Publishers for Historical Society of Montana, 1960), p. 105.

73. Dary, *Cowboy Culture*, p. 155.

74. William MacCann, *Two Thousand Miles' Ride through the Argentine Provinces*, 2 vols. (London: Smith, Elder, 1853), 1:13–14.

75. Fred Ings, "Roundup Days of the 'Eighties," *Canadian Cattlemen* 1:3 (Dec. 1938):133.

76. Remington, *Pony Tracks*, p. 47 (see also p. 60); Rollins, *Cowboy*, p. 121.

77. MacCann, *Two Thousand Miles'*

Ride, 1:2–3; Edward Larocque Tinker, *Horsemen of the Americas and the Literature They Inspired*, 2d ed. (Austin: University of Texas Press, 1967), p. 15.

78. William Henry Hudson, *A Naturalist in La Plata* (New York: Dutton, 1922), pp. 350–351.

79. Head, *Rough Notes*, p. 184; René León Echaiz, *Interpretación histórica del huaso chileno* (Santiago: Editorial Universitaria, 1955), pp. 75–79.

80. Graham, *Paez*, p. 23; Sachs, *De los llanos*, p. 175; José Samper, *Ensayo sobre las revoluciones políticas y la condición social de las repúblicas colombianas* (Paris: Thurnot, 1861), p. 93.

81. Remington, *Pony Tracks*, p. 60; Dary, *Cowboy Culture*, p. 50; Richard E. Ahlborn, "The Hispanic Horseman," *El palacio* 89:2 (Summer 1983):15.

82. Ahlborn, "Hispanic Horseman," p. 14–17. On charro equipment, see James Norman, *Charro: Mexican Horseman* (New York: Putnam, 1969).

83. Dary, *Cowboy Culture*, p. 51; Watts, *Dictionary*, p. 332.

84. Quoted in John K. Rollinson, *Wyoming Cattle Trails: History of the Migration of Oregon-raised Herds to Midwestern Markets* (Caldwell, Idaho: Caxton Printers, 1948), p. 116; Dary, *Cowboy Culture*, pp. 244–245.

85. Theodore A. Dodge, "Some American Riders," *Harper's Magazine*, July 1891:204.

86. Martin, *Paniolo*, pp. 29–37.

87. Sheppard, "Bronco Busters," pp. 186, 251.

Chapter 6. Ranchers and Cowboys

1. Peter Watts, *A Dictionary of the Old West, 1850–1900* (New York: Knopf, 1977), p. 88.

2. John R. Erickson, *The Modern Cowboy* (Lincoln: University of Nebraska Press, 1981), p. 214; David Dary, *Cowboy Culture: A Saga of Five Centuries* (New York: Knopf, 1981), p. 278.

3. Robert P. Matthews, "Los aprietos de la industria ganadera a mediados del siglo XIX," *Boletín histórico* 40 (Jan. 1976):60; José P. Barrán and Benjamín Nahum, *Recuperación y dependencia, 1895–1904*, vol. 3 of *Historia rural del Uruguay moderno* (Montevideo: Banda Oriental, 1973), p. 263.

4. Brian Loveman, *Chile: The Legacy of Hispanic Capitalism* (New York: Oxford University Press, 1979), pp. 88, 95, 99.

5. John Miers, *Travels in Chile and La Plata*, 2 vols. (1826; repr., New York: AMS Press, 1970), 2:345; Richard W. Slatta, *Gauchos and the Vanishing Frontier* (Lincoln: University of Nebraska Press, 1983), pp. 58–59.

6. Carl E. Solberg, *Immigration and Nationalism: Argentina and Chile, 1890–1914* (Austin: University of Texas Press, 1970), pp. 161–162.

7. Slatta, *Gauchos*, pp. 77, 109–110.

8. Alistair Hennessy, *The Frontier in Latin American History* (Albuquerque: University of New Mexico Press, 1978), p. 113; Slatta, *Gauchos*, pp. 34–35.

9. Alexander von Humboldt and Aimé Bonpland, *Personal Narrative of Travels to the Equinoctial Regions of the New Continent, during the Years 1799–1804*, trans. Helen Maria Williams, 4 vols., 2d ed. (London: Longman, Hurst, Rees, Orme, Brown, and Green, 1825), 4:320; Universidad Central de Venezuela, Facultad de Humanidades y Educación, *Mano de obra: Legislación y administración*, vol. 1 of *Materiales para el estudio de la cuestión agraria en Venezuela, 1810–1865* (Caracas, 1979), pp. 113, 533, 640–642; Miguel Izard, *Series estadísticas para la historia de Venezuela* (Merida: Universidad de los Andes, 1970), pp. 69–70; José Antonio de Armas Chitty, *Tucupido: Formación de un pueblo del llano* (Caracas: Universidad Central de Venezuela, 1961), p. 16.

10. Fernando I. Parra Aranguren, *Antecedentes del derecho del trabajo en Venezuela, 1830–1928* (Maracaibo: Universidad de Zulia, 1965), p. 54; William E. Curtis, *Venezuela: A Land Where It's Always Summer* (New York: Harper and Brothers, 1896), p. 159. On elite-mass conflict, see E. Bradford Burns, *The Poverty of Progress: Latin America in the Nineteenth Century* (Berkeley: University of California Press, 1980).

11. William C. Holden, *The Espuela Land and Cattle Company: A Study of a Foreign-Owned Ranch in Texas* (Austin: Texas State Historical Association, 1970), pp. 116, 120.

12. Ibid., pp. 121–122.

13. Simon M. Evans, "The Passing of a Frontier: Ranching in the Canadian West, 1882–1912" (Ph. D. diss., University of Calgary, 1976), p. 52; John R. Craig, *Ranching with Lords and Commons: Or Twenty Years on the Range* (1903; repr., New York: AMS Press, 1971), p. 88.

14. David H. Breen, *The Canadian Prairie West and the Ranching Frontier, 1874–1924* (Toronto: University of Toronto Press, 1983), p. 163; Edna Kells, "Pioneer Interviews" (typescript, Edmonton, ca. 1935, Glenbow Archive, Calgary, D 920 K 29), p. 65.

15. John David Higinbotham, *When the West Was Young: Reminiscences of the Early Canadian West* (Toronto: Ryerson Press, 1933), p. 199.

16. Breen, *Canadian Prairie West*, p. 214.

17. Raúl Jacob, *Consequencias sociales del alambramiento, 1872–1880* (Montevideo: Banda Oriental, 1969), p. 108.

18. Matthews, "Los aprietos," p. 55; José P. Barrán and Benjamín Nahum, *La civilización ganadera bajo Batlle, 1905–1914*, vol. 6 of *Historia rural del Uruguay moderno* (Montevideo: Banda Oriental, 1977), pp. 377–380.

19. Quotation from William T. Hornaday, "The Cowboys of the Northwest," *Cosmopolitan* 2:4 (Dec. 1886):225; Philip Ashton Rollins, *The Cowboy: An Unconventional History of Civilization on the Old-Time Cattle Range* (1922; repr., Albuquerque: University of New Mexico Press, 1979), p. 156.

20. William W. Savage, Jr., ed., *Cowboy Life: Reconstructing an American Myth* (Norman: University of Oklahoma Press, 1975), p. 75; Edward Everett Dale, *The Range Cattle Industry: Ranching on the Great Plains from 1865 to 1925* (1930; repr., Norman: University of Oklahoma Press, 1960), p. 6.

21. Evans, "Passing of a Frontier," p. 205; John W. G. MacEwan, *Between the Red and the Rockies* (1952; repr., Saskatoon: Western Producer Prairie Books, 1979), pp. 127–128.

22. Quotation from John J. Young, "Ranching in the Canadian North-West," in John Castell Hopkins, ed., *Canada: An Encyclopedia of the Country* (Toronto: Linscott, 1899), 5:62.

23. James C. Shaw, "Pioneering in Texas and Wyoming" (unpaginated typescript, Western Range Cattle Industry Study, Colorado Heritage Center, Denver).

24. Westermeier, *Trailing the Cowboy*, p. 41; Craig, *Ranching*, p. 69, David E. Lopez, "Cowboy Strikes and Unions," *Labor History* 18:3 (Summer 1977):328–329.

25. Westermeier, *Trailing the Cowboy*, pp. 132–133.

26. Lopez, "Cowboy Strikes," pp. 336–337; Ernest S. Osgood, *The Day of the Cattleman* (Minneapolis: University of Minnesota Press, 1929), pp. 150–151; Arnold J. Bauer, *Chilean Rural Society from the Spanish Conquest to 1930* (Cambridge: Cambridge University Press, 1975), p. 222; Barrán and Nahum, *La civilización ganadera*, p. 370; Donald Denoon, *Settler Capitalism: The Dynamics of Dependent Development in the Southern Hemisphere* (New York: Oxford University

Press, 1983), pp. 83–84; Slatta, *Gauchos*, pp. 51–56. On the tragic massacres of workers in Patagonia, see Osvaldo Bayer, *La Patagonia rebelde* (Mexico: Nueva Imagen, 1980). The book also was made into a powerful film.

27. John R. Erickson, *The Modern Cowboy* (Lincoln: University of Nebraska Press, 1981), pp. 216–218.

28. Ibid., p. 214.

29. Arnold J. Bauer, "The Hacienda El Huique in the Agrarian Structure of Nineteenth-Century Chile," *Agricultural History* 46:4 (Oct. 1972):460–462; Bauer, *Chilean Rural Society*, pp. 146–147, 160; Bauer, "Chilean Rural Labor in the Nineteenth Century," *American Historical Review* 76:4 (Oct. 1971):1,080–1,081; Loveman, *Chile*, p. 164; René León Echaiz, *Interpretación histórica del huaso chileno* (Santiago: Editorial Universitaria, 1955), p. 69.

30. Loveman, *Chile*, pp. 163, 173.

31. José P. Barrán, *Apogeo y crisis del Uruguay pastoril y caudillesco*, vol. 4 of *Historia uruguaya*, 2d ed. (Montevideo: Banda Oriental, 1975), p. 82.

32. Barrán and Nahum, *Recuperación*, pp. 133–134; Jacob, *Consequencias*, p. 100.

33. Slatta, *Gauchos*, pp. 48–50, 175.

34. Howard R. Lamar, *The Far Southwest, 1846–1912: A Territorial History* (New York: Norton, 1977), p. 27; Remington, *Pony Tracks*, p. 60; Ramirez, "Vaquero," p. 60.

35. H. B. C. Benton, "Letter to Agnes Spring" [Harrison, Idaho, July 3, 1944] (pamphlet, Wyoming: Biography and Ranches, Western Range Cattle Industry Study, Colorado Heritage Center, Denver), p. 2; Holden, *Espuela Land*, p. 117; Maurice W. Frink, W. Turrentine Jackson, and Agnes Wright Spring, *When Grass Was King* (Boulder: University of Colorado Press, 1956), p. 10; John K. Rollinson, *Wyoming Cattle Trails: History of the Migration of Oregon-raised Herds to Midwestern Markets* (Caldwell, Idaho: Caxton Printers, 1948), p. 39.

36. Harry Denning, "Account Book, Lineham, Alberta, 1908–1954" (photocopy, Glenbow Archive, Calgary, BR D 411A), pp. 4–9.

37. Ralph C. Coppock, Leger [*sic*], vol. 1, 1904–1918 (Glenbow Archive, Calgary, BR C 785, Box 1), p. 16.

38. Milton J. Esman, *Landlessness and Near-Landlessness in Developing Countries* (Ithaca, N. Y.: Center for International Studies, Cornell University, 1978), table 3.

39. Mario Góngora, *Vagabundaje y sociedad fronteriza en Chile, siglos XVII a XIX* (Santiago: Universidad de Chile, 1966), pp. 10–11.

40. Bauer, *Chilean Rural Society*, pp. 130–132, 141; Benjamín Vicuña MacKenna, pseud. Daniel J. Hunter, *A Sketch of Chili* (New York: S. Hallet, 1866), pp. 37–38.

41. Loveman, *Chile*, pp. 120–122, 194–195; Bauer, *Chilean Rural Society*, p. 46.

42. Loveman, *Chile*, pp. 220–222; Gonzalo Izquierdo Fernández, *Un estudio de las ideologías chilenas: La sociedad de agricultura en el siglo XIX* (Santiago: Universidad de Chile, 1968), pp. 24–26.

43. Bauer, *Chilean Rural Society*, pp. 59, 78; Loveman, *Chile*, p. 235.

44. Mario Dotta, Duaner Freire, and Nelson Rodríguez, *El Uruguay ganadero: De la explotación primitiva a la crisis actual* (Montevideo: Banda Oriental, 1972), pp. 31–32, 122; Bauer, *Chilean Rural Society*, p. 79.

45. Enrique Mendez Vives, *El Uruguay de la modernización, 1876–1904*, vol. 5 of *Historia uruguaya* (Montevideo: Banda Oriental, 1975), pp. 14–15, 18–19, 25, 114.

46. Miguel Angel Cárcano, *Evolución histórica del régimen de la tierra pública, 1810–1916* (1917; repr., Buenos Aires:

EUDEBA, 1972), pp. 385, 389; Slatta, *Gauchos*, pp. 122–124.

47. *Anales de la Sociedad Rural Argentina*, 16:2 (Feb. 1882):23.

48. F. J. McLynn, "The Frontier Problem in Nineteenth-Century Argentina," *History Today* 30 (Jan. 1980):32; A. F. Zimmerman, "The Land Policy of Argentina, with Particular Reference to the Conquest of the Southern Pampas," *Hispanic American Historical Review* 25 (Feb. 1945):3–26; Cárcano, *Evolución histórica*, pp. 385, 388–389, 516.

49. Julio de Armas, *La ganadería en Venezuela: Ensayo histórico* (Caracas: Congreso de la República, 1974), pp. 139–140; Matthews, "Los aprietos," p. 51; Matthews, "Rural Violence and Social Unrest in Venezuela, 1840–1858: Origins of the Federalist War" (Ph. D. diss., New York University, 1974), pp. 105–107; Julio César Salas, *Civilización y barbarie: Estudios sociológicos americanos* (1919; repr., Caracas: Ediciones Centauro, 1977), pp. 187, 193–194.

50. Jane M. Rausch, *A Tropical Plains Frontier: The Llanos of Colombia, 1531–1831* (Albuquerque: University of New Mexico Press, 1984), p. 211; Federico Brito Figueroa, *Ensayos de la historia social venezolana* (Caracas: Universidad Central de Venezuela, 1960), pp. 235–236, 294; Universidad Central de Venezuela, Consejo de Desarrollo Científico y Humanístico, *Materiales para el estudio de la cuestión agraria en Venezuela, 1800–1830* (Caracas, 1964), pp. 512–513.

51. Matthews, "Los aprietos," p. 54; Matthews, "La turbulenta década de los Monagas, 1847–1858," in *Política y economía en Venezuela* (Caracas: Fundación Boulton, 1976), pp. 118–119; Ramón Losada Aldona, *Venezuela: Latifundio y subdesarrollo: Estudio sociojurídico sobre la cuestión agraria venezolana*, 2d ed. (Caracas: Universidad Central de Venezuela, 1980), pp. 77–78.

52. William H. Dusenberry, *The Mexican Mesta: The Administration of Ranching in Colonial Mexico* (Urbana: University of Illinois Press, 1963), pp. 46–49, 51, 54.

53. Quotation from François Chevalier, *Land and Society in Colonial Mexico*, trans. Alvin Eustis, ed. Lesley Byrd Simpson (Berkeley: University of California Press, 1963), p. 93; Dusenberry, *Mesta*, pp. 51, 64, 143, 207; Eric Van Young, "Mexican Rural History Since Chevalier: The Historiography of the Colonial Hacienda," *Latin American Research Review* 18:3 (1983):5–61.

54. Charles H. Harris III, *A Mexican Family Empire: The Latifundio of the Sánchez Navarro Family, 1765–1867* (Austin: University of Texas Press, 1975), pp. 70–75, 185; Lamar, *Far Southwest*, p. 28.

55. Harris, *Mexican Family Empire*, pp. 27, 310–312.

56. Remington, *Pony Tracks*, p. 47.

57. Dary, *Cowboy Culture*, pp. 140, 318.

58. Sharp, *Whoop-Up Country*, pp. 234–235; Frink, *Grass Was King*, pp. 63–65; Dary, *Cowboy Culture*, pp. 252, 263, 324; Jimmy M. Skaggs, *Prime Cut: Livestock Raising and Meatpacking in the United States, 1607–1983* (College Station: Texas A&M University Press, 1986), pp. 62–63.

59. Dale, *Range Cattle Industry*, pp. 84–89; Osgood, *Day of the Cattleman*, pp. 118–119; James W. Eaton, "The Wyoming Stock Growers Association's Treatment of Nonmember Cattlemen During the 1880s," *Agricultural History* 58:1 (Jan. 1984):70–80.

60. Dary, *Cowboy Culture*, pp. 264–271; Lewis E. Atherton, *The Cattle Kings* (Bloomington: Indiana University Press, 1961), pp. 44–45, 111; Dale, *Range Cattle Industry*, p. 89.

61. Kenneth Coppock, "Early Days Ranching in Canadian West," *Canadian*

Cattlemen 1:1 (June 1938):40–41; Breen, *Canadian Prairie West*, p. 89.

62. Breen, *Canadian Prairie West*, pp. 34, 82–83.

63. Ibid., pp. 43–45, 50–51, 77.

64. Quotation from J. F. Fraser, *Canada as It Is*, reprinted in Lewis H. Thomas, "British Visitors' Perspectives of the West, 1885–1914," in Anthony W. Raspovich and H. C. Klassen, eds., *Prairie Perspectives* (Toronto and Montreal: Holt, Rinehart and Winston, 1973), p. 187; Breen, *Canadian Prairie West*, pp. 95–97, 152–153.

65. Breen, *Canadian Prairie West*, pp. 20–22, 40–41, 47.

Chapter 7. Home on the Range

1. Robert B. Cunninghame Graham, *José Antonio Paez* (London: Heinemann, 1929), p. 18; Alexander von Humboldt and Aimé Bonpland, *Personal Narrative of Travels to the Equinoctial Regions of the New Continent, During the Years 1799–1804*, trans. Helen Maria Williams, 2d ed. (London: Longman, Hurst, Rees, Orme, Brown, and Green, 1825), p. 320; Pál Rosti, *Memorias de un viaje por América*, trans. Judith Sarosi (Caracas: Universidad Central de Venezuela, 1968), p. 167; Karl Sachs, *De los llanos: Descripción de un viaje de ciencias naturales a Venezuela*, trans. José Izquierdo (Caracas and Madrid: Edime, 1955), p. 176.

2. George D. Flinter, *A History of the Revolution of Caracas* (London: Allman, 1819), pp. 102–105, 118–119.

3. Richard W. Slatta, *Gauchos and the Vanishing Frontier* (Lincoln: University of Nebraska Press, 1983), p. 77.

4. Ibid., p. 76; George Byam, *Wanderings in Some of the Western Republics of America* (London: John W. Parker, 1850), pp. 72, 76; Nora E. Ramirez, "The Vaquero and Ranching in the Southwestern United States, 1600–1970" (Ph. D. diss., Indiana University, 1979), p. 171.

5. John Miers, *Travels in Chile and La Plata*, 2 vols. (1826; repr., New York: AMS Press, 1970), 2:310; Arnold J. Bauer, *Chilean Rural Society from the Spanish Conquest to 1930* (Cambridge: Cambridge University Press, 1975), p. 74.

6. F. Warner Robinson, "The New Cattle Country," *Scribner's Magazine* 51:2 (Feb. 1912):177, 185.

7. J. Frank Dobie, *A Vaquero in the Brush Country* (1929; repr., Austin: University of Texas Press, 1957), p. 28; David Dary, *Cowboy Culture: A Saga of Five Centuries* (New York: Knopf, 1981), p. 55.

8. Ramon F. Adams, *Come an' Get It: The Story of the Old Cowboy Cook* (Norman: University of Oklahoma Press, 1952), pp. 85, 88, 91, 96; Peter Watts, *A Dictionary of the Old West, 1850–1900* (New York: Knopf, 1977), p. 308.

9. Quotation from John K. Rollinson, *Wyoming Cattle Trails: History of the Migration of Oregon-raised Herds to Midwestern Markets*, (Caldwell, Idaho: Caxton Printers, 1948), p. 79; Joe B. Frantz and Julian E. Choate, Jr., *The American Cowboy: The Myth and the Reality* (Norman: University of Oklahoma Press, 1955), p. 37.

10. Byam, *Wanderings*, p. 127; Maria Dundas Graham, *Journal of a Residence in Chile* (1824; repr., New York: Praeger, 1969), p. 119; Slatta, *Gauchos*, p. 78.

11. Slatta, *Gauchos*, pp. 78–80.

12. Quotation from Victor M. Ovalles, *El llanero: Estudio sobre su vida, sus costumbres, su carácter y su poesía* (Caracas: Herrera Irigoyen, 1905), pp. 88–90; Sachs, *De los llanos*, p. 91; Rosti, *Memorias*, p. 170.

13. Adams, *Come an' Get It*, pp. 67–68, 72, 75; Watts, *Dictionary*, pp. 11–12.

14. William F. Cochrane, "Letter Book" (MS., Glenbow Archive, Calgary, M234). Doubtful words are indicated by [?].

15. Anon., "Memoirs of an Itinerant Cowhand," *Canadian Cattlemen* 5:3 (Dec. 1942):100; Fred A. Ackland, "Cattle on a

Thousand Hills," *Alberta Historical Review* 19:4 (Autumn 1971):26 (originally published in the Lethbridge *Herald*, Aug. 23, 1906); Clifford P. Westermeier, *Trailing the Cowboy: His Life and Lore as Told by Frontier Journalists* (Caldwell, Idaho: Caxton Printers, 1955), p. 70; Philip Ashton Rollins, *The Cowboy: An Unconventional History of Civilization on the Old-Time Cattle Range*, rev. ed. (Albuquerque: University of New Mexico Press, 1936), pp. 129–130.

16. Fred W. Ings, "Roundup Days of the 'Eighties," *Canadian Cattlemen* 1:3 (Dec. 1938):133.

17. Quotation from Rollins, *Cowboy*, p. 129; Westermeier, *Trailing the Cowboy*, p. 70.

18. Adams, *Come an' Get It*, pp. 76–79, 99, 102, 109–110; Ross Santee, *Cowboy* (1928; repr., Lincoln: University of Nebraska Press, 1977), pp. 88–89, 105; Wesley L. Fankhauser, "Son-of-a-gun to paté de Foie gras: Chow on Early Great Plains Ranches," *Journal of the West* 16:1 (Jan. 1977):29; Westermeier, *Trailing the Cowboy*, p. 45.

19. Joseph G. McCoy, *Cattle Trade of the West and Southwest* (1874; repr., N.p.: Readex Microprint, 1966), p. 137; Theodore Roosevelt, "In Cowboy Land," *The Outlook* 104 (May 24, 1913):150.

20. Sachs, *De los llanos*, p. 91, 125; Ramón Paez, *Wild Scenes in South America; or Life in the Llanos of Venezuela* (London: Sampson Low, 1863), pp. 31, 37.

21. Paez, *Wild Scenes*, pp. 21–22; Sachs, *De los llanos*, p. 72, Rosti, *Memorias*, p 167; Adams, *Come an' Get It*, p. 99.

22. Slatta, *Gauchos*, p. 77.

23. Quotation from Mary Ella Inderwick, "Letter to Alice, May 13, 1884, North Fork Ranch, Alberta" (MS., Glenbow Archive, Calgary, M 559), p. 3; Frantz and Choate, *American Cowboy*, p. 64; Slatta, *Gauchos*, pp. 58–59. Women on the frontier have attracted little study in Latin America. For the United States, see Susan

Armitage and Elizabeth Jameson, eds., *The Women's West* (Norman: University of Oklahoma Press, 1987); Dee Brown, *The Gentle Tamers: Women of the Old Wild West* (Lincoln: University of Nebraska Press, 1958); Julie Ray Jeffrey, *Frontier Women: The Trans-Mississippi West, 1840–1880* (New York: Hill and Wang, 1979); Glenda Riley, ed., "Women in the West," *Journal of the West* 21 (April 1982); Alice Lee Marriott, *Hell on Horses and Women* (Norman: University of Oklahoma Press, 1958); Sandra L. Myres, *Westering Women and the Frontier Experience, 1800–1915* (Albuquerque: University of New Mexico Press, 1982); Joan M. Jensen and Darlis A. Miller, "The Gentle Tamers Revisited: New Approaches to the History of Women in the American West," *Pacific Historical Review* 49:2 (May 1980):173–213; and Sheryll Patterson-Black and Gene Patterson-Black, *Western Women in History and Literature* (Crawford, Neb.: Cottonwood Press, 1978).

24. John Mawe, *Travels in the Interior of Brazil* (London: Longman, Hurst, Rees, Orme and Brown, 1823), p. 26; Charles Darwin, *Journal of Researches into the Geology and Natural History of the Various Countries Visited by H. M. S. Beagle* (1839; facs. ed., New York: Hafner, 1952), p. 149.

25. Slatta, *Gauchos*, pp. 72–73; José P. Barrán and Benjamín Nahum, *La civilización ganadera bajo Batlle*, vol. 6 of *Historia rural del Uruguay moderno* (Montevideo: Banda Oriental, 1977), pp. 377–380.

26. José Antonio Paez, *Autobiografía del General José Antonio Paez*, 2 vols. (1869; facs. ed., Caracas: Academia Nacional de Historia, 1973), 1:6; Robert Ker Porter, *Sir Robert Ker Porter's Caracas Diary, 1825–1842: A British Diplomat in a Newborn Nation*, ed. Walter Dupuoy (Caracas: Walter Dupuoy, 1966), p. 674.

27. Carlos Siso, *La formación del pueblo venezolano: Estudios sociológicos*, 2 vols.

(Madrid: García Enciso, 1953), 2:135; Sachs, *De los llanos*, p. 91.

28. Paez, *Autobiografía*, p. 10; Alejandro Rivas Sosa, *Nuestro ganado vacuno: La ganadería como fuente potencial de riqueza nacional* (Caracas: Elite, 1938), pp. 56–66; Miguel Izard, "La Venezuela del cafe vista por los viajeros del siglo XIX," *Boletín histórico* 7:20 (May 1969): 211, 220.

29. Archivo General de la Nación, Caracas, Secretaría de Interior y Justicia, vol. 995, folios 303–304; vol. 998, folios 247–248; vol. 999, folio 119.

30. Mauricio A. Vila, *Una geografía humano-económica de la Venezuela de 1873* (Caracas: Ministerio de Fomento, 1970), p. 179; Fernando Calzadilla Valdes, *Por los llanos de Apure* (Santiago: Imprenta Universitaria, 1940), p. 35. See photographs of typical ranch buildings in the 1950s in Miguel Acosta Saignes, "La vivienda popular en Barinas," in *Cuadernos Universitarias* (Caracas: Signo, 1955).

31. Frantz and Choate, *American Cowboy*, p. 55; Dary, *Cowboy Culture*, pp. 142, 145.

32. Rollins, *Cowboy*, pp. 163–164; Slatta, *Gauchos*, pp. 70, 77.

33. Duncan McNab McEachran, *Impressions of Pioneers of Alberta as a Ranching Country, Commencing 1881* (Ormstown, Quebec: published by the author, 1916?), p. 7.

34. Fred Ings, "Tales from the Midway Ranch" (typescript, Glenbow Archive, Calgary, M 264-f1, 1933), p. 9.

35. Calgary *Weekly Herald*, Oct. 9, 1902, reprinted in David H. Breen, "The Ranching Frontier in Canada, 1875–1905," in Lewis G. Thomas, ed., *The Prairie West to 1905: A Canadian Sourcebook* (Toronto: Oxford University Press, 1975), p. 303.

36. Ings, "Tales from the Midway Ranch," pp. 44–45.

37. William C. Holden, *The Espuela Land and Cattle Company: A Study of a Foreign-Owned Ranch in Texas* (Austin: Texas State Historical Association, 1970), pp. 157–160; Ramirez, "Vaquero," pp. 192–193, 259; T. H. Whitney, "The White Mud Pool Wagon," *Canadian Cattlemen* 2:1 (June 1939):204.

38. William T. Hornaday, "The Cowboys of the Northwest," *Cosmopolitan* 2:4 (Dec. 1886):223.

39. Slatta, *Gauchos*, p. 57.

40. Rollins, *Cowboy*, pp. 170, 185; Douglas Branch, *The Cowboy and His Interpreters* (New York: Appleton, 1926), p. 103.

41. Samuel L. Fornucci, *A Folk Song History of America: America Through Its Songs* (Englewood Cliffs, N. J.: Prentice-Hall, 1984), pp. 151–169; Charlie Seemann, "The American Cowboy: Image and Reality," liner notes to *Back in the Saddle Again* (New York: New World Records, 1983), p. 1 (a superb collection of authentic cowboy songs recorded from 1928 to 1980); Seemann, telephone conversation with the author, Dec. 8, 1987; Seemann, "Bacon, Biscuits and Beans: Food of the Cattle Trails and Cow Camps as Found in American Cowboy Songs," *Arizona Friends of Folklore World* 4:3 (Fall 1974); Slatta, *Gauchos*, pp. 81–82.

42. Seemann, "American Cowboy," p. 1.

43. John Baumann, "On a Western Ranche," *Fortnightly Review*, April 1, 1887:526–527.

44. Jules Verne Allen, *Cowboy Lore* (San Antonio: Naylor, 1933), p. 144.

45. Rollins, *Cowboy*, p. 267. For more on authentic cowboy work songs, see John I. White, *Get Along Little Doggies: Songs and Songmakers of the American West* (Urbana: University of Illinois Press, 1975); Glen Ohrlin, *The Hell Bound Train: A Cowboy Songbook* (Urbana: University of Illinois Press, 1973); Seemann, "American Cowboy," pp. 1–2.

46. Quoted in Rollinson, *Wyoming Cattle Trails*, pp. 231–232; Stephen Paullada,

Rawhide and Song: A Comparative Study of The Cattle Cultures of the Argentinian Pampa and North American Great Plains (New York: Vantage, 1963), pp. 114–115, 174.

47. Lonn Taylor and Ingrid Maar, The American Cowboy (Washington, D. C.: Library of Congress, 1983), pp. 75–76.

48. Paullada, Rawhide and Song, pp. 175–176, 178, 192; song quoted in Allen, Cowboy Lore, pp. 130–131; Seemann, "American Cowboy," p. 2.

49. Deborah Schwartz, letter to the author, June 16, 1988; Paullada, Rawhide and Song, pp. 107, 162, 164; Tinker, Horsemen, p. 31; Nicolas Slonimsky, Music of Latin America (New York: Crowell, 1945), p. 74.

50. Schwartz, letter; Paullada, Rawhide and Song, pp. 109–111.

51. Paullada, Rawhide and Song, p. 168.

52. Ibid., p. 169.

53. Gerard Behague, Music in Latin America: An Introduction (Englewood Cliffs, N. J.: Prentice-Hall, 1979), pp. 107–108; Schwartz, letter; Schwartz, "The Gauchesco Tradition as a Source of National Identity in Argentine Art Music, ca. 1875–1950" (dissertation proposal, University of Texas, April 1, 1988).

54. Horacio Cabrera Sifontes, La Rubiera (Caracas: N.p., 1972), pp. 79–83; Victor M. Ovalles, El llanero: Estudio sobre su vida, sus costumbres, su carácter y su poesía (Caracas: Herrera Irigoyen, 1905), pp. 75, 134; Luis F. Ramón y Rivera, La música folklórica de Venezuela (Caracas: Monte Avila, 1955), pp. 12, 14; Jesús José Loreto Loreto, El llano y sus costumbres (Caracas: Presidencia de la República Venezuela, 1980), p. 26.

55. Fermín Vélez Boza, El folklore en la alimentación venezolana (Caracas: Instituto Nacional de Nutrición, 1966), pp. 64, 69; José Samper, Ensayo sobre las revoluciones políticas y la condición social de las repúblicas colombianas (Paris: Thurnot,

1861), pp. 94–95; Ovalles, El llanero, pp. 135–137; Slonimsky, Music of Latin America, p. 289.

56. Sachs, De los llanos, p. 65.

57. Slonimsky, Music of Latin America, p. 290; Behague, Music in Latin America, pp. 154–157.

58. Ramirez, "Vaquero," p. 260; Tinker, Horsemen, pp. 83–84; Paul J. Vanderwood, "Nineteenth-Century Mexico's Profiteering Bandits," in Richard W. Slatta, ed., Bandidos: The Varieties of Latin American Banditry (Westport, Conn.: Greenwood, 1987), pp. 16–26; Merle E. Simmons, The Mexican Corrido as a Source for Interpretive Study of Modern Mexico, 1870–1950 (Bloomington: Indiana University Press, 1957).

59. Ramirez, "Vaquero," pp. 258–259.

60. Lynn J. Martin, ed., Nā paniolo o Hawai'i (Honolulu: Honolulu Academy of Arts, 1987), pp. 72, 88–89, 92–93; Nick Tosches, Country: Legends and Dying Metaphors in America's Biggest Music, rev. ed. (New York: Scribner's, 1985), pp. 173–174.

61. Martin, Paniolo, pp. 90–92; Seemann, "American Cowboy," p. 3.

Chapter 8. Horsin' 'Round

1. The differences between play, contests, games, and sport are important in the literature on the history of sport. See Allen Guttmann, From Ritual to Record: The Nature of Modern Sports (New York: Columbia University Press, 1978), pp. 3–5, 7, 9. Other helpful sport history literature includes Richard S. Gruneau, "Freedom and Constraint: The Paradoxes of Play, Games, and Sports," Journal of Sport History 7:3 (Winter 1980):73; Gruneau, "Sport, Social Differentiation, and Social Inequality," in Donald W. Ball and John W. Loy, eds., Sport and Social Order (Reading, Mass.: Addison-Wesley, 1975),

pp. 134–137, 170; Gruneau, *Class, Sports, and Social Development* (Amherst: University of Massachusetts Press, 1983), pp. 69–71, 89, 170; John Hargreaves, "Sport and Hegemony: Some Theoretical Problems," in Hart Cantelon and Richard Gruneau, ed., *Sport, Culture, and the Modern State* (Toronto: University of Toronto Press, 1982), pp. 114–135; and T. J. Jackson Lears, "The Concept of Cultural Hegemony: Problems and Possibilities," *American Historical Review* 90 (June 1985):567–593.

2. Mary Lou LeCompte, "The Hispanic Influence on the History of Rodeo, 1823–1922," *Journal of Sport History* 12 (Spring 1985):21–38; Slatta, "Cowboys and Gauchos," *Américas* 33 (March 1981):3–8; Slatta, "Cowboys, Gauchos, and Llaneros," *Persimmon Hill* 12:4 (1983): 8–23.

3. Claudio Gay, *Historia física y política de Chile: Agricultura*, 2 vols. (Paris: N.p., 1862), 1:387–388; Tomás Lago, *El huaso* (Santiago: Universidad de Chile, 1953), p. 92; George Byam, *Wanderings in Some of the Western Republics of America* (London: John W. Parker, 1850), pp. 57–58; Richard W. Slatta, *Gauchos and the Vanishing Frontier* (Lincoln: University of Nebraska Press, 1983), p. 28.

4. Octavio P. Alais, *Libro criollo: Costumbres nacionales* (Buenos Aires: Bredahl, 1903), pp. 98–101; S. Griswold Morley, "Cowboy and Gaucho Fiction," *New Mexico Quarterly* 16 (Autumn 1946):256; Lago, *Huaso*, pp. 23–24; LeCompte, "Hispanic Influence," p. 22. See the photograph of a ring racer in New Mexico in David R. Phillips, ed., *The Taming of the West: A Photographic Perspective* (Chicago: Regency, 1974), p. 99. Thanks to Mary Lou LeCompte for supplying references on the Mexican vaquero and charro (letters to the author, July 7 and Dec. 8, 1987).

5. Lago, *Huaso*, pp. 22–23; Eugenio Pereira Salas, *Juegos y alegrías coloniales en Chile* (Santiago: Zig-Zag, 1947), pp. 20–24;

Mary Lou LeCompte and William H. Beezley, "Any Sunday in April: The Rise of Sport in San Antonio and the Hispanic Borderlands," *Journal of Sport History* 13:2 (Summer 1986):136; José Cisneros, *Riders Across the Centuries: Horsemen of the Spanish Borderlands* (El Paso: Texas Western Press, 1984), p. 39.

6. John A. Lucas and Ronald A. Smith, *Saga of American Sport* (Philadelphia: Lea and Febiger, 1978), pp. 99–100.

7. Thomas Joseph Hutchinson, *Buenos Ayres and Argentine Gleanings* (London: Edward Stanford, 1865), pp. 51–52; Hutchinson, *The Parana: With Incidents of the Paraguayan War, and South American Recollections, from 1861 to 1868* (London: Edward Stanford, 1868), p. 98; Ysabel F. Rennie, *The Argentine Republic* (New York: Macmillan, 1945), p. 11.

8. Pereira Salas, *Juegos y alegrías*, pp. 20–60; René León Echaiz, *Interpretación histórica del huaso chileno* (Santiago: Editorial Universitaria, 1955), pp. 80–85; Carlos del Campo L. and Luis Durand, *Huasos chilenos: Folklore campesino* (Santiago: Leblanc, 1939), unpag.; Nora E. Ramirez, "The Vaquero and Ranching in the Southwestern United States, 1600–1970" (Ph. D. diss., Indiana University, 1979), p. 208.

9. Quoted in Clifford P. Westermeier, *Trailing the Cowboy: His Life and Lore as Told by Frontier Journalists* (Caldwell, Idaho: Caxton Printers, 1955), pp. 362–363.

10. Ibid., pp. 369–370.

11. Santiago Pérez Triana, *Down the Orinoco in a Canoe* (London: Heinemann, 1902; Spanish ed., 1897), pp. 91–92; Nathaniel H. Bishop, *The Pampas and the Andes: A Thousand Miles' Walk across South America* (1854; 11th ed., Boston: Lee and Shepard, 1883), p. 94; Hutchinson, *The Parana*, pp. 97–98; LeCompte and Beezley, "Any Sunday," pp. 134, 137. The original Mexican term for bull riding, *jari-*

peo, later became a synonym for cha-rreada, or rodeo competition. Today bull riding is called *jineteo de novilla* or *jineteo de toros*.

12. Jesús José Loreto Loreto, *El llano y sus costumbres* (Caracas: Presidencia de la República Venezolana, 1980), p. 92.

13. Edward Sullivan, *Rambles and Scrambles in North and South America*, 2d ed. (London: Robert Bentley, 1852), p. 381.

14. Ramón Paez, *Wild Scenes in South America; or Life in the Llanos of Vene-zuela* (London: Sampson Low, 1863), pp. 183–184.

15. Sir Robert Ker Porter, *Sir Robert Ker Porter's Caracas Diary, 1825–1842: A British Diplomat in a Newborn Na-tion*, ed. Walter Dupuoy (Caracas: Dupuoy, 1966), pp. 324–325; on the equestrian daring of Rosas, see Slatta, *Gauchos*, p. 85.

16. James W. Wells, *Exploring and Travelling Three Thousand Miles Through Brazil*, 2 vols. (London: Sampson Low, Marston, Searle, and Rivington, 1886), 2:239; LeCompte and Beezley, "Any Sun-day," p. 137; Ramirez, "Vaquero," pp. 84–85; Westermeier, *Trailing the Cowboy*, pp. 347–348.

17. Jo Mora, *Californios: The Saga of the Hard-Riding Vaqueros, America's First Cowboys* (Garden City: Doubleday, 1949), pp. 130–135; Ramirez, "Vaquero," pp. 205–206; Peter Watts, *A Dictionary of the Old West, 1850–1900* (New York: Knopf, 1977), pp. 150–151.

18. William MacCann, *Two Thousand Miles' Ride through the Argentine Prov-inces*, 2 vols. (1853; repr., New York: AMS Press, n.d.), 1:14; Robert B. Cunning-hame Graham, "La Pampa," in *Rodeo: A Collection of the Tales and Sketches of R. B. Cunninghame Graham*, ed. A. F. Tschiffely (Garden City: Doubleday, Doran, 1936), pp. 68–70.

19. Thomas Jefferson Page, *La Plata, the Argentine Confederation, and Para-guay* (New York: Harper, 1859), pp. 52–53.

20. MacCann, *Two Thousand Miles' Ride*, 1:14.

21. Emilio Daireaux, *Vida y costum-bres en La Plata*, 2 vols. (Buenos Aires: Lajouane, 1888), 2:230–231; Buenos Aires Province, Ministerio de Gobierno, *Memoria* (Buenos Aires, 1871–1872), pp. 703–704.

22. *Anales de la Sociedad Rural Argen-tina* 16 (July 1882):133–134; Ernesto Raúl Hernández, *Recopilación de leyes agrarias vinculadas a la ganadería* (La Plata?: Mi-nisterio de Asuntos Agrarios de la Provincia de Buenos Aires, 1952), pp. 65–66.

23. Hutchinson, *The Parana*, p. 91; Bishop, *The Pampas and the Andes*, p. 93; Wilfred Latham, *The States of the River Plate*, 2d ed. (London: Longmans, Green, 1868), pp. 56–59; quotation from Gay, *His-toria física*, 1:395.

24. Quote from George A. Peabody, *South American Journals, 1858–1859*, ed. John Charles Phillips (Salem, Mass.: Pea-body Museum, 1937), p. 128.

25. Mora, *Californios*, pp. 70–71; Rami-rez, "Vaquero," pp. 210–211.

26. Hutchinson, *The Parana*, pp. 91–92; Bishop, *The Pampas and the Andes*, p. 93; Latham, *The States*, p. 59; Gay, *Historia física*, 1:395.

27. Samuel C. Reid, Jr., *The Scouting Expeditions of McCulloch's Texas Rang-ers* (Philadelphia: G. B. Zieber, 1847), pp. 58–59.

28. Pereira Salas, *Juegos y alegrías*, p. 59.

29. Echaiz, *Interpretación histórica*, pp. 82–84; Pereira Salas, *Juegos y ale-grías*, pp. 58–59; Campo and Durand, *Huasos chilenos*, unpag.; George M. McBride, *Chile: Land and Society* (New York: American Geographical Society, 1936), p. 159.

30. Joe A. Stout, "Cowboy," in Howard R. Lamar, ed., *The Reader's Encyclopedia*

of the American West (New York: Crowell, 1977), p. 269.

31. Sir Francis Bond Head, *Rough Notes taken during some Rapid Journeys across the Pampas and among the Andes* (London: John Murray, 1826), p. 47.

32. Bishop, *The Pampas and the Andes*, p. 92.

33. Arnold R. Rojas, *The Vaquero* (Santa Barbara, Calif., and Charlotte, N. C.: McNally and Lofton, 1964), pp. 41, 59–63.

34. Dary, *Cowboy Culture*, p. 292; John K. Rollinson, *Wyoming Cattle Trails: History of the Migration of Oregon-raised Herds to Mid-western Markets* (Caldwell, Idaho: Caxton Printers, 1948), pp. 45, 75; Watts, *Dictionary*, pp. 10, 236.

35. Rollinson, *Wyoming Cattle Trails*, p. 75.

36. Robert B. Cunninghame Graham, *José Antonio Paez* (London: Heinemann, 1929), pp. 122–123; José Antonio de Armas Chitty, *Historia del Guárico*, 2 vols. (San Juan de los Morros: Universidad "Rómulo Gallegos," 1978), 1:68–69, Robert Proctor, *Narrative of a Journey across the Cordillera of the Andes, and of a Residence in Lima, and Other Parts of Peru in the Years 1823 and 1824* (London: Constable, 1825), p. 15.

37. William Henry Hudson, *Tales of the Pampa* (New York: Knopf, 1916), pp. 248–251; Lago, *Huaso*, p. 124; Pereira Salas, *Juegos y alegrías*, p. 48.

38. Jorge Paez, *Del truquiflor a la rayuela: Panorama de los juegos y entretenimientos argentinos* (Buenos Aires: Centro Editor de América Latina, 1971), pp. 26–27; Luis García del Soto, "El pato, la fiesta del coraje," *Todo es Historia* 11:127 (Dec. 1977):62–68.

39. Lago, *Huaso*, p. 124; Pereira Salas, *Juegos y alegrías*, pp. 48–49, 57.

40. Reid, *Scouting Expeditions*, pp. 59–60; LeCompte and Beezley, "Any Sunday," pp. 133–134.

41. Westermeier, *Trailing the Cowboy*, p. 355.

42. Ramirez, "Vaquero," p. 208; Mora, *Californios*, p. 69; Charles Frederick Holder, "A Tournament of Roses," *Harper's Weekly*, Feb. 14, 1891:126–127; Beezley and LeCompte, "Any Sunday," pp. 138, 140–141; LeCompte, "Hispanic Influence," pp. 27–28.

43. Slatta, *Gauchos*, p. 51.

44. Bishop, *The Pampas and the Andes*, p. 94; Hutchinson, *The Parana*, pp. 97–98; Victor M. Ovalles, *El llanero: Estudio sobre su vida, sus costumbres, su carácter y su poesía* (Caracas: Herrera Irigoyen, 1905), pp. 56–57.

45. Glenn R. Vernam, *Man on Horseback: The Story of Mounted Men from the Scythians to the American Cowboy* (Lincoln: University of Nebraska Press, 1964), p. 406.

46. LeCompte, "Hispanic Influence," p. 24; Mora, *Californios*, p. 69.

47. Philip Ashton Rollins, *The Cowboy: An Unconventional History of Civilization on the Old-Time Cattle Range*, rev. ed. (1922; repr., Albuquerque: University of New Mexico Press, 1979), p. 181; Lucas and Smith, *Saga*, p. 58; Ramirez, "Vaquero," p. 212.

48. Slatta, *Gauchos*, pp. 25–26. On the importance of knife play, see Ezequiel Martínez Estrada, *X-Ray of the Pampa*, trans. Alain Swietlicki (Austin: University of Texas Press, 1971), pp. 52–53.

49. Guttmann, *From Ritual to Record*, pp. 3–4. See Gruneau, *Class, Sports*, pp. 23–34, for an excellent critique of Huizinga and Novak.

50. William Henry Hudson, *Far Away and Long Ago: A History of My Early Life* (New York: Dutton, 1918), pp. 40–41; Michael G. Mulhall and Edward T. Mulhall, *Handbook of the River Plate Republics* (London: Stafford, 1875), pp. 108–109; Horacio Cabrera Sifontes, *La Rubiera* (Caracas: N.p., 1972), p. 87; Ricardo Güiraldes, *Don Segundo Sombra: Shadows on the Pampas*, trans. Harriet de Onís (New York: Signet, 1966), p. 173.

51. Cabrera Sifontes, *La Rubiera*, p. 87. The novel includes excellent descriptions of llanos life (esp. pp. 79–95).

52. Duthie quoted in Edna Kells, "Pioneer Interviews" (typescript, 1935, Glenbow Archive, Calgary, D 920 K 29), p. 12.

53. J. Frank Dobie, *The Longhorns* (New York: Grosset and Dunlap, 1941), p. 6.

54. Frederic Remington, *Pony Tracks* (Norman: University of Oklahoma Press, 1961), p. 50; LeCompte, "Hispanic Influence," p. 24; Westermeier, *Trailing the Cowboy*, pp. 367–369.

55. *Field and Farm*, July 8, 1899, quoted in Westermeier, *Trailing the Cowboy*, p. 345.

56. Robert J. Higgs, *Sports: A Reference Guide* (Westport, Conn.: Greenwood Press, 1982), p. 17; Lucas and Smith, *Saga*, pp. 29–30, 93.

57. Benjamin Rader, *American Sports: From the Age of Folk Games to the Age of Spectators* (Englewood Cliffs, N. J.: Prentice-Hall, 1983), p. 19.

58. Paez, *Del truquiflor*, pp. 26–27; John Arlott, ed., *The Oxford Companion to World Sports and Games* (London: Oxford University Press, 1975), p. 791.

59. J. Macnie, *Work and Play in the Argentine* (London: Werner Laurie, 192?), pp. 142–143; Echaiz, *Interpretación histórica*, pp. 87–89.

60. Bartolomé Gutiérrez, "Del folklore de la pampa, las deportes del gaucho," *La Nación*, July 16, 1927; Macnie, *Work and Play*, p. 144; Arlott, *Oxford Companion*, p. 791; Patrick A. Dunae, *Gentlemen Emigrants: From the British Public Schools to the Canadian Frontier* (Vancouver and Toronto: Douglas and McIntyre, 1980), p. 91.

61. H. Piercy Douglas, "The Hurlingham Club of Buenos Ayres," *Outing Magazine* 34:1 (April 1899):73–76; James R. Scobie, *Buenos Aires: Plaza to Suburb, 1870–1910* (New York: Oxford University Press, 1974), p. 234; Arlott, *Oxford Companion*, p. 503.

62. Scobie, *Buenos Aires*, pp. 119, 190; Rader, *American Sports*, p. 20.

63. *El orden* (Buenos Aires), Jan. 6, 1909; *El municipio* (Buenos Aires), Sept. 8 and 19, 1909; Michael Moody, "Rodeo is Hot—in Chile," *Persimmon Hill* 15:3 (Autumn 1987):3–17.

64. Pedal, "El ciclismo olavarriense," *La patria* (Olavarría), June 29, 1899; see also issues of July 2, 1899, and Feb. 15, 1900.

65. Arnold J. Bauer, *Chilean Rural Society from the Spanish Conquest to 1930* (Cambridge: Cambridge University Press, 1975), p. 166. For a description of earlier Chilean equestrian games, see Pereira Salas, *Juegos y alegrías*.

66. McBride, *Chile*, pp. 159–160.

67. Ings, "Tales from the Midway Ranch," pp. 77, 79–80; Kells, "Pioneer Interviews," p. 7.

68. Dunae, *Gentlemen Emigrants*, p. 91.

69. LeCompte, "Hispanic Influence," p. 35; Paul F. Long, "From Sagebrush to Sawdust: The Circus Cowboys," *Persimmon Hill* 15:1 (1987): 10–19.

70. Elizabeth Atwood Lawrence, *Rodeo: An Anthropologist Looks at the Wild and the Tame* (Chicago: University of Chicago Press, 1984), p. 45; Bruce A. Rosenberg, *The Code of the West* (Bloomington: Indiana University Press, 1982), p. 35; LeCompte and Beezley, "Any Sunday," p. 141.

71. The quoted phrase is the subtitle from Rader, *American Sports*. See Gruneau, "Sport," pp. 136, 170.

Chapter 9. Hellin' 'Round

1. Quoted from issue of Oct. 3, 1882, in Clifford P. Westermeier, ed., *Trailing the Cowboy: His Life and Lore as Told by Frontier Journalists* (Caldwell, Idaho: Caxton Printers, 1955), p. 50; Thomas J. Noel, *The City and the Saloon: Denver, 1858–1916* (Lincoln: University of Nebraska Press, 1982), p. 2; Richard Erdoes,

Saloons of the Old West (New York: Knopf, 1969), p. 76.

2. Quote from Thomas J. Hutchinson, *Buenos Ayres and Argentine Gleanings* (London: Edward Stanford, 1865), p. 283. For other unflattering images of pulpería life, see Richard W. Slatta, "Pulperías and Contraband Capitalism in Nineteenth-Century Buenos Aires Province," *The Americas* 38 (Jan. 1982):352–356.

3. Ricardo Güiraldes, *Don Segundo Sombra: Shadows on the Pampas*, trans. Harriet de Onís (New York: Signet, 1966), p. 51.

4. On the tenuous theory of male bonding, see Lionel Tiger, *Men in Groups*, 2d ed. (New York: M. Moyars/Scribner's, 1984) and the critique by Rae Lesser Blumberg, *Stratification: Socioeconomic and Sexual Inequality* (Dubuque, Iowa: William C. Brown, 1978), pp. 6–10. See also Noel, *City and the Saloon*, p. 91; Sherri Cavan, *Liquor License: An Ethnography of Bar Behavior* (Chicago: Aldine, 1966), p. 67; William B. Taylor, *Drinking, Homicide, and Rebellion in Colonial Mexican Villages* (Stanford: Stanford University Press, 1979), p. 65; and Robert J. Glynn et al., "Social Contexts and Motives for Drinking in Men," *Journal of Studies on Alcohol* 44 (Nov. 1983):1,021–1,022.

5. Quote from Ramon F. Adams, *Western Words: A Dictionary of the American West* (Norman: University of Oklahoma Press, 1968), p. 96; see also pp. 39, 190; Elliott West, *The Saloon of the Rocky Mountain Mining Frontier* (Lincoln: University of Nebraska Press, 1979), pp. 19–21.

6. Quote from T. H. Whitney, "The White Mud Pool Wagon," *Canadian Cattlemen* 2:1 (June 1939):204–205; Joe B. Frantz and Julian Ernest Choate, Jr., *The American Cowboy: The Myth and the Reality* (Norman: University of Oklahoma Press, 1955), pp. 96–97; Paul F. Sharp, *Whoop-Up Country: The Canadian-American West, 1865–1885* (Helena: His-torical Society of Montana, 1960), pp. 173–174.

7. Edward Larocque Tinker, *The Horsemen of the Americas and the Literature They Inspired*, 2d ed. (Austin: University of Texas Press, 1967), p. 21; Ezequiel Martínez Estrada, *X-Ray of the Pampa*, trans. Alain Swietlicki (Austin: University of Texas Press, 1971), p. 52.

8. Henry Caven, "Recollections" (typescript, Glenbow Archive, Calgary, D 636.081 M 621); Marcos de Estrada, *Apuntes sobre el gaucho argentino* (Buenos Aires: Ministerio de Cultura y Educación, 1981), p. 155; Fred Ings, "Tales from the Midway Ranch" (typescript, 1933, Glenbow Archive, Calgary, M 264-f1), pp. 53–54; Richard W. Slatta, *Gauchos and the Vanishing Frontier* (Lincoln: University of Nebraska Press, 1983), p. 118; Nora E. Ramirez, "The Vaquero and Ranching in the Southwestern United States, 1600–1970" (Ph. D. diss., Indiana University, 1979), pp. 184–185.

9. Buenos Aires Province, Comisión de Hacendados del Estado de Buenos Aires, *Antecedentes y fundamentos del proyecto de código rural* (Buenos Aires, 1864); letter from Mauricio Díaz, Bahía Blanca, March 6, 1850, juez de paz de Azul 9-4-4; reports of juez de crimen 1872, 38-4-313; Archivo Histórico de la Provincia de Buenos Aires "Ricardo Levene" (La Plata, Argentina); police reports of March, June, July 1852, Policía, 1852, Archivo Histórico Municipal de Tandil (Tandil, Argentina).

10. Eugenio Pereira Salas, *Juegos y alegrías coloniales en Chile* (Santiago: Zig-Zag, 1947), pp. 256–257.

11. Taylor, *Drinking*, pp. 65–66, 156; Michael C. Scardaville, "Alcohol Abuse and Tavern Reform in Late Colonial Mexico City," *Hispanic American Historical Review* 60 (Nov. 1980):644–645, 670–671.

12. Richard Maxwell Brown, "Saloon," in Howard R. Lamar, ed., *The Reader's Encyclopedia of the American West* (New York: Crowell, 1977), p. 1,062.

13. Craig MacAndrew and Robert Edgerton, *Drunken Comportment: A Social Explanation* (Chicago: Aldine, 1969), pp. 36, 60, 165; David Mandelbaum, "Alcohol and Culture," in Mac Marshall, ed., *Beliefs, Behaviors, and Alcoholic Beverages: A Cross-Cultural Survey* (Ann Arbor: University of Michigan Press, 1979), pp. 17–18; R. O. Pihl, Mark Smith, and Brian Farrell, "Alcohol and Aggression in Men: A Comparison of Brewed and Distilled Beverages," *Journal of Studies on Alcohol* 45 (May 1984):278, 281.

14. MacAndrew and Edgerton, *Drunken Comportment*, pp. 82, 90–94, 171–173; Taylor, *Drinking*, p. 66; Slatta, *Gauchos*, p. 118.

15. Allan M. Winkler, "Drinking on the American Frontier," *Quarterly Journal of Studies on Alcohol* 29 (June 1968):416–417.

16. Laurence Ivan Seidman, *Once in the Saddle: The Cowboy's Frontier, 1866–1896* (New York: Knopf, 1973), p. 86; Charles W. Harris and Buck Rainey, eds., *The Cowboys: Six Shooters, Songs and Sex* (Norman: University of Oklahoma Press, 1976), p. 87; E. C. Abbott and Helena Huntington Smith, *We Pointed Them North* (Norman: University of Oklahoma Press, 1939), p. 52; Noel, *City and the Saloon*, pp. 30–31.

17. Taylor, *Drinking*, p. 41; Thomas J. Hutchinson, *The Parana: With Incidents of the Paraguayan War, and South American Recollections, from 1861 to 1868* (London: Edward Stanford, 1868), p. 89; quote from Nathaniel Holmes Bishop, *The Pampas and the Andes: A Thousand Miles' Walk Across South America*, 11th ed. (Boston: Lee and Shepard, 1883), pp. 98–99.

18. William MacCann, *Two Thousand Miles' Ride Through the Argentine Provinces*, 2 vols. (1853; repr., New York: AMS Press, n.d.), 2: 282, 285. Quote from Robert B. Cunninghame Graham, "La Pulperia," in John Walker, ed., *The South American Sketches of R. B. Cunninghame Graham* (Norman: University of Oklahoma Press, 1978), p. 63.

19. George D. Flinter, *A History of the Revolution of Caracas* (London: Allman, 1819), pp. 119–120.

20. Fermín Vélez Boza, *El folklore en la alimentación venezolana* (Caracas: Instituto Nacional de Nutrición, 1966), p. 75.

21. Erdoes, *Saloons*, pp. 25–26; David Dary, *Cowboy Culture: A Saga of Five Centuries* (New York: Knopf, 1981), p. 211; quote from Adams, *Western Words*, p. 34; see also pp. 178–179.

22. Balzac quoted in Darrell W. Bolen, "Gambling: Historical Highlights and Trends and Their Implications for Contemporary Society," in William R. Eadington, ed., *Gambling and Society: Interdisciplinary Studies on the Subject of Gambling* (Springfield, Ill.: Charles C. Thomas, 1976), p. 12; J. Philip Jones, *Gambling Yesterday and Today: A Complete History* (Newton Abbot, England: David and Charles, 1973), pp. 13–14, 64, 84. For a critique of various theories of gambling, see Tomás M. Martínez, *The Gambling Scene: Why People Gamble* (Springfield, Ill.: Charles C. Thomas, 1983), pp. 108–131.

23. Robert K. De Arment, *Knights of the Green Cloth: The Saga of the Frontier Gamblers* (Norman: University of Oklahoma Press, 1982), pp. 227–229; Pereira Salas, *Juegos y alegrías*, pp. 189–191, 222–232; Jesús José Loreto Loreto, *El llano y sus costumbres* (Caracas: Presidencia de la República Venezolana, 1980), p. 108; MacCann, *Two Thousand Miles' Ride*, 1:47; Slatta, "Pulperías," p. 352; Jorge Paez, *Del truquiflor a la rayuela: Panorama de los juegos y entretenimientos argentinos* (Buenos Aires, Centro Editor de América Latina, 1971), pp. 35–40.

24. Quoted in De Arment, *Knights*, pp. 41 (see also pp. 75–85); Brown, "Saloon," p. 1,062.

25. Dary, *Cowboy Culture*, p. 214; William H. Forbis, *The Cowboys* (Alex-

andria, Va.: Time-Life Books, 1973), pp. 82, 170; Adams, *Western Words*, pp. 48, 55, 167, 231.

26. Westermeier, *Trailing the Cowboy*, pp. 144–145.

27. Duncan McNab McEachran, "A Journey over the Plains from Fort Benton to Bow River and Back" (Glenbow Archive, Calgary, pamphlet 971.23 M 141j), p. 12; "George" quoted in John R. Craig, *Ranching with Lords and Commons; or, Twenty Years on the Range* (1903; repr., New York: AMS Press, 1971), pp. 89–90, 97.

28. Jules Verne Allen, *Cowboy Lore* (San Antonio: Naylor, 1950), p. 120.

29. Bolen, "Gambling," p. 16; Hutchinson, *The Parana*, p. 91; Madaline Wallis Nichols, *The Gaucho: Cattle Hunter, Cavalryman, Ideal of Romance* (1942; repr., New York: Gordian Press, 1968), p. 14; Tinker, *Horsemen*, p. 24; Paez, *Truquiflor*, pp. 40–46; Oreste Plath, *Folklore chileno*, 3d ed. (Santiago: Editorial Nascimento, 1969), pp. 191–193.

30. Pereira Salas, *Juegos y alegrías*, pp. 110–122; Allen F. Gardiner, *A Visit to the Indians on the Frontiers of Chili* (London: Seeley and Burnside, 1841), p. 77; Karl Sachs, *De los llanos: Descripción de un viaje de ciencias naturales a Venezuela*, trans. José Izquierdo (Caracas and Madrid: Edime, 1955), pp. 181–184; Plath, *Folklore*, pp. 193–195.

31. Erdoes, *Saloons*, p. 182.

32. Quoted in George M. Blackburn and Sherman L. Ricards, "The Prostitutes and Gamblers of Virginia City, Nevada: 1870," *Pacific Historical Review* 48 (May 1979):241.

33. *Rocky Mountain News*, July 23, 1889, quoted in Noel, *City and the Saloon*, p. 86; Adams, *Western Words*, p. 51; Erdoes, *Saloons*, p. 189; Abbott, *We Pointed Them North*, p. 108; Sharp, *Whoop-Up Country*, p. 174; Dary, *Cowboy Culture*, p. 217. See also Marion S. Goldman, *Gold Diggers and Silver Miners: Prostitution and Social Life on the Comstock Lode* (Ann Arbor: University of Michigan Press, 1981) and Anne E. Butler, *Daughters of Joy, Sisters of Misery: Prostitutes in the American West, 1865–90* (Urbana: University of Illinois Press, 1985).

34. Edward Brado, *Cattle Kingdom: Early Ranching in Alberta* (Toronto and Vancouver: Douglas and McIntyre, 1984), pp. 230–231.

35. Martínez Estrada, *X-Ray of the Pampa*, p. 205. On the many barriers to gaucho family life, see Slatta, *Gauchos*, pp. 58–60.

36. Slatta, *Gauchos*, pp. 66–67; Tinker, *Horsemen*, p. 27; Jorge Bossio, *Historia de las pulperías* (Buenos Aires: Plus Ultra, 1972), p. 61.

Chapter 10. Cowboys and Indians

1. Wallace Stegner, *Wolf Willow: A History, a Story and a Memory of the Last Prairie Frontier* (Toronto: Macmillan, 1955), p. 73; Harold B. Barclay, *The Role of the Horse in Man's Culture* (London: J. A. Allen, 1980), pp. 165–188; Theodore A. Dodge, "Some American Riders," *Harper's New Monthly Magazine*, June 1891: 854–862; Allen F. Gardiner, *A Visit to the Indians on the Frontiers of Chili* (London: Seeley and Burnside, 1841), p. 97; J. W. G. MacEwan, "The Story of the Horse on the North American Continent," *Canadian Cattlemen* 4:3 (Dec. 1941):93, 128; Alistair Hennessy, *The Frontier in Latin American History* (Albuquerque: University of New Mexico Press, 1978), pp. 62–63.

2. Hennessy, *Frontier*, pp. 45–46; Silvio R. Duncan Baretta and John Markoff, "Civilization and Barbarism: Cattle Frontiers in Latin America," *Comparative Studies in Society and History* 20:4 (Oct. 1978):595–597, 602–605.

3. Robert M. Denhardt, *The Horse of*

the Americas, rev. ed. (Norman: University of Oklahoma Press, 1975), p. 160; Miguel Izard, "Sin domicilio fijo, senda segura, ni destino conocido: Los llaneros de Apure a finales del período colonial," *Boletín americanista* 33 (1983):21–33; Miguel Izard, *El miedo de la revolución: La lucha por la libertad en Venezuela, 1777–1830* (Madrid: Tecnos, 1979), p. 176.

4. Richard W. Slatta, *Gauchos and the Vanishing Frontier* (Lincoln: University of Nebraska Press, 1983), p. 59. For details on the Argentine case, see Kristine L. Jones, "Conflict and Adaptation in the Argentine Pampas, 1750–1880" (Ph. D. diss., University of Chicago, 1984).

5. Slatta, *Gauchos*, pp. 8–9.

6. Robert B. Cunninghame Graham, *The South American Sketches of R. B. Cunninghame Graham*, ed. John Walker (Norman: University of Oklahoma Press, 1978), pp. 25–26. For additional examples, see Félix Coluccio, *Diccionario folklórico argentino*, 2 vols. (Buenos Aires: Lassarre, 1964).

7. José Antonio de Armas Chitty, *Vocabulario del hato* (Caracas: Universidad Central de Venezuela, 1966), pp. 13–14; René León Echaiz, *Interpretación histórica del huaso chileno* (Santiago: Editorial Universitaria, 1955), pp. 93–95.

8. Gardiner, *A Visit to the Indians*, pp. 97–98. Compare the descriptions in Slatta, *Gauchos*, p. 74, and William H. B. Webster, *Narrative of a Voyage to the Southern Atlantic Ocean*, 2 vols. (London: Richard Bentley, 1834), 1:81.

9. Roberto H. Marfany, *El indio en la colonización de Buenos Aires* (Buenos Aires: Comisión Nacional de Cultura, 1940), pp. 62–63, 67–68; Madaline Wallace Nichols, "The Spanish Horse of the Pampas," *American Anthropologist* 41 (Jan. 1939):119–129; Juan Carlos Walther, *La conquista del desierto*, 2d ed. (Buenos Aires: Círculo Militar, 1964), pp. 118–119, 139. Walther's work, available in several

editions, provides good descriptions of military actions on the Argentine Indian frontier. Also useful is Dionisio Schöo Lastra, *El indio del desierto, 1535–1879* (Buenos Aires: Agencia General, 1928).

10. Alfred Tapson, "Indian Warfare on the Pampa during the Colonial Period," *Hispanic American Historical Review* 42 (Feb. 1962):8–9; Alfred Hasbrouck, "The Conquest of the Desert," ibid. 15 (May 1935):205.

11. Argentine Republic, Ejercito, *Política seguida con el aborigen*, 3 vols. (Buenos Aires: Círculo Militar, 1973), 1:121; Ricardo Rodríguez Molas, *Historia social del gaucho* (Buenos Aires: Marú, 1968), pp. 27, 66–70, 135; Juan Carlos Vedoya et al., *La campaña del desierto y la tecnificación ganadera* (Buenos Aires: EUDEBA, 1979), pp. 17–18. See also Roberto H. Marfany, "El cuerpo de blandengues de la frontera de Buenos Aires, 1752–1810," *Humanidades* 23 (1933): 313–373.

12. Louis de Armond, "Frontier Warfare in Colonial Chile," *Pacific Historical Review* 23:2 (May 1954):128–131; George M. McBride, *Chile: Land and Society* (New York: American Geographical Society, 1936), p. 114.

13. Jones, "Conflict," p. 27; Tapson, "Indian Warfare," p. 13; Vedoya, *Campaña*, p. 18.

14. Decree of Aug. 30, 1815, "Gobierno," X-8-9-3, Archivo General de la Nación, Buenos Aires; Ataulfo Pérez-Aznar, "La política tradicional y la Argentina moderna," *Revista de la universidad* 20–21 (Jan. 1966–July 1967):207–208; Walther, *Conquista*, pp. 191–192.

15. Sandra L. Myres, *The Ranch in Spanish Texas, 1691–1800* (El Paso: Texas Western Press, 1969), pp. 24–25; Edward Larocque Tinker, *The Horsemen of the Americas and the Literature They Inspired*, 2d ed. (Austin: University of Texas Press, 1967), p. 100; Robert B. Cunning-

hame Graham, *José Antonio Paez* (London: Heinemann, 1929), p. 25; Slatta, *Gauchos*, pp. 7–8.

16. John Mawe, *Travels in the Interior of Brazil* (London: Longman, Hurst, Rees, Orme and Brown, 1823), p. 34; Francis Bond Head, *Rough Notes taken during Some Rapid Journeys across the Pampas and among the Andes*, 2d ed. (London: John Murray, 1826), pp. 44–45; Robert Ker Porter, *Sir Robert Ker Porter's Caracas Diary, 1825–1842: A British Diplomat in a Newborn Nation*, ed. Walter Dupuoy (Caracas: Walter Dupuoy, 1966), p. 150; William E. Curtis, *Venezuela: A Land Where It's Always Summer* (New York: Harper, 1896), pp. 250–251.

17. Graham, *South American Sketches*, p. 25; Brian Loveman, *Chile: The Legacy of Hispanic Capitalism* (New York: Oxford University Press, 1979), pp. 56, 59, 70; Richard M. Morse, ed., *The Bandeirantes: The Historical Role of the Brazilian Pathfinders* (New York: Knopf, 1965), pp. 81–91, 100–113.

18. Quoted in Eloy G. González, *Historia estadística de Cojedes desde 1771* (Caracas: Americana, 1911), pp. 29–30.

19. Miguel Izard, "Ni cuatreros ni montoneros, llaneros," *Boletín americanista* 31 (1981):125. See also Germán Carrera Damas, *Boves: Aspectos socio-económicos de la guerra de independencia*, 3d ed. (Caracas: Universidad Central de Venezuela, 1972).

20. Izard, "Ni cuatreros," p. 138.

21. Slatta, *Gauchos*, pp. 13, 182–183; G. Reid Andrews, *The Afro-Argentines of Buenos Aires, 1800–1900* (Madison: University of Wisconsin Press, 1980), pp. 215–216.

22. Reginald Horseman, *Race and Manifest Destiny: The Origins of American Racial Anglo-Saxonism* (Cambridge: Harvard University Press, 1981), pp. 209–214; Patricia Nelson Limerick, *The Legacy of Conquest: The Unbroken Past of the American West* (New York: Norton, 1987), pp. 240–241; Cecil Robinson, *Mexico and the Hispanic Southwest in American Literature* (Tucson: University of Arizona Press, 1977), pp. 33–68. See also Arnoldo DeLeon, *They Called Them Greasers: Anglo Attitudes Toward Mexicans in Texas, 1821–1900* (Austin: University of Texas Press, 1983); Arnoldo DeLeon and Kenneth L. Stewart, "Lost Dreams and Found Fortunes: Mexican and Anglo Immigrants in South Texas, 1850–1900," *Western Historical Quarterly* 14:3 (July 1983):291–310.

23. Nora E. Ramirez, "The Vaquero and Ranching in the Southwestern United States, 1600–1970" (Ph. D. diss., Indiana University, 1979), p. 119; Joseph G. McCoy, *Cattle Trade in the West and Southwest* (1874; repr., N.p.: Readex Microprint, 1966), p. 375 (see also p. 373); José E. Limón, "Folklore, Social Conflict, and the U. S.-Mexican Border," in Richard M. Dorson, ed., *Handbook of American Folklore* (Bloomington: Indiana University Press, 1983), pp. 216–226; William W. Savage, Jr., ed., *Cowboy Life: Reconstructing an American Myth* (Norman: University of Oklahoma Press, 1975), p. 147.

24. Theodore Dodge, "Some American Riders," *Harper's New Monthly Magazine* July 1891:211.

25. Ramirez, "Vaquero," pp. 70–75, 104–105, 135; Kenneth W. Porter, "Negro Labor in the Western Cattle Industry, 1866–1900," *Labor History* 10:3 (Summer 1969):351, 359, 363.

26. Julian Somora, Joe Bernal, and Albert Peña, *Gunpowder Justice: A Reassessment of the Texas Rangers* (Notre Dame: University of Notre Dame Press, 1979), pp. 10–11, 15–18; 28–29, 34–35, 52–55; Stephen B. Oates, "Los Diablos Tejanos: The Texas Rangers in the Mexican War," *Journal of the West* 9:4 (Oct. 1970): 492, 496, 499, 504.

27. Thomas J. Noel, *The City and the Saloon: Denver, 1858–1916* (Lincoln: University of Nebraska Press, 1982), pp. 23–

29; David Dary, *Cowboy Culture: A Saga of Five Centuries* (New York: Knopf, 1981), p. 211.

28. Ramirez, "Vaquero," p. 130; Arnold R. Rojas, *The Vaquero* (Santa Barbara, Calif., and Charlotte, N. C.: McNally and Loftin, 1964), p. 71; letter to the author from John Scharff, Burns, Oregon, July 1, 1974; Richard W. Slatta, "Chicanos in the Pacific Northwest: An Historical Overview of Oregon's Chicanos," *Aztlán* 6:3 (Fall 1975):328; David Braly, "Cattle Barons of Early Oregon" (mimeograph, Prineville, Oreg.: American Media, 1978), pp. 17–18, 21, 39.

29. Philip Durham and Everett L. Jones, *The Negro Cowboys* (Lincoln: University of Nebraska Press, 1965), pp. 3, 15, 17, 143.

30. Porter, "Negro Labor," pp. 347–348, 363, 366; Joe A. Stout, "Cowboy," in Howard R. Lamar, ed., *The Reader's Encyclopedia of the American West* (New York: Crowell, 1977), p. 268; Durham and Jones, *Negro Cowboys*, pp. 3, 45.

31. W. Sherman Savage, *Blacks in the West* (Westport, Conn.: Greenwood Press, 1976), p. 88; Durham and Jones, *Negro Cowboys*, pp. 24, 153.

32. Durham and Jones, *Negro Cowboys*, p. 17.

33. Ibid., pp. 209–211, 218.

34. Ibid., pp. 189, 200–210; Savage, *Blacks in the West*, p. 90.

35. H. Frank Lawrence, "Early Days in the Chinook Belt," *Alberta Historical Review* 13:1 (1965):12; J. W. G. MacEwan, *John Ware's Cattle Country* (Saskatoon: Western Producer Prairie Books, 1960), pp. 1, 10–17; Fred Ings, "Tales from the Midway Ranch" (typescript, 1933, Glenbow Archive, Calgary, M 264-f1), p. 18 (serialized in *Canadian Cattlemen* beginning June 1941).

36. Duncan McNab McEachran, "A Journey Over the Plains from Fort Benton to Bow River and Back" (Glenbow Archive, Calgary, pamphlet 971.23 M 141j), pp. 8, 12–13; William F. Cochrane to J. M.

Browning, March 29, 1885, "Letter Book," (MS., Glenbow Archive, Calgary, M 234), p. 113.

37. *Macleod Gazette*, Oct. 2, 1890:2; see also the issue of March 24, 1893:2.

38. Paul Sharp, "The Northern Great Plains: A Study in Canadian-American Regionalism," *Mississippi Valley Historical Review* 39:1 (June 1952):64–65; John L. Tobias, "Protection, Civilization, Assimilation: An Outline History of Canada's Indian Policy," *Western Canadian Journal of Anthropology* 6:2 (1976):13–30; Tobias, "Canada's Subjugation of the Plains Cree," *Canadian Historical Review* 64:4 (Dec. 1983):519–521, 526, 548.

39. On Indian-white relations, see Robert M. Utley, *The Indian Frontier of the American West, 1846–1890* (Albuquerque: University of New Mexico Press, 1984) and Brian W. Dippie, *The Vanishing American: White Attitudes and U. S. Indian Policy* (Middletown, Conn.: Wesleyan University Press, 1982).

40. *Las Vegas Daily Optic*, Dec. 17, 1883, repr. in Westermeier, *Trailing the Cowboy*, p. 166; *New Mexico Stock Grower*, Dec. 19, 1885, quoted in Maurice Frink, W. Turrentine Jackson, and Agnes Wright Spring, *When Grass Was King* (Boulder: University of Colorado Press, 1956), p. 19.

41. Manuel J. Olascoaga, *Estudio topográfico de la pampa y Río Negro*, vol. 1 of Argentine Republic, Ministerio de Guerra y Marina, *La conquista del desierto*, 4 vols. (Buenos Aires: Arajuo, 1939), pp. 160–163 (quote from p. 69); Adolfo A. Alsina, *La nueva linea de la frontera* (1877; repr., Buenos Aires: EUDEBA, 1977), pp. 25–29, 369; John E. Hodge, "The Role of the Telegraph in the Consolidation and Expansion of the Argentine Republic," *The Americas* 41 (July 1984):68–69, 72, 80; Hasbrouck, "Conquest," p. 217.

42. Roca's presidential message reprinted in Nestor Tomás Auza, *Documentos para la enseñanza de la historia argen-*

tina, 1852–1890, 2 vols. (Buenos Aires: Pannedille, 1970), 1:212; *La Campaña* (Buenos Aires), April 25 and 29, 1883.

43. On legal repression, see Richard W. Slatta, "Rural Criminality and Social Conflict in Buenos Aires Province," *Hispanic American Historical Review* 60 (Aug. 1980):450–472; and Rodríguez Molas, *Historia social*, pp. 41–42, 75, 83–85, 102, 112–114.

44. Slatta, *Gauchos*, pp. 25–28, 118; Marcos de Estrada, *Apuntes sobre el gaucho argentino* (Buenos Aires: Ministerio de Cultura y Educación, 1981), p. 155.

45. Slatta, *Gauchos*, pp. 43–45; quote from Walther, *Conquista*, p. 798; Julio Aníbal Portas, *Malón contra malón: La solución final del problema del indio en la Argentina* (Buenos Aires: La Flor, 1967), pp. 58–60.

46. Hennessy, *Frontier*, pp. 19, 146–147.

47. Jones, "Conflict," pp. 69–72, 85–87. For a perceptive interpretation of frontier conflict, see Baretta and Markoff, "Civilization and Barbarism," pp. 587–620.

Chapter 11. Riding into the Sunset

1. Juan Iturbe, "Nuestros llanos: Apuntes fisiográficas, biológicas y agropecuarias" (Caracas: La Nación, 1942), p. 21; Miguel Izard, "Ni cuatreros ni montoneros, llaneros," *Boletín americanista* 31 (1981):118–122; Jane M. Rausch, *A Tropical Plains Frontier: The Llanos of Colombia, 1531–1831* (Albuquerque: University of New Mexico Press, 1984), pp. 198, 211–212; Robert P. Matthews, "Los aprietos de la industria ganadera a mediados del siglo XIX," *Boletín histórico* 40 (Jan. 1976):72–73.

2. Miguel Izard and Richard W. Slatta, "Banditry and Social Conflict on the Venezuelan Llanos," in Slatta, ed., *Bandidos: The Varieties of Latin American Banditry*

(Westport, Conn.: Greenwood Press, 1987), pp. 40–44.

3. Germán Arciniegas, "La guerra y la carne," *El nacional*, Jan. 5, 1969:A-4.

4. José María Colina to president of Guárico, July 15, 1878, Secretaría de Instrucción y Justicia, vol. 976, p. 163, Archivo General de la Nación, Caracas; Karl Sachs, *De los llanos: Descripción de un viaje de ciencias naturales a Venezuela*, trans. José Izquierdo (Caracas and Madrid: Edime, 1955), p. 87.

5. Raye Platt, "Opportunities for Agricultural Colonization in the Eastern Valleys of the Andes," in W. L. G. Joerg, ed., *Pioneer Settlement* (New York: American Geographical Society, 1932), pp. 87–90; Alejandro Rivas Sosa, *Nuestro ganado vacuno: La ganadería como fuente potencial de riqueza nacional* (Caracas: Elite, 1938), p. 20; Catherine LeGrand, *Frontier Expansion and Peasant Protest in Colombia, 1850–1936* (Albuquerque, University of New Mexico Press, 1986), pp. 8–9, 210.

6. Brian Loveman, *Chile: The Legacy of Hispanic Capitalism* (New York: Oxford University Press, 1979), pp. 142–143; José Pedro Barrán, *Apogeo y crisis del Uruguay pastoril y caudillesco, 1839–1875*, vol. 4 of *Historia uruguaya*, 2d ed. (Montevideo: Banda Oriental, 1975), pp. 50, 131–132.

7. Arnold J. Bauer, *Chilean Rural Society from the Spanish Conquest to 1930* (Cambridge: Cambridge University Press, 1975), pp. 66–70, 77, 102–104, 179–181, 211–212; Loveman, *Chile*, pp. 100, 104, 107; Teodoro Schneider, *La agricultura en Chile en los últimos cincuenta años* (Santiago: Barcelona, 1904), p. 68.

8. Ricardo Rodríguez Molas, *Historia social del gaucho* (Buenos Aires: Marú, 1968), pp. 185–192; Jonathan C. Brown, *A Socioeconomic History of Argentina, 1776–1860* (Cambridge: Cambridge University Press, 1979), pp. 46–52.

9. Federico Brito Figueroa, *Ensayos de*

historia social venezolana (Caracas: Universidad Central de Venezuela, 1960), p. 235; Rodríguez Molas, *Historia social*, pp. 190–192.

10. Charles H. Harris, *A Mexican Family Empire: The Latifundio of the Sánchez Navarro Family, 1765–1867* (Austin: University of Texas Press, 1975), pp. 203–204, 302–307.

11. Benjamin Keen and Mark Wasserman, *A Short History of Latin America*, 3d ed. (Boston: Houghton Mifflin, 1988), pp. 210–218.

12. Paul J. Vanderwood, *Disorder and Progress: Bandits, Police, and Mexican Development* (Lincoln: University of Nebraska Press, 1981), pp. 79–82, 94–97.

13. Manual A. Machado, Jr., *The Mexican Cattle Industry, 1910–1975: Ideology, Conflict, and Change* (College Station: Texas A&M University Press, 1981), pp. 2–3, 6–13.

14. Ibid., pp. 19–20, 27, 125.

15. Ibid., pp. 123–124.

16. Enrique Mendez Vives, *El Uruguay de la modernización, 1876–1904*, vol. 5 of *Historia uruguaya* (Montevideo: Banda Oriental, 1975), p. 20; Raúl Jacob, *Consequencias sociales del alambramiento, 1872–1880* (Montevideo: Banda Oriental, 1969), pp. 35, 38.

17. Thomas Woodbine Hinchliff, *South American Sketches* (London: Longman, Green, Longman, Roberts, and Green, 1863), p. 103.

18. Richard W. Slatta, *Gauchos and the Vanishing Frontier* (Lincoln: University of Nebraska Press, 1983), pp. 148–150.

19. Maurice W. Frink, W. Turrentine Jackson, and Agnes Wright Spring, *When Grass Was King* (Boulder: University of Colorado Press, 1956), pp. 56–57; Charles L. Wood, *The Kansas Beef Industry* (Lawrence: Regents Press of Kansas, 1980), p. 24; Frederic L. Paxson, "The Cow Country," *American Historical Review* 22:1 (Oct. 1916):71–72; Edward Everett

Dale, *The Range Cattle Industry: Ranching on the Great Plains from 1865 to 1925* (Norman: University of Oklahoma Press, 1960), p. 109.

20. Fred Ings, "Tales from the Midway Ranch" (typescript, 1933, Glenbow Archive, Calgary, M 264-f1), p. 88.

21. Quoted in Simon M. Evans, "Canadian Beef for Victorian Britain," *Agricultural History* 53:4 (Oct. 1979):759.

22. Santiago Pérez Triana, *Down the Orinoco in a Canoe* (London: Heinemann, 1902), pp. 89–90; Fernando Calzadilla Valdes, *Por los llanos de Apure* (Santiago: Imprenta Universitaria, 1940), pp. 255–256, 266–268.

23. David Dary, *Cowboy Culture: A Saga of Five Centuries* (New York: Knopf, 1981), pp. 310–311; Sandra L. Myres, *The Ranch in Spanish Texas, 1691–1800* (El Paso: Texas Western Press, 1969), p. 29.

24. Dary, *Cowboy Culture*, pp. 310–311; David H. Breen, *The Canadian Prairie West and the Ranching Frontier, 1874–1924* (Toronto: University of Toronto Press, 1983), pp. 51, 70.

25. Quoted in Loveman, *Chile*, pp. 123–124; Charles C. Griffin, "Francisco Encina and Revisionism in Chilean History," *Hispanic American Historical Review* 37:1 (Feb. 1957):1–28. On changing Chilean and Argentine attitudes toward immigrants, see Carl E. Solberg, *Immigration and Nationalism: Argentina and Chile, 1890–1914* (Austin: University of Texas Press, 1970).

26. Quoted in Carl E. Solberg, "A Discriminatory Frontier Land Policy: Chile, 1870–1914," *The Americas* 26:2 (Oct. 1969):122.

27. Ibid., pp. 125–127; Solberg, *Immigration and Nationalism*, p. 24; David Rock, *Argentina, 1516–1987: From Spanish Colonization to Alfonsín*, rev. ed. (Berkeley: University of California Press, 1987), p. 179.

28. Magnus Morner and Harold Sims,

Adventurers and Proletarians: The Story of Migrants in Latin America (Pittsburgh: University of Pittsburgh Press, 1985), pp. 36, 40–41.

29. Quotation from Terry Jordan, *Trails to Texas: Southern Roots of Western Cattle Ranching* (Lincoln: University of Nebraska Press, 1981), p. 21; Slatta, *Gauchos*, pp. 158–160.

30. Slatta, *Gauchos*, p. 154; Rock, *Argentina*, pp. 137–139. Major studies of Argentine agriculture include Carl E. Solberg, *The Pampas and the Prairies: Agrarian Policy in Canada and Argentina, 1880–1930* (Stanford: Stanford University Press, 1987); James R. Scobie, *Revolution on the Pampas: A Social History of Argentine Wheat, 1860–1910* (Austin: University of Texas Press, 1964); Carl C. Taylor, *Rural Life in Argentina* (Baton Rouge: Louisiana State University Press, 1948); Ezequiel Gallo, *Farmers in Revolt: The Revolution of 1893 in the Province of Santa Fe, Argentina* (London: Athlone, 1976); Horacio Giberti, *El desarrollo agrario argentino* (Buenos Aires: EUDEBA, 1964); Gastón Gori, *El pan nuestro: Panorama social de las regiones cerealistas argentinas* (Buenos Aires: Galatea, 1958); and Mark Jefferson, *Peopling the Pampa* (New York: American Geographical Society, 1926).

31. José P. Barrán and Benjamín Nahum, *Recuperación y dependencia, 1895–1904*, vol. 3 of *Historia rural del Uruguay moderno* (Montevideo: Banda Oriental, 1973), pp. 298–299; Domingo Ordoñana, *Pensamientos rurales sobre necesidades sociales y economicas de la República*, 2 vols. (Montevideo: Imprenta Rural, 1892), 1:394.

32. Miguel Izard, "La Venezuela del cafe vista por los viajeros del siglo XIX," *Boletín histórico* 7:20 (May 1969):191, 197; Francisco Depons, *Viaje a la parte oriental de Tierra Firme*, trans. Enrique Planchart (1806; repr., Caracas: Tipografía Americana, 1930), p. 315.

33. Leszek M. Zawisza, "Colonización agricola en Venezuela," *Boletín histórico* 13:37 (Jan. 1975):19, 22–23.

34. Reports by Governor Rafael Hermoso, Secretaría de Instrucción y Justicia, vol. 38, 1831, pp. 5–8, Archivo General de la Nación, Caracas; Antonio Arellano Moreno, *Las estadísticas de las provincias en la época de Paez* (Caracas: Academia Nacional de Historia, 1973), p. 135.

35. Hermoso reports, Archivo General de la Nación, Caracas, Instrucción y Justicia, vol. 38, pp. 6, 10.

36. Ibid., pp. 14, 20, 40, 52, 57–58, 63–111; Zawisza, "Colonización agricola," pp. 34–36, 44.

37. Manuel Pérez Vila, "El gobierno deliberativo: Hacendados, comerciantes y artesanos frente a la crisis, 1830–1848," in *Política y Economía en Venezuela* (Caracas: Foundación Boulton, 1976), p. 48; Izard, "La Venezuela del cafe," pp. 207–210; Marco Aurelio Vila, *Una geografía humano-económica de la Venezuela de 1873* (Caracas: Ministerio de Fomento, 1970), pp. 140–141.

38. The best overview of elite-mass conflict and changes forced upon the rural masses is E. Bradford Burns, *The Poverty of Progress: Latin America in the Nineteenth Century* (Berkeley: University of California Press, 1980).

39. Buenos Aires Province, *Registro oficial* (Buenos Aires, 1822), pp. 69, 170, 277; Benito Díaz, *Juzgados de paz de la campaña de la Provincia de Buenos Aires, 1821–1854* (La Plata: Universidad Nacional de La Plata, 1959), pp. 105–106, 202–203.

40. Rodríguez Molas, *Historia social*, pp. 229–234; Alfredo J. Montoya, *Historia de los saladeros argentinos* (Buenos Aires: El Coloquio, 1970), pp. 45–46, 57, 60. The rural code of Buenos Aires province is reprinted in Ernesto Raúl Hernández, *Recopilación de leyes agrarias vinculadas a la ganadería: Período comprendido entre los años 1856 a 1952* (La Plata?: Ministerio

de Asuntos Agrarios de la Provincia de Buenos Aires, 1952), pp. 8–45.

41. A. R. Fernández, *Prontuario informativo de la provincia de Buenos Aires* (Buenos Aires: Campañía Sud-Americana de Billetes de Banco, 1903), 2:37–38; Godofredo Daireaux, *La cría de ganado en la estancia moderna*, 3d ed. (Buenos Aires: Prudent Brothers and Moetzel, 1904), p. 96; Francisco Bauzá, *Estudios literarios* (Montevideo: Librería Nacional, 1885), pp. 249–250.

42. John W. White, *Argentina: The Life Story of a Nation* (New York: Viking, 1942), p. 73.

43. Hinchliff, *South American Sketches*, pp. 89, 195; Robert Crawford, *Across the Pampas and the Andes* (London: Longmans, Green 1884), pp. 115–116; Carlos D'Amico, *Siete años en el gobierno de la Provincia de Buenos Aires* (Buenos Aires: Peuser, 1895), p. 99.

44. Fletcher quoted in William W. Savage, Jr., ed., *Cowboy Life: Reconstructing an American Myth* (Norman: University of Oklahoma Press, 1975), p. 130.

45. Jack Parsons and Michael Earney, *Land and Cattle: Conversations with Joe Pankey, a New Mexico Rancher* (Albuquerque: University of New Mexico Press, 1978), pp. 15–16.

46. Rodney O. Davis, "Before Barbed Wire: Herd Law Agitations in Early Kansas and Nebraska," *Journal of the West* 6:1 (Jan. 1967):49–50.

47. *Denver Republican*, Dec. 9, 1900, reprinted in Westermeier, *Trailing the Cowboy*, pp. 179–180.

48. David Braly, "Cattle Barons of Early Oregon" (mimeograph, Prineville, Oreg.: American Media, 1978), p. 50; Oscar H. Flagg, *A Review of the Cattle Business in Johnson County, Wyoming Since 1892 and the Causes That Led to the Recent Invasion* (New York: Arno Press and the New York Times, 1969).

49. Slatta, *Gauchos*, pp. 142–143.

50. Alexander Begg, "Stock Raising in the Bow River District Compared with Montana," in John Macoun, ed., *Manitoba and the Great North West* (Guelph, Ontario: World Publishing, 1882), p. 278; *Yellowstone Journal* (Miles City), April 18, 1882, quoted in Leland Everett Stuart, "Men and Cattle on the Northern Plains, 1860–1887" (thesis, University of Oregon, 1971), p. 26.

51. Lonn Taylor and Ingrid Maar, *The American Cowboy* (Washington, D. C.: Library of Congress, 1983), pp. 18–19; Ernest S. Osgood, *The Day of the Cattleman* (Minneapolis: University of Minnesota Press, 1929), p. 229; John T. Schlebecker, *Cattle Raising on the Plains, 1900–1961* (Lincoln: University of Nebraska Press, 1963), pp. 7, 113; Dale, *Range Cattle Industry*, pp. 92, 94, 97.

52. Craig Miner, *West of Wichita: Settling the High Plains of Kansas, 1865–1890* (Lawrence: University Press of Kansas, 1986), pp. 176–177.

53. Regulations reprinted in Dary, *Cowboy Culture*, pp. 303–307.

54. Deane, "Reminiscences of a Mounted Police Officer" (typescript, Glenbow Archive, Calgary, M 311); Breen, *Canadian Prairie West*, pp. 64, 67, 74.

55. Calgary *Herald*, April 9, 1885 (typescript copy, Glenbow Archive, Calgary, M 419).

56. Simon M. Evans, "American Cattlemen on the Canadian Range, 1874–1914," *Prairie Forum* 4:1 (Spring 1979):132–133; Breen, *Canadian Prairie West*, pp. 127–135.

57. H. M. Hatfield, "Diaries" (typescript, Glenbow Archive, Calgary, M 480); Breen, *Canadian Prairie West*, pp. 145–149.

58. Katherine Hughes, "The Last Great Roundup," *Alberta Historical Review* 11:2 (Spring 1963):1; Fred Ings, "Tales from the Midway Ranch," p. 13.

59. Wesley F. Orr, "Letter Books, 1888–1897," 5 vols. (Glenbow Archive, Calgary, O 75 A), 3:169.

60. Simon M. Evans, "The End of the Open-Range Era in Western Canada," *Prairie Forum* 8:1 (Spring 1983):71–72; Charles M. MacInnes, *In the Shadows of the Rockies* (London: Rivingtons, 1930), pp. 241–245.

61. Quoted in Breen, *Canadian Prairie West*, p. 168.

Chapter 12. The Cowboy Rides Again

1. Theodore Roosevelt, "In Cowboy Land," *The Outlook* 104 (May 24, 1913):150; Douglas Branch, *The Cowboy and His Interpreters* (New York: Appleton, 1926), p. 190; David B. Davis, "Ten-Gallon Hero," in James K. Folsom, ed., *The Western: A Collection of Critical Essays* (Englewood Cliffs, N. J.: Prentice-Hall, 1979), pp. 17–19, 26–29; Lonn Taylor and Ingrid Maar, *The American Cowboy* (Washington, D. C.: Library of Congress, 1983), p. 17.

2. Elizabeth Atwood Lawrence, *Rodeo: An Anthropologist Looks at the Wild and the Tame* (Chicago: University of Chicago Press, 1984), pp. 46–47; William W. Savage, Jr., ed., *Cowboy Life: Reconstructing an American Myth* (Norman: University of Oklahoma Press, 1975), pp. 6, 8; Robert W. Dubose, "Updating the Cowboy," *Southern Folklore Quarterly* 26:1 (March 1962):189; Don Russell, *The Wild West: A History of the Wild West Shows* (Fort Worth: Amon Carter Museum of Western Art, 1970); Prentiss Ingraham, *Buck Taylor, King of the Cowboys* (New York: Beadle's Half-Dime Library, 1887).

3. See Taylor and Maar, *American Cowboy,* for a quick survey of the cowboy's cultural pervasiveness.

4. Jack Nachbar, "Horses, Harmony, Hope, and Hormones: Western Movies, 1930–1946," *Journal of the West* 22:4 (Oct. 1983):30; John H. Lenihan, "Classics and Social Commentary: Postwar Westerns, 1946–1960," ibid., p. 35; Michael P. Rogin,

Ronald Reagan, the Movie and Other Episodes in Political Demonology (Berkeley: University of California Press, 1987), pp. 25, 38.

5. Rogin, *Ronald Reagan, the Movie,* p. 189; Michael E. Welsh, "Western Film, Ronald Reagan, and the Western Metaphor," in Archie P. McDonald, ed., *Shooting Stars: Heroes and Heroines of Western Film* (Bloomington: Indiana University Press, 1987), p. 148.

6. Roy A. Jordan and Tim R. Miller, "The Politics of a Cowboy Culture," *Annals of Wyoming* 52:1 (Spring 1980):44. On John Wayne, see Maurice Zolotow, *Shooting Star* (New York: Simon and Schuster, 1974); George Carpozi, *The John Wayne Story* (New Rochelle, N.Y.: Arlington House, 1972); Archie P. McDonald, "John Wayne: Hero of the Western," *Journal of the West* 22:4 (Oct. 1983):53–63; John Boswell and Jay David, *Duke: The John Wayne Album* (New York: Ballantine, 1979).

7. Boswell and David, *Duke*, p. 15; Rogin, *Ronald Reagan, the Movie,* pp. 249–250; Archie P. McDonald, "John Wayne: Hero of the Western," in McDonald, *Shooting Stars*, pp. 124–125.

8. Boswell and David, *Duke*, pp. 125–129; Rogin, *Ronald Reagan, the Movie,* pp. 188–189.

9. David G. Pugh, *Sons of Liberty: The Masculine Mind in Nineteenth-Century America* (Westport, Conn.: Greenwood Press, 1983), pp. 132, 135; John G. Cawalti, *The Six-Gun Mystique* (Bowling Green: Bowling Green University Press, n.d.), pp. 38–39; Jordan and Miller, "Politics," p. 45.

10. Paul A. Hutton, "From Little Big Horn to Little Big Man: The Changing Image of a Western Hero in Popular Culture," *Western Historical Quarterly* 7:1 (Jan. 1976):45; Edward Countryman, "Westerns and United States' History," *History Today* 33 (March 1983):18–23.

11. Michael Mason, ed., *The Country*

Music Book (New York: Scribner's, 1985), pp. 7, 10, 12, 42–48, 58; Charlie Seemann, "The American Cowboy: Image and Reality," liner notes to *Back in the Saddle* (New York: New World Records, 1983), p. 1.

12. Michael Murphey, *Peaks, Valleys, Honky-tonks & Alleys* (New York: Epic Records/CBS, 1979).

13. William W. Savage, Jr., *The Cowboy Hero: His Image in American History and Culture* (Norman: University of Oklahoma Press, 1979), pp. 3–4; Taylor and Maar, *Cowboy*, pp. 78–79; Roland Marchand, *Advertising the American Dream: Making Way for Modernity, 1920–1940* (Berkeley: University of California Press, 1985). Typical ads can be seen accompanying virtually any televised professional football contest.

14. See the Compaq ad in *PC Week*, Oct. 13, 1987:195. The Dell ads appear in *PC Magazine*, Nov. 1987:224–225, and in *PC Week*, Nov. 10, 1987:84, 89. The Northern Telecom ad appears in *PC Week Connectivity Buyer's Guide*, Nov. 10, 1987:C/26–C/27.

15. Richard Drinnon, *Facing West: The Metaphysics of Indian-Hating and Empire-Building* (Minneapolis: University of Minnesota Press, 1980), pp. 368, 450–451; Richard S. Slotkin, *The Fatal Environment: The Myth of the Frontier in the Age of Industrialization, 1800–1890* (New York: Atheneum, 1985), pp. 16–19.

16. Drinnon, *Facing West*, p. 435.

17. Taylor and Maar, *American Cowboy*, p. 78; Ray Merlock, "Gene Autry and the Coming of Civilization," in McDonald, *Shooting Stars*, pp. 87–108.

18. Seemann, "American Cowboy," p. 4.

19. "The Fourth Cowboy Poetry Gathering" (promotional pamphlet); Charlie Seemann, telephone conversation with the author, Dec. 8, 1987.

20. "Fourth Cowboy Poetry Gathering;" Jeff Adler and Jeff B. Copeland, "Git Along, Little Doggerels," *Newsweek*, Feb. 11, 1985:77; Gwen Petersen, "Git Along Li'l Doggerels: Cowboys and Poetry," *Per-*simmon Hill* 16:1 (Spring 1988):28–37; Edward Hoagland, "Buckaroo Poets: Whoop-ee-ti-yi-yo, Git Along, Little Doggerel," *New Yorks Times Book Review*, Jan. 8, 1989: 3, 17.

21. The fundamental work on the nativist backlash to immigration is Carl E. Solberg, *Immigration and Nationalism: Argentina and Chile, 1890–1914* (Austin: University of Texas Press, 1970).

22. Herbert Gibson, "The Evolution of Live-Stock Breeding in the Argentine," in Argentine Republic, *Stock-breeding and Agriculture in 1909: Monographs*, vol. 3 of *Censo agropecuario nacional: La ganadería y la agricultura en 1908* (Buenos Aires: Argentine Meteorological Office, 1909), p. 73.

23. Slatta, *Gauchos*, pp. 176–179; Slatta, "The Gaucho in Argentina's Quest for National Identity," *Canadian Review of Studies in Nationalism* 12:1 (1985):99–101.

24. Leopoldo Lugones, *El payador*, 4th ed. (Buenos Aires: Huemul, 1972), pp. 49, 66; Ricardo Rojas, *Los gauchescos* (Buenos Aires: Losada, 1948), p. 549; Slatta, "Gaucho in Argentina's Quest," pp. 99–122; Hebe Clementi, "National Identity and the Frontier," *American Studies International* 18:3–4 (1981):36–44.

25. *Nativa* 50 (Feb. 29, 1928); Julian O. Miranda, *Apuntes sobre historia de la República Oriental del Uruguay*, 7th ed. (Montevideo: Barreiro y Ramos, 1904), pp. 45–47; Slatta, "Gaucho in Argentina's Quest," p. 108; Mario Sambarino, *La cultura nacional como problema* (Montevideo: Nuestra Tierra, 1970). Contrast the views of the gaucho in Vicente Rossi, *El gaucho: Su orígen y evolución* (Córdoba: Río de la Plata, 1921); Alberto Zum Felde, *Proceso intelectual del Uruguay y crítica de su literatura*, 2 vols. (Montevideo: Imprenta Nacional Colorado, 1930); and Emilio P. Corbière, *El gaucho: Desde su origen hasta nuestros dias* (Buenos Aires: Rosso, 1929).

26. Ezequiel Martínez Estrada, *X-Ray*

of the Pampa, trans. Alain Swietlicki (Austin: University of Texas Press, 1971), p. 375.

27. Slatta, "Gaucho in Argentina's Quest," pp. 116–119; J. C. M. Ogelsby, "'Who Are We?': The Search for a National Identity in Argentina, Australia and Canada, 1870–1950," in D. C. M. Platt and Guido DiTella, eds., *Argentina, Australia and Canada: Studies in Comparative Development, 1870–1965* (London: Macmillan, 1985), pp. 115–117.

28. Madaline Wallis Nichols, *The Gaucho: Cattle Hunter, Cavalryman, Ideal of Romance* (1942; repr., New York: Gordian Press, 1968), p. 62; Slatta, "Gaucho in Argentina's Quest," pp. 106–107.

29. Alberto Gerchunoff, *The Jewish Gauchos of the Pampas*, trans. P. de Pereda (New York: Abelard-Schuman, 1955); Robert Weisbrot, *The Jews of Argentina from the Inquisition to Perón* (Philadelphia: Jewish Publication Society of America, 1979), pp. 214–222; Juan Goyechea, *Los gauchos vascos* (Buenos Aires: Editorial Vasca Ekin, 1975).

30. Mary Lombardi, "The Frontier in Brazilian History: An Historiographical Essay," *Pacific Historical Review* 44:4 (Nov. 1975):450–454.

31. *Nativa* 50 (Feb. 29, 1928).

32. José María Samper, *Ensayo sobre las revoluciones políticas y la condición social de las repúblicas colombianas* (Paris: Thurnot, 1861), pp. 93–94; Manuel Tejera, *Venezuela pintoresca e ilustrada* (Paris: Librería Española, 1875), p. 250.

33. Samper quoted in Jane M. Loy, "Horsemen of the Tropics: A Comparative View of the Llaneros in the History of Venezuela and Colombia," *Boletín Americanista* 31 (1981):165–166; José E. Machado, "El gaucho y el llanero," in Daniel Mendoza, *El llanero: Ensayo de sociología venezolana* (Buenos Aires: Editorial Venezuela, 1947), p. 12.

34. Laureano Vallenilla Lanz, *Disgrega-ción e integración: Ensayo sobre la formación de la nacionalidad venezolana*, 2 vols. (Caracas: Tipografía Universal, 1930), 1:171, 191–192.

35. René León Echaiz, *Interpretación história del huaso chileno* (Santiago: Editorial Universitaria, 1955), p. 106; Hernán Godoy Urzua, *El carácter chileno* (Santiago: Editorial Universitaria, 1976, 1982). The folklorist Tomás Lago asserts that the huaso is a Chilean national symbol. I disagree. See Michael Moody, "Rodeo is Hot—in Chile," *Persimmon Hill* 15:3 (Autumn 1987):11.

36. Guillermo Feliú Cruz, *Patria y chilenidad: Ensayo histórico y sociológico sobre los orígenes de estos sentimientos nacionales afectivos* (Santiago: Biblioteca Nacional, 1966), pp. 160–161; Tomás Lago, *El huaso* (Santiago: Universidad de Chile, 1953), p. 207.

37. For the viewpoint of an outraged Canadian, see Pierre Berton, *Hollywood's Canada: The Americanization of Our National Image* (Toronto: McClelland and Stewart, 1975).

38. Paul F. Sharp, *Whoop-Up Country: The Canadian-American West, 1865–1885* (Helena: Historical Society of Montana, 1960), p. 240; Simon M. Evans, "American Cattlemen on the Canadian Range, 1874–1914," *Prairie Forum* 4:1 (Spring 1979): 126–127; Evans, "The Passing of a Frontier: Ranching in the Canadian West, 1882–1912" (Ph. D. diss., University of Calgary, 1976), pp. 242–243.

39. Sharp, *Whoop-Up Country*, p. 240; David H. Breen, "The Turner Thesis and the Canadian West: A Closer Look at the Ranching Frontier," in Lewis H. Thomas, ed., *Essays on Western History in Honour of Lewis Gwynne Thomas* (Edmonton: University of Alberta Press, 1976), pp. 149–150.

40. Breen, *Canadian Prairie West*, pp. 64–67; Carl E. Solberg, "Peopling the Prairies and the Pampas: The Impact of

Immigration on Argentine and Canadian Agrarian Development, 1870–1930," *Journal of Inter-American Studies and World Affairs* 24:2 (May 1982):140.

41. On the political economy of ranching, see Jimmy M. Skaggs, *Prime Cut: Livestock Raising and Meatpacking in the United States, 1607–1983* (College Station: Texas A&M University Press, 1986).

42. Philip Durham and Everett L. Jones, *The Negro Cowboys* (Lincoln: University of Nebraska Press, 1965), pp. 222–224.

43. Quoted in John K. Rollinson, *Wyoming Cattle Trails: History of the Migration of Oregon-raised Herds to Midwestern Markets* (Caldwell, Idaho: Caxton Printers, 1948), p. 159. See also Roy Harvey Pearce, *Savagism and Civilization: A Study of the Indian and the American Mind* (1953; repr., Berkeley: University of California Press, 1988).

44. Nora E. Ramirez, "The Vaquero and Ranching in the Southwestern United States, 1600–1970" (Ph. D. diss., Indiana University, 1979), pp. 123–127.

45. Jack Jackson, *Los Mesteños: Spanish Ranching in Texas, 1721–1821* (College Station: Texas A&M University Press, 1986), pp. 588–595; Arnoldo DeLeon, *They Called Them Greasers: Anglo Attitudes Toward Mexicans in Texas, 1821–1900* (Austin: University of Texas Press, 1983), pp. 3–13, 17, 25; Cecil Robinson, *Mexico and the Hispanic Southwest in American Literature* (Tucson: University of Arizona Press, 1963), pp. 33–68. See also Francis Paul Prucha, *The Indians in American Society from the Revolutionary War to the Present* (Berkeley: University of California Press, 1985).

46. Manuel Patricio Servin, "California's Hispanic Heritage: A View into the Spanish Myth," in David J. Weber, ed., *New Spain's Far Northern Frontier: Essays on Spain in the American West, 1540–1821* (Albuquerque: University of New Mexico Press, 1979), pp. 119–120.

47. John W. White, *Argentina: The Life Story of a Nation* (New York: Viking, 1942), pp. 66–67.

48. Branch, *Cowboy*, p. 181; Ray A. Billington, *Land of Savagery; Land of Promise: The European Image of the American Frontier in the Nineteenth Century* (New York: Norton, 1981), pp. 170.

49. Taylor and Maar, *Cowboy*, pp. 67–68.

50. Billington, *Land of Savagery*, pp. 172–173.

51. Gary Topping, "The Rise of the Western," *Journal of the West* 19:1 (Jan. 1980):30; Don D. Walker, *Clio's Cowboys: Studies in the Historiography of the Cattle Trade* (Lincoln: University of Nebraska Press, 1981), pp. 113–123; quotation from David Mogen, "Owen Wister's Cowboy Heroes," in James K. Folsom, ed., *The Western: A Collection of Critical Essays* (Englewood Cliffs, N. J.: Prentice-Hall, 1979), p. 57; John R. Milton, *The Novel of the American West* (Lincoln: University of Nebraska Press, 1980), pp. 20–21, 32.

52. Don D. Walker, "Criticism of the Cowboy Novel: Retrospect and Reflections," *Western American Literature* 11:4 (Feb. 1977):281–284; Mody C. Boatright, "The American Myth Rides the Range: Owen Wister's Man on Horseback," *Southwest Review* 36:3 (Summer 1951):157–193; Jackson K. Putnam, "Historical Fact and Literary Truth: The Problem of Authenticity in Western American Literature," *Western American Literature* 15:1 (May 1980):17–23.

53. Richard M. Dorson, *America in Legend: Folklore from the Colonial Period to the Present* (New York: Pantheon, 1973), pp. 129–131.

54. Milton, *Novel*, p. 35; Branch, *Cowboy*, p. 210; Edward Larocque Tinker, *The Horsemen of the Americas and the Literature They Inspired*, 2d ed. (Austin: University of Texas Press, 1967), pp. 112–113.

55. John Dinan, "The Pulp Cowboy,"

Persimmon Hill 15:3 (Autumn 1987):18–26.

56. J. Frank Dobie, *Guide to Life and Literature in the Southwest* (1942; repr., Dallas: Southern Methodist University Press, 1974) remains a useful reference on Western literature.

57. Walker, "Criticism," p. 77; Walter Clemons, "Saga of a Cattle Drive," *Newsweek*, June 3, 1985:74.

58. Myron I. Lichtblau, "Formation of the Gaucho Novel in Argentina," *Hispania* 41:3 (Sept. 1958):297–298; S. Morley Griswold, "Cowboy and Gaucho Fiction," in James K. Folsom, ed., *The Western: A Collection of Critical Essays* (Englewood Cliffs, N. J.: Prentice-Hall, 1979), pp. 19–22.

59. Horacio Jorge Becco, "La poesía gauchesca en el Río de la Plata," *Inter-American Review of Bibliography* 24:2 (1974):135–146; Slatta, *Gauchos*, pp. 191–192; Solberg, *Immigration and Nationalism*, pp. 141–144; Ricardo Rojas, *Los gauchescos* (Buenos Aires: Losada, 1948).

60. Tinker, *Horsemen*, pp. 57–60.

61. Slatta, *Gauchos*, pp. 184–188.

62. Morley, "Cowboy and Gaucho Fiction," in Folsom, *The Western*, pp. 118–121; Jean Franco, *The Modern Culture of Latin America: Society and the Artist* (Harmondsworth, England: Penguin, 1970), pp. 18–19, 71, 104–105, 144; Ricardo Güiraldes, *Don Segundo Sombra: Shadows on the Pampas*, trans. Harriet de Onís (New York: Signet, 1966), pp. 16–17.

63. José Ramón Medina, *Ochenta años de literatura venezolana, 1900–1980* (Caracas: Monte Avila, 1980), pp. 142–145, 174–175; Lowell Dunham, "Rómulo Gallegos: Creador de la literatura nacional venezolana," *Revista nacional de cultura*, 26 (May 1964):36.

64. John E. Englekirk, "Doña Bárbara: Legend of the Llanos," *Hispania* 31:1 (1948):260–261, 268–269.

65. Rómulo Gallegos, *Doña Bárbara*, trans. Robert Malloy (New York: Peter Smith, 1948), p. 138; Juan Liscano, "La obra literaria de Rómulo Gallegos," *Inter-American Review of Bibliography* 16:2 (1966):123–143.

66. Robinson, *Mexico and the Hispanic Southwest*, pp. 141–142.

67. Mary J. Cannizzo, "*Costumbrismo* in Chilean Prose Fiction" (Ph. D. diss., Columbia University, 1972), p. 488.

68. Taylor and Maar, *American Cowboy*, p. 77. Recent studies of rodeo include Kristine Fredriksson, *American Rodeo: From Buffalo Bill to Big Business* (College Station: Texan A&M University Press, 1984); Lawrence, *Rodeo*; Vella C. Munn, *Rodeo Riders: Life on the Rodeo Circuit* (New York: Harvey House, 1982); Bob St. John, *On Down the Road: The World of the Rodeo Cowboy* (Englewood Cliffs, N. J.: Prentice-Hall, 1977); and Joe Englander, *They Ride the Rodeo: The Men and Women of the American Amateur Rodeo Circuit* (New York: Collier, 1979).

69. Charles W. Furlong, *Let 'er Buck: A Story of the Passing of the Old West* (New York: Putnam's, 1923), pp. 16, 138.

70. Fredriksson, *American Rodeo*, pp. 13–18, 109.

71. Ibid., pp. 51, 147–148, 172; Ron Givens, "In the School of Hard Knocks," *Newsweek on Campus*, Oct. 1984:22–24.

72. Fredriksson, *American Rodeo*, pp. 40–48, 86–88; Virginia Cowan-Smith and Bonnie Domrose Stone, *Aloha Cowboy* (Honolulu: University of Hawaii Press, 1988), pp. 44, 116.

73. Guy Weadick, "The Origin of the Calgary Stampede," *Alberta Historical Review* 14:4 (Autumn 1966):5, 13, 21–23; Leroy V. Kelly, *The Range Men: The Story of the Ranchers and Indians of Alberta* (1913; repr., New York: Argonaut Press, 1965), pp. 431–439.

74. Kenneth Coppock, "The Calgary Stampede: A Western Institution," *Cana-*

dian Cattlemen 1:1 (June 1938):36, 51; Hugh A. Dempsey, "Calgary's First Stampede," *Alberta Historical Review* 3:3 (Summer 1955):3–13.

75. Ivan D. Inman, "The Rancher's Roundup," *Alberta History* 23:3 (Summer 1975):1–6; Coppock, "Stampede," p. 51; Theodore Barris and Robert Semeniuk, *Rodeo Cowboys: The Last Heroes* (Edmonton, Alberta: Executive Sport Publications, 1981), pp. 1–33.

76. Lawrence, *Rodeo*, pp. 61–63, 87, 129, 142, 159–160.

77. Fredriksson, *American Rodeo*, p. 4; Mary Lou LeCompte, "The Hispanic Influence on the History of Rodeo, 1823–1922," *Journal of Sport History* 12:1 (Spring 1983):21–23.

78. LeCompte, "Hispanic Influence," pp. 21–23; James Norman, *Charro: Mexican Horseman* (New York: Putnam's, 1969), pp. 41–42, 51–55, 91–92.

79. Norman, *Charro*, pp. 15, 93–94.

80. Ibid., pp. 95–97; José Alvarez de Villar, *Men and Horses of Mexico: History and Practice of Charrería* (Mexico: Ediciones Lara, 1979), pp. 46–47; Mary Lou LeCompte, letter to the author, Dec. 8, 1987.

81. Givens, "School of Hard Knocks," pp. 22–24. See also Teresa Jordan, *Cowgirls: Women of the American West: An Oral History* (Garden City: Doubleday, 1982); Elizabeth Van Steenwyk, *Women in Sports: Rodeo* (New York: Harvey House, 1978); Lynn Haney, *Ride 'em Cowgirl* (New York: Putnam's, 1975).

82. Norman, *Charro*, pp. 89. 96–97; LeCompte, letter to the author, Dec. 8, 1987.

83. Moody, "Rodeo," pp. 6–7.

84. Ibid., pp. 6–10.

85. Ibid., pp. 11, 14–15.

86. Ibid., pp. 16–17.

87. This discussion of the Western film has been influenced by several works, including John Tuska, *The Filming of the West* (Garden City: Doubleday, 1976); John H. Lenihan, *Showdown: Confronting Modern America in the Western Film* (Urbana: Illinois University Press, 1980); James R. Parish and Michael C. Pitts, *The Great Western Pictures* (Metuchen, N. J.: Scarecrow Press, 1976); George N. Fenin and William K. Everson, *The Western: From Silents to the Seventies* (New York: Grossman, 1973); Richard W. Etulain, "Changing Images: The Cowboy in Western Films," *Colorado Heritage* 1 (1981): 36–55; Les Adams and Buck Rainey, *Shoot 'em Ups: The Complete Reference Guide to Westerns of the Sound Era* (New Rochelle, N. Y.: Arlington House, 1978); Wayne M. Sarf, *God Bless You, Buffalo Bill: A Layman's Guide to History and the Western Film* (New Brunswick: Cornwall Books, 1983); Etulain, "Western Films: A Brief History," special issue of *Journal of the West* 22:4 (Oct. 1983); and McDonald, *Shooting Stars*.

88. Richard W. Slatta, "Tar Heels Ride with the Cowboys," *The State* (Raleigh, N. C.), Aug. 1982:17–18.

89. Thomas N. Walters, *Seeing in the Dark* (Durham, N. C.: Moore Publishing, 1972), p. 16.

90. Mason, *County Music Book*, pp. 42–45, 397; Seemann, "American Cowboy," p. 1.

91. Lenihan, *Showdown*, pp. 4, 176; Gary A. Yoggy, "When Television Wore Six-Guns: Cowboy Heroes on TV," in McDonald, *Shooting Stars*, pp. 218–261; Lawrence R. Borne, *Dude Ranching: A Complete History* (Albuquerque: University of New Mexico Press, 1983).

92. Berton, *Hollywood's Canada*, pp. 15, 247.

93. Ibid., pp. 120, 210, 217, 230.

94. William Mark McCaffrey, "The Gaucho from Literature to Film: Martín Fierro and Juan Moreira" (Ph. D. diss., University of California at San Diego, 1983), pp. 45, 48–49, 103, 118; Dennis West,

"Cinemagraphic Images of Nineteenth-Century Argentina" (conference paper, LaCrosse, Wis., April 16, 1988).

95. McCaffrey, "Gaucho from Literature to Film," pp. 48–49, 103, 118.

96. Carl J. Mora, *Mexican Cinema: Reflections of a Society, 1896–1980* (Berkeley: University of California Press, 1982), p. 47.

97. *Persimmon Hill* 15:4 (Winter 1987):46–51; Dinan, "Pulp Cowboy," p. 26. See also Mary Young, "The West and American Cultural Identity," *Western Historical Quarterly* 1 (1970):137–161; and Don D. Walker, "History and Imagination: The Prose and Poetry of the Cattle Industry, 1895–1905," *Pacific Historical Review* 45:3 (Aug. 1976):379–397.

Chapter 13. Conclusions

1. For a concise explication of the "cowpens" theory, see Terry G. Jordan, "The Origin of Anglo-American Cattle Ranching in Texas: A Documentation of Diffusion from the Lower South," *Economic Geography* 45 (Jan. 1969):65.

2. William Eugene Hollon, *The Great American Desert Then and Now* (New York: Oxford University Press, 1966), pp. 130–131.

3. David H. Breen, "The Turner Thesis and the Canadian West: A Closer Look at the Ranching Frontier," in Lewis H. Thomas, ed., *Essays on Western History in Honour of Lewis Gwynne Thomas* (Edmonton: University of Alberta Press, 1976), pp. 151–152; William F. DeVerell, "To Loosen the Safety Valve: Eastern Workers and Western Lands," *Western Historical Quarterly* 19:3 (Aug. 1988):285; Robert A. Burchell, "Opportunity and the Frontier: Wealth-Holding in Twenty-Six Northern California Counties, 1848–1880," *Western Historical Quarterly* 18:2 (April 1987):194–196.

4. F. J. McLynn, "The Frontier Problem in Nineteenth-Century Argentina," *History Today* 30 (Jan. 1980):32.

5. Jane M. Rausch, *A Tropical Plains Frontier: The Llanos of Colombia, 1531–1831* (Albuquerque: University of New Mexico Press, 1984), pp. 209, 211–212, 241–242; Richard W. Slatta, "Rural Criminality and Social Conflict in Nineteenth-Century Buenos Aires Province," *Hispanic American Historical Review* 60:3 (Aug. 1980):450–472; Raúl Jacob, *Consequencias sociales del alambramiento, 1872–1880* (Montevideo: Banda Oriental, 1969), p. 18.

6. Breen, "Turner Thesis," p. 156.

7. Carl Berger, *The Writing of Canadian History: Aspects of English-Canadian Writing, 1900–1970* (Toronto: Oxford University Press, 1976), p. 175; Breen, "Turner Thesis," p. 149; Robin W. Winks, "Frontier, Canada," in Howard R. Lamar, ed., *The Reader's Encyclopedia of the American West* (New York: Crowell, 1977), pp. 416–418.

8. David J. Weber, "Turner, the Boltonians, and the Borderlands," *American Historical Review* 91:1 (Feb. 1986):81; Silvio Duncan Baretta and John Markoff, "Civilization and Barbarism: Cattle Frontiers in Latin America," *Comparative Studies in Society and History* 20 (Oct. 1978):593–595.

9. Richard W. Slatta and Arturo Alvarez D'Armas, "El llanero y el hato venezolano: Aportes bibliográficos," *South Eastern Latin Americanist* 29:2–3 (Sept. 1985):33–35.

10. Ibid., pp. 34–35; bibliography, pp. 36–41.

11. Richard J. Morrisey, "The Shaping of Two Frontiers," *Américas* 3:1 (Jan. 1951):3–6, 41–42.

12. Walter Prescott Webb, *The Great Frontier* (Austin: University of Texas Press, 1979), pp. 8–28; David M. Potter, *People of Plenty: Economic Abundance and the American Character* (Chicago:

University of Chicago Press, 1973), pp. 124, 155–165.

13. James Norman, *Charro: Mexican Horseman* (New York: Putnam's, 1969), pp. 47–48.

14. Weber, "Turner, the Boltonians, and the Borderlands," pp. 70, 73; John Francis Bannon, *The Spanish Borderlands Frontier, 1513–1821* (New York: Holt, Rinehart and Winston, 1970), p. 5; Herbert Eugene Bolton, *The Spanish Borderlands: A Chronicle of Old Florida and the Southwest* (New Haven: Yale University Press, 1921), pp. 233–234.

15. Marvin W. Mikesell, "Comparative Studies in Frontier History," *Annals of the Association of American Geographers* 50:1 (March 1960):62–74; Weber, "Turner, the Boltonians, and the Borderlands," p. 72. The notes to the Weber essay offer an excellent guide to the most important frontier historiography.

16. Miguel Izard, "Ni cuatreros ni montoneros, llaneros," *Boletín americanista* 31 (1981):109–113; Julio de Armas, "Nacimiento de la ganadería venezolana," *Revista Shell* 3:11 (June 1954):35; David Rock, *Argentina, 1516–1987: From Spanish Colonization to Alfonsín*, rev. ed. (Berkeley: University of California Press, 1987), pp. 34–35, 54.

17. Thomas Falkner, *A Description of Patagonia and Adjoining Parts of South America* (1774; facs. ed., Chicago: Armann and Armann, 1935); Rock, *Argentina*, p. 17.

18. Ricardo Caillet-Bois, "Dictamen imparcial sobre los gauchos," *Boletín del Instituto de Investigaciones Históricas* 5:29 (July 1926):103.

19. Izard, "Ni cuatreros," pp. 90–91; José E. Machado, "El gaucho y el llanero," in Daniel Mendoza, *El llanero: Ensayo de sociología venezolana* (Buenos Aires: Editorial Venezuela, 1947), pp. 20–21; Joe B. Frantz and Julian E. Choate, Jr., *The American Cowboy: The Myth and the Reality* (Norman: University of Oklahoma Press, 1955), p. 64; quotation from Clifford P. Westermeier, ed., *Trailing the Cowboy: His Life and Lore as Told by Frontier Journalists* (Caldwell, Idaho: Caxton Printers, 1955), p. 250.

20. See Daniel Granada, *Reseña histórico-descriptiva de antiguas y modernas supersticiones del Río de la Plata* (Montevideo: Barreiro y Ramos, 1896); Westermeier, *Trailing the Cowboy*, pp. 231–232.

21. Arnold J. Bauer, *Chilean Rural Society from the Spanish Conquest to 1930* (Cambridge: Cambridge University Press, 1975), p. 160.

22. Slatta and Alvarez D'Armas, "El llanero," p. 33; Eleazar Córdova-Bello, *Aspectos históricos de la ganadería en el Oriente venezolano y Guayana* (Caracas: Tipografía Remar, 1962), p. 3; Rafael Ramón Castellanos, "Bolívar Coronado y otros seudonimos," *El universal*, Aug. 15, 1978:1–5; Rafael Bolívar Coronado, *Parnaso boliviano* (Barcelona: Maucci, [1920?]), pp. 6–7.

23. Richard W. Slatta, *Gauchos and the Vanishing Frontier* (Lincoln: University of Nebraska Press, 1983), p. 182.

24. Marshall W. Fishwick, "The Cowboy: America's Contribution to the World's Mythology," *Western Folklore* 11:2 (April 1952):77–92.

25. Quoted in Weber, "Turner, the Boltonians, and the Borderlands," p. 79.

26. Rausch, *Tropical Plains Frontier*, p. 241; Slatta, *Gauchos*, p. 193; Kenneth W. Porter, *The Negro on the American Frontier* (New York: Arno Press and the New York Times, 1971), p. 495.

Acción. License to hunt wild cattle in the colonial Río de la Plata.

Alpargatas. Sandals (in Chile, ojotas; in Mexico, huaraches).

Amansador. Horse tamer.

Amo. Master.

Apartar. Separate or sort cattle.

Araucanians. Indians of southern Chile and western Argentina.

Arbuckle's. Brand of coffee favored by the American cowboy.

Arepa. Filled corn cakes eaten in Venezuela.

Argentinidad. "Argentinity"; the essense of Argentine national character.

Asado. Río de la Plata barbecue; beef quick-roasted over an open fire.

Bagual. Gaucho term for wild horse.

Banda Oriental. "Eastern Bank"; modern-day Uruguay.

Bandeirante. Slave hunter and explorer from colonial São Paulo, Brazil.

Blandengue. Argentine gaucho militiaman of the colonial era.

Bolas. Also boleadoras; weapon used by gauchos and Indians of the Río de la Plata to entangle the feet of rheas (ostriches), horses, or cattle.

Bombachas. Baggy, bloused trousers adopted by the gaucho to replace the traditional diaper-like chiripá.

Bombilla. Hollow tube tipped with an infuser used to sip mate.

Botas de potro. Supple gaucho boots made from the legskin of a calf.

Cabildo. Town council in Spanish America.

Cacao. Plant that yields chocolate; important in Venezuela.

Campanha. Rolling plains ranching area of Rio Grande do Sul, in southern Brazil.

Caña. Rum, sugarcane liquor.

Capataz. Ranch foreman who works under the manager (mayordomo).

Caporal. Range boss in charge of seasonal roundup (rodeo).

Castas. Non-white, lower classes of colonial Spanish America.

Caudillo. Local or regional military chieftain in Spanish America.

Chaparejos. Also chaparreras; chaps, usually leather, worn to protect the legs.

Charango. Small, guitar-like instrument fashioned from an armadillo shell.

Charrería. Also charreada; charro rodeo competition and riding exhibition.

Charro. Gentleman rider of Mexico.

Chichimecs. Indians of northern New Spain (Mexico).

Chiripá. Large, diaper-like cloth worn by gauchos in lieu of trousers.

Cinchada. Gaucho tug-of-war on horseback.

Cobija. Poncho or cape worn on the llanos.

Colear. Throw a bull or cow to the ground by grasping the tail.

Correr el gallo. "Chicken pull" or "chicken race"; Mexican equestrian game.

Corrido. Mexican folksong.

Cowpen. Enclosure to hold cattle in the colonial Carolinas.

Criollo. Creole, American-born; applied to people, cattle, and horses.

Cuarta de cordón. Riding whip; Anglicized to "quirt."

Cueca. Typical folk dance of Chile.

Curandero. Folk healer, medicine man.

Dally. Wrap the end of the rope around the saddle horn when roping a cow; from the Spanish phrase "dar la vuelta."

Desgracia. Gaucho term for an unfortunate accident.

Desjarretadera. Hocking knife used to down cattle in colonial Spanish America.

Domador. Gaucho broncobuster.

Encomienda. Royal grant of Indian labor made to Spanish conquerers.

Estancia. Cattle or sheep ranch in the Río de la Plata.

Estanciero. Rancher in the Río de la Plata.

Facón. Gaucho's long, sword-like knife.

Fundo. Cattle ranch or estate in Chile.

Gachupín. Derogatory term for Spaniard.

Garrocha. Pike used to prod cattle in colonial Spanish America.

Gauchesco. Literary genre that uses gaucho themes and/or dialect.

Gaucho. Horseman/ranchworker of Argentina and Uruguay.

Gaúcho. Horseman/ranchworker of the campanha region of Rio Grande do Sul, Brazil.

Gauderio. Eighteenth-century pejorative term for gaucho.

Greaser. Derogatory Anglo term for Mexican.

Gringo. Term for foreigner in Spanish America.

Hatero. Ranch owner on the llanos.

Hato. Cattle ranch on the llanos.

Hierra. Also yerra; branding season in the Río de la Plata.

Huaraches. See *alpargatas*.

Huaso. Also guaso; Chilean horseman.

Inquilino. Tenant tied to a large estate in Spanish America.

Jáquima. Rope placed over a horse's head; Anglicized to "hackamore".

Jinetea. Short-stirruped riding style passed by the Moors to the Spaniards and thence to Spanish America.

Joropo. Venezuelan folk dance.

Juego de cañas. Equestrian joust with canes.

Juez de campo. Roundup judge or overseer in Spanish America.

Latifundia. Large, landed estates that dominate the Latin American countryside.

Lei. Garland of colorful flowers or shells worn by Hawaiian cowboys on their hats.

Llanero. Horseman of the llanos.

Llanos. Tropical inland plains of Venezuela and Colombia.

Longhorn. Wild, rangy cattle of northern Mexico; product of interbreeding between animals of Anglo and Mexican settlers.

Métis. Mixed blood, Indian-French inhabitants of western Canada.

Machismo. Ideal type of extreme, sometimes violent behavior to prove manliness in Latin America.

Malón. Indian raid.

Manta. More costly, finely made poncho used on the llanos.

Maroma. Gaucho sport of dropping from a corral gate onto a wild animal.

Matadero. Slaughterhouse.

Matanza. Slaughter of wild cattle for their hides and tallow.

Mate. Highly caffeinic tea made from leaves of the holly-like Ilex paraguariensis.

Matrero. Gaucho outlaw, fugitive, murderer.

Mayordomo. Ranch manger in Spanish America.

Mecate. Fine, horsehair rope; Anglicized to "McCarty".

Mescal. Alcoholic beverage distilled from the maguey plant.

Mesta. Rancher's organization and lobby in Spain and New Spain.

Mesteño. Translated as "mustang"; wild Spanish cattle in New Spain.

Mestizo. Racially mixed, of Indian and Spanish heritage.

Mingaço. Agricultural harvest in Chile.

Minifundia. Tiny, subsistence plots of land farmed by Latin American peasants.

Montonera. Popular uprising against the government led by a caudillo.

Mustang. See *mesteño*.

Ñandú. Rhea or ostrich of the pampas.

Nighthawk. Rider who watches horses on a trail drive at night.

Ojotas. See *alpargatas*.

Ombu. Large, twisted tree-like shrub of the pampa.

Pampa. Fertile, grassy plains of the Río de la Plata.

Paniolo. Also paniola; horseman of Hawaii.

Paso de muerte. Bareback wild-horse ride performed at the Mexican charrería.

Pato. Equestrian gaucho game in which riders contest the possession of a duck sewn into a hide.

Patrón. Boss, ranch owner.

Payador. Gaucho troubador, folksinger.

Peón. Worker, generally landless.

Pechando. "Breasting"; equestrian gaucho game in which riders run their horses into one another.

Pialar. Gaucho equestrian game.

Pingo. Gaucho term for his horse.

Porteño. Resident of Buenos Aires, capital of Argentina.

Pulpería. Tavern-cum-general store.

Pulpero. Tavernkeeper, operator and sometimes owner of a pulpería.

Río de la Plata. The region drained by the river of that name in southern South America.

Reata. Rawhide rope; Anglicized to "lariat".

Recado. Soft, multilayered gaucho saddle.

Resero. Also tropero; trail driver, man who moves cattle.

Retobado. Someone who, according to gaucho superstition, could not be injured by firearms.

Riña de gallos. Cockfight.

Road ranching. Raising cattle along emigration routes in the American West.

Rodeo. Roundup of cattle, usually for branding.

Roto. "Broken one"; landless rural worker in Chile.

Saladero. Meat-salting plant.

Serape. Mantle or cape worn in Mexico.

Sertão. "Backlands"; dry inland plains of northeastern Brazil.

Slow elk. Beef poached by unemployed cowboy.

Sombrero. Wide-brimmed Mexican hat.

Sortija. Equestrian ring race.

Swampers. Wild cattle of the east Texas Gulf Coast.

Taba. Dice-like game of throwing the knucklebone of a cow.

Tapaderas. Long, pointed leather coverings that hang from the stirrups of a Mexican saddle.

Tasajo. Jerky, dried meat; also charqui or carne seca.

Terrateniente. Member of the landed elite in Spanish America.

Tienda de raya. Company store of a large Mexican estate.

Tirador. Broad leather belt worn by gauchos and vaqueros.

Topeo. Huaso game of pushing each other's horses along a rail.

Tres Marías. "The three Marys"; gaucho term for boleadoras.

Tropilla. Gaucho's herd of remounts.

Vago y mal entretenido. "Vagrant and ne'er-do-well"; legal classification of vagrant imposed on the unemployed gaucho.

Vaqueiro. Horseman of northeastern Brazil.

Vaquería. Wild-cattle hunt (called rebuque in Chile).

Vaquero. Horseman of Mexico.

Vizcacha. Prairie dog of the pampas.

Wrangler. Man or boy in charge of extra mounts on a trail drive.

The history of the Americas takes in many cultures, centuries, and countries. These bibliographical suggestions are for readers who wish to read more about specific countries or cowboy types. Since I began this project, many ranching studies have appeared. This felicitous boom in frontier historiography allowed me to draw more heavily upon published sources than I had originally planned.

But many cowboy figures still await substantial treatments, particularly in English. The Chilean huaso, the Brazilian vaqueiro and gaúcho, the Mexican vaquero, and the llanero of Colombia and Venezuela still lack major historical studies supported by manuscript and archival research. Many of the existing Spanish and Portuguese studies tend toward the impressionistic and lack a solid basis of archival evidence. I hope that *Cowboys of the Americas* will serve as an impetus for other scholars to fill in the many missing pages in the histories of these colorful figures.

The readings suggested below are limited to books and a few articles in English. The select bibliography that follows gives additional Spanish-language sources and a fuller rendering of the intellectual debts that I incurred in researching this volume.

General and Comparative Studies

Lack of extensive archival materials makes comparative frontier study a risky undertaking. But for Latin America, several attempts have been made. For breadth of vision in conceptualizing the impact of the frontier, we return to Walter Prescott Webb's *Great Frontier*. Edward Larocque Tinker's pioneering works, *Horsemen of the Americas* and *Centaurs of Many Lands*, compare the lives, literature, and legends of several cowboy types. Alistair Hennessy surveys many types of frontiers in *The Frontier in Latin American History*. Robert Denhardt includes valuable information on equestrian life in *The Horse of the Americas*. On changing equestrian equipment, see *Man on Horseback* by Glenn R. Vernam.

My edited volume *Bandidos: The Varieties of Latin American Banditry* offers a comparative perspective on rural crime and criminality. The collection includes essays on the llanero and the gaucho. Robert B. Cunninghame Graham wrote many delightful sketches and vignettes of cowboy life in both North and South America. His writings have been reprinted in several volumes edited by John D. Walker.

United States

The best overview of the American cowboy, demonstrating an appreciation of his Hispanic roots, is David Dary's *Cowboy Culture*. Jack Jackson's heavily documented *Los Mesteños* offers further evidence of the Hispanic roots of Texas ranching.

The American Cowboy, by Lonn Taylor and Ingrid Maar, is a wonderful collection of illustrations with a minimal text. It is the catalog for a major cowboy exhibit sponsored by the American Folklife Center of the Library of Congress. Russell Martin's coffee-table publication *Cowboy* contains some four hundred illustrations. Another well-illustrated volume with substantial historical text is *The Cowboys*, a Time-Life publication written by William H. Forbis.

The documents collected by William W. Savage, Jr., in *Cowboy Life: Reconstructing an American Myth* contribute stimulating firsthand descriptions and opinions. *The Cowboy Hero*, also by Savage, is an important study of the cowboy's cultural significance. Other firsthand observations, many quoted in this book, are the newspaper reports reprinted by Clifford P. Westermeier in *Trailing the Cowboy: His Life and Lore as Told by Frontier Journalists*.

Canada

Happily, the livestock industry of western Canada is the subject of several excellent books and articles. Most important is David Breen's outstanding study *Canada's Prairie West*. Simon Evans has written many useful articles on Alberta ranching. Less scholarly (without citations) but informative is Edward Brado's *Cattle Kingdom*. The books of Grant MacEwan, such as *Blazing the Old Cattle Trail*, offer enjoyable, often humorous sketches of cowboy and ranch culture in Alberta. In 1987 the Glenbow Museum in Calgary published a thirty-six-page pamphlet by Sheilagh Jameson called *Ranches, Cowboys, and Characters: Birth of Alberta's Western Heritage*.

Argentina and Uruguay

The Gaucho: Cattle Hunter, Cavalryman, Ideal of Romance, by Madaline Wallis Nichols, is a brief, older study that touches on the gaucho's rise in the eighteenth century. Nichols includes a bibliography of more than fourteen hundred items covering all aspects of gaucho life. Those who can read Spanish should not miss *Historia social del gaucho* by Ricardo Rodríguez Molas. My own book *Gauchos and the Vanishing Frontier* offers the best information on the nineteenth-century decline of the Argentine gaucho. *Don Segundo Sombra*, the touching story of a boy growing to gaucho manhood by Ricardo Güiraldes, conveys much of the flavor of gaucho character and values.

Benjamín Nahum, José P. Barran, and Fernando Assunção have written extensively in Spanish on Uruguayan rural history. Little on the Uruguayan gaucho in history or literature has reached us in English.

Chile

The Chilean huaso still awaits substantial treatment in either English or Spanish. Aside from brief glimpses by European travelers and impressionistic works of folklore, little has been written. Michael Moody briefly has described modern Chilean rodeo.

Brazil

John Chasteen's dissertation "Twilight of the Lances: The Saravia Brothers and Their World" describes the ranching borderlands of southern Brazil and northern Uruguay during the nineteenth and early twentieth centuries. The many regional histories of Brazil generally fail to treat cowboy figures. Portuguese-language studies of Rio Grande do Sul present something of gaúcho folklore and culture. But the vaqueiro of the Northeast remains a shadowy figure.

Venezuela and Colombia

As with many of these cowboy figures, we know more about the llanero's folklore and myth than about his history. Miguel Izard has written extensively in Spanish about the Venezuelan llanero. The dissertation by Robert P. Matthews, "Rural Unrest and Social Violence in Venezuela," reveals much about economic and political disruptions on the llanos in the first half of the nineteenth century. But no significant study of the llanero has yet appeared in English.

Arturo Alvarez D'Armas and I list mostly Spanish sources in "El llanero y el hato venezolano: Aportes bibliográficos." *A Tropical Plains Frontier: The Llanos of Colombia, 1531–1831*, Jane M. Rausch's fine history of the early llanos includes limited material on ranch life. Historians look forward to a second volume that will continue the story through the nineteenth century. *Doña Bárbara*, the captivating novel by Rómulo Gallegos, well conveys the power, mystery, and superstitions of the llanos.

Mexico

As with Canada, we have studies of ranching but little specifically about the cowboy. In fact, the Mexican charro (gentleman rider) has attracted more attention than the vaquero (working cowboy). Most accessible are *Charro: Mexican Horseman* by James Norman and articles by Mary Lou LeCompte.

On early Spanish ranching in Texas, see *Los Mesteños* by Jack Jackson. Another excellent rural study is *A Mexican Family Empire: The Latifundio of the Sánchez Navarro Family, 1765–1867*, by Charles H. Harris III. Although good on ranching and ranchers, both volumes make only scattered references to the lives and work of ranch hands.

Nora E. Ramirez blends folklore and history in her dissertation "The Vaquero and Ranching in the Southwestern United States, 1600–1970." *Californio* by Jo Mora and the several books of Arnold R. Rojas examine the vaquero in California.

Hawaii

Hawaii's paniolo remained largely invisible outside the islands until recently. *Nā Paniolo o Hawai'i*, edited by Lynn J. Martin, relates much of the folklore of the Hawaiian cowboy and something of his history. The Hawaiian cowboy and his ties to the Mexican vaquero await further study. Virginia Cowan-Smith and Bonnie Domrose Stone have written a popular history of horsemanship in Hawaii called *Aloha Cowboy*.

Modern-Day Cowboys

On the latter-day cowboy in the United States, see the excellent descriptions by Fay E. Ward in *The Cowboy at Work* and by John R. Erickson in *The Modern Cowboy*. Bart

McDowell's *American Cowboy in Life and Legend* mixes paintings, photographs, and a lively text. William D. Wittliff presents contemporary photographs of latter-day Texas vaqueros in *Vaquero: Genesis of the Texas Cowboy*. Few equivalent works exist for other areas.

A photo essay on today's Argentine gaucho appeared in *National Geographic* in October 1980. Additional books of photographs aimed at tourists have been published with minimal, often romanticized texts. Peter Rivière describes twentieth-century ranch life in the Brazilian northeast in *The Forgotten Frontier: Ranchers of Northern Brazil*.

SELECT BIBLIOGRAPHY

This select bibliography includes archival collections and major books and articles. See the endnotes for citations to manuscript sources and specialized articles. In the second section of the bibliography, I have included a few relevant books that appeared after I completed the manuscript. The section opens with general and comparative studies. The remaining citations are arranged by geographical region, from Canada in the north to Chile and Argentina in the south. Studies of the cowboy in the United States and of the gaucho in Argentina and Uruguay are further subdivided into the topical categories of history and literature/popular culture.

Note on Archives

To complete this book, I used manuscripts, newspapers, and other printed sources at the following research collections:

Glenbow Archives, Calgary, Alberta, Canada

University of Calgary Library, Alberta, Canada

Western Range Cattle Industry Study, Colorado Heritage Center, Denver

Library of Congress, Washington, D. C.

Benson Latin American Collection, University of Texas, Austin

Library, Fundación Boulton, Caracas, Venezuela

Archivo General de la Nación, Caracas, Venezuela

Biblioteca Nacional, Caracas, Venezuela

Archivo General de la Nación, Buenos Aires, Argentina

Biblioteca Nacional, Buenos Aires, Argentina

Library, Universidad Nacional de la Provincia de Buenos Aires, La Plata, Argentina

Archivo Histórico de la Provincia de Buenos Aires "Ricardo Levene," La Plata, Argentina

Books and Articles

GENERAL AND COMPARATIVE STUDIES

Baretta, Silvio Duncan, and John Markoff. "Civilization and Barbarism: Cattle Frontiers in Latin America." *Comparative Studies in Society and History* 20 (Oct. 1978): 587–620.

Billington, Ray Allen, ed. *The Frontier Thesis: Valid Interpretation of American History?* New York: Krieger, 1977.

Cronon, William. "Revisiting the Vanishing Frontier: The Legacy of Frederick Jackson Turner." *Western Historical Quarterly* 18:2 (April 1987): 157–176.

Denhardt, Robert M. *The Horse of the Americas*. Rev. ed. Norman: University of Oklahoma Press, 1975.

Dinsmore, Wayne. *The Horses of the Americas*. Norman: University of Oklahoma Press, 1978.

Donahue, John. *Don Segundo Sombra y el Virginiano: Gaucho y cowboy.* Madrid: Editorial Pliegos, 1988.

Graham, Robert B. Cunninghame. *The South American Tales and Sketches of Robert B. Cunninghame Graham.* Ed. John Walker. Norman: University of Oklahoma Press, 1978.

Guichard du Plessis, Jean, and Jo Mora. *Cowboys et gauchos des Amériques.* Paris: André Bonne, 1968.

Hennessy, Alistair. *The Frontier in Latin American History.* Albuquerque: University of New Mexico Press, 1978.

Jackson, W. Turrentine. "A Brief Message for the Young and/or Ambitious: Comparative Frontiers as a Field of Investigation." *Western Historical Quarterly* 9:1 (Jan. 1978): 5–18.

Lawrence, Elizabeth Atwood. *Hoofbeats and Society: Studies of Human-Horse Interactions.* Bloomington: Indiana University Press, 1985.

Pady, Donald Stuart. *Horses and Horsemanship.* Ames: Iowa State University Press, 1973.

Paullada, Stephen. *Rawhide and Song: A Comparative Study of the Cattle Cultures of the Argentinian Pampa and North American Great Plains.* New York: Vantage, 1963.

Rouse, John E. *World Cattle.* Norman: University of Oklahoma Press, 1970.

Slatta, Richard W. "Comparative Frontier Social Life: Western Saloons and Argentine Pulperías." *Great Plains Quarterly* 7:3 (Summer 1987): 155–165.

———. "Gauchos, llaneros y cowboys: Un aporte a la historia comparada." *Boletín Americanista* 34 (1984): 193–208.

Slatta, Richard W., ed. *Bandidos: The Varieties of Latin American Banditry.* Westport, Conn.: Greenwood Press, 1987.

Slotkin, Richard. *The Fatal Environment: The Myth of the Frontier in the Age of Industrialization, 1800–1890.* New York: Atheneum, 1985.

Smith, Dwight L., ed. *The American and Canadian West: A Bibliography.* Santa Barbara: ABC–Clio Press, 1979.

Solberg, Carl W. *Immigration and Nationalism: Argentina and Chile, 1890–1914.* Austin: University of Texas Press, 1970.

———. *The Pampas and the Prairies: Agrarian Policy in Canada and Argentina, 1880–1930.* Stanford: Stanford University Press, 1987.

Tinker, Edward Larocque. *The Horsemen of the Americas and the Literature They Inspired.* Rev. ed. Austin: University of Texas Press, 1967.

Towne, Charles W., and Edward N. Wentworth. *Cattle and Men.* Norman: University of Oklahoma Press, 1955.

Vernam, Glen R. *Man on Horseback: The Story of the Mounted Man from the Scythians to the American Cowboy.* Lincoln: University of Nebraska Press, 1964.

Webb, Walter Prescott. *The Great Frontier.* Austin: University of Texas Press, 1951.

CANADA

Berton, Pierre. *Hollywood's Canada: The Americanization of Our National Image.* Toronto: McClelland and Stewart, 1975.

Brado, Edward. *Cattle Kingdom: Early Ranching in Alberta.* Vancouver and Toronto: Douglas and MacIntyre, 1984.

Breen, David H. *The Canadian Prairie West and the Ranching Frontier, 1874–1924.* Toronto: University of Toronto Press, 1983.

Craig, John R. *Ranching with Lords and Commons; or Twenty Years on the Range.* 1903. Reprint. New York: AMS Press, 1971.

Cross, Michael S., ed. *The Turner Thesis and the Canadas: The Debate on the Impact of the Canadian Environment.* Toronto: Copp Clark, 1970.

Dunae, Patrick A. *Gentlemen Emigrants: From the British Public Schools to the Canadian Frontier.* Vancouver and Toronto: Douglas and McIntyre, 1981.

Evans, Simon M. "The Passing of a Frontier: Ranching in the Canadian West, 1882–1912." Ph. D. diss., University of Calgary, 1976.

Grant, Ted, and Andy Russell. *Men in the Saddle: Working Cowboys of Canada.* Toronto and New York: Van Nostrand Reinhold, 1978.

Jameson, Sheilagh. *Ranches, Cowboys, and Characters: The Birth of Alberta's Western Heritage.* Calgary: Glenbow Museum, 1987.

Kelly, Leroy Victor. *The Range Men: The Story of the Ranchers and Indians of Alberta.* 1913. Reprint. New York: Argonaut Press, 1965.

Lavington, H. Dude. *Nine Lives of a Cowboy.* Victoria: Sono Nis Press, 1982.

Long, Philip Sheridan. *The Great Canadian Range.* Toronto: Ryerson Press, 1963.

Lupton, Austin A. "Cattle Ranching in Alberta, 1874–1910: Its Evolution and Migration." *Albertan Geographer* 3 (1966–1967):48–58.

MacEwan, John Walter Grant. *Blazing the Old Cattle Trail.* 1962. Reprint. Saskatoon: Western Producer Prairie Books, 1975.

Macoun, John, ed. *Manitoba and the Great North West.* Guelph, Ontario: World Publishing, 1882.

Sharp, Paul F. *Whoop-Up Country: The Canadian-American West, 1865–1885.* Helena: Historical Society of Montana, 1962.

Stegner, Wallace. *Wolf Willow: A History, a Story, and a Memory of the Last Plains Frontier.* 1955. Reprint. Toronto: Macmillan, 1977.

Thomas, Gregory E. G. "The British Columbia Ranching Frontier, 1858–1896." M. A. thesis, University of British Columbia, 1976.

Thomas, Lewis H., ed. *Essays on Western History in Honour of Lewis Gwynne Thomas.* Edmonton: University of Alberta Press, 1976.

———. *The Prairie West to 1905: A Canadian Sourcebook.* Toronto: Oxford University Press, 1975.

Weir, Thomas R. *Ranching in the Southern Interior Plateau of British Columbia.* Ottawa: Queen's Printer, 1964.

UNITED STATES: HISTORY

Abbott, Edward Charles. *We Pointed Them North: Recollections of a Cowpuncher.* Norman: University of Oklahoma Press, 1939.

Ackerman, Joe A., Jr. *Florida Cowman: A History of Florida Cattle Raising.* Kissimmee: Florida Cattlemen's Association, 1976.

Adams, Andy. *The Log of the Cowboy: A Narrative of the Old Trail Days.* 1903. Reprint. Lincoln: University of Nebraska Press, 1964.

Adams, Ramon F. *Come an' Get It: The Story of the Old Cowboy Cook.* Norman: University of Oklahoma Press, 1952.

———. *Western Words: A Dictionary of the Range, Cowcamp, and Trail.* 1945. Reprint. Norman: University of Oklahoma Press, 1968.

Arnade, Charles. "Cattle Raising in Spanish Florida, 1513–1763." *Agricultural History* 35:3 (July 1961):116–124.

Athearn, Robert G. *The Mythic West in Twentieth-Century America*. Lawrence: University Press of Kansas, 1986.

Branch, Douglas. *The Cowboy and His Interpreters*. 1926. Reprint. New York: Appleton, 1961.

Brennan, Joseph. *Paniolo*. Honolulu: Topgallant, 1978.

Brimlow, George F. *Harney County, Oregon, and Its Range Land*. Portland: Binsford and Mort, 1951.

Cowan-Smith, Virginia, and Bonnie Domrose Stone. *Aloha Cowboy*. Honolulu: University of Hawaii Press, 1988.

Dale, Edward Everett. *The Range Cattle Industry: Ranching on the Great Plains from 1865 to 1925*. 1930. Reprint. Norman: University of Oklahoma Press, 1960.

Dary, David. *Cowboy Culture: A Saga of Five Centuries*. New York: Knopf, 1981.

Durham, Philip, and Everett L. Jones. *The Negro Cowboys*. Lincoln: University of Nebraska Press, 1965.

Forbis, William H. *The Cowboys*. Rev. ed. Alexandria, Va.: Time-Life Books, 1978.

Frantz, Joe B., and Julian E. Choate, Jr. *The American Cowboy: The Myth and the Reality*. Norman: University of Oklahoma Press, 1955.

Frink, Maurice, W. Turrentine Jackson, and Agnes Wright Spring. *When Grass Was King*. Boulder: University of Colorado Press, 1956.

French, Giles. *Cattle Country of Peter French*. Portland: Binsford and Mort, 1964.

Guice, John D. W. "Cattle Raisers of the Old Southwest: A Reinterpretation." *Western Historical Quarterly* 8:2 (April 1977):167–187.

Holden, William C. *The Espuela Land and Cattle Company: A Study of a Foreign-Owned Ranch in Texas*. 1934. Reprint. Austin: Texas State Historical Association, 1970.

Hough, Emerson. *The Story of the Cowboy*. New York: Appleton, 1898.

James, Will. *Cow Country*. New York: Scribner's, 1927.

Jordan, Terry G. *Trails to Texas: Southern Roots of Western Cattle Ranching*. Lincoln: University of Nebraska Press, 1981.

Lamar, Howard R. "Much to Celebrate: The Western History Association's Twenty-Fifth Birthday." *Western Historical Quarterly* 17:4 (Oct. 1986):397–416.

Lamar, Howard R., ed. *The Reader's Encyclopedia of the American West*. New York: Crowell, 1977.

Lopez, David E. "Cowboy Strikes and Unions." *Labor History* 18:3 (Summer 1977): 325–340.

Martin, Lynn J., ed. *Nā Paniolo o Hawai'i*. Honolulu: Honolulu Academy of Arts, 1987.

Martin, Russell. *Cowboy: The Enduring Myth of the Wild West*. New York: Stewart, Tabori and Chang, 1983.

McCoy, Joseph G. *Cattle Trade of the West and Southwest*. 1874. Reprint. N.p.: Readex Microprint, 1966.

McLoughlin, Denis. *Wild and Woolly: An Encyclopedia of the Old West*. New York: Doubleday, 1975.

Oliphant, J. Orin. *On the Cattle Ranges of the Oregon Country*. Seattle: University of Washington Press, 1968.

Paul, Rodman W. *The Far West and the Great Plains in Transition*. New York: Harper and Row, 1988.

Rollins, Philip Ashton. *The Cowboy: An Unconventional History of Civilization on the*

Old-Time Cattle Range. 1922. Reprint. Albuquerque: University of New Mexico Press, 1979.

Santee, Ross. *Cowboy.* 1928. Reprint. Lincoln: University of Nebraska Press, 1977.

Savage, William W., Jr., ed. *Cowboy Life: Reconstructing an American Myth.* Norman: University of Oklahoma Press, 1975.

Steffen, Jerome O., ed. *The American West: New Perspectives, New Dimensions.* Norman: University of Oklahoma Press, 1981.

Watts, Peter. *A Dictionary of the Old West, 1850–1900.* New York: Knopf, 1977.

Westermeier, Clifford P., ed. *Trailing the Cowboy: His Life and Lore as Told by Frontier Journalists.* Caldwell, Idaho: Caxton Printers, 1955.

Worster, Donald. "New West, True West: Interpreting the Region's History." *Western Historical Quarterly* 18:2 (April 1987):141–156.

Young, Mary. "The West and American Cultural Identity: Old Themes and New Variations." *Western Historical Quarterly* 1:2 (April 1970):137–160.

UNITED STATES: LITERATURE AND POPULAR CULTURE

Adams, Les, and Buck Rainey. *Shoot 'em Ups: The Complete Reference Guide to Westerns of the Sound Era.* New Rochelle, N. Y.: Arlington House, 1978.

Allard, William A. *Vanishing Breed: Photographs of the Cowboy and the West.* New York: Little, Brown, 1982.

Bold, Christine. *Selling the Wild West: Popular Western Fiction, 1860–1960.* Bloomington: Indiana University Press, 1987.

Borne, Lawrence R. *Dude Ranching: A Complete History.* Albuquerque: University of New Mexico Press, 1983.

Cawalti, John G. *The Six-Gun Mystique.* Bowling Green: Bowling Green University Press, n.d.

Dinan, John. "The Pulp Cowboy." *Persimmon Hill* 15:3 (Autumn 1987):18–26.

Dobie, J. Frank. *Guide to Life and Literature of the Southwest.* Rev. ed. Dallas: Southern Methodist University Press, 1952.

Dusard, Jay. *The North American Cowboy: A Portrait.* Prescott, Ariz.: Consortium, 1983.

Erickson, John R. *The Modern Cowboy.* Lincoln: University of Nebraska Press, 1981.

Etulain, Richard W. "Changing Images: The Cowboy in Western Films." *Colorado Heritage* 1 (1981):36–55.

Etulain, Richard W., ed. "Western Films: A Brief History." *Journal of the West* 22:4 (Oct. 1983).

Everson, William K. *A Pictorial History of the Western Film.* New York: Citadel Press, 1969.

Fishwick, Marshall W. "The Cowboy: America's Contribution to the World's Mythology." *Western Folklore* 11:2 (April 1952):77–92.

Folsom, James K. *The American Western Novel.* New Haven: Yale University Press, 1966.

Folsom, James K., ed. *The Western: A Collection of Critical Essays.* Englewood Cliffs, N. J.: Prentice-Hall, 1979.

Fredriksson, Kristine. *American Rodeo: From Buffalo Bill to Big Business.* College Station: Texas A&M University Press, 1984.

Harris, Charles W., and Buck Rainey, eds. *The Cowboy: Six-shooters, Songs, and Sex.* Norman: University of Oklahoma Press, 1976.

Johnston, Moira. *Ranch: Portrait of a Surviving Dream.* Garden City: Doubleday, 1983.

Jordan, Roy A., and Tim R. Miller. "The Politics of a Cowboy Culture." *Annals of Wyoming* 52:1 (Spring 1980):40–45.

Lawrence, Elizabeth Atwood. *Rodeo: An Anthropologist Looks at the Wild and the Tame.* Chicago: University of Chicago Press, 1984.

Lenihan, John H. *Showdown: Confronting Modern America in the Western Film.* Urbana: University of Illinois Press, 1980.

Lomax, John A., and Alan Lomax, comps. *Cowboy Songs and Other Frontier Ballads.* New York: Macmillan, 1938.

McDonald, Archie P., ed. *Shooting Stars: Heroes and Heroines of Western Film.* Bloomington: Indiana University Press, 1987.

McMurtry, Larry. *Lonesome Dove.* New York: Simon and Schuster, 1985.

Mason, Michael, ed. *The Country Music Book.* New York: Scribner's, 1985.

Milton, John R. *The Novel of the American West.* Lincoln: University of Nebraska Press, 1980.

Petersen, Gwen. "Git Along Li'l Doggerels: Cowboys and Poetry." *Persimmon Hill* 16:1 (Spring 1988):28–37.

Rector, Margaret, ed. *Cowboy Life on the Texas Plains: The Photographs of Ray Rector.* College Station: Texas A&M University Press, 1982.

Remington, Frederic. *Pony Tracks.* 1895. Reprint. Norman: University of Oklahoma Press, 1961.

Rogin, Michael P. *Ronald Reagan, the Movie and Other Episodes in Political Demonology.* Berkeley: University of California Press, 1987.

Savage, William W., Jr. *The Cowboy Hero: His Image in American History and Culture.* Norman: University of Oklahoma Press, 1979.

Seemann, Charlie, producer. *Back in the Saddle Again.* New York: New World Records, 1983.

Taft, Robert. *Artists and Illustrators of the Old West, 1850–1900.* 1953. Reprint. Princeton: Princeton University Press, 1982.

Taylor, Lonn, and Ingrid Maar. *The American Cowboy.* New York: Harper and Row, 1983.

Tosches, Nick. *Country: Living Legends and Dying Metaphors in America's Biggest Music.* Rev. ed. New York: Scribner's, 1985.

Tuska, John. *The Filming of the West.* Garden City: Doubleday, 1976.

Tyler, Ronnie C. *American Frontier Life: Early Western Painting and Prints.* Fort Worth: Amon Carter Museum, 1987.

Walters, Thomas N. *Seeing in the Dark.* Durham, N. C.: Moore Publishing, 1972.

Wright, Will. *Sixguns and Society: A Structural Study of the Western.* Berkeley: University of California Press, 1977.

MEXICO

Ahlborn, Richard E. "The Hispanic Horseman." *El palacio* 89:2 (Summer 1983):12–21.

Almaráz, Félix D., Jr. *The San Antonio Missions and Their System of Land Tenure.* Austin: University of Texas Press, 1989.

Alvarez de Villar, José. *Men and Horses of Mexico: History and Practice of Charrería.* Mexico City: Ediciones Lara, 1979.

Ballesteros, José Ramón. *Origen y evolución del charro mexicano.* Mexico City: Manuel Porrúa, 1972.

Bishko, Charles J. "The Peninsular Background of Latin American Cattle Ranching." *Hispanic American Historical Review* 32:4 (Nov. 1952):491–515.

Brand, Donald D. "The Early History of the Range Cattle Industry in Northern Mexico." *Agricultural History* 35:3 (July 1961):132–139.

Burchan, L. T. "Cattle and Range Forage in California, 1770–1880." *Agricultural History* 35:3 (July 1961):140–149.

Cisneros, José. *Riders Across the Centuries: Horsemen of the Spanish Borderlands*. El Paso: Texas Western Press, 1984.

Dobie, J. Frank. "The Mexican Vaquero of the Texas Border." *Southwestern Political and Social Science Quarterly* 8:1 (June 1927):1–12.

———. "Ranch Mexicans." *Survey* 66 (May 1, 1931):167–170.

Dusenberry, William H. *The Mexican Mesta: The Administration of Ranching in Colonial Mexico*. Urbana: University of Illinois Press, 1963.

Faulk, Odie B. "Ranching in Spanish Texas." *Hispanic American Historical Review* 45:2 (May 1965):257–266.

Fugate, Francis L. "Origins of the Range Cattle Era in South Texas." *Agricultural History* 35:3 (July 1961):155–158.

Harris, Charles H. III. *A Mexican Family Empire: The Latifundio of the Sánchez Navarro Family, 1765–1867*. Austin: University of Texas Press, 1975.

Jackson, Jack. *Los Mesteños: Spanish Ranching in Texas, 1721–1821*. College Station: Texas A&M University Press, 1986.

LeCompte, Mary Lou. "The Hispanic Influence on the History of Rodeo, 1823–1922." *Journal of Sport History* 12:1 (Spring 1985):21–38.

LeCompte, Mary Lou, and William H. Beezley. "Any Sunday in April: The Rise of Sport in San Antonio and the Hispanic Borderlands." *Journal of Sport History* 13:2 (Summer 1986):128–146.

Machado, Manuel A., Jr. *The North Mexican Cattle Industry, 1910–1975: Ideology, Conflict, and Change*. College Station: Texas A&M University Press, 1981.

Mora, Carl J. *Mexican Cinema: Reflections of a Society, 1896–1980*. Berkeley: University of California Press, 1982.

Mora, Joseph J. *Californios: The Saga of the Hard-Riding Vaqueros, America's First Cowboys*. Garden City: Doubleday, 1949.

Morrisey, Richard J. "The Early Range Cattle Industry in Arizona." *Agricultural History* 24:3 (July 1950):151–156.

———. "The Northward Expansion of Cattle Raising in New Spain, 1550–1600." *Agricultural History* 25:3 (July 1951):115–121.

Myres, Sandra L. *The Ranch in Spanish Texas, 1691–1800*. El Paso: Texas Western Press, 1969.

———. "The Spanish Cattle Kingdom in the Province of Texas." *Texana* 4:3 (Fall 1966):233–246.

Norman, James. *Charro: Mexican Horseman*. New York: Putnam's, 1969.

Ramirez, Nora E. "The Vaquero and Ranching in the Southwestern United States, 1600–1970." Ph. D. diss., Indiana University, 1979.

Rincón Gallardo, Carlos. *El libro del charro mexicano*. 3d ed. Mexico City: Porrúa, 1960.

Rojas, Arnold R. *The Vaquero*. Charlotte, N. C.: McNally and Loftin, 1964.

Wagoner, Junior Jean. *History of the Cattle Industry in Southern Arizona, 1540–1940*. Tucson: University of Arizona Press, 1952.

Weber, David J. *The Mexican Frontier, 1821–1846: The American Southwest Under Mexico*. Albuquerque: University of New Mexico Press, 1982.

———. "Mexico's Far Northern Frontier, 1821–1854: Historiography Askew." *Western Historical Quarterly* 7:3 (July 1976):279–293.

Wittliff, William D. *Vaquero: Genesis of the Texas Cowboy*. San Antonio: Institute of Texan Cultures, 1972.

Worcester, Don. *The Spanish Mustang: From the Plains of Andalusia to the Prairies of Texas*. El Paso: Texas Western Press, 1986.

VENEZUELA AND COLOMBIA

Appun, Karl Ferdinand. "Los llanos de El Baúl." Trans. Federica de Ritter. *Anales de la Universidad Central de Venezuela* 32 (Jan. 1953):155–242.

Armas, Julio de. *La ganadería en Venezuela: Ensayo histórico*. Caracas: Congreso de la República, 1974.

———. "Nacimiento de la ganadería venezolana." *Revista Shell* 3:11 (June 1954):26–35.

Armas Chitty, José Antonio de. *Tucupido: Formación de un pueblo del llano*. Caracas: Universidad Central de Venezuela, 1961.

———. *Vocabulario del hato*. Caracas: Universidad Central de Venezuela, 1966.

Bolívar Coronado, Rafael (pseud. Daniel Mendoza). *El llanero: Estudio de sociología venezolana*. Caracas: Cultura Venezolana, 1922.

Briceño, Tarcila. *La ganadería en los llanos centro-occidentales venezolanos, 1900–1935*. Caracas: Biblioteca de la Academia Nacional de la Historia, 1985.

Calzadilla Valdés, Fernando. *Por los llanos de Apure*. Santiago: Imprenta Universitaria, 1940.

Carvallo, Gastón. *El hato venezolano, 1900–1980*. Caracas: Fondo Editorial Tropykos, 1985.

Depons, Francisco. *Viaje a la parte oriental de Tierra Firme*, 1806. Trans. Enrique Planchart. 2 vols. Caracas: Tipografía Americana, 1930.

Díaz, José Antonio. *El agricultor venezolano ó lecciónes de agricultura práctica nacional*. 2 vols. Caracas: Rojas Brothers, 1877.

Gallegos, Rómulo. *Doña Bárbara*. Trans. Robert Malloy. New York: Peter Smith, 1948.

Graham, Robert Bontine Cunninghame. *José Antonio Paez*. London: Heinemann, 1929.

Humboldt, Alexander von, and Aimé Bonpland. *Personal Narrative of Travels to the Equinoctial Regional of the New Continent, During the Years 1799–1804*. Trans. Helen María Williams. 2d ed. 4 vols. London: Longman, Hurst, Rees, Orme, Brown and Green, 1825.

Izard, Miguel. "Mi coronel, hasta aquí le llegaron las matemáticas: Los llaneros del Apure." In Izard, comp. *Marginados, fronterizos, rebeldes y oprimidos*. 2 vols. Barcelona: Ediciones del Serbal, 1985.

———. "Ni cuatreros ni montoneros: Llaneros." *Boletín americanista* 31 (1981):83–142.

———. "Oligarcas temblad, viva la libertad: Los llaneros de Apure y la Guerra Federal." *Boletín americanista* 32 (1982):227–277.

———. "Sin domicilio fijo, senda segura, ni destino conocido: Los llaneros del Apure a finales del período colonial." *Boletín americanista* 33 (1983):13–83.

Loy, Jane M. "Horsemen of the Tropics: A Comparative View of the Llaneros in the History of Venezuela and Colombia." *Boletín americanista* 31 (1981):159–171.

Mantilla Trejos, Eduardo. *Sobre los llanos*. Caracas: Fotomecánica Industrial, 1988.

Matthews, Robert Paul. *Violencia rural en Venezuela, 1840–1858: Antecedentes socio-económicas de la Guerra Federal.* Caracas: Monte Avila, 1977.

Mayer, John. "El llanero." *Atlantic Monthly* 3 (Feb. 1859):174–188.

Ovalles, Victor Manuel. *El llanero: Estudio sobre su vida, sus costumbres, su carácter y su poesía.* Caracas: Herrera Irigoyen, 1905.

Paez, Ramón. *Wild Scenes in South America, or Life in the Llanos of Venezuela.* London: Sampson Low, 1863.

Porter, Robert Ker. *Sir Robert Ker Porter's Caracas Diary, 1825–1842: A British Diplomat in a Newborn Nation.* Ed. Walter Dupuoy. Caracas: Dupuoy, 1966.

Rausch, Jane M. *A Tropical Plains Frontier: The Llanos of Colombia, 1531–1831.* Albuquerque: University of New Mexico Press, 1984.

Rivas Sosa, Alejandro. *Nuestro ganado vacuno: La ganadería como fuente potential de riqueza nacional.* Caracas: Elite, 1938.

Rosti, Pál. *Memorias de un viaje por América.* 1861. Trans. Judith Sarosi. Caracas: Universidad Central de Venezuela, 1968.

Sachs, Karl. *De los llanos: Descripción de un viaje de ciencias naturales a Venezuela.* 1878. Trans. José Izquierdo. Caracas and Madrid: Edime, 1955.

Sambrano Urdaneta, Oscar. *El llanero: Un problema de crítica literaria.* Caracas: Cuadernos Literarios, 1952.

Samper, José María. *Ensayo sobre las revoluciones políticas y la condición social de las repúblicas colombianas.* Paris: Thurnot, 1861.

Slatta, Richard W., and Arturo Alvarez D'Armas. "El llanero y el hato venezolano: Aportes bibliográficos." *South Eastern Latin Americanist* 29:2–3 (Sept. 1985):33–41.

Urbaneja Achelpohl, Luis Manuel. *El gaucho y el llanero.* Caracas: Elite, 1926.

Vallenilla Lanz, Laureano. *Disgregación e integración: Ensayo sobre la formación de la nacionalidad venezolana.* 2 vols. Caracas: Tipografía Universal, 1930.

Vila, Pablo. *Visiones geohistóricas de Venezuela.* Caracas: Ministerio de Educación, 1969.

CHILE

Bauer, Arnold J. *Chilean Rural Society from the Spanish Conquest to 1930.* Cambridge: Cambridge University Press, 1975.

Byam, George. *Wanderings in Some of the Western Republics of America.* London: John W. Parker, 1850.

Campo L., Carlos del, and Luis Durand. *Huasos chilenos: Folklore campesino.* Santiago: Leblanc, 1939.

Denhart, Robert M. "The Chilean Horse." *Agricultural History* 24:3 (July 1950):161–165.

Echaiz, René León. *Interpretación histórica del huaso chileno.* Santiago: Editorial Universitaria, 1955.

Gardiner, Allen Francis. *A Visit to the Indians on the Frontiers of Chili.* London: Seeley and Burnside, 1841.

Góngora, Mario. *Vagabundaje y sociedad fronteriza en Chile, siglos XVII a XIX.* Santiago: Universidad de Chile, 1966.

Guarda, Gabriel. *La sociedad en Chile astral antes de la colonización alemana, 1645–1845.* Santiago: Andres Bello, 1979.

Lago, Tomás. *El huaso.* Santiago: Universidad de Chile, 1953.

Loveman, Brian. *Chile: The Legacy of Hispanic Capitalism.* 2d ed. New York: Oxford University Press, 1988.

Moody, Michael. "La fiesta huasa." *Américas* 38: 1 (Jan. 1986):20–24, 46.

———. "Rodeo is Hot—in Chile." *Persimmon Hill* 15:3 (Autumn 1987): 5–17.

Pereira Salas, Eugenio. *Juegos y alegrías coloniales en Chile*. Santiago: Zig-Zag, 1947.

Prado P., Uldaricio. *El caballo chileno, 1541 a 1914: Estudio zootécnico e histórico hípico*. Santiago: Imprenta Santiago, 1914.

Solberg, Carl E. "A Discriminatory Frontier Land Policy: Chile, 1870–1914." *The Americas* 26:2 (Oct. 1969):115–133.

ARGENTINA AND URUGUAY: HISTORY

Assunção, Fernando. *El gaucho*. Montevideo: Imprenta Nacional, 1963.

———. *El gaucho: Estudio socio-cultural*. 2 vols. Montevideo: Dirección General de Extensión Universitaria, 1978–1979.

———. *Pilchas criollas: Usos y costumbres del gaucho*. Rev. ed. Montevideo: Master Fer, 1979.

Azcuy Armeghino, Eduardo. *Artigas en la historia argentina*. Buenos Aires: Ediciones Corregidor, 1986.

Barrán, José Pedro, and Benjamín Nahum. *Historial rural del Uruguay moderno*. 7 vols. Montevideo: Ediciones de la Banda Oriental, 1967–1978.

———. "Uruguayan Rural History." *Hispanic American Historical Review* 64:4 (Nov. 1984):655–674.

Busaniche, José Luis., ed. *Estampas del pasado: Lecturas de historia argentina*. 1959. Reprint. Buenos Aires: Solar-Hachette, 1971.

Cárcano, Miguel Angel. *Evolución histórica del régimen de la tierra pública, 1810–1916*. 1917. Reprint. Buenos Aires: EUDEBA, 1972.

Coluccio, Félix. *Diccionario folklórico argentino*. 2 vols. Buenos Aires: Lasserre, 1964.

Chasteen, John C. "Twilight of the Lances: The Saravia Brothers and Their World." Ph. D. diss., University of North Carolina, 1988.

Daireaux, Emilio. *Vida y costumbres en La Plata*. 2 vols. Buenos Aires: Lajouane, 1888.

Giberti, Horacio. *Historia económica de la ganadería argentina*. 1954. Reprint. Buenos Aires: Solar-Hachette, 1970.

Gori, Gastón. *Vagos y mal entretenidos: Aporte al tema hernandiano*. 2d ed. Santa Fe, Argentina: Colmegna, 1965.

Jones, Kristine L. "Conflict and Adaptation in the Argentine Pampas, 1750–1880." Ph. D. diss., University of Chicago, 1984.

Laxalt, Robert. "The Gauchos: Last of a Breed." *National Geographic* 158:4 (Oct. 1980):478–501.

Molinari, Ricardo Luis. *Biografía de la pampa: Cuatro siglos de historia del campo argentino*. Buenos Aires: Arte Gaglianone, 1988.

Nichols, Madaline Wallis. *The Gaucho: Cattle Hunter, Cavalryman, Ideal of Romance*. 1942. Reprint. New York: Gordian Press, 1968.

Paladino Giménez, José M. *El gaucho: Reseña fotográfica, 1860–1930*. Buenos Aires: Palsa, 1971.

Pérez Amuchástegui, Antonio Jorge. *Mentalidades argentinas, 1860–1930*. 2d ed. Buenos Aires: EUDEBA, 1970.

Pinto, Luis C. *El gaucho rioplatense, frente a los malos historidadores*. Buenos Aires: Ciordia y Rodríguez, 1944.

———. *El gaucho y sus detractores: Defensa de las tradiciones argentinas; reivindicación del gaucho*. Buenos Aires: Ateneo, 1943.

Rapoport, Mario, comp. *Economía e historia: Contribuciones a la historia económica argentina*. Buenos Aires: Editorial Tesis, 1988.

Rock, David. *Argentina, 1516–1987: From Spanish Colonization to Alfonsín*. Rev. ed. Berkeley: University of California Press, 1987.

Rodríguez Molas, Ricardo. *Historia social del gaucho*. Buenos Aires: Marú, 1968.

Saubidet, Tito. *Vocabulario y refranero criollo*. 7th ed. Buenos Aires: Rafael Palumbo, 1975.

Slatta, Richard W. "'Civilization' Battles 'Barbarism': Argentine Frontier Strategies, 1516–1880." *Inter-American Review of Bibliography* 39:2 (1989).

———. "The Demise of the Gaucho and the Rise of Equestrian Sport in Argentina." *Journal of Sport History* 13:2 (Summer 1986):97–110.

———. "The Gaucho in Argentina's Quest for National Identity." *Canadian Review of Studies in Nationalism* 21:1 (Spring 1985):99–122.

———. *Gauchos and the Vanishing Frontier*. Lincoln: University of Nebraska Press, 1983.

ARGENTINA AND URUGUAY: LITERATURE

Argentine Republic, Embassy. *Martín Fierro en su centenario*. Buenos Aires: Francisco A. Colombo, 1973.

Becco, Horacio Jorge. "La poesía gauchesca en el Río de la Plata." *Inter-American Review of Bibliography* 24:2 (April 1974):135–146.

Becco, Horacio Jorge, ed. *Antología de la poesía gauchesca*. Madrid: Aguilar, 1972.

Borges, Jorge Luis, and Adolfo Bioy Casares, eds. *Poesía gauchesca*. 2 vols. Mexico City: Fondo de Cultura Económica, 1955.

Furt, Jorge M. *Cancionero popular rioplatense*. 2 vols. Buenos Aires: Roldán, 1923.

Garganigo, John F. *Javier de Viana*. New York: Twayne, 1972.

Güiraldes, Ricardo. *Don Segundo Sombra: Shadows on the Pampas*. Trans. Harriet de Onís. 1935. Reprint. New York: Signet, 1966.

Hernández, José. *The Gaucho Martín Fierro*. Trans. Walter Owen. 1935. Reprint. Buenos Aires: Pampa, 1960.

Lichtblau, Myron I. *The Argentine Novel in the Nineteenth Century*. New York: Hispanic Institute in the United States, 1959.

Lugones, Leopoldo. *El payador*. 4th ed. Buenos Aires: Huemul, 1972.

Martínez Estrada, Ezequiel. *Muerte y transfiguración de Martín Fierro*. 2 vols. Mexico City: Fonda de Cultura Económica, 1948.

———. *X-Ray of the Pampa*. Trans. Alain Swietlicki. Austin: University of Texas Press, 1971.

Pages Larraya, Antonio. *Prosas de Martín Fierro*. Buenos Aires: Raigal, 1952.

Rojas, Ricardo. *Historia de la literatura argentina: Ensayo filosófico sobre la evolución de la cultura en el Plata*. 4 vols. Buenos Aires: Coni, 1917–1922.

Sarmiento, Domingo F. *Life in the Argentine Republic in the Days of the Tyrants; or Civilization and Barbarism*. Trans. Mrs. Horace (Mary) Mann. 1868. Reprint. New York: Hafner, 1971.

Sava, Walter. "A History and Interpretation of Literary Criticism of 'Martín Fierro.'" Ph. D. diss., University of Wisconsin, 1973.